Scattered Finds

Scattered Finds

Archaeology, Egyptology and Museums

Alice Stevenson

First published in 2019 by
UCL Press
University College London
Gower Street
London WC1E 6BT

Available to download free: www.ucl.ac.uk/ucl-press

Text © Alice Stevenson, 2019
Images © Copyright holders named in captions, 2019

Alice Stevenson has asserted her right under the Copyright, Designs and Patents Act 1988 to be identified as author of this work

A CIP catalogue record for this book is available from The British Library. This book is published under a Creative Commons 4.0 International license (CC BY 4.0). This license allows you to share, copy, distribute and transmit the work; to adapt the work and to make commercial use of the work providing attribution is made to the authors (but not in any way that suggests that they endorse you or your use of the work). Attribution should include the following information:

Stevenson, A. 2019. *Scattered Finds: Archaeology, Egyptology and Museums*. London, UCL Press. https://doi.org/10.14324/111. 9781787351400

Further details about Creative Commons licenses are available at http://creativecommons.org/licenses/

ISBN: 978-1-78735-142-4 (Hbk.)
ISBN: 978-1-78735-141-7 (Pbk.)
ISBN: 978-1-78735-140-0 (PDF)
ISBN: 978-1-78735-143-1 (epub)
ISBN: 978-1-78735-144-8 (mobi)
ISBN: 978-1-78735-145-5 (html)
DOI: https://doi.org/10.14324/111. 9781787351400

Acknowledgements

I first conceived of this book during my postdoctoral research in the Pitt Rivers Museum at the University of Oxford between 2009 and 2012. Towards the end of my contract, funding from an anonymous benefactor and support from Michael O'Hanlon allowed me to undertake a pilot project to develop a grant proposal for the UK's Arts and Humanities Research Council (AHRC). This was to look more closely at the history of finds distribution from British excavations in Egypt to museums worldwide. I feel enormously fortunate to have been able to spend my early career at the Pitt Rivers Museum, an institution that has shaped my own thinking and practice. I am especially grateful to Jeremy Coote, Dan Hicks, Alison Petch and Chris Morton, together with the University of Oxford's early history of anthropology research group, for discussions over the years.

With backing from John Baines, the application to the AHRC was successful, and the 'Artefacts of Excavation' project was funded between 2014 and 2017. By that time I had taken up the curatorship of UCL's Petrie Museum of Egyptian Archaeology, and a full-time postdoctoral researcher, Emma Libonati, took on responsibility for a key element of the project: digitizing and uploading archives from the Petrie Museum to a newly created online resource, the Artefacts of Excavation website, hosted by the University of Oxford's Griffith Institute (http://egyptartefacts.griffith.ox.ac.uk/), initially designed by our part-time researcher Sarah Glover. Volunteer Alix Robinson, meanwhile, digitized the finds distribution archives of the Egypt Exploration Society, with help from Carl Graves, and Emma Libonati once again took on the arduous task of making these accessible on the website. The site is intended to provide information that might help identify material excavated in Egypt by British organizations in museum collections worldwide. Additionally, it provides an overview of the scope of distribution, the history, politics and significance of which are analysed in this book. I am hugely grateful to John Baines for his unwavering support for the project, as well as to Emma Libonati for the many long hours spent provisioning the website with such a considerable amount of material, identifying destination names in the archives, and ensuring that the project's conference, held at UCL in April 2016, was such a success. It was Emma who first suggested the term 'object habit' for this symposium, a concept that I have developed further in this book. Emma also contributed to research on the history of objects sent to Italian institutions, discussed in Chapter Three.

Thanks are due to the staff (past and present) of the Petrie Museum of Egyptian Archaeology at UCL: Debbie Challis, Pia Edqvist, Anna Garnett, Tracey Golding, Helen Pike, Maria Ragan, Briony Webb and Alice Williams. Towards the end of the project, additional assistance was received from Massimiliano Pinarello and Heba Abd El Gawad. Similarly, the project could not have succeeded without the help of the Egypt Exploration Society – Carl Graves, Chris Naunton and Cedric Goebell – and the staff of the Griffith Institute in Oxford – Liam McNamara, Francisco Bosch-Puche and Cat Warsi. A steering committee, including Liam McNamara, John Taylor and Alison Petch, was especially helpful in the early stages of the project's development.

In undertaking the research for this book I have been in correspondence with dozens of curators and archivists at institutions ranging from the USA's White House and Britain's Royal Palaces to universities in Japan and local museums in Cornwall. Special mention, however, goes to Ashley Cooke, Carl Graves, Faye Kalloniatis, Margaret Maitland, and Campbell Price, who were always exceedingly generous with the information that they shared about the collections and archives they look after. Thanks are due to Lawrence Berman of the Boston Museum of Fine Arts, and Adela Oppenheim of the Metropolitan Museum of Art, for assistance during a research visit in April 2015; to Anlen Boshoff, Esther Esmyol and Lambert Vorster for assistance in South Africa during research visits in 2014 and 2017; to the University of Kyoto for the invitation to participate in their symposium in February 2016, and to the museum staff at the University for the opportunity to study the University's collections there; and to Prince Lawerh and Irene Morfini for help in the National Museum of Ghana during a research visit in September 2017. Brian Weightman and Meg Wilson were very generous in sharing transcriptions of the archives at the Kelvingrove Museum in Glasgow, and Christina Donald helped with explorations of the collections at the McManus Museum and Art Gallery's stores in Dundee. For assistance identifying further archival sources, museum objects and references I would like to acknowledge Louise Allen, Maura Anderson, Brigitte Balanda, Yekaterina Barbash, Stephanie Boonstra, Michael Carver, Chris Davey, Josh Emmitt, Ben Harer, Angela Houghton, Sue Giles, Imogen Gunn, Gabrielle Heffernan, Maarten Horn, John J. Johnson, Gina Laycock, Steven Lubar, Jennifer McCormick, Samantha Masters, Peter Morris, Mark Norman, Alessandro Pezzati, Nathan Schlanger, Jon Schmitz, Sarah Scott, Paul Smith, Angela Stienne, Veronica Tamorri, John Taylor, Ross Thomas, Amara Thornton, Carolyn Thorp, Alexandra Villing, Marianne Weldon and Martha Zierden.

My own linguistic inadequacies have left me indebted to more able colleagues who have translated texts from various corners of the globe. For help with Japanese sources I am very grateful to Kento Zenihiro, Noriyuki Shirai, Hyung Il Pai, Ryan Botta, and especially to Tomoaki Nakano. I would like to thank Chloe Ward for French translations, Elizabeth Wood for German, Anlen Boshoff for Afrikaans, and Heba Abd El Gawad and Ahmed Mekawy Ouda for Arabic.

Several individuals kindly commented on earlier chapter drafts and shared references, unpublished papers and archival sources. I am grateful for their expertise and advice: Tine Bagh, John Baines, Wendy Doyon, Heba Abd El Gawad, Thomas Gertzen, Daniela Picchi, Christina Riggs, Kathleen Sheppard, Stephen Quirke and Alice Williams.

My final thanks, as ever, goes to my husband Paul. He has been my soul companion and support throughout my career, and I dedicate this book to him.

Contents

List of figures	ix
Introduction	1
Chapter 1: Trinkets, Trifles and Oddments: The Material Facts of History (1880–1914)	25
Chapter 2: Collecting in America's Progressive and Gilded Eras (1880–1919)	69
Chapter 3: International, Colonial and Transnational Connections (1880–1950)	105
Chapter 4: A Golden Age? (1922–1939): Collecting in the Shadow of Tutankhamun	145
Chapter 5: Ghosts, Orphans and the Dispossessed: Post-war Object Habits (1945–1969)	181
Chapter 6: Legacies and Futures (1970–)	217
Conclusion	253
Appendix A: Legislation relating to the excavation and export of Egyptian antiquities	259
Appendix B: Ancient Egyptian chronology	261
Bibliography	263
Index	297

List of figures

Introduction

Fig. 0.1 Advertisement for Thomas Cook Nile tours, circa. 1890–1. Courtesy of the Thomas Cook Archives. 7

Fig. 0.2 Photograph of archaeological finds in a dig-house courtyard at Abydos, circa. 1900. Courtesy of the Petrie Museum of Egyptian Archaeology, UCL. 8

Fig. 0.3 Photograph of Hilda Petrie at Abydos, circa 1903. Courtesy of the Petrie Museum of Egyptian Archaeology, UCL. 12

Fig. 0.4 Egyptian shabti acquired from the Egypt Exploration Fund by Sir Henry Rider Hagaard around 1900, now in Liverpool's World Museum (museum number 56.22.603). Courtesy of National Museums Liverpool, World Museum. 15

Fig. 0.5 Photographs of Egyptian work teams on site at Egypt Exploration Fund excavations at Abydos, 1911–12. Courtesy of the Egypt Exploration Society, (ABNeg.11.0240). 19

Chapter 1

Fig. 1.1 Lower part of a seated royal statue of a Hyksos king of the mid-second millennium BC at Bubastis 1888–89, with Egyptian workmen in background. Courtesy of the Egypt Exploration Society (BUB.NEG.15). 26

Fig. 1.2 Foundation deposit from the pylon of the sanctuary of Amun-Ra, built under Ptolemy II Philadelphu (285–246 BC), photographed by Flinders Petrie in 1885. Courtesy of the Petrie Museum of Egyptian Archaeology, UCL (PMAN 2680). 27

Fig. 1.3 Landscape around Tanis after a rainstorm. Photograph taken by Flinders Petrie February 1884. Courtesy of the Egypt Exploration Society (DE.NEG.193a). 31

Fig. 1.4 Acknowledgement certificate dated 1904 from Bankfield Museum for objects presented by the Egypt Exploration Fund. The vignettes illustrate the dense, universalist displays of world culture UK municipal museums aspired to in the early twentieth century. Courtesy of the Egypt Exploration Society (DIST 21.36). 43

Fig. 1.5 The Qurna burial group, *in situ*, shortly after discovery. Courtesy of the Petrie Museum of Egyptian Archaeology, UCL (PMAN 2851). 45

Fig. 1.6 Distribution grid from 1901, organizing the dispatch of artefacts from royal second dynasty tombs at Abydos to museums around the UK. Courtesy of the Petrie Museum of Egyptian Archaeology, UCL (PMA/WFP1/D/9/9.1). 47

Fig. 1.7 Photographic view of Amelia Edwards's study at her home, The Larches, in Bristol. Courtesy of the Principal and Fellows of Somerville College, Oxford. 51

Fig. 1.8 Photograph of Hilda Petrie's sister, Amy Urlin, in the mess room of the Abydos dig-house, circa. 1903. Courtesy of the Petrie Museum of Egyptian Archaeology, UCL. 59

Fig. 1.9 Photograph of Beatrice Orme in Egypt in the early years of the twentieth century. On the back of the photograph is written 'The best length for a skirt in Egypt!!'. Courtesy of the Petrie Museum of Egyptian Archaeology, UCL. 59

Chapter 2

Fig. 2.1 Photograph of a statue of Ramesses II (museum number 87.111) excavated by Petrie's team at Tell Nebesheh as displayed in the original Museum of Fine Art building on Copley Square, Boston in 1903. Photograph © 2018 Museum of Fine Arts Boston (Negative number E15692). 71

Fig. 2.2 Photograph of University of Pennsylvania's exhibit at the 1893 Columbian World Exposition taken by Jas. H. Crockwell, Salt Lake City, Utah. Courtesy of Penn Museum (image #174642). 73

Fig. 2.3 Photograph of material received by the University of Chicago in 1896 from the Egypt Exploration Fund's work at the Ramesseum. Courtesy of the Oriental Institute, Chicago. 77

Fig. 2.4 Photograph of one of the press cuttings in Amelia Edwards's scrapbook taken from the *Daily Graphic*, 11 January 1890, showing Edwards lecturing in New York. Courtesy of the Principal and Fellows of Somerville College, Oxford.   80

Fig. 2.5a & b Front and back of a 'tomb card' from EES Abydos excavations, 1908–09. Courtesy of the Egypt Exploration Society (AB.TC.E.0011).   92

Fig. 2.6 Photograph of payday at Balabish, March 1915. Courtesy of the Egypt Exploration Society (BAL.NEG.10).   95

Fig. 2.7 Pectoral and necklace of Queen Sithathoryunet with the name of Senwosret II (c. 1887 BC) (museum number 16.1.3a, b) excavated by the British School of Archaeology in Egypt team at Lahun in 1914. Creative Commons Zero (CC0) The Metropolitan Museum of Art, New York.   98

Chapter 3

Fig. 3.1 Glyptotek Museum conservator 'Elo' with mummy (museum number AE1425), excavated by the British School of Archaeology in Egypt at Hawara in 1911. Archive photo held by Royal Library and Courtesy of Tine Bagh, Glyptotek Museum.   115

Fig. 3.2 Photograph of the interior of McGill University's Redpath Museum, circa 1893. Through the open door of the museum hall is the room devoted to archaeological and ethnological material. Courtesy of Notman Photographic Archives, McCord Museum of Canadian History, Montreal (view 2604).   121

Fig. 3.3 Roman era terracotta figurine excavated in 1908–09 by Flinders Petrie's teams at Memphis. Described by Petrie as 'Indian'. Courtesy of the Petrie Museum of Egyptian Archaeology (UC8932).   129

Fig. 3.4 Photograph of antiquities displays inside the Exhibition Hall at Kyoto University's Faculty of Letters, circa 1923. Courtesy of the University of Kyoto.   131

Fig. 3.5 Letter from University of Tokyo acknowledging the donation of antiquities from the Egypt Exploration Fund's 1906–07 excavation seasons. Courtesy of the Egypt Exploration Society (EES.DIST.28.10b).   134

Chapter 4

Fig. 4.1 Relief carving showing Akhenaten and Nefertiti, found during the Egypt Explorations Society's 1926–7 excavations at Amarna. Courtesy of the Egypt Exploration Society (TA.NEG.26-27-073). 149

Fig. 4.2 Report in the Australian *Sunday Times* of Lord Carnarvon's death and treasure for museums, 20 May 1923. Reproduced with permission of the Griffith Institute, University of Oxford. 152

Fig. 4.3 Predynastic ceremonial mace-head excavated at Hierakonpolis in 1897–8 (museum number AN.1896-1908/E3632-a), reconstructed by Ashmolean restorer W. H. Young. Image © Ashmolean Museum, University of Oxford. 159

Fig. 4.4 (i) Plaster cast of a Badarian ivory figurine made by Ashmolean restorer W. H. Young now in the Petrie Museum of Egyptian Archaeology (museum number UC19638); (ii) a second copy of the same figurine from the National Museum of Scotland, shown here with Young's trademark signature, NEOS, inscribed on base (museum number A.1926.722). The original is in the British Museum (museum number EA59648). 160

Fig. 4.5 Amarna vase (museum number AN.1926.109-a) restored by the Ashmolean Museum's restorer W. H. Young. Image ©Ashmolean Museum, University of Oxford. 161

Fig. 4.6 Object card from Egypt Exploration Society's 1931–2 Tell el-Amarna excavations showing an object selected for the Wellcome Historical Medical Museum. Courtesy of the Egypt Exploration Society (TA.OC.31-32.443). 164

Chapter 5

Fig. 5.1 Bomb damage in Liverpool Museum. A member of the auxiliary fire service carrying a ceramic coffin lid from Garstang's 1906 excavations at Esna on 4 May 1941. A seated statue of the lioness-headed goddess Sekhmet is visible in the background. Courtesy of National Museums Liverpool, World Museum (16.11.06.403). 182

Fig. 5.2 The former Stepney Borough Natural History Study Museum in London's St George in the East cemetery. Photograph © Alice Stevenson, 2017.   193

Fig. 5.3 Example of a pre-war display at the Ashmolean Museum, 1939. Image © Ashmolean Museum, University of Oxford.   197

Fig. 5.4 Diorama commissioned by Cyril Aldred to illustrate late Predynastic king Scorpion performing an agricultural ceremony © National Museums Scotland (V.2013.68).   197

Fig. 5.5 Photograph of an architect's model showing part of a proposed new building for the Pitt Rivers Museum, designed by Pier Luigi Nervi, Powell and Moya, circa 1967. Courtesy of the Pitt Rivers Museum, University of Oxford (photograph number 2008.74.5).   204

Fig. 5.6 Outside the National Museum of Ghana. Photograph © Alice Stevenson, 2017.   206

Fig. 5.7 'Save the monuments of Nubia': Ghanaian stamps dated 1963. Photograph © Alice Stevenson 2017.   209

Chapter 6

Fig. 6.1 Beads made of meteoric iron by Diane Johnson. Courtesy of the Petrie Museum of Egyptian Archaeology, UCL (museum number UC80628–9).   233

Fig. 6.2 Modern Egypt project display in the British Museum, 2017. Courtesy of the Trustees of the British Museum.   235

Fig. 6.3 Poster advertising the 2013 'Afro-combs' exhibition. Reproduced with the kind permission of The Fitzwilliam Museum and the Museum of Archaeology and Anthropology, Cambridge.   244

Introduction

Statues of ancient Egyptian rulers and their gods can be encountered in the grandiose galleries of the Metropolitan Museum of Art on Manhattan's traffic-choked Fifth Avenue. More humble grave goods, excavated from tombs along the Nile, can be found in homemade cabinets in a South African barn at the end of a dirt track road. Several hundred artefacts made of pottery, stone and metal are displayed in the wood-panelled vitrines of one of Japan's oldest universities, while a single, 5000-year-old ceramic vessel is tucked away in a shed in a quiet Cornish village. Scattered between national museums, public schools, masonic lodges, royal palaces, universities and auction houses are hundreds of thousands of archaeological finds from Egypt. Some are unassuming fragments, others are monumental works of art. All were caught up in a massive network of financial sponsorship and patronage for British archaeological fieldwork that propelled these things far from the cemeteries, temples and towns from which they had been excavated. Over the course of a century, an estimated 350 institutions across twenty-seven countries in five continents benefited materially from these excavations. And this excludes the waifs and the strays: those small 'duplicate' items that became personal gifts, diplomatic concessions or quietly procured souvenirs. Taken together, no other endeavour in world archaeology is comparable in terms of its scope and material legacy.

The history of this material diaspora can be told from any number of perspectives. Most accounts that have touched on this story have done so from the point of view of specific archaeological sites – in an effort to reconstruct them – or else from the perspective of particular institutions – in order to explain the origins of their collection. No study has attempted to take a holistic view of the practice as a historical phenomenon, one intimately linked both to the development of archaeology as a discipline and to the museum as an institution. The most common departure points for these histories have been the establishment of the London-based Egypt Exploration Fund (EEF) in 1882 and the career of one of its most prominent field directors, the unconventional archaeologist Sir William

Matthew Flinders Petrie (1853–1942). Both are key to accounts that link objects and people across the globe, but they are no more than colourful threads in a complex tapestry. A more fully textured history must incorporate a much wider cast of characters, in a greater diversity of contexts, than has been acknowledged before.

This book is an attempt to relocate this narrative and to do so with greater sensitivity to the historical conditions that enabled and shaped the nature of Egyptian archaeology in the field, in the museum and in many spaces in between. In other words, it is what anthropologists have called a 'multi-sited' project, which allows for 'the layering of partly incommensurable experiences in different places through time, and tracing the connections and disjunctions between them'.[1] Such an approach is valuable when attempting to navigate a course between sweeping imperial and colonial endeavours in Egypt, on the one hand, and smaller scale institutional politics and personal relationships, on the other. Drawing on case studies that are geographically and chronologically divergent in this way serves as a foil to shallow claims that there exists some sort of vague 'eternal fascination' with the land of the pharaohs when, historically, Egyptian material culture has occupied a considerably more vexed position.[2] Depending on circumstances, archaeological finds could be burdensome, contested or of marginal interest. Widespread distribution did not necessarily reflect an inherent interest in Egypt's past. Instead, it actively constituted particular geographies of knowledge or power, and it is by examining the passage of artefacts through alternative trajectories that it becomes possible to identify how such interests were cultivated in the first place.

Object Habits

Central to my argument is the concept of the 'object habit', a shorthand for referring to an area's or a community's attitude to things, affecting what was collected, when and why.[3] It takes into account factors that influenced the types of things chosen; motivations for collecting; mechanisms of acquisition; temporal variations in procurement; styles of engagements with artefacts; their treatment, documentation and representation; and attitudes to their presentation and reception. These practices emerge not only within the museum or out in the field, but also, significantly, between the two within the wider world.

It is not my intention to theorize objects themselves.[4] My interest is in how people engaged with them, and in the worldviews that were reflected and constituted by their presence. Furthermore, I want to be able to say something about the ways in which the dividends of archaeological fieldwork shaped conceptions of the past, and how such things were brought into dialogue with the present. In this framework, ancient Egyptian material culture is not only the product of long-gone societies, but it is also a result of more recent cultures of collecting. There is nothing revolutionary in these lines of thought. That objects do not simply illustrate history, but also generate it, is the mainstay of a considerable body of cultural and critical theory. In this vein, the discourses expounded in this book owe a major debt to the biographical approaches instigated by the anthropologists Arjun Appadurai and Igor Kopytoff.[5] Three decades of scholarship have built upon their insights into object biographies, and have resulted in several productive analytical frameworks for understanding how museum collections form.[6] These include the model of the relational museum developed at the Pitt Rivers Museum in Oxford,[7] and sociological investigations inspired by Bruno Latour's Actor-Network-Theory (ANT).[8] Such models have brought into relief the shifting value of artefacts throughout their life-courses, and they highlight how museums operate within extensive networks that link collecting in the field with institutions. However, instead of examining the ways in which a single institution drew into itself complexes of people and things, my analysis encompasses a transnational system of exchange that cross-cuts a multitude of organizations and fields of relations.

Situating the distribution of finds within the full agency of the world also has the effect of re-conceptualizing the relationship of the museum to international fieldwork. There is a common misconception that 'museums have always been, and continue to be, a relatively peripheral player in archaeological motivation'.[9] I disagree. While it is tempting to envisage such dispersals as a linear transmission of objects from the field to the museum, throughout this book are numerous examples of how excavation and curatorial practices are informed by related practices of knowledge. This study therefore complements other histories of archaeology that have sought to triangulate museums and colonial fieldwork.[10] It is clear that both arenas of activity ultimately impinged upon each other in highly complex ways. 'These worlds', as Chris Wingfield has commented, 'have never been quite as distinct as they might appear'.[11]

Not only were such routes of transmission not linear, they were also far from flat. Artefacts travelled along paths determined by wealth, cultural authority and social opportunity. In this context it is striking just how many women enthusiastically championed organizations like the EEF. Consequently, the historical prospects for women to become involved in the archaeological process forms a key theme for discussion at several points throughout this book. The project of recognizing women's contribution to archaeology has usually proceeded by identifying those pioneers, the 'trowel-blazers', who participated in or led excavations.[12] However, there were greater numbers of women involved both in establishing the tenets of the discipline and in the production of archaeological knowledge than these efforts might suggest. This is an oversight attributable not only to sex, but also to the fact that the part of archaeology that many chose to work in, or were restricted to, was the museum. Realigning the position of museums in archaeological histories, as well as in practice, is therefore not simply a disciplinary project, it is equally a feminist one. More specifically, it can be characterized as being sympathetic to third wave feminism, which recognizes that there is never one viewpoint, but multiple perspectives, dependent upon dynamics such as those of class, sex, religion and ethnicity.[13] This stance is appropriate for this work because I aim to engage with a fuller spectrum of interests, concerns and characters (not just female) that variously intersected with the movement of Egyptian antiquities out of the field and into institutions. Moreover, feminist traditions of critical analysis have long emphasized the connection between the social context of research and the nature of knowledge production.[14]

In view of these concerns I have tried to be sensitive to diffuse sets of historical contingencies in order to understand the development of institutions and the varied reception of the artefacts acquired by them. And this is where I think the potential of the object habit concept really comes to the fore, namely in its ability to open up what otherwise might become circumscribed and inward-looking areas of enquiry, isolated from parallel and related phenomena in the wider world. Furthermore, the idea of the object habit foregrounds the nature of things – in the widest possible sense – against the grain of studies that are frequently more attentive to the social relationships forged during processes of collecting than to the material prerequisites of those relationships. Museum Studies literature has become more attuned to the properties of things,[15] and this realignment is a reminder that the articles involved in such enquiries need not be limited to antiquities. Archaeological and museum activities produce, manage and interpret a range of materials – photographs, field notes, biological specimens and plaster casts – that are variously implicated in mediations between past, present and future. These too circulated away from field sites alongside antiquities. All have a physicality, be it in their size, weight, fragility, reproducibility, ornamentation or condition, that had (and continues to have) direct, and historically dependent, effects at various points in the distribution network.

The approach that I take, therefore, constitutes something of a counterpoint to over-determined accounts in which 'disciplinary' museums act as powerful 'purveyors of ideology and of a downward spread of knowledge to the public'.[16] Certainly, museums did act as sites that shaped behaviours and consciousness, but there were additional, external dynamics that conditioned visitors' and curators' attitudes to things. In adopting this line of enquiry I have, following several other scholars, favoured a general emphasis on historical and cultural geographical approaches to museums and collections, rather than adopting a stance taken from critical theory. For instance, Michelle Henning has emphasized that museums need to be understood in relation to the wider culture of which they are part,[17] Andrea Witcomb reminds us that museums have always been subject to contradictory influences,[18] John Mackenzie has cautioned that museums function in the real world and scholars should not claim too much for them, [19] and Anthony Shelton has argued that collections are not simply paradigmatic representations subject to particular disciplinary constraints.[20] For Egyptian antiquities specifically, Elliot Colla identifies forms of 'artifaction' that were 'neither single-minded nor centralized'.[21] Instead, he notes that antiquities were subject to ongoing, and often incomplete, processes of recontextualization and reframing. My account of the distribution of finds from British excavations in Egypt seeks to be cognizant of these positions.

Chronological and Geographical Scope

The fates of archaeological finds are narrated across six chapters organized loosely by chronology and geography, beginning in late Victorian England, and moving across four phases of distribution activity through to the present day. My decision to commence the study in the 1880s is not an arbitrary one, but a deliberate periodization that acknowledges a confluence of trends across political agendas, social mores, intellectual discourses and economic developments that together created the ideal conditions for a fresh reception of Egyptian material.

For the century leading up to 1880, Stephanie Moser has charted attitudes to Egyptian antiquities in the British Museum, from their being presented and consumed as enigmatic 'wondrous curiosities'[22] towards being appreciated through more historically informed notions of Egypt as an autonomous culture, outside the shadow of Classical art.[23] Moser deliberately closes her account in 1880, because it was at that juncture that the museological construction of ancient Egypt came to include a different character of antiquity, one that was created through innovative excavation procedures and which represented new forms of evidential meaning. In the Egyptological world, the 1880s began with a sharp generational turnover as many of the old guard passed away, including Auguste Mariette (1821–81), the founder of Egypt's Department of Antiquities (Service des Antiquités). His death in January 1881, coupled with Egyptian financial instability and a physically crumbling museum at Bulaq in Cairo, left archaeology in Egypt in a precarious situation, according to historian Jason Thompson.[24] While Thompson leaves his first volume of *The History of Egyptology* at this bleak cliffhanger, David Gange's characterization of the possibilities for British Egyptology in the early 1880s strikes a more positive tone, noting that 'ancient Egypt's reception was strikingly different after 1880 from everything it had been in the mid century'.[25]

Indeed, looking beyond Egyptology it is clear that other forces of change were fostering a far more favourable environment for new archaeological practices. Significant here was Britain's involvement in the elaboration of Egypt's infrastructure, with initiatives in transportation and communication fuelling the flow of people, information and, crucially, things. The British travel agent Thomas Cook (1808–92) was one of the chief protagonists of modernity's drive in Egypt, and his September 1880 edition of *The Excursionist* proudly declared that 'a contract has been signed by the Government, handing over to us the entire control of the steamboat service of the Nile for a period of ten years'. As a result, the 1880–1 season witnessed the largest number of passengers ever to have gone up the Nile by steamer. Archaeologists working in Egypt became increasingly reliant upon this company for communications and the management of money, as well as transport to and from sites along what became known to many in Britain as 'Cook's Canal' (Fig. 0.1).

British foreign policy also became progressively entangled with that of Egypt in the wake of the British bombardment of Alexandria in July 1882. The attack was in response to Ahmad 'Urabi (1841–1911), Egypt's Minister of War, who, together with a nationalistic faction, had been asserting power over the country where Britain had financial and expansionist interests, especially in relation to the Suez Canal. When Cairo fell a few months after the British military assault, Egypt became a 'veiled protectorate' that lasted for almost seventy-five years.[26] Nevertheless, archaeological activities were not financially sponsored by

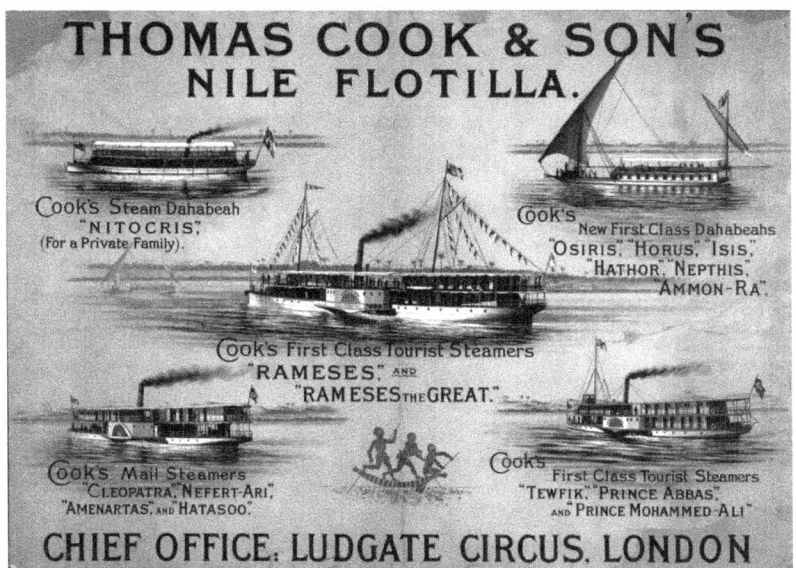

Fig. 0.1 Advertisement for Thomas Cook Nile tours, circa. 1890–1. Courtesy of the Thomas Cook Archives.

the British government; antiquities remained under the control of the French, and Egyptian laws against the export of antiquities prevented the wholesale removal of its heritage abroad (Appendix A). Chapter One therefore explores how the practice of 'partage', through which the spoils of fieldwork were divided between Egyptian institutions and foreign excavators, prevailed in such circumstances. The success of partage led to the most intense and diverse phase of finds distribution, which lasted from 1884 up until the First World War. As such, it is covered by Chapters One, Two and Three.

Scholars have recognized the omnivorous amassing of cultural artefacts and natural specimens in the nineteenth century as symptomatic of an 'epistemology of things' that structured the emergent disciplines of anthropology and archaeology.[27] In other words, it is well-documented that Victorian knowledge about the world was thought to be convincingly and objectively demonstrated by marshalling brute material facts. Politics and disciplinary advancement were not, however, the only forces driving material out of Egypt. Chapter One's review of the range of attitudes that motivated the acquisition of such artefacts in Britain suggests that this was as much an ontological turn within Victorian society at large, as it was an epistemological one within the academy. Archaeology, as an artefact-driven enterprise in the nineteenth century (Fig. 0.2), led to an influx of antiquities that influenced and resonated with Victorian culture

Fig. 0.2 Photograph of archaeological finds in a dig-house courtyard at Abydos, circa. 1900. Courtesy of the Petrie Museum of Egyptian Archaeology, UCL.

on multiple levels. Supply was met by new forms of demand, informed by the perceived ability of objects to communicate, to educate and to affect, especially when deployed within the fast developing museum world.

Archaeological societies in Britain capitalized on what were initially very liberal partage arrangements, using the material gains from excavation as a means of leveraging interest and funding from parties throughout Britain, Europe, the British Empire and eventually also the Far East. The United States later became a particularly serious competitor for Egyptian antiquities, and Chapter Two examines this aspect of the changing relationship between Britain and the USA, from the late nineteenth century through to the end of the First World War, together with the divergent museological and archaeological strategies that emerged on either side of the Atlantic. Institutions in a further 26 countries were the beneficiaries of finds from the EEF's excavations. In exploring this practice, Chapter Three presents a series of case studies from a selection of these countries in order to examine how and why Egyptian archaeological objects came to be grounded in European institutions, in colonial museums and in Asian universities. It further considers how the value and status of these antiquities became contingent upon relationships with local interests, regional politics and alternative bodies of knowledge.

Chapters Four and Five draw into relief the relationship between political, cultural and social developments, on the one hand, and shifts in archaeological and museum practice, on the other. During the inter-war years (the subject of Chapter Four), the coincidence of the discovery of Tutankhamun's tomb with an upsurge of Egyptian nationalism sets the scene for a series of tensions around Egyptian antiquities; between popular and academic, between art and science, and between original and reproduction. In order to explore these conceptual fault lines, this chapter turns to the roles that restorers, administrators and replica objects played in the distribution network, aspects that have been largely neglected in histories of collecting. Such a focus also makes it possible to examine the strategies that were adopted during what can be characterized as a second phase of finds distribution, during which antiquities exports from Egypt were progressively curtailed. Chapter Five tackles the post-war decades, which have received more limited attention in accounts of museum development and archaeological practice than the Victorian, Edwardian and inter-war periods. This period was anything but quiet. There was a sea-change in attitudes towards the integrity and purpose of museum collections, combined with a profound shift in the way society at large valued objects. In this third phase of distribution, Britain's transnational networks contracted substantially. Partly in parallel, across a large number of institutions in Britain and America, Egyptian objects were actively disposed of. What also emerged during this time, however, were new contexts for collecting in decolonizing nations.

The chronicle of patterns of collecting across these five chapters brings to the fore the parallels in periodization between certain ancient epochs (Appendix B) and particular modern trends, whether they be the intense interest in Egypt's prehistory in the late nineteenth century or the global fascination with the Amarna Age in the 1920s. These phases constitute the object habits of particular moments. Yet while attentions may have ebbed and flowed across the decades, ignoring some materials and celebrating others, none were ever completely disregarded. The final chapter, Chapter Six, gathers these various strands together to take the story from the 1970s through into the present day. Distribution was brought to a complete halt during this phase. This chapter, therefore, reflects on the legacy of partage, the antiquities markets through which Egyptian material continues to circulate, and the possibilities for new research and fresh displays based upon collections dispersed many decades ago. Although in many ways this final discussion is a historical one, Chapter Six is also a call to re-evaluate how Egypt is collected and treated in, and as, archaeological practice in the contemporary world.

Mechanisms of Collecting and Distributing Egypt

The Egypt Exploration Fund (EEF) was founded in 1882 through the initiative of Victorian novelist and travel writer Amelia Edwards (1831–92), with the support of Reginald Stuart Poole (1832–95) of the Department of Coins and Medals at the British Museum, and with advice from Gaston Maspero (1846–1916), Head of the Service des Antiquités de l'Égypte.[28] It was one of the earliest excavation committees established in Britain, following the Palestine Exploration Fund and the Roman Exploration Fund in the 1860s,[29] and is, as the Egypt Exploration Society (EES),[30] still active today. Edwards spent much of 1881 and early 1882 building support for this enterprise through a tenacious letter-writing campaign, the responses to which were encouraging: the sensationalist archaeologist Heinrich Schliemann wrote from Troy to say that he had read her letter with 'profound interest'; Sir Erasmus Wilson, surgeon and financial sponsor of Cleopatra's Needle's exile from the Nile to the Thames, forwarded 100 pounds for the cause; Robert Browning, the English poet and playwright, had no objection; the Archbishop of Canterbury was happy to lend his name, as was the Chief Rabbi; Lord Carnarvon was on board, together with the excavator of Nineveh, Sir Henry Layard; and 'Darwin's bulldog', Professor Thomas Huxley, would promote the cause. With such backing, Edwards submitted a notice to *The Times*, published on 30 March 1882, heralding a new Society 'for the purpose of excavating the ancient sites of the Egyptian Delta'.

In 1886, the EEF's memorandum listed three aims: to organize excavations in Egypt, to publish the sites explored and to 'ensure the preservation of such antiquities by presenting them to museums and similar public institutions'.[31] Relative to goals one and two, this latter objective quickly assumed prime importance. In return for financial sponsorship of the Fund, or else by offering to defray its considerable transport costs, museums, libraries, universities or schools could secure antiquities for their collections. The demographic profile of the many hundreds of individual subscribers to the Fund also acted as a guide to local interest, allowing suitable nearby institutions to be identified.[32]

A separate sub-branch of the EEF, the Graeco-Roman Branch, was founded in 1897 to manage the specific interest in the vast caches of papyri unearthed in the Fayum under the leadership of papyrologists Bernard P. Grenfell (1869–1926) and Arthur Hunt (1871–1934). The pair commenced investigations in abandoned villages of the Greek and Roman periods in 1895–6, including at Oxyrhynchus and el-Hibeh. The distributions that they managed independently of the main EEF committee encompassed an even larger number of institutions than the EEF's archaeological missions, with libraries worldwide seeking examples of ancient texts, especially Christian and literary papyri in Greek. The networks that Grenfell and Hunt cultivated for the circulation of these ancient texts ran parallel to, and overlapped with, the ones that are the focus of this book, and are worthy of a separate study as particular types of objects in their own right.[33] Although the distribution of papyri is not addressed explicitly in this account, it should be noted that Grenfell and Hunt did retain mummies, pottery and other artefacts as additional incentives for eliciting funds, and much of this non-papyrological material was fed into the main EEF distribution network.

By the early 1900s, the EEF was not the only organization arranging the transport of large numbers of objects. Flinders Petrie's relationship with the Fund was fractious, and amid arguments over financial arrangements in the late 1880s he sought to work independently. He came to rely on the private patronage of two wealthy industrialists, Jesse Haworth (1835–1921) and Henry Martyn Kennard (1833–1911), leading to a three-way split of all objects permitted to leave Egypt in the late 1880s and 1890s. On his appointment as the first Edwards Professor of Egyptian Archaeology and Philology at University College London (UCL) in 1892, Petrie was able to establish the Egypt Research Account (ERA) to support the training of a new generation of archaeologists. The ERA was essentially just a bank account, but it formed the foundation of the British School of Archaeology in Egypt (BSAE) in 1905. This new organization, like the EEF, had no physical base in Egypt, and like the EEF it used archaeological finds as leverage to finance future archaeological campaigns. It was managed by Flinders Petrie, or more usually his wife Hilda (1871–1956; Fig. 0.3), latterly with help from a young Olga Tufnell (1905–85), rather than by committee like the EEF. The BSAE was formally wound up in 1956, whereupon its assets were handed over to UCL's Petrie Museum of Egyptian Archaeology.

One of the first students trained using ERA funds was Oxford University mathematics graduate John Garstang (1876–1956). The 23-year-old joined Petrie's team at Abydos in 1899 and within three years had been appointed as Honorary Reader in Egyptian Archaeology at the University of Liverpool. By 1907 he was Professor of the Methods and Practice of Archaeology. In the decade prior to the First World War, Garstang's own fieldwork in Egypt relied upon the backing of wealthy 'excavation committees'. Here too finds were a resource for educing funding, but his management of artefact distributions deviated from the methods adopted by the EEF and Petrie's ERA/BSAE. In place of

Fig. 0.3 Photograph of Hilda Petrie at Abydos, circa 1903. Courtesy of the Petrie Museum of Egyptian Archaeology, UCL.

sponsors, Garstang's terms of contract referred to 'shareholders', while his excavation committee and initial backers were referred to as a 'syndicate'.[34] At first, he did implement a fairly altruistic philosophy for the distribution of finds. For the 1902–3 season at Beni Hasan, Garstang sent a short, five-line letter to the editor of *The Times,* published under the headline 'Gift of Egyptian Antiquities to Museums'.[35] It was promptly picked up by the local and international media, from the *Lancashire Press* to the *Frankfurter Zeitung*:

> The Beni Hasan Excavations Committee finds itself able to offer to a number of museums in the United Kingdom and the colonies, a set of a ancient Egyptian pottery, typical work of the XIth Dynasty, dating about 2,300 B.C. The gifts will be allotted to the public museums firstly, by which is understood museums of towns or institutions which are open free of charge to the public. Education institutions accessible to limited number are not debarred, but no grant can be made under any circumstances to private individuals. Applications from the continent of Europe or from America subject to these conditions would be considered equally.

More than 143 institutions responded, including museums in British Guiana, Jamaica, India, Australia and South Africa.[36] A more business-orientated approach, however, was adopted thereafter, as Garstang established division parties hosted in Liverpool's Adelphi hotel. At these events archaeological finds would be divided into lots, spread across up to a dozen tables and allocated to his patrons by means of a tombola. Garstang's efforts by this time were explicitly more commercial ventures than archaeological research exercises. This is all the more apparent in one undated letter in the Garstang Museum archives that describes ongoing work at Beni Hassan, in which the boast was made that £11,000 worth of antiquities had been excavated.[37]

By the First World War, a complex patchwork of British-headed excavations and international webs of finds distribution had emerged. The legacy of the partitioning of artefacts across so vast a network is a daunting phenomenon to address, not least because the process occurred on multiple scales. Single objects might be divided up, such as a pair of ivory clappers from a tomb excavated at Rifeh in 1907, one half of which remained in Cairo while the other was shipped to London.[38] Some were even cut up, such as textiles or mosaics, as discussed in this example from 1886:

> ... among the things exhibited is a square cane of glass mosaic... Petrie suggested that it should be sliced into ten or twelve pieces, to be mounted on glass with balsam, as he did with the Tanis mosaic, for it is useless to keep it as it is, whereas we might distribute the sections, which would be facsimiles and all equally valuable. I went to see Mr. Head today and we decided that it should be done, so we shall be able to give to all our chief museums.[39]

Individual tomb assemblages were frequently broken up, such as the remains from a First Dynasty tomb found at Abydos in 1922, the human skeleton and pottery from which were sent to Kyoto, Japan, while the copper implements remained at UCL. Scale these processes up to the level of the site, and then the more than 150 sites that were excavated over the course of a century, and the formidable task of tracing allotments quickly becomes apparent. Moreover, the processes of archaeological assembly and disaggregation occurred at several junctures, extending the work of curation across multiple locations. Decisions were made across excavation field sites as to what to retain and what to leave behind; in Cairo as to what would be sent to the Egyptian Museum and what would be released for export; in London as to what would be exhibited at the temporary exhibitions and what would not; and in the distribution network as to what objects institutions should or should not receive.

The mechanisms of circulation were equally complex. The benign-sounding term 'collecting' masks a multitude of paths via which institutions and individuals procured antiquities.[40] For example, although individuals were not intended to be the beneficiaries of partage, in practice private gifts of 'duplicates' were common. From the 1899 season at Abydos, for instance, one particular class of funerary artefacts now ubiquitous in collections worldwide – miniature human statuettes called *shabtis* or *ushabtis* – were so numerous that the EEF was able to present examples to every single subscriber. The personable quality of these little blue figurines gave them a uniquely popular appeal, and the Fund's subscriptions increased as a result. In 1925 the gimmick was repeated with some 400 shabtis, this time specifically for an American audience, as the American branch of the EES believed it needed 'all the help these little mascots usually bring over to us'.[41] Shabtis were placed in ancient Egyptian tombs to undertake work on behalf of the deceased in the afterlife, but their afterlives were far more diverse than the ancient Egyptians would have ever entertained. The novelist H. Rider Haggard (1856–1925) was just one of hundreds of recipients, and his petite, blue-glazed shabti, noted to be from Abydos cemetery D tomb 11, eventually found its way into the collection of Liverpool Museum and Art Gallery (Fig. 0.4).[42] Likewise, dignitaries who visited active digs, such as Princess Henry of Battenberg, who witnessed some of the excavations at Deir el-Bahri in 1904, might be presented with personal gifts. The EEF later sent a small crate to Buckingham Palace, containing beads, scarabs, a bronze cat's head, amulets and a stone statue of a couple.[43]

Haggard's shabti has a material presence in Liverpool Museum, but Princess Henry's gifts are, at present, only traceable in the archives. The afterlives of many artefacts plucked from the field are even more elusive. In part, this is due to the nature of the documentation. The archive, as

Fig. 0.4 Egyptian shabti acquired from the Egypt Exploration Fund by Sir Henry Rider Hagaard around 1900, now in Liverpool's World Museum (museum number 56.22.603). Courtesy of National Museums Liverpool, World Museum.

Jacques Derrida observed,[44] is conditioned by social, economic, political and technological forces.[45] The departure points for this project – the records held by the EES, the Petrie Museum and the Garstang Museum – are the product of different agencies, and they comprise a variety of files, letters and miscellaneous paper scraps. Chronologically, these range from carefully inked, albeit vague, references to 'a selection of minor antiquities' in Victorian ledgers of the 1880s, to green-striped, itemized lists produced using dot-matrix printers a century later. Most files on finds distribution are only partial, as these were created not for historical posterity, but as an expedient institutional instrument for performing obligations. The pro rata dispersal system required forging equivalences between sponsorship money and cultural value, making many lists a perfunctory requirement of financial accountancy or organizational propriety, rather than archaeological procedure. By the 1960s, legal accountability for artefacts, instead of financial imperatives, became the main driving force in the creation of lists, with archival practice materializing shifts in power and cultural authority over Egyptian material from British to Egyptian agencies. How artefacts are described, enumerated or ignored in these sources provides further insights into different modes of valuation, delineating the fungible from the inimitable. Almost exclusively they deal with material after partage negotiations, with little mention of artefacts that were to remain in Egypt, or the agencies involved in that process. Another notable omission in almost all lists are mummified remains, a popular museum requisition, and a common encounter on archaeological sites, yet surprisingly absent in the majority of the records. Perhaps they were seen as too popular for organizations like the EEF that prided themselves on their scientific credentials, despite museum demand. Other materials, such as specimens sent for identification at the Natural History Museum, were similarly excluded. The archive is never an objective source. Instead, it is constituted by value judgements as to what was worthy of record and which materials required particular forms of control.

Some articles circulated away from field sites through opaque networks never subject to archival reckoning. One route out of Egypt was with dig participants, who frequently acquired mementoes from the sites they worked on, artefacts that sometimes re-emerged decades later in museum collections, auction houses or private hands. The connection of such individuals to fieldwork is easily overlooked, given the tendency to ascribe heroic status to excavation directors under whose names field seasons were credited. Early archaeological digs, however, were vast undertakings, involving hundreds of native workers divided into multiple teams, working on separate areas of large archaeological concessions. A handful of Western personnel administered activities on site, including both male and female assistants, who took charge of photography, drawing or the documentation of finds both *in situ* and back at the dig-house. Their contributions are mentioned in passing in the opening chapters of most fieldwork memoirs. Some, like Hilda Petrie, were indispensable members of the archaeological team for decades, while others stayed for shorter intervals, like T. E. Lawrence (later of Arabia (1888–1935)), who spent six weeks in 1913 working at the BSAE excavations in cemeteries around Tarkhan. Other names which stray across these records are more obscure and harder to pin down. The 1894–5 season at the prehistoric cemeteries of Naqada and Ballas, for instance, was documented by six individuals: James and Kate Quibell, Flinders Petrie, Bernard P. Grenfell, Garrow Duncan and Hugh Price. The first four names have detailed entries in the compendium *Who Was Who in Egyptology*,[46] while the last two are absent.

Reverend John Garrow Duncan (1872–1951) was an ordained minister from Aberdeen who had been admitted to the British School of Athens in 1894. During this time he joined Petrie's team at Naqada for six weeks, motivated in large measure by the link between Egypt and the Old Testament. According to Petrie he was an 'active and precise observer, making excellent notes of the graves',[47] and he conducted fieldwork with Petrie again in 1905.[48] There is no record of Garrow Duncan receiving objects from these excavations, but in the stores of Dundee's McManus Art Gallery and Museum are numerous Egyptian artefacts donated by him. What links these objects back to specific excavation sites is not his name, but the ciphers scrawled onto their bases – short sequences of numbers and letters indicative of specific field seasons. A flat, grey-stone palette in the shape of fish, numbered '31', links it to a prehistoric tomb documented at Naqada, while the inked marking 'B119' relates a black-topped pottery vessel to a grave excavated nearby at Ballas. It is likely that Hugh Price similarly acquired souvenirs, but his appearance in the annals of archaeology is fleeting, and they are frustratingly silent about his movements after 1896.

Archaeological work in Egypt propelled objects out of the country in other unintended ways. For instance, in 1906 Flinders Petrie planned an Old Kingdom tomb on the southern edge of Gebel Qibili, Giza. He had hoped to remove some portions of the wall, but lacked the resources to do so and refilled the tomb with sand. Soon afterwards, reportedly at the request of foreign antiquities dealers, robbers hacked the reliefs from the tomb's walls and they were whisked away. They found their way to the Brooklyn Museum, which in turn sold them to the Colombian National Museum in Bogota.[49]

Egypt and Egyptians

The focus of this book is the scattering of Egypt's heritage beyond its national borders. It is important to remember, however, that the majority of finds, or what were regarded as the most unique, were supposed to be retained within Egypt, the proportions of which were, from 1835, regulated by national legislation and later by international conventions (see Appendix A). Moreover, the release of antiquities under partage did not pass without criticism in Egypt itself. Heba Abd El Gawad is currently investigating the range of historical and modern Egyptian perspectives on the diaspora of the country's heritage, from those who consider such acts 'legal thefts'[50] to those that regard artefacts abroad as ambassadors for the country. She has noted that the very act of removal itself, more often than not, arouses suspicion in Egypt that the antiquities hosted outside the country are of a higher cultural value and meaning than those in Egypt. El Gawad's ongoing work will add a crucial counterpoint to the account presented here, and an opportunity to further open up dialogue on these issues.

It is equally vital to acknowledge the role that Egyptian workforces have played in enabling and shaping the production of archaeology. As Christina Riggs has remarked, Egyptian voices are largely absent from accounts of the 'discovery of Egypt', despite the fact that their images are ever-present in photographs of fieldwork (Fig. 0.5).[51] The actions of British archaeological teams not only disciplined objects; they also disciplined people and communities. Donald Reid has undertaken important work to redress the lacunae of Egyptian scholars in disciplinary histories of Egyptology, archaeology and museums,[52] while Stephen Quirke has drawn attention to the 'hidden hands' behind Petrie's excavations – the *Quftis* and *reis* of the Egyptian workforce – that foreign missions depended on.[53] Sometimes their names are recorded in field notes (for the purposes of calculating wages), making it possible to relate particular workmen, such as Petrie's *reis* (foreman) Ali Suefi, to specific finds. Nevertheless, these identifications never travelled out of the country with the objects. Financial transactions, intellectual traditions and colonial archival systems, compounded by domestic power struggles, alienated Egyptians from archaeological discoveries and their heritage. More typically, it

Fig. 0.5 Photographs of Egyptian work teams on site at Egypt Exploration Fund excavations at Abydos, 1911–12. Courtesy of the Egypt Exploration Society, (ABNeg.11.0240).

is the excavation director's association with artefacts that has become part of their congealed value, especially in the case of Flinders Petrie, with several specimens around the world simply bearing his name as the crucial vector of an object's significance.

Increasingly, the broader agencies behind collections are being recognized.[54] In the context of British excavations in Egypt they emerge from the system of exchange values instituted by Flinders Petrie, which had a profound influence on the nature of what was retrieved from the field. Petrie's practice of paying tips (*baksheesh*) to his workmen, with the aim of enticing them to bring finds to him rather than to a dealer, meant that locals in Egypt could significantly shape the sorts of objects that made it to foreign display cases. *Quftis* closely monitored what would appeal to Petrie's purse. Several were quick to observe that nothing excited the Professor more than objects that were in some ways indexical, whether that was conferred by the presence of a name, title or date. A fragment of red polished pottery now on display in the Petrie Museum of Egyptian Archaeology is a case in point.[55] It had been presented to Flinders Petrie during the clearance of the tombs of First Dynasty rulers at Abydos during the 1899–1900 season. The sherd itself is genuine, made of marl clay typical of the early third millennium BC, but the inscription is more recent. Purportedly a symbol of First Dynasty king Semerkhet, the unusually stark incision would have caught Petrie's eye, but closer inspection by curator Barbara Adams seventy years later demonstrated that the etching could not have been ancient.[56] If it was a genuine inscription it would have been upside down. No doubt the workers were familiar with the sorts of signs being unearthed at Abydos and knew that Petrie would pay more for pieces bearing them.

Identifying Egyptians within these histories does not necessarily take a trained curator's eye or an archivist's ability to discern Arabic names scrawled hastily in Victorian notebooks. These hands are in fact hiding in plain sight. They are attested by the physical presence of hundreds of thousands of artefacts now spread amongst the world's museums. Collectively, this mass of material things demanded a huge labour force to recover, pack and transport it. Individually, some finds are so immense that they can only owe their current presence to large work crews. Take, for instance, the 12,700 kg (28,000 lb.) granite stone capital now towering over the sculpture gallery of the Boston Museum of Fine Arts.[57] Yet too often the artefacts that come to rest in museums find themselves in locations where all of that effort – the hundreds of campaign letters written, the thousands of miles travelled, the dozens of work teams employed, the weeks of arduous fieldwork, the tonnes of earth shifted, the mounting costs of packing and shipping, the months of drawing and writing, and the many hours of draining diplomacy – dissolves away into a singular accomplishment. It takes renewed and ongoing efforts to make visible the mediations and the multiplicity of interventions that collections embody. This book is just one attempt to that end.

Notes

1. Candea, M. 2013. The fieldsite as device. *Journal of Cultural Economy* 6(3): 252. See also Marcus, G. E. 1995. Ethnography in/of the world system: the emergence of multi-sited ethnography. *Annual Review of Anthropology* 24: 95–117; Stevenson, A., Libonati, E. and Williams, A. 2016 'A selection of minor antiquities': a multi-sited view on collections from excavations in Egypt. *World Archaeology* 48(2): 282–95.
2. University College London's (UCL) eight book series Ucko, P. 2003. (ed.) *Encounters with Ancient Egypt*. London: UCL Press, also sought to challenge this with numerous case studies of changing attitudes to ancient Egypt across time and space.
3. Stevenson, A., Libonati, E. and Baines, J. 2017. Object habits: legacies of fieldwork and the museum. *Museum History Journal* 10(2): 113–26. The term was coined by Emma Libonati who was reminded, during the course of our conversations on motivations for collecting, of the concept of the 'epigraphic habit' used by ancient historians (MacMullen, R. 1982. The epigraphic habit in the Roman Empire. *The American Journal of Philology* 103(3): 233–46). The 'epigraphic habit' seeks to draw attention to the larger set of influences that led to the creation of a text and the different audiences which produced and encountered it.
4. For discussions regarding object agency in the context of museum assemblages see overview in Harrison, R. 2013. Reassembling ethnographic museum collections. In Harrison, R., Byrne, S. and Clarke, A. (eds.) *Reassembling the Collection: Ethnographic Museums and Indigenous Agency*. Santa Fe: SAR Press, pp. 15–17.
5. Kopytoff, I. 1986. The cultural biography of things: commoditization as process. In Appadurai, A. (ed.) *The Social Life of Things: Commodities in Cultural Perspective*. Cambridge: Cambridge University Press, pp. 64–91.
6. Gosden, C. and Marshall, Y. 1999. The cultural biography of objects. *World Archaeology* 31(2): 169–78; Joy, J. 2009. Reinvigorating object biography: reproducing the drama of object lives. *World Archaeology* 41(4): 540–6; Harrison, Reassembling ethnographic museum collections.
7. Gosden, C. and Larson, F. 2007. *Knowing Things: Exploring the Collections at the Pitt Rivers Museum 1884–1945*. Oxford: Oxford University Press; Larson, F., Petch, A. and Zeitlyn, D. 2007. Social networks and the creation of the Pitt Rivers Museum. *Journal of Material Culture* 12(3): 211–39.
8. Latour, B. 2005. *Reassembling the Social: An Introduction to Actor-Network-Theory*. Oxford: Oxford University Press. Examples of its use in museum studies include: Bennett, T. 2014. Liberal government and the practical history of anthropology. *History and Anthropology* 25 (2): 150–70; Waller, L. 2016. Curating actor-network theory testing object-oriented sociology in the Science Museum. *Museum and Society* 14(1): 193–206.
9. Swain, H. 2007. *An Introduction to Museum Archaeology*. Cambridge: Cambridge University Press, p. 12.
10. E.g. Çelik, Z. 2016. *About Antiquities: Politics of Archaeology in the Ottoman Empire*. Austin: University of Texas Press; Guha, S. 2015. *Artefacts of History: Archaeology, Historiography and Indian Pasts*. New Dehli: Sage; Riggs, C. 2014. *Unwrapping Ancient Egypt*. London: Bloomsbury; Shaw, W. 2003. *Possessors and Possessed: Museums, Archaeology and the Visualization of History in the Late Ottoman Empire*. Berkeley: University of California Press.
11. Wingfield, C. 2018. Collection as (Re)assemblage: refreshing museum archaeology. *World Archaeology* 49(5): 594–607.
12. Available at: http://trowelblazers.com/ [accessed 27 January 2018]; Hassett, B., Birch, S. P., Herridge V. and Wragg Sykes R. 2018. TrowelBlazers: accidentally crowdsourcing an archive of women in archaeology. In Apaydin V. (ed.) *Shared Knowledge, Shared Power*. New York: Springer, pp. 129–142.
13. Meskell, L. 1999. *Archaeologies of Social Life*. Oxford: Blackwell, pp. 54–6.
14. Gero, J. 1985. Socio-politics and the woman-at-home ideology. *American Antiquity* 50(2): 342–50; Moser, S. 1996. Science, stratigraphy and the deep sequence: excavation vs regional survey and the question of gendered practice in archaeology. *Antiquity* 70(270): 813–23.
15. See for example Dudley, S. (ed.) 2010. *Museum Materialities: Objects, Engagements, Interpretations*. London and New York: Routledge.
16. Kaplan, F. E. S. 1994. Introduction. In Kaplan, F. E. S. (ed.) *Museums and the Making of Ourselves: The Role of Objects in National Identity*. London and New York: Leicester University Press, p. 3. Many such accounts stem from the application of Foucault's concept of the modern

episteme to the history of collections. See Foucault, M. 1989 [1966]. *The Order of Things.* English reprint. London and New York: Routledge. Foucault's schema was applied explicitly to museums by Hooper-Greenhill, E. 1992. *Museums and the Shaping of Knowledge.* London and New York: Routledge; A more nuanced, although still top-down, application is found in Bennett, T. 1995. *The Birth of the Museum: History, Theory, Politics.* London and New York: Routledge.

17 Henning, M. 2006. *Museums, Media and Cultural Theory.* Maidenhead: Open University Press, p. 3.
18 Witcomb, A. 2003. *Re-Imagining The Museum: Beyond The Mausoleum.* London and New York: Routledge, p. 5.
19 MacKenzie, J. M. 2009. *Museums and Empire: Natural History, Human Cultures and Colonial Identities.* Manchester: Manchester University Press, p. 8.
20 Shelton, A. 2000. Museum ethnography: an imperial science. In Hallam, E. and Street, B. (eds.) *Cultural Encounters: Experiencing Otherness.* London and New York: Routledge, p. 186.
21 Colla, E. 2007. *Conflicted Antiquities: Egyptology, Egyptomania, Egyptian Modernity.* Durham: Duke University Press, p. 177.
22 Moser, S. 2006. *Wondrous Curiosities: Ancient Egypt at the British Museum.* London and Chicago: University of Chicago Press.
23 See also Riggs, C. 2010. Ancient Egypt in the museum: concepts and constructions. In Lloyd, A. (ed.) *A Companion to Ancient Egypt.* Chichester: Blackwell, pp. 1129–53.
24 Thompson, J. 2015. *Wonderful Things: A History of Egyptology 1: From Antiquity to 1881.* Cairo: American University Press in Cairo, p. 172.
25 Gange, D. 2013. *Dialogues with the Dead: Egyptology in British Culture and Religion 1822–1922.* Oxford: Oxford University Press, p. 152.
26 Daly, M. W. 1998. The British occupation, 1882–1922. In Daly, M. W. (ed.) *The Cambridge History of Egypt, Volume Two: Modern Egypt from 1517 to the End of the Twentieth Century.* Cambridge: Cambridge University Press, pp. 239–51.
27 For example: Henare, A. 2005. *Museums, Anthropology and Imperial Exchange.* Cambridge: Cambridge University Press, pp. 121–46; Evans, C. 2007. Delineating objects: nineteenth-century antiquarian culture and the project of archaeology. In Pearce, S. (ed.) *Visions of Antiquity: The Society of Antiquaries of London 1707–2007.* London: Society of Antiquaries of London, pp. 267–305; Conn, S. 1998. *Museums and Intellectual Life, 1876–1926.* Chicago and London: The University of Chicago Press.
28 For a fuller discussion of the very difficult circumstances in which the society was established and the delicate negotiations necessary in order to obtain permission to excavate in Egypt see Drower, M. 1982. Gaston Maspero and the birth of the Egypt Exploration Fund (1881–3). *Journal of Egyptian Archaeology* 68: 299–317.
29 For a full list and discussion of these committees see Thornton, A. 2013. '…a certain faculty for extricating cash': collective sponsorship in late 19th and early 20th century British archaeology. *Present Pasts* 5(1): 1–12.
30 The EEF's name was changed in 1919.
31 EEF 1887. *Egypt Exploration Fund Report of the Fifth Annual General Meeting.* London: Egypt Exploration Fund, p. 25.
32 Individual subscribers are first listed in the EEF Annual Report for 1885, in which 572 people across the UK and the USA are named as donating money.
33 Aspects of the histories of papyri circulation are explored in the following, which also touch on associated artefacts: Hickey, T. M. and Kennan, J. G. 2016. At the creation. Seven letters from Grenfell, 1897. *Analecta Papyrologica* 28: 352–82; Johnson, W. A. 2012. The Oxyrhynchus distributions in America: papyri and ethics. *The Bulletin of the American Society of Papyrologists.* 49: 209–22; Schork, R. J. 2008. The singular circumstance of an errant papyrus. *Arion* 16: 25–47.
34 University of Liverpool, Garstang Museum archives, Beni Hasan paper JG/2/2.
35 *The Times*, 18 February 1904, p. 7.
36 University of Liverpool, Garstang Museum Archives, C: Museum/Archives/MusCorr.
37 Garstang Museum archives, University of Liverpool, miscellaneous.
38 Petrie Museum accession number UC36314 and Cairo Museum accession number JE 69230. See Petrie, W. M. F. 1907. *Gizeh and Rifeh.* London: British School of Archaeology in Egypt, p. 23.
39 Letter from E. Gilbertson to Amelia Edwards, 3 September 1886, EES.CORR.9.a.42.

40 Serpico, M. 2013/2014. Re-excavating Egypt: unlocking the potential in ancient Egyptian collections in the UK. *Egyptian and Egyptological Documents Archives Libraries* 4:131–42.
41 Letter from M. Buckman to M. Jonas, 18 August 1925, EES.USA.COR.
42 Object number 56.22.603, with thanks to curator Ashley Cooke for identifying.
43 EES.DIST.21.43.
44 Derrida, J. 1995. *Archive Fever: A Freudian Impression*. Translated Eric Prenowitz. Chicago and London: University of Chicago Press.
45 For further critical consideration of the nature of the archive see Baird, J. and McFadyen, L. 2014. Towards an archaeology of archaeological archives. *Archaeological Review from Cambridge* 29(2): 14–32; Dirks, N. 2015. *Autobiography of an Archive: A Scholar's Passage to India*. New York: Columbia University Press; Stoler, A. L. 2010. *Along the Archival Grain: Epistemic Anxieties and Colonial Common Sense*. Princeton: Princeton University Press.
46 Bierbrier, M. 2012. *Who Was Who in Egyptology*. Fourth Revised Edition. London: Egypt Exploration Society.
47 Petrie, W. M. F. and Quibell, J. 1896. *Naqada and Ballas*. London: Bernard Quaritch, p. vii.
48 Petrie, W. M. F. and Duncan, G. 1906. *Hyksos and Israelite Cities*. London: British School of Archaeology in Egypt.
49 el Saddik, W. 2017. *Protecting Pharaoh's Treasures: My Life in Egyptology*. Cairo: The American University Press in Cairo. pp. 84–98.
50 أشرف العشماوي 2012. سرقات مشروعة. حكايات عن سرقة آثار مصر وتهريبها ومحاولات استردادها. القاهرة: الدار المصرية اللبنانية. [In Arabic] [Ashmawi, A. 2012. *Legal Thefts: Stories of Thefts of Egyptian Antiquities, Their Smuggling and Attempts to Recover Them*. Cairo: Egyptian Lebanese Publishing House]. With thanks to Heba Abd El Gawad for the reference and synopsis.
51 Riggs, C. 2017. Shouldering the past: photography, archaeology and collective effort at the tomb of Tutankhamun. *History of Science* 55(3): 336–63.
52 Reid, D. 2002. *Whose Pharaohs? Archaeology, Museums and Egyptian National Identity from Napoleon to World War I*. Berkeley and Los Angeles: University of California Press.
53 Quirke, S. 2010. *Hidden Hands: Egyptian Workforces in Petrie Excavation Archives, 1880–1924*. London: Duckworth. *Quftis* are Egyptian workmen specializing in archaeological excavation. They are named after the village of Quft in Upper Egypt, where Petrie recruited men from in 1893 to work on excavation and who he continued to employ for the rest of his career.
54 E.g. Harrison, Reassembling ethnographic collections; Thomas, N. 1991. *Entangled Objects: Exchange, Material Culture, and Colonialism in the Pacific*. Cambridge, MA: Harvard University Press, pp. 83–124.
55 Object number UC36756, Petrie Museum of Egyptian Archaeology, UCL.
56 Adams, B. 1993. Potmark forgery: a serekh of Semerkhet from Abydos. *Discussions in Egyptology* 25: 1–12.
57 Museum number 89.555. From the great temple of Bastet, Bubastis, excavated by Édouard Naville's teams in 1887–8 for the Egypt Exploration Fund.

Chapter 1
Trinkets, Trifles and Oddments: The Material Facts of History (1880–1914)

It must have been quite a sight that cold March morning in 1889 on Liverpool's Huskisson Dock. A colossal, two-tonne red granite torso of a pharaoh lay on the open quay. Towering over him was a pair of enormous black granite legs set upon an imposing throne. Large chunks of temple wall, fragments of shrines and massive stone columns carved deeply with hieroglyphs lay like felled trees around this awkward royal gathering. A finely dressed, middle-aged lady strode among the monuments, inspecting the recently disembarked cargo. With some difficulty she made her way up onto a nearby scaffold and stared over the dock. From here, her gaze fell upon an immense wooden crate lying open below, from where, nestled within the packaging, a flawless six-foot stone face of an Egyptian goddess stared upwards at the grey English sky. Nearby, the lady found a warehouse full of crates replete with an assortment of bronze effigies, blue glazed scarabs and innumerable stone beads. The museums, she might have thought to herself, would be pleased.

Amelia Blanford Edwards's account of the steamship *Mareotis*'s cargo of monuments from Bubastis (Fig. 1.1) was read at the sixth annual general meeting of the London-based Egypt Exploration Fund (EEF).[1] As a versatile, prolific and successful Victorian writer, her reports are vivid and passionate. She devoted the latter part of her life to tirelessly promoting archaeological work in Egypt, following a sojourn up the Nile taken on a whim in 1873, and she was instrumental in the foundation of the EEF. The new organization was announced in London's *The Times* newspaper on 30 March 1882 under the enticing headline 'Egyptian Antiquities'. But despite this eye-catching declaration the last sentence of the article confessed that 'it must be distinctly understood that by the law of Egypt no antiquities can be removed from the country'.[2] So what had happened? What had allowed these monuments to end up so many thousands of miles away from where they were once erected?

In beginning to address these questions it is tempting to appeal to the role of international state diplomacy in negotiating access to such

Fig. 1.1 Lower part of a seated royal statue of a Hyksos king of the mid-second millennium BC at Bubastis 1888–89, with Egyptian workmen in background. Courtesy of the Egypt Exploration Society (BUB.NEG.15).

artefacts, to Britain's imperial privileges or to nationalistic rivalries. These all had a part to play. Yet what ultimately cleaved open the passage for Egypt's heritage abroad was the cordial bargaining for what are referred to in contemporary correspondence as trinkets, trifles or oddments that took place in Paris one afternoon in November 1883 between a Frenchman and an Englishman. The 'partage' arrangements that these two men eventually reached set a legal precedent that permitted Flinders Petrie to export from Egypt vast amounts of the sorts of finds for which he is renowned today, the 'small things forgotten'[3] of past lives. It was these seemingly incidental 'trinkets' (Fig. 1.2) that made up the vast bulk of objects distributed by the EEF, the legacy of which is no less monumental than the statues and temple walls that sat on Liverpool's quay.

This is still not a fully satisfactory account of how hundreds of thousands of Egyptian objects came to be so widely dispersed. Collections are not simply the result of a one-directional movement of things from the field into the museum. The laws of supply and demand still apply. And archaeological discoveries were not just waiting to be found: they had to be recognized as such. What, then, made the quotidian or the

Fig. 1.2 Foundation deposit from the pylon of the sanctuary of Amun-Ra, built under Ptolemy II Philadelphu (285–246 BC), photographed by Flinders Petrie in 1885. Courtesy of the Petrie Museum of Egyptian Archaeology, UCL (PMAN 2680).

'duplicate' worthy of museum acquisition in the first place? Petrie's offerings were a stark contrast to what Stephanie Moser has referred to as the 'wondrous curiosities'[4] with which the heroics of mid-nineteenth century archaeology furnished the British Museum. Not that everything acquired before 1880 was monumental, though. Europe in the 1820s had been enthralled by the opening up of wealthy, intact New Kingdom tombs around Luxor (ancient Thebes), that provided galleries in 1830s London, Paris and Turin with a diverse assortment of domestic furnishings, what Moser refers to as 'accessible oddities'.[5] These, however, were primarily crafts belonging to the ancient Egyptian elite, and were still regarded as 'unique', albeit secondary to colossal works. The material Petrie marshalled – hundreds of plain pottery vessels and sherds, worn bronze implements, and a multiplicity of amulets and beads – was fundamentally more ordinary. While commonplace relics might be deemed valuable by today's archaeological standards, Victorians and Edwardians looked upon them with different sensibilities.

This chapter situates Britain's acquisition of Egyptian finds first within the disciplinary context of late Victorian and Edwardian archaeology, and then within the burgeoning topography of British museums during the long nineteenth century. Archaeological practice and museum professionalism, however, need further qualification as scholars have tended to examine both in somewhat intellectually circumscribed ways. Museums, for instance, have frequently been portrayed as institutions of the Enlightenment whose authority to acquire and display things was intimately linked to imperialism and capitalism, and which deployed ordered knowledge within institutionally controlled spaces. But it is within the broader object habits of the late Victorian era that 'the coming into being'[6] of archaeological things should be more fully appraised. Diverse Victorian and Edwardian attitudes both influenced and interrupted attempts to understand the position and value of newly excavated finds. The same item could be a sacred biblical relic in one context, but an unprepossessing domestic accoutrement in another. The account here, therefore, explores the variegated motivations for acquiring and domesticating these seemingly unimpressive things, cross-cutting a wide range of interests. These include Flinders Petrie's emphasis on the value of scientific 'material facts', provincial towns' celebrations of industrial progress, gothic fantasies about Egypt during the *fin de siècle*, occult and biblical fascinations with the power of objects to reveal truths, British educational reforms through 'object lessons' and women's suffrage campaigns empowered by the achievements of women in ancient civilizations.

Diplomatic Gifts: The British Museum

Three months after the EEF's foundation in April 1882, Admiral Beauchamp Seymour signalled to the *HMS Alexandria* to commence bombing her namesake's fortifications. The ensuing fire from Britain's military assault engulfed much of the city of Alexandria, which burned for days before troops landed. Cairo fell a few months later, and British officials were installed in most areas of Egyptian administration. One department, however, remained under French supervision: the Service des Antiquités de l'Égypte. The organization's dominance over the cultural life of Egypt was later more formally recognized in the Anglo-French Treaty of 1904. This partitioning of diplomatic responsibilities was symptomatic of a deeper-seated tension in the two European countries regarding the status of archaeology. The French tradition was underpinned by centralized administration and government funding;[7] British interests had to be maintained by private, middle- and upper-class initiatives. From the outset then, the EEF's work faced a double bind of not only having to maintain scientific authority, but also of having to attract popular support.

Given these concerns, the EEF's short *Times* column was carefully penned. It was embedded within wider trends in mid-nineteenth-century British cultural practice, including an appeal to the familiarity of biblical and Classical narratives,[8] the use of an imperial rhetoric of preservation[9] and in garnering signatories whose antiquarian exploits in other countries had previously caught the public imagination.[10] These signatories included Charles Newton (1816–94), renowned excavator of Halicarnassus and Cnidus in the 1850s, and Austen H. Layard (1817–94), whose discoveries at Nineveh were reported as a national event in the *Illustrated London News*[11] and were the subject of the best-selling 1849 book *Nineveh and its Remains*. Layard's endeavours were one of a series of large-scale excavations of Classical antiquities that resulted in a significant expansion of the holdings of the British Museum, which was the primary space for the display of archaeology in England until 1880.

The EEF's keenness to capitalize on the success of such 'hero archaeologists' is evident from its first choice of excavator, Heinrich Schliemann (1822–90), the celebrated discoverer of Troy. But Schliemann's love of publicity, his controversial newspaper articles and constant self-promotion were too much for the Head of the Service des Antiquités, Gaston Maspero, who vetoed the suggestion almost immediately. He appealed to Amelia Edwards to consider an alternative expedition leader:

> I have therefore thought of asking you for a young man who has made proficient classical studies, who is interested in the history and languages of the East, and who, with a little goodwill, could soon become something of an Egyptologist.[12]

In the end it was Édouard Naville (1844–1926), a Swiss Egyptologist, who was deemed to fit this profile, and he led the EEF's maiden excavation to Tell el-Maskhuta in 1883.

Tell el-Maskhuta was one of several Delta sites that the EEF focused its early attentions on, ostensibly because it could be shrewdly marketed as a region ripe for new investigations of Classical and biblical histories. It was also a site whose name Edwards asked her audiences to recall from the British Army's advance on Tell el-Kebir only three months earlier, during which Tell el-Maskhuta had played an important role.[13] By placing archaeological work beside military success, the EEF secured for its British audience a sense of authority and legitimacy in trenching the site. The choice of the Delta masked the competitive political geography of archaeological endeavours: Maspero had ensured that the Nile Valley remained the preserve of French teams. The archaeological landscape of Lower Egypt that was left to the British was markedly different from the southern Egyptian Nile. The latter had been the setting for earlier renowned encounters with ancient Egypt, such as those of Giovanni Belzoni (1778–1823), whose adventures took place among the imposing temples and rock-cut tombs of ancient Thebes, and David Roberts (1796–1864), who took Upper Egypt's monuments as the subject of his popular drawings. In contrast, the Delta's flat, frequently water-logged landscape conceals ancient remains within mounds (Tells), rendering it a more daunting, uninspiring terrain to explore than the better-preserved and drier contexts that tend to characterize the Nile Valley.

Naville was not best suited to this challenge. He was an epigrapher rather than an archaeologist, and he was more comfortable among the splendour of monuments and the detail of hieroglyphic texts than he was amid the chattels of past activities.[14] Driven by his own intense religious convictions, he sought to establish tangible links between Egypt and the Bible, and so was quick to herald (erroneously) Tell el-Maskhuta as the location of the storehouses of ancient Pithom, the Hebrew-built 'treasure cities' of Exodus.[15]

In accordance with Egyptian legislation the harvest of monuments cleared by Naville's team was sent to Cairo. The exception were two pieces that the Khedive, Muhammed Tewfik Pasha (1852–92), granted to England through the mediation of Maspero, following patient and tactful diplomacy.[16] After the deliberations concluded, the EEF's President, Sir W. J. Erasmus Wilson,[17] was finally able to express 'great pleasure' in informing the EEF committee that a pair of granite sculptures – one of a falcon with the name of Pharaoh Ramesses II, and a block statue[18] – were to be dispatched to the British Museum. Given all of the political manoeuvrings required to assure this outcome, this first acquisition essentially constituted a diplomatic gift, and it fulfilled the typical narrative of Victorian heroic archaeology that had characterized previous decades.[19]

The following season Naville, anxious to complete his edition of the *Book of the Dead,* decided to remain in Europe. Others opined that Naville's real concern was to avoid the unappealing prospect of coping with life in the desolate marshland around San el-Hagar (Tanis) where the EEF had prospects (Fig. 1.3). In his stead the EEF recruited the more frugal and hardy Flinders Petrie, who was fresh from completing his survey of the Giza pyramid. As an active member of the Plymouth Brethren, like his father before him, Petrie was sympathetic to the underlying biblical narrative promulgated by the EEF, and he was eager to return to Egypt. He was far less sympathetic to Naville's excavation strategies, and he adopted a very different approach in order to 'raise from the dust the body of material facts of history'.[20]

Fig. 1.3 Landscape around Tanis after a rainstorm. Photograph taken by Flinders Petrie February 1884. Courtesy of the Egypt Exploration Society (DE.NEG.193a).

The attention Flinders Petrie gave to fragmentary material facts is eulogized in histories of archaeology, but is rarely examined critically. Such an affinity for material remains, as opposed to the ancient texts that occupied the attention of most mid-nineteenth-century Egyptologists, could be attributed to Petrie's informal education at home, where he had been largely left to his own devices. While a child he collected minerals, fossils and coins, and throughout his teenage years he frequented his local antiquities dealer, N. T. Riley, based in Lee (now in South East London). As Petrie's interest in the ancient world matured he was able to occupy a niche within the emerging discipline of archaeology. Since archaeology was, at that time, a subject formed outside universities, it had an individualistic and informal character that required no primary knowledge or training in the Classics. All that was needed was a great deal of meticulous fieldwork, skills in classification and attention to detail. Petrie obsessively honed these abilities by surveying earthworks and churches in the Kentish landscape, frequenting the British Museum and attending talks of the Royal Archaeological Institute, where men such as Lt-General A. H. Lane Fox Pitt-Rivers (1827–1900) and Sir John Evans (1823–1908) debated archaeological matters, flourishing the objects they had collected as they did so.[21]

In his autobiography Petrie reflected upon these early years and the skills that had served him over the course of his long career. Out of five subjects it was 'the fine art of collecting' that he placed first and foremost, which entailed 'securing all the requisite information, of realising the importance of everything found... of securing everything of interest not only to myself but to others'.[22] When Petrie's field methodology is further scrutinized it becomes apparent that it was this imperative to provide for collections that was in his mind's eye when he embarked upon his excavations, not the archaeological landscape that might be revealed. Contrary to popular or generic histories of archaeology in which he emerges as a founding father of systematic field excavation, Petrie actually devoted little time to the interpretation of archaeological features, or reconstructions of the manner in which sites formed.[23] He rarely measured or visualized stratigraphic profiles or sections.[24] Rather, the digs Petrie directed were fundamentally concerned with the retrieval of objects.[25] The field site merely provided a point of contextual reference for extrapolating sequences:

> Here lies, then, the great value of systematic and strict excavation, in the obtaining of a scale of comparison by which to arrange and date the various objects we already possess. A specimen may be

inferior to others already in a museum, and yet it will be worth more than all of them if it has its history; and it will be the necessary key, to be preserved with the better examples as a voucher of their historical position... The aim, then, in excavating should be to obtain and preserve such specimens in particular as may serve as keys to the collections already existing.[26]

Received wisdom concerning the development of the discipline of archaeology has tended to privilege fieldwork as its central advancement, and the more celebrated discoveries have long been staples of archaeological legend. But, as the above quotation reveals, there were related sites of knowledge production that equally drove the formation of professional archaeology, prominent among which was the museum.[27] Indeed, it was the British Museum's Keeper of Oriental Antiquities, Samuel Birch, who suggested to Petrie, prior to the latter's first visit to Egypt, that pottery collected from the field should be tagged with a note of its find-spot, in order for the British Museum's material to be better dated.[28] For Flinders Petrie, then, the telos of fieldwork was the displayed collection, whether on the printed page of an excavation memoir,[29] or in a museum cabinet back in England.

There was also a certain opportunism to Petrie's interest in the portable material facts that Naville and most of his colleagues had disregarded, as these had more potential, physically and politically, to circumnavigate Egypt's antiquities laws than any colossal or unique finds. The ability of such objects to transcend borders was not solely due to their essential qualities, however. It also depended upon institutional infrastructures, political situations, personal relationships and scientific knowledge. The same set of objects could be characterized as banal in one situation, but lauded as exceptional in another. During Petrie's first seasons of excavation, the tactic he adopted to secure the release of objects from state control was to present them as things that were ordinary and unexceptional, duplicates of material already held in the main museum at Bulaq.

The task of delineating categories of things that could be brought to England occupied the nine months between October 1883 and July 1884. It was the first order of business when Petrie visited Maspero in Paris on his passage to Egypt in November 1883,[30] a cordial meeting that was followed up in January 1884 with a signed agreement. The contract reaffirmed that while 'all objects of any nature, value, or age, discovered in working belong to the Egyptian Government and must be deposited at Bulak', objects that were purchased by Petrie 'in places where he makes his excavations must be submitted to the administration with the right of choice and purchase or reimbursement'.[31] Effectively, archaeological finds passed through what social anthropologist Arjun Appadurai has called a 'commodity phase',[32] in which the fate of the antiquities was governed by economic rather than political mechanisms.

After two months of excavations at San el-Hagar, a Third Intermediate Period temple and town site in the Nile Delta, Petrie wrote assuredly to Reginald Stuart Poole at the British Museum:

> I reckon on bringing home a quantity of little things; I have many pounds weight of draughtsmen, pendants, little figures, ring bezels, pieces of cut glass, rosettes, scraps of bronze work, beats, etc., etc.: all valueless to any large museum, but – when properly labelled – quite an attraction – little local museums, whose sole specimen from Egypt is perhaps a poor blue ushabti, or a hand of a mummy… People want something tangible to finger and stare at; books alone are not enough.[33]

It was evident to Petrie that these things would have widespread appeal that might leverage funding for future excavations. In order to guarantee permission to ship such artefacts out of Egypt, Petrie petitioned Maspero again in June 1884, identifying those items that he would send to Cairo for the Bulaq Museum, and those 'objects of no particular value, but worth taking to England'.[34] The idea of the 'duplicate' was a key concept in these deliberations, a mutable object status that was bound up as much with who had the authority to classify material as such, as it was with the context in which that was decided. Petrie was ultimately successful in his bid, and that autumn sixteen crates of pottery and small objects left Egypt for Great Britain, a hoard of things that was laboriously enumerated in the excavation memoir.[35]

Petrie's strategy had been successful for ensuring export, but on their import into Britain many of these same relics, which often offered little to the naked eye, had to be rehabilitated as appealing items worthy of scientific engagement, museum value and public interest. In some respects Petrie and his colleagues had their work cut out for them, given that earlier in the nineteenth century the British Museum had been reluctant to accept minor antiquities or indeed anything unrelated to Greek or Roman art. In the 1840s, for example, the British Museum had instructed those working at Nineveh to gather only objects that 'either from superiority of workmanship, or from historical connection, or from elucidation of the peculiar manners of the age are most remarkable'.[36]

These attitudes had not entirely dissipated by the 1880s. Although some articles from Petrie's first EEF excavations were put on public display almost immediately, such as Greek vase fragments from the 1884–5 season at Naukratis, there were protests at the 'vast quantity of pottery and small objects' which were deemed to be 'worthless'.[37] Charles Newton, the British Museum's Keeper of Greek and Roman Antiquities (1861–88), went as far as to describe a group of iron tools brought back by Petrie from Naukratis as 'ugly', and he promptly disposed of them.[38]

There was also the issue that not everyone agreed on the judiciousness of the mass export of finds in the first place. The removal of so many things from Egypt sat uncomfortably with the EEF's other excavator, Naville:

> I do not share your point of view as to the great desirability of carrying away great many small things, say several thousands in order to enrich a score of museums... I very well understand that the system of plunder as you call it promotes the welfare of the Fund in England; but you must not forget that it greatly endangers it in Egypt and it might easily someday wreck the entente cordiale which we have always had with the museum.[39]

Of greater import, perhaps, were the British consulate's own misgivings. Sir Evelyn Baring (1841–1917), later Lord Cromer, the powerful British consular general – and de facto ruler – of Egypt, preferred to defer to the French in most matters concerning antiquities, in order to secure political concessions elsewhere. For Cromer, antiquities were 'more trouble than anything else',[40] and he was frequently exasperated by requests for British intervention to ensure access to sites and objects. He did agree to put pressure on Maspero when a member of the British Parliament expressed a desire to explore Egypt, despite that being a 'mere looting operation',[41] but otherwise he often remained rather distant. Colonial fieldwork practices were as much a means of exercising control over the present as they were the past.

There were, however, also opportunities for the EEF to present its work outside the British Museum. Temporary exhibitions showcasing the results of archaeological fieldwork were held during the 'London Season',[42] a term used to describe the cultural landscape of public display and performances during the summer months, which had become firmly established in Britain's capital by the late nineteenth century. The first of these temporary exhibitions was installed at the Royal Archaeological Institute's offices in Oxford Mansions. It was a rather low key affair, designed to appeal to intellectual circles and to act as an intermediary space of post-excavation study between the field and the museum, rather than function as a form of public engagement. The response to this and the succeeding temporary exhibitions was not universally positive. One concerned EEF subscriber, an automobile businessman and son of a biblical antiquities collector, called J. Offord, wrote to Amelia Edwards enquiring:

> Are any of the large things coming from San? I do not ask because I want to see them but because from a business point of view I think one large object would gratify many subscribers more than any number of small ones.[43]

Offord's remarks typify contemporary public expectations of museum displays, which had created a visual codification of ancient Egypt associated with monumentality and endurance. The fragile, fragmentary and humble nature of the remains Petrie showcased went against the grain of such anticipations.[44] Fortunately, Amelia Edwards shared Petrie's view of the value of minor antiquities, and she, being 'the only romanticist in the world who is also an Egyptologist',[45] was able to articulate it in more passionate prose. While the tone of her promotion was derided by some of her colleagues at the British Museum as 'emotional archaeology',[46] Edwards's influence in advocating the value of such finds within and beyond the academy justifies the acknowledgement that she was as much of a participant in the production of archaeological knowledge as those in the field. Edwards, far more than Petrie at that time, was at the forefront of establishing within wider public consciousness what an archaeological object was. She provided florid articles about the EEF's discoveries for magazines such as *Harper's Bazar* [sic] and in detailed newspaper columns for *The London Times* and *The New York Times*. In her emotive and graphic accounts of ancient times she repeatedly emphasized the science of things and the worth of incidental finds. For instance, to promote the first instalment of archaeological finds delivered from Tanis and Naukratis to the Boston Museum of Fine Arts Edwards noted, in a letter published in the *Boston Daily Advertiser* on 18 December 1885, that

> …it is hard to make people understand that very small things, of no intrinsic value, can be precious… You have some very curious and precious specimens of Egyptian glass… these look like chips and rubbish, but they testify to the level which the art of glass working had reached.

What Amelia Edwards also recognized was that it would be in the provinces, not the metropole, that these unexceptional trinkets, trifles and oddments would find new significance, as she reported to the EEF Committee in 1888:

> ...wherever there is a local museum, there is an eager desire on the part of the authorities and townsfolk to obtain objects for their museum... I have repeatedly been promised subscriptions and donations, if a contribution of objects is likely to follow.[47]

While overseeing the division of finds in 1886, Edwards therefore prudently suggested

> ...laying aside, for stores – six sets of ushabti of all types, six sets of arrow head types, six sets representative pottery, & six sets of minor bronzes – for future museums. We shall have subscriptions & requests for donations in abundance – & it is well to be provided.[48]

Such 'trinkets' would have been less attractive to large national museums, but they could more easily be accommodated within the new municipal institutions that were springing up around Britain. As Kate Hill has observed, historical and museological commentators have largely neglected the study of these municipal museums.[49] Likewise, historical accounts of collecting and empire have tended to present a somewhat restricted view of the relationship between the field and empire's 'centres of calculation',[50] usually focusing solely upon the British Museum.[51] However, participation in the new discipline of archaeology, and the opportunity to collect directly from the field in Egypt, was a far more diffuse phenomenon that requires a broader scope of analysis. This should include a middle register of museums in economic hubs such as Bristol, Liverpool and Manchester, or intellectual centres such as Cambridge and Oxford, alongside a much larger number of regional museums and private foundations.

'By the gains of industry we promote art': Beyond the British Museum

Amelia Edwards was prodigious in her output. Between 1877 and 1891 she authored more than 100 signed articles for *The Academy* (in addition to unsigned notes), 74 articles for *The Times* and a series of 16 articles for *Knowledge* over six months in 1882.[52] When not promoting the

Fund's activities in the media, Edwards's administrative responsibilities occupied a considerable amount of her time elsewhere. Reams of her handwritten lists survive in the University of Oxford's Somerville College archives, giving one small insight into the enormous amounts of labour that archaeological finds demanded long after they had left the field, but before they made it to the museum. These lists also offer a glimpse of the volume of material flowing into England from the EEF's first excavations. One set of manuscripts neatly details every one of the 613 objects sent to the British Museum from Petrie's 1884 Tanis excavations, with a note of their features and dimensions. The other catalogues 312 artefacts sent to Bristol Museum and Art Gallery that same year.[53]

Edwards's surviving inventories particularize what is otherwise nonchalantly recorded in the EEF's own distribution records as 'a selection of minor antiquities'. Between 1884 and 1901, the EES distribution lists mention 49 other British institutions that received finds, including ones in Sheffield, Dundee, Macclesfield, York, Liverpool and Bolton, highlighting the coincidence of the influx of material from Egypt into Britain and the steady growth in the number of local museums across the country. Within five years of the EEF's foundation, the committee noted with satisfaction that 'the public, in subscribing to the Egypt Exploration Fund, appreciated the fact that they were making a good investment for the British Museum and for our provincial collections'.[54] By the end of the nineteenth century a national network of 24 honorary EEF secretaries had been established across Britain to manage this local interest,[55] and the EEF was regularly receiving subscriptions directly from provincial museums keen to expand their collections.

A symbiotic dependency between the Fund and museums was soon established, with the result that the financial imperative to provide for museums took precedence over pretensions to scientific archaeological practice. The EEF had become an association of donors that 'unearthed treasures in order to give them away'.[56] The administration of distributions became more logistically complex, with the result that mistakes in the allocation of material were frequently made and insufficient care taken to ensure the safe transport of delicate antiquities. Edwards's distribution lists were neatly scripted ledgers, deliberate and conscious records written with a sense of archival purpose. Petrie and his colleagues' later, hastily scribbled inventories on the backs of invitations, scrapped correspondence and lecture programmes betray the impatient and now taken-for-granted task of dispersing things. A 1905 letter from the Liverpool Museum paints one image of the sort of chaos that ensued:

...the vase duly arrived here but in such a shattered condition that the post office officials had to place a piece of brown paper around it to keep the case in the box; if any scarabs were enclosed, they must have been lost in transit.[57]

Museums themselves also became ever more demanding, and this pressure to provide for them weighed upon excavators. Naville, for instance, pleaded at the EEF's 1910 annual general meeting 'not to owe us a grudge if we do not send numerous boxes of antiquities', emphasizing that 'archaeology is not the art of finding objects so as to make collections and fill museums'.[58]

To understand the roots of this eager municipal museum movement, and the museums' interest in acquiring 'selections of minor antiquities', it is necessary to go back to the mid-nineteenth century, when the British Government attempted to address the effects of the industrial revolution and the major population centres outside London that it had created. The 1836 *Report from the Select Committee on Arts and their Connexion with Manufactures* argued that regional museums were required to support industry at the local level, while the 1845 Public Museums Act made provision for these new centres wherever the population exceeded 10,000 inhabitants. Uptake was slow at first,[59] but between 1870 and 1910 there was an exponential growth in the number of museums founded by municipal authorities.[60] A report from 1888 noted that of 211 provincial museums in England, Ireland, Scotland and Wales, nearly 100 had been built since 1872.[61] By 1914 around 115 more museums had been founded across the country.[62]

Several of these new museums developed out of earlier nineteenth-century local societies, absorbing their collections as they did so. For example, the collection of Warrington Museum in Cheshire grew from the local Natural History Society's. Other fledgling institutions shared a genealogical origin with the World Fairs, including 'modernity's most unsurpassable artifact',[63] the 1851 Great Exhibition at Crystal Palace. Such expositions are frequently characterized as showcases that had been engineered to demonstrate the industrial progress of a nation and its manufacturing prowess. Many early municipal museums have similarly been portrayed as political instruments, designed to discipline the population – particularly the working classes – to the benefit of a burgeoning middle class. This well-worn focus of museological analysis, initiated by scholars such as Tony Bennett,[64] variously draws on post-colonialist, structuralist and post-structuralist theory, and is heavily influenced by the writings of Foucault.[65] Although these approaches were largely developed in relation to national museums, and tend to overlook the complex ways in which visitors engaged with them, they can nevertheless usefully frame the emergence of specifically technical museums in the provinces within which 'scientific and technical instruction must above all subjects be given in object lessons'.[66] Several institutions of this sort were linked with the Arts and Crafts Movement, and followed the likes of William Morris and John Ruskin in placing a new emphasis on the value of labour, the pleasures of craftsmanship and the appeal of natural materials. In this context trade and labour were not just economic enterprises, but central concerns of Victorian culture.[67]

Late nineteenth-century Birmingham Museum was among the first municipal museums to acquire material from the EEF, only a few months after the Prince of Wales opened its galleries in November 1885. With its foundation stone bearing the motto 'by the gains of industry we promote art' the museum encapsulates many of the trends of industrial art and municipal museums. Its end of year report for 1891, for instance, described Birmingham Museum as one of

> … the finest museums which exists in the provinces… [it] lives and prospers solely by its artistic industries' in the development of public instruction… The aim of the Museum is very clear, and strikes the visitor at once. It is desired to form a true Museum of Art and Industry. All the collections tend to this end, by their nature, their classification, and the manner in which they are exhibited. It is sought to give the public, the artists, and the artizans models of industrial art of the purest taste, the most beautiful forms, and the highest execution.[68]

Other large town museums housed contemporary collections of industrial art and consumer goods, including samples of modern ironwork, textiles and jewellery, together with the tools of manufacture. Petrie's excavation returns of ancient production resonated with such modern assemblages, and it is no coincidence that the first modest artefacts sent from his excavations at Tanis to the iron and steel centre of Sheffield, for example, comprised four iron knives, a nail, and an iron hook, together with seven bronze nails of varying patterns.[69] Similarly, the textile production hub of Bolton received numerous samples of ancient linen.

Britain's industrial success influenced the membership of the EEF committee and its subscribers, affecting patterns in the traffic of finds. The manager of West Street Brewery in Brighton, Henry Willet (1823–1905), was an early enthusiast of the EEF, promising £500 to the

Fund if £250 more were subscribed within a fortnight.[70] He was also a founding member of Brighton Museum and, by 1885, Vice President of the Fund. Equally notable is the high concentration of Egyptological material sent to the Greater Manchester region in North West England, underscoring the link between the archaeological exploration of Egypt and wealthy industrialists.[71] Similarly, Macclesfield benefited from its connection with Marianne Brocklehurst (1832–98), whose father was a silk manufacturer. She had met Amelia Edwards in Egypt and was one of the earliest contributors to the EEF, as well as one of its local honorary secretaries. In the textile manufacturing centre of Dundee, the museum secretary at the then Albert Institute (now the McManus Museum and Art Gallery), proudly linked ancient Egyptian textile manufacture – 'the oldest in the world, exquisitely fine linens' – to the local flax industries led by the Baxter Brothers.[72]

Object Sequences: Lieutenant-General Pitt-Rivers

Within this industrial narrative of progress ancient Egypt held a privileged position as the fount of civilized society. In his *Companion to the Crystal Palace Egyptian Collection*, Gardner Wilkinson noted that the

> ... great antiquity of Egypt, and its well-known connection with early sacred history, invest it with an interest which no other country possesses... [it has] the oldest existing monuments, [which] prove it to have arrived, even in those remote days, at a point of civilization which continued long to distinguish it among the nations of antiquity.[73]

This pivotal place within world history permitted Egypt to occupy a secure intellectual niche within the culture-evolutionary framework that structured the emerging discipline of anthropology, of which British Egyptology was then considered part. Looming large within this academic milieu was the 'patron saint of curators',[74] Lieutenant-General Pitt-Rivers, an ardent advocate of the idea that technologies and cultures evolved gradually from the primitive to the civilized, or could degenerate in the other direction. His own collection, first displayed at the South Kensington Museum in 1874, was classified into object series demonstrating these principles, juxtaposing things deemed to be at a similar level of advancement, regardless of their age or origin. In Pitt-Rivers's own words,

> The collection does not contain any considerable number of unique specimens... ordinary and typical specimens, rather than rare objects, have been selected and arranged in sequence, so as to trace, as far as practicable, the succession of ideas by which the minds of men in a primitive condition of culture have progressed from the simple to the complex, and from the homogeneous to the heterogeneous.[75]

The influence of these ideas on museum classifications was widespread, with museums in Brighton, Edinburgh, Liverpool and Warrington adopting this comparative perspective for the organization of their displays (Fig. 1.4).[76] Notably, Pitt-Rivers shared the widespread view that Egypt was 'the cradle of western civilisation, certainly the land in which western culture first began to put forth its strong shoots'.[77]

Shortly after coming into his fortune at the Rushmore Estate in 1881, Pitt-Rivers booked passage to Egypt with Thomas Cook, and while he was there he located and published the first examples of Egyptian Palaeolithic implements found *in situ*. Arguments in favour of a prehistoric era in Egypt had been gathering pace in intellectual circles since J. J. A. Worsaae first drew attention to flint tools discovered on the borders of Egypt in 1867.[78] Despite such reports, several prominent Egyptologists, blinkered by the country's mass of monuments and tombs, still rejected the very idea of a Stone Age in the Nile Valley.[79] Instead, scholars such as Auguste Marriette argued that Egyptian flint implements had only been used in the historical periods for the construction of tombs, or had been employed during mummification rituals. The debate echoed through the meeting rooms of the *Anthropological Institute of Great Britain and Ireland* throughout the 1870s.[80] The flints that Pitt-Rivers recovered in Egypt were embedded in the same gravel into which had been cut ancient Egyptian tombs of the New Kingdom. This juxtaposition of prehistoric with historic evidence neatly encapsulates the dual conceptual significance that Egypt held at this point in Victorian discussions of the past: the antiquity of man on the one hand, and the origin and spread of civilization on the other.

Pitt-Rivers became a sponsor of the EEF, through which he acquired numerous finds that he used as the first artefacts in several of his museum arrangements that aimed to demonstrate the evolutionary development of culture. At King John's House on his own estate, for instance, he installed a series of paintings 'illustrating the history of painting from the earliest times, commencing with Egyptian painting of mummy heads of the Twentieth and Twenty-Sixth Dynasties.'[81] Similarly, his unrealized plans for a new museum situated Egypt at the fulcrum between prehistory, as it was then understood, and history, as represented by civilization.[82] Museums around the country looked towards Egypt in a similar manner.

Fig. 1.4 Acknowledgement certificate dated 1904 from Bankfield Museum for objects presented by the Egypt Exploration Fund. The vignettes illustrate the dense universalist displays of world culture UK municipal museums aspired to in the early twentieth century. Courtesy of the Egypt Exploration Society (DIST 21.36).

Disciplinary Fault Lines

The importance of objects to Victorians within these sorts of discourses has been commented on widely by historians, literary scholars, geographers, anthropologists and archaeologists who have explored this 'era of the object'.[83] Social anthropologist Amiria Henare, in an account of ethnographic collecting in Scotland and New Zealand, has highlighted the centrality of artefact-based research in the late nineteenth century, and the role of objects as ideal scientific data, unmediated by the opinions of travellers, colonial officials and missionaries. Cross-cultural methods of this nature permitted anthropologists to collapse spatial and temporal distance by bringing together objects for comparative study into the various 'stages of civilization', mostly famous outlined by Oxford's 'father of anthropology' Edward Tylor. Such a 'material anthropology'[84] meant that objects were key to the way in which the world was understood. Similarly, geographer David Livingstone has acknowledged that the object-based approach to knowing seized upon by late nineteenth-century museums 'constituted a remarkable experiment in visual encyclopedism'.[85] It was embodied in the dense displays of the period, the minimal labelling (especially for finds like pottery) and the absence of interpretive text panels or indeed any form of contextualization other than the setting of the museum and the vitrines themselves.

Despite the widespread conviction that objects were able to impart scientific and objective knowledge, the frameworks within which antiquities were to be deployed in these museums were in a state of flux. The nascent academic disciplines of anthropology, archaeology and Egyptology were still being configured within new institutional settings, and what constituted an ethnographic, art historical or archaeological object was ambiguous. Museums themselves, as Christopher Whitehead comments, were sites where academic disciplines were being mapped out and subject areas connected, but when it came to Egypt its antiquities 'occupied uncertain terrain'.[86] The accommodation of the realistic Roman era mummy portrait panels, recovered by Petrie's teams at Hawara in 1888, into the exhibitionary order of London's museums is just one example. Eleven of these vivid representations entered London's National Gallery, where they were displayed as a link between Classical and Renaissance art in the Western tradition. Not everyone agreed with the move. The acquisition was criticized in particular by several gallery trustees, who felt the finds were more archaeological than artistic and argued that the panels only belonged in the British Museum.[87] Even within a single institution like the British Museum, however, taxonomic ambivalences existed as to where Egypt belonged within particular categories of Western knowledge. Notwithstanding the existence of a department dedicated to Egyptian and Assyrian Antiquities, offerings from Petrie and the EEF were able to be slotted into the British Museum's other divisions: Coins and Medals; Greek and Roman Antiquities; and British and Mediaeval Antiquities and Ethnography Departments.

These debates continued into the Edwardian period, and came into stark relief in the South Kensington Museum's deliberations on the future of its Egyptian collections. In a museum Board of Education minute paper dated 12 June 1907 it was noted that

> we [South Kensington Museum] have no right to an Egyptian collection here from a purely archaeological point of view, a such a collection belongs to the British Museum... [But] there does not seem to be any reason why we should not have specimens which (1) are of artistic merit or (2) which illustrate some particular technique in art industry.

The following year the museum's resolve on these points was tested when it was presented with a unique opportunity to acquire what was described at the time as 'the richest' undisturbed burial recorded from Egypt: the Qurna burial group (Fig. 1.5).[88] In 1908 Petrie's BSAE teams uncovered

Fig. 1.5 The Qurna burial group, *in situ*, shortly after discovery. Courtesy of the Petrie Museum of Egyptian Archaeology, UCL (PMAN 2851).

an intact royal burial in Western Thebes dating to the sixteenth century BC. It comprised a young woman's gilded coffin, together with that of a child, accompanied by golden jewellery, a finely crafted wooden headrest and delicate pottery beakers. Petrie was keen to retain the integrity of the find, and approached Cecil Smith, South Kensington's Director. Internal memos indicated that Smith was tempted. He equivocated, but eventually replied that

> I cannot help thinking that the great interest which attaches to this series of antiquities is an interest primarily historical and Egyptological, and I doubt whether they should not be in the British Museum…[89]

But the British Museum had also declined, and Petrie was frustrated that London's museums were preferring to sort their holdings by material rather than by period. 'I had hoped,' Petrie retorted 'that one at least would follow the modern interest in rooms and groups of single periods'.[90] This 'modern interest' was a continental museum model known as *Kulturgeschichte*, the goal of which was to convey the sense of period through the comparison of a range of artefacts in period rooms and composite displays. It had a greater impact on the structuring of American collections than British ones, which remained trussed more strongly to industrial, evolutionary narratives.[91]

These debates in turn led Egyptian finds to form key touchstones for wider-ranging treatises on the general structure of museum display. At the Museums Association's 1908 Ipswich conference, the Director of Manchester Museum, William E. Hoyle, presented a paper on 'the arrangement of an Egyptological collection'.[92] He identified three possible schemes: chronological according to period; topical based on an object's nature and use; and ideal, presenting objects within settings evocative of the period. The lively discussion following the talk reflected on the problems and possibilities for each suggestion, noting capacity issues as well as intellectual ones in achieving their goals. Flinders Petrie's own views were conveyed in a letter to the symposium. He argued that any scheme should depend on the purpose of the collection:

> whether it be (1) Artistic, as South Kensington Museum, or (2) Historical, as the British Museum, or (3) Cultural, as an Ethnographic series, or (4) Technical, such as Jermyn Street Museum; or of some special class as (5) to illustrate development, like the Pitt Rivers Museum, Oxford.[93]

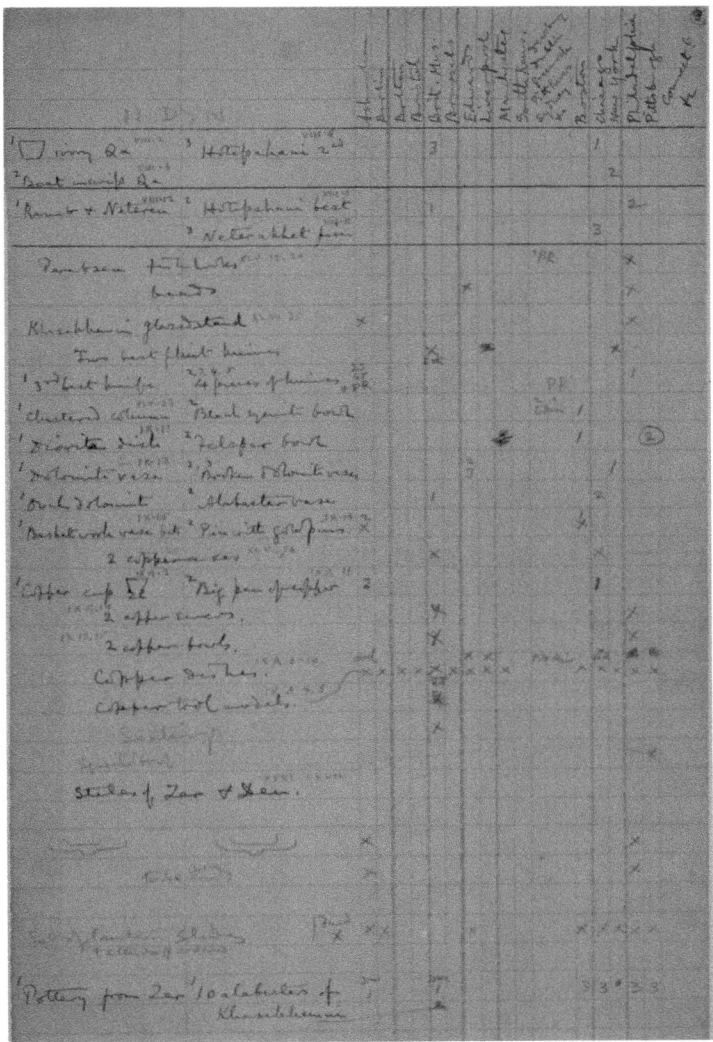

Fig. 1.6 Distribution grid from 1901, organizing the dispatch of artefacts from royal second dynasty tombs at Abydos to museums around the UK. Courtesy of the Petrie Museum of Egyptian Archaeology, UCL (PMA/WFP1/D/9/9.1).

The malleable status of Egyptian objects in this context is visualized most clearly in Petrie's early twentieth-century, grid-like BSAE distribution manuscripts (Fig. 1.6). Along the left-hand side he listed broad artefact classes like flint knives, stone bowls or beads, while along the top he scribbled the names of institutions. It was a convenient method of dividing up a season's finds, assigning very similar objects to very different institutions. Catalogue-based classification methods such as this, Catherine Nichols suggests, helped to create the very idea of 'duplicates', thereby shaping the possibilities for dispersal, exchange and circulation of artefacts.[94] By these means, copper dishes excavated in 1900 from the Second Dynasty royal tombs at Abydos, for instance, could be allocated to national museums and small regional museums alike. Equally, they were able to be dispatched both to museums focusing on art and history, like the Ashmolean, and to those that constructed comparative sequences of culture, like Pitt-Rivers' Museum in Farnham or the British Museum's 'Ethnological Department' (Ethnography), on the other.[95]

***

The industrial economy underpinned the logistics of international fieldwork, museum building and intellectual deliberation in the late nineteenth century. Imperial politics facilitated the circulation of finds, and scholarly frameworks privileged object knowledge in a diversity of schemes. It is easy to understand, therefore, why accounts of the formation of collections tend to be discussed in terms of the discursive formation of power, structured from the top down by wealthy industrialists' money, cultural-evolutionary rhetoric and curatorial agencies. Whether archaeologically, anthropologically or art historically focused, accounts of museum acquisition in this period do not generally probe the deeper questions of how or why such a framework based on object knowledge came to be so ingrained within Victorian worldviews. Such omissions are part of a tendency for histories of academic disciplines to be isolated from contingent phenomena in the wider world that informed their development. An obsession with things was not the sole prerogative of the academy, but a pervasive feature of the period. Recognition of this can go some way towards addressing the question as to why the Victorian public might even want to see the EEF's trinkets, trifles and oddments in the first place.

Object Habits: Beyond the Museum

From the 1880s onwards there was an increasing appetite for tangible goods across society, as tastes and attitudes became affected by industrialization. Mass consumption led to new social practices as disposable income was spent on consumer goods rather than making-do with re-usable items, a trend apparent today in the large amounts of packaging datable to the 1880s and 1890s itself recovered archaeologically.[96] At the same time the rapid production of imperial geographical knowledge encouraged exotic and eclectic trends in collecting. These volatile object habits infused Victorian culture, in turn producing the artefacts of archaeological enquiry.

It is well established that this Victorian consumerism was nurtured by the development of advertising, arcades and department stores,[97] which all fostered particular modes of looking, what Tony Bennett has called the 'exhibitionary complex'.[98] The parallel between museums and department stores, and between Victorian commerce and ancient Egyptian industry, is neatly encapsulated in a review of Petrie's temporary exhibition of finds from Kahun and Gurob at Oxford Mansions in 1890:

> It is, indeed a singular experience to pass from the stream of modern life in Oxford Street, with its roar of traffic and shop windows, smart with the latest novelties, and then at the distance of a few paces to find oneself surrounded by the tools and utensils, the dresses and ornaments, the objects pertaining to ritual observance, the talismans, the charms against unseen and malevolent influences, and even the coffins and funeral paraphernalia of a populace which, at an interval of more than forty centuries, was as brisk and busy as our own.[99]

The British home itself had, from the mid-nineteenth century onwards, become more museum-like, with eclecticism and exoticism being advocated in numerous titles of the day, such as Mary Haweis's (1881) *The Art of Decoration* or Clarence Cook's (1878) *The House Beautiful*. Domestic space was linked to social advancement and aspiration through a clutter of diverse ornaments placed in halls, parlours and dining rooms, a form of 'bric-a-brac consumption'.[100] Popular art of the period, such as was being produced by Dutch and Belgian-trained artist Lawrence Alma-Tadema (1836–1912), also situated antiquity comfortably within the home. Through his careful observation of antiquities in museums and his knowledge of archaeological discoveries, Alma-Tadema developed an acute sense of tactility that infused his oil paintings. The scenes of the ancient past that he rendered incorporated domestic artefacts in striking detail, echoing the Arts and Crafts movement's appreciation of the ordinary.[101] Alma-Tadema, along with influential painters who were equally attentive to archaeological detail like Edward Poynter and Henry Wallis, were staunch supporters of the EEF, appearing regularly as subscribers and as visitors to the annual exhibitions. The development of props for theatre performances of the 'Orient' was similarly observant of archaeological pieces.[102] It was all part of the 'world-as-exhibition', an 'objectness' to Victorian social life which, through a variety of mechanisms, 'rendered things up as its object' for public consumption, education and entertainment.[103]

Other forms of engagement with artefacts are apparent from fiction writing. The acquired taste for diverse domestic paraphernalia, for instance, pervades the literature of the period.[104] In Bram Stoker's (1897) *The Jewel of Seven Stars*, for example, the character of Margaret Trelawny remarks of her domestic space that 'I sometimes don't know whether I am in a private house or the British Museum'. Abercrombie Smith of Arthur Conan Doyle's (1892) *Lot No. 249* observed a similar transformation of the home, when he encountered 'a museum rather than a study' where the 'walls and ceiling were thickly covered with a thousand strange relics from Egypt and the East'.[105] What is clear from these tales is that objects were not merely symbols of status, but were vital to understanding and intense relationships were forged between people and things. Even a fragment or small relic offered the seductive possibility of an unmediated connection to the past. In his best-selling novel *She* (1887), H. Rider Haggard wove his narrative around the discovery of 'The Sherd of Amenartas', and devoted a dozen pages to describing this single fragmentary relic.[106] The EEF's own secretary, Emily Paterson (1861–1947), composed whimsical poems about the power of simple objects, including 'On a mummy bead', published in *Biblia* in 1901. Objects in these stories were fetishized as sources of power and meaning, suggesting a more privileged ontological status for material culture in Victorian culture in comparison to later periods.[107] Amelia Edwards's description of her own residence in Bristol, The Larches, which was 'filled and over-filled with curiosities of all descriptions',[108] encapsulates popular Victorian attitudes (Fig. 1.7):

> Each object recalls the place and circumstances of its purchase, brings back incidents of foreign travel, and opens up long vistas of delightful memories. For me, every bit of old pottery on the tops of the bookcases has its history.

In the same article Edwards remarked that there were two mummified human heads concealed within her bedroom wardrobe which 'perhaps, talk to each other in the watches of the night, when I am sound asleep'. While this may seem exceptionally macabre, the world of the dead was comfortably accommodated within the nineteenth-century domestic

Fig. 1.7 Photographic view of Amelia Edwards's study at her home, The Larches, in Bristol. Courtesy of the Principal and Fellows of Somerville College, Oxford.

sphere, where keepsakes of hair, teeth and other human remains acted as intimate connections between the living and the dead. In this Victorian relic culture, things were cherished for their ability to store memories and to tell stories.[109]

At their most extreme these beliefs found expression in the widely circulated theory of 'psychometry', the idea that psychic traces of human memories could be found on personal possessions. As psychometry percolated into popular engagements with spiritualism during the *fin de siècle*, curios like jewellery became commonplace focuses for psychic readings and ghostly encounters.[110] Similarly, esoteric outfits, such as the fraternal Hermetic Order of the Golden Dawn, founded in London in the 1887, relied heavily upon antiquities for spiritual epiphany. Members maintained an arcane image of Egypt, fusing cryptic and Egyptological presentations of Egypt within their rituals. Belief in communication with the dead formed one cornerstone of the hermetic foundations of the organization. Knowledge was acquired not by reason, but through revelation, including long hours spent among Egyptian antiquities in places such at the British Museum,[111] a location favoured also by London spiritualists like Thomas Douglas Murray and William T. Stead.[112] Boundaries between the esoteric and scientific were not always pronounced. One of the EEF's Archaeological Survey participants, Marcus W. Blackden (1864–1934), was ordained into the Hermetic Order of the Golden Dawn in 1896, while Petrie's student and later academic colleague at UCL, Margaret Murray (1863–1963),[113] famously influenced the development of Wicca. Battiscombe Gunn (1883–1953), one of Murray's protégés, who excavated with the BSAE just prior to the First World War before becoming Professor of Egyptology at Oxford, had more than a passing interest in theosophy,[114] and was seemingly well acquainted with the infamous Aleister Crowley in his youth.[115] Hilda Petrie's unconventional colleague Lina Eckenstein (1857–1931), who participated in excavations at Abydos at the turn of the century, also knew Crowley. Her brother, Oskar Eckenstein (1859–1921), was one of Crowley's few close friends; they would go rock climbing together.

Although seemingly antithetical to the occult's claims to knowing the past, those drawn towards Egypt's biblical connections were equally enticed by the efficacy of things to reveal knowledge, despite the vexed relationship many Christian denominations had had with the material world since the Reformation. Nineteenth-century 'higher criticism' had mounted challenges to the authority and historical truth of the Bible, challenges that archaeologists sought to counter with the brute facts of concrete places and authentic things. In this way, as historian David Gange has argued, biblical Egyptology directly supported a revival of traditional Old Testament Christianity in the closing decades of the nineteenth century.[116] This was a rationale that initially drove both Naville and Petrie's explorations of 'sacred geography', and which brought numerous men of the cloth to not only contribute financially to the EEF, but also to make pilgrimages to the sites it excavated. These enthusiasts included Canon Hardwicke Rawnsley (1851–1920), founder of the National Trust, while others even participated in excavations, as was the case with the

Reverend Garrow Duncan. Edwards and Poole were both acutely aware of the appeal of this narrative of ancient Egypt to a population deeply familiar with biblical narratives, in part due to the success of the Sunday School Movement in Britain, begun a century before. Most famously, both Edwards and Poole enthusiastically petitioned Naville to return from Tell el-Maskhuta with thousands of bricks, which were then to be distributed among EEF supporters. Even these most mundane of objects were construed as an evocative testament to the labours of Hebrew slaves under the Pharaohs: 'the bricks which they had to make, and did make, without straw, while their hands were bleeding and their hearts were breaking'.[117] These artefacts, Edwards proclaimed, were 'a sermon in bricks', thereby underscoring the way in which objects were able to speak to people.

It is unsurprising too, therefore, that several Sunday Schools around Britain requested loans of objects from the EEF. Most notable was the museum at the Sunday School Teachers' Institute on Fleet Street, which was devoted to the explanation and illustration of the scriptures, and which received numerous finds from Petrie's 1880s excavation seasons. A review of the museum's rooms in Serjeants' Inn describes the many models, casts and objects that were on display, emphasizing the value for each in realizing the reality of the bible, such as a 'signet ring of a Pharaoh recalling that which was placed on the hand of Joseph when he became viceroy of Egypt'.[118] Its curator, the Reverend J. G. Kitchin, published a handbook on *The Bible Student in the British Museum*,[119] which promised to 'assist readers in studying the Holy Scriptures', as well as *Scripture Teaching Illustrated by Models and Objects*. He passionately believed in the value of 'stone witnesses' and he extolled the virtues of using objects to teach children, preaching that 'Is not our Lord's life itself one long object-lesson?'[120] He further suggested that all Sunday Schools ought to possess a little museum, since 'teaching by the help of visible objects is stamped with the Divine approval and authority'.[121] As a religion of the Word, Protestant Christianity had dismissed Catholicism's attribution of divine power to artefacts and images, but Kitchin's object lessons were developed through the co-performance of word and object, thereby revealing theological truths in ways that would not contradict the immateriality of Protestantism.[122]

Artefacts were also popularly absorbed into public education more broadly as the British Government promoted 'object lessons' in which direct contact with things was deemed fundamental to children's education. The idea of the object lesson was central to the pedagogical methods promoted by Swiss social reformer J. H. Pestalozzi (1746–1827), who believed that individuals developed through concrete engagements with the world. By the end of the nineteenth century his ideas had become orthodoxy, and object lessons were made compulsory in British state schools in 1895.[123] Government-issued instructions for school inspectors further encouraged teachers to arrange for museum excursions that could count towards the school day.[124] The growth of object lessons inside elementary school curriculums led to schools scrambling to acquire commonplace things to use in class, and trying to source makeshift museum-like storage.[125] For the independently wealthy all-boys public schools of Harrow, Eton, Rugby and Charterhouse, this was not a problem: students had their own private museums furnished with genuine ancient finds procured through the EEF. These and many other schools, such as Merchant Taylor's School in Rickmansworth, Salt Schools in Shipley and Broughton Beck School in Lancashire, eagerly responded to John Garstang's 1904 offer in national and local newspapers of Middle Kingdom pottery. The Headmaster of Broughton Beck School reported that there was a 'very nice museum in connection with the schools and would deem it a very great favour if we are favoured with some specimens'.[126] In Haslemere, the Quaker surgeon Sir Jonathan Hutchinson (1828–1913) even created a museum exam for local children, to encourage observation, reading and discussion, and his small private museum was arranged in open display to enable people to learn through their hands as well as their eyes. His collection included four shabtis from the EEF's excavations at Deir el-Bahri.[127]

Higher education was similarly eager for objects to use in teaching, research and for the development of social policies. At University College London, Petrie became acquainted with the polymath Francis Galton (1822–1911), creator of the first weather map, developer of the scientific basis of fingerprinting and inventor of several statistical concepts such as correlation. Galton was also responsible for coining the term, and propagating the theory of, eugenics. In the context of Victorian society's anxieties about population degeneration and the growth of criminal classes, Galton sought to improve human populations through selective breeding. Flinders Petrie was one of his most prestigious advocates. These goals became entangled in university collections and museum arrangements of Egyptian finds. Prehistoric skulls were hoarded from Naqada for craniological measurements, Late Period terracotta heads from Memphis were organized into a series of racial types, and the Roman era mummy portraits from Hawara were scrutinized for attributes of character. Extrapolating from material such as this to the present day, Petrie saw 'one great lesson… the necessity of weeding'.[128] Egyptian things, Debbie Challis concludes, were being used 'as a tool to attempt to influence modern governance and systems of living'.[129]

From the arts to education, and from religion to social engineering, things from the past were integrated into the present. The reverse, though, is also true. Archaeologists like Tim Murray and Christopher Evans have argued that not only did fictional authors such as H. Rider Haggard draw from the form and content of accounts of scientific exploration, but also that contemporary creative works influenced archaeologists themselves.[130] This was achieved through the application of comparable narrative structures and a shared cultural context in which fiction could give shape to an unintelligible, remote and unfamiliar past. Martin Willis, for instance has noted how relic culture – a key feature of Gothic sensibility, that celebrated the uncanny, the sublime and the boundary between life and death – permeated the prose of Petrie's observations, demonstrating how Victorian fiction informed 'material facts'.[131] Likewise, Dominic Montserrat has shown how Petrie's effusive 1892 descriptions of the painted pavement from Akhenaten and Nefertiti's Great Palace at Amarna are suffused with references to the art nouveau movement – the 'naturalistic grace of the plants' and 'the new style of art'.[132] The resonance between ancient and modern times was not necessarily simply a casual or convenient point of reference, but implied a comparable ideology that rejected designs predicated upon Renaissance or Classical dictums.[133] Object habits came full circle in making the archaeological artefact. In so doing, they transformed mundane items into multivalent touchstones across the long Victorian period in a variety of contexts.

***

Pride and Prejudice: Negotiating Status Through Finds Distribution

Against this background of intense and diverse convictions around the power of objects, the EEF's 1882 *Times* newspaper headline 'Egyptian Antiquities' takes on a richer meaning, and the public enthusiasm for the EEF's initiatives becomes more understandable. Moreover, it helps provide a clearer picture of how civic investment could directly influence the trajectories of object dispersal. Prominent individual subscribers to the EEF could nominate local institutions to be the recipients of their share of finds, or else the demographic profile of donations would be utilized as one point of reference in EEF committee decisions to recommend donations to specific locations. Alternatively, if someone was prepared to defray the often exorbitant costs of freight, then those persons could direct material to the institution of their choice. In 1890, for instance, the McLean Museum in Greenock acquired a bas-relief slab from the site of the great temple of Bubastis, 'owing to the generosity of John Scott Esq. C.B., who paid for the cost of transporting the said block'.[134] These practices dispersed and localized the agency for collecting Egyptian material among a range of protagonists. As the volume of artefacts coming from Egypt increased, and as museums became far more numerous, ordinary citizens had greater opportunities to participate vicariously in archaeological discovery and its public presentation. In some cases the distribution of humble offerings of incidental things significantly empowered such citizens, and collections could be deployed as leverage for bigger campaigns, such as calls for new museum buildings or for women's suffrage.

That external agencies could influence the strategies of museum authorities challenges the main thrust of the literature inspired by Foucault that assumes that museums were responsible for regulating knowledge and exercising power over discourses. Sam Alberti[135] provides a counterexample of how, although Manchester Museum's Board actively resisted the expansion of the Egyptian collection in the 1890s, it eventually had to concede to both popular pressure and economic opportunism. The presence of a significant Egyptological collection in Manchester was the result of the patronage of successful local cotton merchant, Jesse Haworth, who had become enthralled with ancient Egypt after reading Edwards's *A Thousand Miles Up the Nile*. Haworth, together with Henry Martyn Kennard, financially backed Flinders Petrie's independent excavations in the 1880s and 1890s, with the portion of finds allocated after partage being divided equally between the three men. Haworth had loaned his share of the finds to Manchester's Owens College, even though the museum's principal audience at that time was science students. In 1892 the museum formed a sub-committee with a view to disposing of the Egyptian collection, as it was felt to be irrelevant for teaching, since neither archaeology nor Egyptology were then subjects of study at the College – which was later to become Manchester University. Even when Haworth offered to donate his entire collection to the museum, the science professors refused. His second offer of £5000 for a new building, however, clinched Manchester Museum's commitment to curating an Egyptian collection, and when the new building opened in 1912 its collecting remit had to be reformulated. The management of the collection also required new staffing, at which point Winifred Crompton (1870–1932), was appointed assistant in charge. Museums then, as now, constituted 'sites of struggle between curators, academics, sponsors, and the general public, all of whom had different aspirations for the institutions'.[136]

A second example of civic and urban development built on Egyptian collections occurred in Rochdale. Charles Heape, co-owner of Manchester's Strines Calico Printing Company, secured for the local library a selection of pottery from Petrie's excavations at Dendereh, and advocated for a new museum in the town. When it eventually opened in 1903, Charles and his brother ensured that it subscribed to the BSAE.[137] In Macclesfield, Amelia Edwards's friend, Marianne Brocklehurst, also had a passion for collecting Egyptian material, and was one of the earliest subscribers to the EEF and to Flinders Petrie's ERA. Brocklehurst campaigned for a new museum to house her private collection, and approached her local council with money for the venture. After several years of disputes, the West Park Museum was opened in 1898 with the financial aid of Ellen Philips, the wife of a local manufacturer.[138] The large sums of money that could be invested by these wealthy patrons also meant that many fine objects were sent to the regions, in addition to the more frequently allocated sets of amulets, shabtis, beads and pottery.

This last example highlights one of the most striking features of the development of collections of Egyptian archaeology in the late Victorian period: the extent of women's agency in the production of archaeology. So notable was this influence that it has been remarked that Egyptology, more than any other museum discipline, was created by women.[139] Just to take one snapshot, the EEF annual report for 1899–1900 records 29 local honorary secretaries across Britain, more than half of whom were women. Five women were full EEF committee members, and of the 559 subscribers, at least 176 can be identified from their salutations as female. Certain of these women were especially active, such as Annie Barlow (1863–1941), the EEF secretary for Bolton, whose efforts ensured that Bolton Museum was richly rewarded with finds. Such examples underscore Kate Hill's observation that these museums were not just places where national identity or scientific objectivity were produced, but that they were also where local communities could be enacted, with women taking a leading role. As the distinction between public and private blurred, as affluent homes became more 'museum-like' and museums more 'home-like', women emerged as one of the primary agents behind the domestication of museum knowledge: 'women's fascination with "authenticity" as a material quality relating to oldness, personal associations and "aura" enabled a significant change in the idea of the museum object'.[140]

Notably, many of the most active female supporters of museums were also energetic campaigners for women's rights, meaning that fundraising and collecting for museums potentially empowered other politically motivated agendas. Amelia Edwards herself was Vice President of the Bristol and West of England National Society for Women's Suffrage, and she left her collection to University College London in 1892 precisely because it was the only university in England that gave women degrees on an equal basis with men. Edwards also sought the support of leading women's suffrage activists for the EEF's cause. In 1887, for example, she approached executive council member of the London National Society for Women's Suffrage, Frances Power Cobbe (1822–1904), to become a member of the EEF: 'I assure you,' Edwards wrote, 'it is not your money or your life that I want – but your *name*… especially the names of eminent women'. Cobbe in return requested information about Egyptian female rulers, to which Edwards enthusiastically responded: 'the whole scheme of Ancient Egyptian law as regards women was most extraordinary.. [her] independence – nay her *supremacy* – even in private life, was absolute'.[141]

It was not just the seemingly enviable position of women in ancient times that attracted females to Egyptology. More important, perhaps, was its accessibility as a relatively new and ambiguous subject which, until Flinders Petrie's appointment as Edwards Chair of Egyptian Archaeology and Philology in 1892, was one that developed independently of universities. Therefore, while Amelia Edwards has been considered a 'radical nonconformist' and one of a handful of 'women in unusual paths' by the standards of Victorian Britain,[142] in the field of Egyptian archaeology she was not alone by any means. Numerous women were active participants throughout the entire finds distribution network, from fieldwork to raising funds for archaeological investigations to securing finds for local museums.[143]

Beginning with the field, Flinders Petrie's excavations were populated by female staff (Fig. 1.8). It is often claimed that women's lack of acceptance within fieldwork was 'a serious obstacle to women's full integration in archaeology',[144] but there were in fact numerous opportunities for their involvement at the turn of the century, especially in Egypt. The 1898–99 EEF season at the cemeteries of Hu, for instance, included not only Flinders Petrie and his new wife Hilda, but also Beatrice Orme and Henrietta Lawes. A photograph of Orme at the excavation site survives in the Petrie Museum of Archaeology, picturing her in a masculine shirt and tie, a look adopted by many 'new women' of the period who were entering the world of work and higher education (Fig. 1.9).[145] Another strong-minded new woman of the Victorian era was Lina Eckenstein,[146] who excavated alongside Margaret Murray and the artist Winifred Freda Hansard at the EEF's 1903 excavations at Abydos and Saqqara. Eckenstein formed a strong alliance with Hilda Petrie, who she accompanied to Sinai on camel-back, traversing rough mountain terrain and red sandstone gorges equipped with a whip

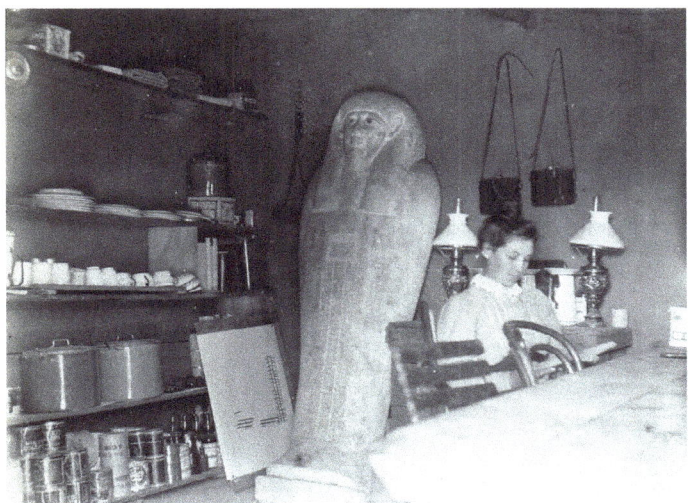

Fig. 1.8 Photograph of Hilda Petrie's sister, Amy Urlin, in the mess room of the Abydos dig-house, circa. 1903. Courtesy of the Petrie Museum of Egyptian Archaeology, UCL.

Fig. 1.9 Photograph of Beatrice Orme in Egypt in the early years of the twentieth century. On the back of the photograph is written 'The best length for a skirt in Egypt!!'. Courtesy of the Petrie Museum of Egyptian Archaeology, UCL.

and a revolver. She too was vigorously involved in the suffrage movement, a cause that she drew Hilda into with her.

In addition to sharing in the spartan life of the field, these women held several responsibilities alongside male participants, such as marking objects with context numbers, drawing and photographing finds, packing crates of artefacts, surveying sites, and occasionally directing fieldwork itself. Excavations in Egypt produced masses of finds, and it was often the women who were responsible for the heavy burden of ensuring 'the general orderliness of the ever-growing collections'.[147] This is clear from Petrie's introductions to his archaeological memoirs, like that for *Abydos*, published in 1901:

> My wife drew all the plans, besides doing much in sorting and arranging material. Miss Orme's help was more valuable than ever, as she developed all my photographs, and inked in fifty-seven plates of my pencil drawings, beside drawing marks and pottery and helping in sorting the stone vase fragments. Without her doing such a great mass of work, this volume could not have appeared till many weeks later. Miss A. Urlin sorted much of the vase fragments, and joined many complex fractures, besides doing a great part of the daily marking of objects.[148]

Petrie's account of his working day for that same season differs little from what he described of the women's work: 'the general course of work was, that I photographed in the morning, sorted and drew stone vases in the evening'.[149]

The marking of objects was an especially important form of authentication through which a curio or unprepossessing article could be transformed into a certified archaeological object, distinguishing it from the miscellaneous mass of relics that had otherwise percolated haphazardly into museum collections. Whereas antiquities could be 'wondrous curiosities', excavated trinkets, trifles and oddments required the support of these markings in order to be made meaningful. The role of Hilda Petrie, Beatrice Orme, Henrietta Lawes, Amy Urlin, Margaret Murray, Freda Hansard and a whole host of others in attending to these matters therefore made them more than simply site caretakers or handmaidens to the real business of archaeological excavation. As noted above, excavation was then understood primarily as involving the retrieval of objects, and archaeological inference did not usually occur at the trowel's edge. Rather, finds organization was key to the very production of knowledge. In any case, the actual digging was carried out by a workforce gathered together by the world's first trained field professionals: Egyptian *Quftis*.

Those neat ciphers inked onto finds in the dusty shade of makeshift dig-houses remain vital clues a century later for re-establishing connections between orphaned objects now in museum stores and these field histories. Although archaeologists tend to think of context as the static find-spot, in examining the diaspora of Egypt's excavated objects the term's original Latin meaning (*contexere*) is more appropriate, because it emphasizes the process of connecting or weaving together.[150] By tacking back and forth between object and archive – which is what object marks enable – archaeological context is continuously performed and object biographies enriched.

Some connections are stronger than others, and of the huge volume of finds distributed, several objects have a greater biographical weight because they can be connected to specific individuals. The 'valuable collection of Egyptian antiquities and specimens of sepulchral alabaster' that Reading Town Hall obtained in 1900 from Hu, for example, was a direct result of Henrietta Lawes's participation in the 1898–99 season.[151] Bucks County Museum received sets of faience beads from Freda Hansard's participation in fieldwork at Saqqara, led by Hilda Petrie and Margaret Murray, while Liverpool Museum has some 470 Egyptian objects in its collection associated with Hilda's sister Amy Urlin, who participated in the EEF's second season at Abydos.

Although gendered differences in spatial praxis on excavations were far less pronounced than is often assumed, other barriers to the acknowledgement of women's archaeological contribution clearly existed. Most problematic in this regard was the place of universities, within which knowledge and academic status were institutionalized in the early decades of the twentieth century. Margaret Murray's career, as presented by Kate Sheppard, highlights the issue.[152] Murray came to UCL in 1894 as one of the first of many female students to study Egyptology. She became an assistant to Petrie, and in 1899 she was appointed to a junior lectureship, making her the first female lecturer in archaeology in Britain. Her role in the university, however, was tenuous, and her contract was not made permanent until the 1920s. Nevertheless, during her time Murray supported the development of many women's careers and interests, including those who were unable to participate in fieldwork, but who underpinned the financial basis of British archaeological work.

One such woman was Glaswegian Janet May Buchanan (1866–1913). She is largely responsible for the size and significance of Glasgow Museum's Egyptology collection today, where an estimated 1000 artefacts are attributable to her efforts.[153] May Buchanan founded both the Glasgow and Edinburgh branches of the Egyptian Research Students Association (ERSA),[154] and organized a special exhibition in Kelvingrove Museum to showcase British archaeological work in Egypt. This opened in November 1912, with loans of objects presented by Amy Urlin, Hilda Petrie and Margaret Murray. That other women rallied round to ensure that this display materialized is no coincidence: it was a political statement. This is made clear in the catalogue Murray wrote to accompany the exhibition, in which she made explicit the connection between the suffragist cause and ancient Egypt in a section entitled 'Women's role in Egypt':

> The standard of civilisation in any country is judged to a very great extent by the position of the women. Where the women are treated as inferiors, they become inferior and the nation suffers accordingly; where women are treated as equals, the nation improves and advances.[155]

Tragically, just weeks after the exhibition opened Buchanan was struck by car and killed. In her memory the two branches of the ERSA created a fund for the purchase of Egyptian objects for permanent display in Glasgow museums. Unlike Manchester though, this local support was ignored by city museum managers, and most of the May Buchanan collection was left to languish in store. The memorial funds were ultimately directed towards the University of Glasgow's Hunterian Museum instead. Whether the neglect shown by Glasgow museums to May Buchanan's legacy was a political decision is unknown, but had she been a wealthy male patron one suspects her contribution would have been more visible.

***

Late Victorian feminist-derived culture challenged social inequalities in diverse ways, and Egyptian archaeology, together with its material products, offered just one platform among many. It should not be assumed, however, that there was a shared sense of purpose among these individuals. Class, education and religious background coloured worldviews, and consequently, as this chapter has emphasized, there were a multitude of perspectives on things that informed the collection and understanding of Egyptian archaeology across Britain before the First World War. Such adaptability made Egyptology a liminal subject, at once esoteric and scientific, Classical and biblical, popular and academic. Some of these interests were complementary, others contradictory, but all had a part to play in the spread of ancient Egyptian culture throughout Britain, a legacy that is today present in at least 112 museum collections.[156] There are undoubtedly many more still to be relocated and recontextualized.

Notes

1. Moon, B. 2006. *More Usefully Employed: Amelia B. Edwards, Writer, Traveller and Campaigner for Ancient Egypt*. London: Egypt Exploration Society.
2. The law referred to here is the Khedivial Decree of 19 May 1880, which expressly forbade the export of 'toute sorte d'objets rentrant sous le domaine de l'Ígyptologie tels que monnaies, inscriptions anciennes et en general les objets de la meme nature que ceux qui se trouvent deposes au Musee de Boulaq'. See Khater, A. 1960. *Le regime juridique des fouilles et des antiquités en Égypt*. Cairo: Institut Français d'Archéologie Orientale, p. 280.
3. Deetz, J. 1977. *In Small Things Forgotten: The Archaeology of Early American Life*. New York: Anchor Books.
4. Moser, S. 2006. *Wondrous Curiosities: Ancient Egypt at the British Museum*. London and Chicago: University of Chicago Press.
5. Moser, *Wondrous Curiosities*, pp. 125–70.
6. Daston, L. 1999. Introduction: the coming into being of scientific objects. In Daston, L. (ed.) *Biographies of Scientific Objects*. Chicago: The University of Chicago Press, pp. 1–14.
7. Kohl, P. L. and Fawcett, C. 1996. *Nationalism, Politics and the Practice of Archaeology*. Cambridge: Cambridge University Press; Diaz-Andreu, M. 2007. *A World History of Nineteenth-century Archaeology: Nationalism, Colonialism and the Past*. Oxford: Oxford University Press.
8. Gange, D. 2013. *Dialogues with the Dead: Egyptology in British Culture and Religion*. Oxford: Oxford University Press.
9. Swenson, A. and Mandler, P. 2013. *Britain and the Heritage of Empire, c. 1800–1940*. Oxford: Oxford University Press.
10. Malley, S. 2012. *From Archaeology to Spectacle in Victorian England: The Case of Assyria, 1845–1854*. Farnham: Ashgate.
11. Anon. 1852. Reception of Nineveh sculptures at the British Museum. *Illustrated London News* 28 February 1852: 184.
12. Letter from Maspero to Edwards, 15 April 1882. Amelia Edwards archive, Somerville College, University of Oxford.
13. Dixon, D. M. 2003. Some Egyptological sidelines on the Egyptian War of 1882. In Jeffreys, D. (ed.) *Views of Ancient Egypt Since Napoleon Bonaparte: Imperialism, Colonialism and Modern Appropriations*. London: UCL Press, pp. 87–94. Edwards had even gone as far as suggesting that soldiers might be employed as the excavation work force. See Drower, M. 1982. Gaston Maspero and the birth of the Egypt Exploration Fund (1881–3). *Journal of Egyptian Archaeology* 68: 311.
14. Virenque, H. 2015. Edouard Naville (1844–1926) in the Delta. In Cooke, N. and Daubney, V. (eds.) *Every Traveller Needs a Compass: Travel and Collecting in Egypt and the Near East*. Oxford: Oxbow Books, pp. 190–5.
15. Pithom is mentioned in Exodus 1:1 as the city built by the forced labour of Israelites for the pharaoh. Naville, E. 1885. *The Store-City of Pithom and the Route of the Exodus*. London: Egypt Exploration Fund.
16. Letters from Maspero to Edwards, 26 June 1883 and 23 August 1883, Amelia Edwards archive Somerville College, University of Oxford.
17. Wilson, an English surgeon and dermatologist, was as enamoured by the monumentality of Egypt's past as was Naville, having already personally financed the transportation of an Egyptian obelisk – one of 'Cleopatra's Needles' – from the Nile River to the Thames.
18. Accession numbers 1883.1107.2 and 1883.1107.1.
19. On the 'hero archaeologist' see Challis, D. 2008. *From the Harpy Tomb to the Wonders of Ephesus: British Archaeologists in the Ottoman Empire 1840–1880*. London: Duckworth.
20. Flinders Petrie in his 1893 inaugural address at UCL as the Edwards Professor of Egyptian Archaeology and Philology, a copy of which was published in Janssen, R. 1992. *The First Hundred Years: Egyptology at University College London 1892–1992*. London: UCL Press, pp. 98–102. See also Petrie, W. M. F. 1904. *Methods and Aims in Archaeology*. London: Macmillan and Co., pp. 138–9.
21. Stevenson, A. 2012. 'We seem to be working in the same line': A. H. L. F Pitt-Rivers and W. M. Flinders Petrie. *Bulletin of the History of Archaeology* 22(1): 4–13.
22. Petrie, W. M. F. 1931. *Seventy Years in Archaeology*. London: Sampson, Low and Marston, p. 106.

23 Lucas, G. 2001. *Critical Approaches to Fieldwork: Contemporary and Historical Archaeological Practice*. London and New York: Routledge, p. 25.
24 Petrie's 1892 season at Tell el-Hesy in Palestine is the exception rather than the rule.
25 This focus upon objects remained an integral part of Petrie's approach to fieldwork for the rest of his career. See for instance his work in Palestine as explored by Sparks, R. 2013. Flinders Petrie through word and deed: re-evaluating Petrie's field techniques and their impact on object recovery in British Mandate Palestine. *Palestine Exploration Quarterly* 145(2): 143–59.
26 Petrie, W. M. F. 1888. *Tanis II*. London: Egypt Exploration Fund, p. vii.
27 Livingstone, D. N. 2003. *Putting Science in its Place: Geographies of Scientific Knowledge*. Chicago and London: University of Chicago Press.
28 Drower, M. 1985. *Flinders Petrie: A Life in Archaeology*. London: Victor Gollancz, p. 43.
29 Petrie, *Methods and Aims in Archaeology*, p. 114.
30 Undated statement signed by Petrie and Maspero EES.COR.016.f.06.
31 Letter from Petrie to Poole, 28 January 1884, EES.COR.16.f.17.
32 Appadurai, A. 1986. Introduction: commodities and the politics of value. In Appadurai, A (ed.) *The Social Life of Things: Commodities in Cultural Perspective*. Cambridge: Cambridge University Press, pp. 3–63.
33 Letter from Petrie to Poole, 29 May 1884, EES.COR.16.f.32.
34 Letter from Petrie to Maspero, 9 June 1884, EES.COR.16.f.34.
35 Petrie, W. M. F. 1885. *Tanis. Part 1, 1883-84*. London: Egypt Exploration Fund.
36 Quoted in Brusius, M. 2012. Misfit objects: Layard's excavations in ancient Mesopotamia and the biblical imagination in mid-nineteenth century Britain. *Journal of Literature and Science* 5: 45–6.
37 Drower, *Flinders Petrie: A Life in Archaeology*, p. 105.
38 Villing, A. n.d. Reconstructing a 19th-century excavation: problems and perspectives. http://www.britishmuseum.org/research/online_research_catalogues/ng/naukratis_greeks_in_egypt/introduction/reconstructing_an_excavation.aspx [accessed 28 Jan 2015].
39 Letter from Naville to Edwards, 14 February 1887, EES.COR.5.e.8.
40 Reid, D. 2002. *Whose Pharaohs? Archaeology, Museums and Egyptian National Identity from Napoleon to World War I*. Berkeley and Los Angeles: University of California Press. p. 181.
41 Goode, J. F. 2007. *Negotiating for the Past: Archaeology, Nationalism, and Diplomacy in the Middle East, 1919–1941*. Austin: University of Texas Press, p. 71.
42 Thornton, A. 2015. Exhibition season: annual archaeological exhibitions in London, 1880s–1930s. *Bulletin of the History of Archaeology* 25(2): 1–18.
43 Letter from J. Offord Junior to Amelia Edwards, 29 August 1885, EES.COR.006.g.
44 Williams, A. 2019. *Exhibiting Archaeology: Constructing Knowledge of Egypt at Temporary Exhibitions in London, 1884-1939*. DPhil Thesis. Oxford: University of Oxford.
45 Cited in Melman, B. 1992. *Women's Orients: English Women and the Middle East, 1718–1918, Sexuality, Religion and Work*. Ann Arbor: University of Michigan Press, p. 258.
46 In what was clearly a none-too-veiled put-down that Amelia Edwards was a woman and not a serious scholar. See James, T. G. H. (ed.) 1982. *Excavating in Egypt: The Egypt Exploration Society*. London: Egypt Exploration Society, p. 14.
47 James, *Excavating Egypt*, p. 33.
48 Letter from Edwards to Griffith, 29 October 1885, EES.COR.3.a.45.
49 Hill, K. 2005. *Cultural and Class in English Public Museums, 1850–1914*. London: Ashgate.
50 Latour's oft-cited term for key nodes in geographic networks through which knowledge is received and distributed. Latour, B. 1987. *Science in Action. How to Follow Scientists and Engineers Through Society*. Cambridge: Harvard University Press.
51 See for example Jasanoff, M. 2006. *Edge of Empire: Conquest and Collecting in the East 1750– 1850*. London: Harper Perennial; Colla, E. 2007. *Conflicted Antiquities: Egyptology, Egyptomania, Egyptian Modernity*. Durham: Duke University Press.
52 Moon, *More Usefully Employed*, p. 182.
53 These are the only two surviving lists in Oxford. Another similar list by Edwards is held in the archives of the Egyptology Department of the Boston Museum of Fine Arts.
54 EEF 1887. *Report of the Fifth Annual General Meeting*. London: Egypt Exploration Fund, p. 15.
55 In the EEF annual report for 1899–1900 these are listed as: Aberdeen, Ayr, Belfast, Birmingham, Bolton (Lancs), Bristol and Clifton, Cambridge, Carlisle, Cheltenham, Dewsbury, Dublin, Dundee, Edinburgh, Glasgow, Greenock, Liverpool, London, Manchester, Nottingham, Oldham, Tamworth, South Wales, Weston-Super-Mare and York.

56 EEF 1887. *Report of the Fifth Annual General Meeting*. London: Egypt Exploration Fund, p. 15.
57 EES.DIST.24.39.
58 Naville, E. 1910. Naville's Address. In *Report of the Twenty-Fifth Ordinary General Meeting. 1910–11*. London: Egypt Exploration Fund, p. 22.
59 Snape, R. 2010. Objects of utility: cultural responses to industrial collections in municipal museums 1845–1914. *Museum and Society* 8(1): 18–36.
60 The uptake from 1891 was additionally facilitated by the Museums and Gymnasiums Act that made it easier for municipalities to establish museums. See Lewis, G. 1992. Museums in Britain: a historical survey. In Thompson, J. M. A. (ed.) *Manual of Curatorship: A Guide to Museum Practice*. Oxford and Boston: Butterworth-Heinemann, pp. 22–46; Hill, *Cultural and Class in English Public Museums*, p. 36.
61 Hill, *Culture and Class*, p. 36, citing the *Report of the 57th Meeting of the British Association for the Advancement of Science* (1888), pp. 97–130.
62 Kavanagh, G. 2000 *Dream Spaces: Memory and the Museum*. London: Leicester University Press, p. 58.
63 Preziosi, D. 2003. *Brain of the Earth's Body: Art, Museums, and the Phantasms of Modernity*. Minneapolis: University of Minnesota Press, p. 96.
64 Bennett, T. 1995. *The Birth of the Museum*. London and New York: Routledge.
65 Hooper-Greenhill, E. 1992. *Museums and the Shaping of Knowledge*. London and New York: Routledge.
66 MacLauchlan, J. 1903. Technical museums. *Museums Journal* 2(12): 163–74. See also Caddie, A. J. 1910. The board of education and provincial museums. *Museums Journal* 10(11): pp. 128–9, who comments that 'I would urge that at any rate the great industrial areas should first of all confine themselves to collecting material illustrative of the local industries'.
67 Kriegel, L. 2008. *Grand Designs: Labour, Empire, and the Museum in Victorian Culture*. Durham and London: Duke University Press.
68 Anon, 1901. *Borough of Birmingham Museum and School of Art Committee Report for the year ending March 31, 1891*. Birmingham: Birmingham Museum, p. 7.
69 Petrie, *Tanis. Part I*, p. 41.
70 EEF 1884. *Report of the Second Annual General Meeting*. London: Egypt Exploration Fund, p. 11.
71 Anon. 2008. *What's in Store: Collections Review in the Northwest*. London: Museums, Libraries and Archives.
72 MacLauchlan, Technical museums.
73 Wilkinson, J. G. 1857. *The Egyptians in the Time of the Pharaohs: Being a Companion to the Crystal Palace Egyptian Collections*. London: Bradbury and Evans, p. 1.
74 Keith, A. 1913. 'What should museums do for us?' cited in Bennett, T. 2004. *Pasts Beyond Memory: Evolution, Museums, Colonialism*. London and New York: Routledge, p. 65.
75 Lane Fox [Pitt-Rivers], A. H. 1875. On the principles of classification adopted in the arrangement of his anthropological collection, now exhibited in the Bethnal Green Museum. *Journal of Anthropological Institute* 4: 293–4.
76 Shelton, A. 2000. Museum ethnography: an imperial science. In Street, B. and Hallam, E. (eds.) *Cultural Encounters: Representing 'Otherness'*. London and New York: Routledge, pp. 155–93.
77 Lane Fox [Pitt-Rivers], A. H. 1875. On early modes of navigation. *The Journal of the Anthropological Institute of Great Britain and Ireland* 14: 413.
78 Anon. 1868. The International Congress of Archaic Anthropology. *Anthropological Review* 6: 203–15; Jukes Brown, A. J. 1878. On some flint implements from Egypt. *The Journal of the Anthropological Institute of Great Britain and Ireland* 7: 396–412.
79 Lepsius, R. 1870. Ueber die Annahme eines sogenannten prähistorischen Steinalters in Aegypten. *Zeitschrift für Ägyptische Sprache und Altertumskunde* 8: 89–107; Mariette, A. 1876. *Notice des principaux monuments exposés dans les galeries provisoires de S. A. le Khédive a Boulaq*. Sixth Edition. Le Caire: A. Mourès.
80 Burton, R. 1879. Stones and bones from Egypt and Midian. *The Journal of the Anthropological Institute of Great Britain and Ireland* 8: 290–319; Lubbock, J. 1875. Notes on the discovery of stone implements in Egypt. *The Journal of the Anthropological Institute of Great Britain and Ireland* 4: 215–22.
81 Pitt-Rivers, A. H. L. F. 1890. *King John's House, Tollard Royal, Wilts*. Printed privately.

82 Pitt-Rivers, A. H. L. F. 1888. Presidential address British Association for the Advancement of Science, Section H, Anthropology, 1888. *Report of the British Association for the Advancement of Science*, pp. 825–8.
83 Henare, A. 2005. *Museums, Anthropology and Imperial Exchange*. Cambridge: Cambridge University Press, pp. 121–46; Evans, C. 2007. Delineating objects: nineteenth-century antiquarian culture and the project of archaeology. In Pearce, S. (ed.) *Visions of Antiquity: The Society of Antiquaries of London 1707-2007*. London: Society of Antiquaries of London, pp. 267–305; Conn, S. 1998. *Museums and Intellectual Life, 1876–1926*. Chicago and London: The University of Chicago Press; Livingstone, *Putting Science in its Place*; Willis, M. 2011. *Vision, Science and Literature, 1870–1920*. London: Pickering and Chatto.
84 To use a phrase employed by Gosden, C. and Larson, F. 2007. *Knowing Things: Exploring the Collections of the Pitt Rivers Museum*. Oxford: Oxford University Press, p. 122.
85 Livingstone, *Putting Science in its Place*, p. 40.
86 Whitehead, C. 2009. *Museums and the Construction of Disciplines: Art and Archaeology in Nineteenth-Century Britain*. London: Duckworth, p. 92.
87 Challis, D. 2015. What's in a face? Mummy portrait panels. In Carruthers, W. (ed.) *Histories of Egyptology: Disciplinary Measures*. London and New York: Routledge, pp. 227–41. See also Riggs, C. 2010. Ancient Egypt in the museum: concepts and constructions. In Lloyd, A. (ed.) *A Companion to Ancient Egypt*. Chichester: Blackwell, pp. 1129–31. This was a long-running quandary, and the portraits did eventually get transferred from the National Gallery to the British Museum in the 1990s.
88 Petrie, W. M. F. 1908 *Qurneh*. London: British School of Archaeology in Egypt, p. 10.
89 Letter from Cecil Smith to Flinders Petrie, 4 August 1909, V&A archives, copies held in UCL Petrie Museum of Egyptian Archaeology.
90 Letter from Flinders Petrie to Cecil Smith, 9 August 1909, V&A archives, copies held in UCL Petrie Museum of Egyptian Archaeology.
91 Curran, K. 2016. *The Invention of the American Art Museum: From Craft to Kulturgeschichte. 1870–1930*. Los Angeles: Getty Research Institute. See Chapter Two of this book for further discussion on this point.
92 Hoyle, W. E. 1908. The arrangement of an Egyptological collection. *The Museums Journal* 8(11): 152–62.
93 Hoyle, The arrangement of an Egyptological collection, p. 162. Jermyn Street Museum was the Geological Museum, which transferred to South Kensington in 1935.
94 Nichols, C. A. 2016. Exchanging anthropological duplicates at the Smithsonian Institute. *Museum Anthropology* 39(2): 130–46.
95 PMA/WFP1/D/9/7.
96 Licence, T. 2015. *What the Victorians Threw Away*. Oxford: Oxbow Books.
97 Thomas, D. W. 2004. *Cultivating Victorians: Liberal Culture and the Aesthetic*. Philadelphia: University of Pennsylvania Press; Benson, J. 1994. *The Rise of Consumer Society in Britain, 1880–1980*. London: Longman; Thomas, R. 1990. *The Commodity Culture of Victorian England: Advertising and Spectacle 1851–1914*. Stanford: Stanford University Press; Cohen, D. 2006. *Household Gods: The British and their Possessions*. New Haven: Yale University Press; Edwards, C. 2005. *Turning Houses into Homes. A History of the Retailing and Consumption of Domestic Furnishings*. London: Ashgate, pp. 166–72.
98 Bennett, *The Birth of the Museum*.
99 Anon. 1890. Mr. Petrie's forthcoming exhibition of Egyptian Antiquities. *Athenaeum* 96: 297–8.
100 Mullins, P. R. 2002. Racializing the parlor: race and Victorian bric-a-brac consumption. In Orser, C. E. (ed.) *Race and the Archaeology of Identity*. Salt Lake City: University of Utah Press, pp. 158–76.
101 Moser, S. 2016. Archaeology and ancient Egypt. In Prettejohn, E. and Trippi, P. (eds.) *Lawrence Alma-Tadema: At Home in Antiquity*. Munich: London and New York: Prestel, pp. 52–3; Alma-Tadema became acquainted with Flinders Petrie in the late 1880s and is known to have visited his temporary exhibitions. See Drower, *Flinders Petrie*, p. 142.
102 Ziter, E. 2003. *The Orient on the Victorian Stage*. Cambridge: Cambridge University Press.
103 Mitchell, T. 2004. Orientalism and the exhibitionary order. In Preziosi, D. and Farago, C. J. (eds.) *Grasping the World: The Idea of the Museum*. Aldershot: Ashgate Publishing, p. 445.
104 Shears, J. and Harrison, J. (eds.) 2013. *Literary Bric-à-Brac and the Victorians: From Commodities to Oddities*. London and New York: Routledge.

105 Both quoted in Daly, N. 1994. The obscure object of desire: Victorian commodity culture and fictions of the mummy. *NOVEL: A Forum on Fiction* 28(1): 33; See further examples from Victorian fiction in Black, J. B. 2000. *On Exhibit: The Victorians and Their Museums*. Charlottesville and London: University Press of Virginia, pp. 76–94; Hoberman, R. 2003. In quest of a museal aura: turn of the century narratives about museum-displayed objects. *Victorian Literature and Culture* 31(2): 467–82.
106 Willis, *Vision, Science and Literature, 1870–1920*.
107 In particular after the Second World War. See Chapter Five.
108 Edwards, A. B. 1891. My home life. *Arena Magazine* 4: 304.
109 Lutz, D. 2015. *Relics of Death in Victorian Literature and Culture*. Cambridge: Cambridge University Press.
110 See, for example, the story related by author Marie Corelli's companion Bertha Vyver concerning an Egyptian necklace and a supernatural visitation in Hutchison, S. and Brown, R. (eds.) 2015. *Monsters and Monstrosity from the Fin de Siècle to the Millennium: New Essays*. Jefferson: McFarland, p. 29.
111 Tully, C. J. 2010. Walk like an Egyptian: Egypt as authority in Aleister Crowley's reception of the book of law. *The Pomegranate: International Journal of Pagan Studies* 12(1): 20–47.
112 Luckhurst, R. 2012. Counter-narrative in the Egyptian rooms of the British Museum. *History and Anthropology* 23(2): 257–69.
113 Sheppard, K. L. 2013. *The Life of Margaret Alice Murray: A Woman's Work in Archaeology*. Lanham: Lexington Books.
114 A movement associated with Helena Blavatsky (1831–91) and the teaching of the underlying unity of global religious and esoteric traditions.
115 Vinson, S. and Gunn, J. 2015. Studies in esoteric syntax. The enigmatic friendship of Aleister Crowley and Battiscombe Gunn. In Carruthers, W. (ed.) *Histories of Egyptology: Interdisciplinary Measures*. London: Routledge, pp. 96–112.
116 Gange, D. 2006. Religion and science in late nineteenth-century Egyptology. *The Historical Journal* 49(4): 1083–103. See also Goldhill, S. 2014. *The Buried Life of Things*. Cambridge: Cambridge University Press.
117 Edwards, A. B. 1891. *Pharaohs, Fellahs and Explorers*. New York: Harper and Brothers, p. 50.
118 Anon. 1893. A Sunday-school teachers' museum. *Quiver* 28(301): 403.
119 Kitchin, J. G. 1893. *The Bible Student in the British Museum*. London: Cassell and Company.
120 Lester, H. A. 1912. *Sunday School Teaching: Its Aims and its Methods*. London: Longmans, Green and Co., p. 67.
121 Kitchin, J. G. 1891. *Scripture Teaching, Illustrated by models and objects*. London: Church of England Sunday School Institute, p. 3.
122 A very similar set of Christian object habits characterized religious education in the United States. See Hasinoff, E. 2011. *Faith in Objects: American Missionary Expositions in the Early Twentieth Century*. New York: Palgrave Macmillan.
123 Lawn, M. 2005. A pedagogy for the public: the place of objects, observation, mechanical production and cupboards. In Lawn, M. and Grosvenor, I. (eds.). *Materialities of Schooling: Design, Technology, Objects, Routines*. Didcot: Symposium Books, p. 147.
124 HMI 1899. *Revised Instructions Issued to Her Majesty's Inspectors, and Applicable to the Code of 1899*. London: Eyre & Spottiswoode.
125 Lawn, M. 2013. A pedagogy for the public: the place of objects, observation, mechanical production and cupboards. *Revista Linhas* 14(26): 244–64.
126 Letter from William Redhead to John Garstang, 24 February 1904, Garstang Museum archives.
127 Swanton, E. W. 1947. *A Country Museum: The Rise and Progress of Sir Jonathan Hutchinson's Educational Museum* at Haslemere. Haslemere: Educational Museum.
128 Petrie, W. M. F. 1906. *Migrations: The Huxley Lecture of 1906*. London: Anthropological Institute of Great Britain, p. 32a. Petrie's eugenic principles were laid out most clearly in his 1907 publication *Janus in Modern Life*. London: G. P. Putnam.
129 Challis, D. 2013. *The Archaeology of Race: The Eugenic ideas of Francis Galton and Flinders Petrie*. London: Bloomsbury, p. 197.
130 Murray, T. 1993. Archaeology and the threat of the past: Sir Henry Rider Haggard and the acquisition of time. *World Archaeology* 25(2): 175–86; Evans, C. 1989. Digging with the pen. Novel archaeologies and literary traditions. *Archaeological Review from Cambridge* 8(20):186-211.
131 Willis, *Vision, Science and Literature*, p. 155.

132 Montserrat, D. 2000. *Akhenaten: History, Fantasy and Ancient Egypt*. London and New York: Routledge, pp. 68–9.
133 Montserrat, *Akhenaten*, pp. 68–9.
134 McLean Institute accession records. John Scott (1830–1903) was a well-known shipbuilder and engineer in Greenock.
135 Alberti, S. J. M. M. 2012. *Nature and Culture: Objects, Disciplines and the Manchester Museum*. Manchester: Manchester University Press, p. 68.
136 Livingstone, *Putting Science in its Place*, p. 37.
137 Serpico, M. and El Gawad, H. 2016. *Beyond Beauty: Transforming the Body in Ancient Egypt*. London: Two Temple Place, pp. 87–9.
138 Serpico and El Gawad, *Beyond Beauty*, pp. 69–73.
139 Hill, K. 2016. *Women and Museums 1850–1914: Modernity and the Gendering of Knowledge*. Manchester: Manchester University Press, p. 167; see also Whitelaw, A. 2013. Women, museums and the problems of biography. In Hill, K. (ed.) *Museums and Biographies: Stories, Objects, Identities*. Woodridge: Brewer and Brewer, pp. 75–86.
140 Hill, *Women and Museums*, p. 220.
141 Cited in Mitchell, S. 2004. *Frances Power Cobbe: Victorian Feminist, Journalist, Reformer*. Charlottesville and London: University of Virginia Press, pp. 322–3.
142 Willard, F. E. 1897. *Occupations for Women: A Book of Practical Suggestions for the Material Advancement, The Mental And Physical Development, and the Moral and Spiritual Uplift Of Women*. New York: The Success Company.
143 See Hill, *Women and Museums*, pp. 166–9 for further examples of the role of women in the EEF.
144 Hamilton, S. 2007. Women in practice: women in British contract field archaeology. In Hamilton, S., Whitehouse, R. and Wright, K. I. (eds.) *Archaeology and Women: Ancient and Modern Issues*. Walnut Creek: Left Coast Press, p. 122.
145 With thanks to Amara Thornton for drawing this to my attention.
146 Oldfield, S. 2004. Eckenstein, Lina Dorina Johanna (1857–1931). In *Oxford Dictionary of National Biography (Online ed.)* Oxford: Oxford University Press. DOI: http://dx.doi.org/10.1093/ref:odnb/59940 [accessed 12 May 2016].
147 Petrie, W. M. F. 1901. *Diospolis Parva*. London: Egypt Exploration Fund, p. 2.
148 Petrie, W. M. F. 1901. *The Royal Tombs of the Earliest Dynasties*. London: Egypt Exploration Fund, p. 1.
149 Petrie, *Royal Tombs of the Earliest Dynasties*, p. 1.
150 Hodder, I. 1986. *Reading the Past*. Cambridge: Cambridge University Press, p. 122.
151 Letter from Reading Town Council to EES, 5 October 1899, EES.DIST.17.26a.
152 Sheppard, *The Life of Margaret Alice Murray*.
153 Weightman, B. and Wilson, M. 2016. Janet May Buchanan. Scotland's forgotten heroine of Egyptology. Available at: http://egyptartefacts.griffith.ox.ac.uk/?q=resources/janet-may-buchanan-scotlands-forgotten-heroine-egyptology [accessed 9 August 2016].
154 The ERSAs were initially established in many cities, mostly connected with the British School of Archaeology in Egypt to which they contributed.
155 Murray, M. 1912. *Guide for 'Egyptian Research Students' Association' and a Catalogue of Loan Collection of Egyptian Antiquities Held in Kelvingrove Museum*. Glasgow: Glasgow Museums, p. 20.
156 Serpico, M. 2006. *Past, Present and Future: An Overview of Ancient Egyptian and Sudanese Collections in the UK*. London: Museums, Libraries and Archives Council.

Chapter 2
Collecting in America's Progressive and Gilded Eras (1880–1919)

Mark Twain only wrote one work of collaborative fiction, *The Gilded Age*, a title that has come to characterize American excess between roughly the 1870s and the 1900s.[1] His lesser-known co-author was the editor and publisher Charles Dudley Warner (1829–1900), a man who later became a Vice President of the American Branch of the Egypt Exploration Fund (EEF). Through such prominent connections, Britain's EEF was zealously promoted and its subscriber base swelled. By the beginning of the twentieth century it could even count among its numbers the President of the United States himself.[2] This intense interest coincided with the beginning of an expansion in the American museum sector,[3] and out of all the countries that participated in Britain's finds distribution network, it was the USA that became the most earnest competitor for a share of the finest discoveries. The result was that an estimated 60 institutions across 23 US states received Egyptian antiquities through British organizations between 1880 and the early 1920s.

This chapter traces these transfers and the transatlantic dialogues that accompanied them. At first, the US was largely reliant upon British fieldwork to provide it with excavated material to feed the American museum movement. By the early twentieth century, however, these institutions began to work independently in Egypt without intermediaries. British colonial structures, together with French and Egyptian ones, made this possible, but it was the Americans who capitalized upon it, industrializing archaeology on a massive scale. With the onset of the First World War, the balance of archaeological opportunity between the nations shifted further, and the USA took the leading role.

Throughout these structural realignments, local interests and idiosyncratic personalities continually re-shaped the receptions of, and practices around, antiquities, both in the field and in the museum. Many of the underlying motivations for the acquisition of Egyptian things in the United States ran parallel to the ambitions of British institutions, with a similar 'bourgeois acquisitiveness',[4] a strong interest from well-organized women's movements and a marked influence of female curatorial staff who engaged with archaeological finds in innovative ways. Nevertheless, there remained fundamental differences between the two countries. Perhaps the most important of these was the alternative geographies of urban aspiration that drove many wealthy US city patrons to invest in their local museums. Unlike museum growth in Britain, which was facilitated by government initiatives as well as by the occasional wealthy donor, America's institutions depended almost exclusively on the capitalist venture of private philanthropy. Moreover, such competition existed not only between cities, but also within them, with multiple institutions vying for the most striking artefacts. Another distinctive trend in the United States was its development of fine art museums, whose evolving ethos came to shape particular attitudes to Egyptian material. In the longer term it is arguably this development that continues to define a distinctly American approach to Egypt.

'I look on chisell'd histories': The American Branch of the EEF

In 1888, a large granite statue of one of Egypt's most infamous New Kingdom pharaohs, Ramesses II, was installed in Boston's Museum of Fine Arts (MFA, Fig. 2.1). Most visitors were unlikely to have been able to read the hieroglyphic rendering of the king's names, but they would not have missed the prominent label on the plinth below. It declared that the monument was a 'Gift of the Egypt Exploration Fund through W. C. Winslow. AM. Vice Pres^{dt}.'. The man mentioned alongside the ancient ruler, the Reverend William Copley Winslow (1840–1917), was a local Episcopal priest and the self-appointed founder of the EEF's American Branch. He had been immediately attracted to the EEF's biblical mandate, and in 1883 commenced an effusive correspondence with Amelia Edwards. Winslow's endeavours became ever more solipsistic over the years. He earnestly hankered after honorary degrees and tediously bemoaned his lack of recognition, insisting that all large objects the EEF sent to Boston should bear his name.[5] His relationship with the EEF became strained, and after a protracted period of accusations and insinuations, Winslow was dismissed from the Fund in 1902. Little insight into the machinations of Egyptology, archaeology or museums is revealed by the mass of archival correspondence relating to this unfortunate episode.[6] As the Director of Carnegie Museum commented in 1901, 'We would be very glad to be spared the trouble of reading letters constituting chapters

Fig. 2.1 Photograph of a statue of Ramesses II (museum number 87.111) excavated by Petrie's teams at Tell Nebesheh as displayed in the original Museum of Fine Art building on Copley Square, Boston in 1903. Photograph © 2018 Museum of Fine Arts Boston (Negative number E15692).

in the history of the same. They make us tired.'[7] Working through these letters more than a century later, this statement remains true.

There is no denying, however, that Winslow's vigorous campaigning was of enormous benefit to the Fund. Within a year Edwards was able to report to the EEF Committee the 'discovery of a silver mine in the United States of America from which the ore is conveniently extracted in a ready minted condition, and every blow of the pick produces a yield of shining American dollars'.[8] By the end of the century there were 67 areas of the US with multiple local honorary secretaries, and by 1890, 57 per cent of all EEF subscribers were American. Winslow himself managed to raise an estimated $130,000 from American subscriptions, a sum equivalent to more that $3 million today. Such amounts surpassed those mustered in Britain, so much so that it became a source of considerable consternation when it came to deciding the division of finds between Britain and its partners across the Atlantic. It also resulted in lengthy tussles as various parties attempted to establish equivalences between sponsorship money, ancient finds and museum values.

There had been few major Egyptology collections in the US previously. The oldest collection of Egyptian material in America had come to the Peabody Essex Museum in Salem, Massachusetts, in the early 1800s. It had been inherited from the East India Marine Society, whose members presented Egyptian curios picked up during their travels. There was also the private collection of Henry Abbott (1812–59), a British physician who had resided in Cairo for twenty years, and who shipped several hundred antiquities across the Atlantic in the early 1850s after the British Museum refused to buy them. The Abbott collection ended up in the care of New York's Historical Society. In Boston, the Museum of Fine Art's Egyptian collection was founded in 1872, and contained around a thousand antiquities acquired from a Scottish artist, Robert Hay (1799–1863), and presented to Boston after its exhibition at London's Crystal Palace. Tourist souvenirs from Egypt (especially mummy parts)[9] were also scattered across the United States, but large, permanent arenas for their display did not exist until the latter part of the century.[10] Their founding was coincident with the rich harvest of finds reaped by the EEF, which in many cases supplied major new American institutions with their first Egyptian antiquities, providing the impetus and means for American museums to undertake more systematic collecting in ancient Egypt.

This is not to say that Egypt had not been an integral part of American cultural life for much of the nineteenth century. Despite the absence of large collections or professional positions in Egyptology or archaeology there was an awareness of European-led expeditions. American travelogues about Egypt were in fact as numerous, if not more so, than their British counterparts at this time, and were fuelled by a burgeoning periodical press that gave regular attention to the land of the pharaohs.[11] George Gliddon toured a moving 'Panorama of the Nile' – a large-scale painting moved between two vertical rollers – from 1849, accompanied by popular lectures, exhibitions and mummy unwrappings.[12] The celebrated American poet Walt Whitman read widely in Egyptology in the 1840s and 1850s, and frequented Dr Abbott's collection in New York, leading to Egyptological references in popular works such as *Salut au Monde!*: 'I look on chisell'd histories, records of conquering kings, dynasties, cut in slabs of sand-stone, or on granite-blocks'.[13] Egyptian revival architecture of the early to mid-nineteenth century was visible across the United States, in monumental gateways of rural cemeteries and in commemorative obelisks erected for great men. The debates surrounding the merits of such appropriations, including the controversial building of the Washington Monument, ensured that Egypt remained in the public eye right through to the 1880s and 1890s.[14] Such works, as in Europe, familiarized readers with the distant land of Egypt, and may have contributed to a sense of entitlement and ownership over the sites, monuments and artefacts encountered.[15]

Expectations surrounding Egypt's representation at Philadelphia's 1876 Centennial Exhibition, America's first major international exhibition, were primed by this interest. In execution, however, the Egyptian section's eclectic mix of plaster casts, illustrations and photographs, arranged by the German Egyptologist Heinrich Brugsch (1827–94), was considered somewhat feeble.[16] In contrast, Chicago's 1893 Columbian World Exposition presented Egypt as a grandiose spectacle with a bustling 'Cairo Street' and a monumental replica of the Luxor Temple, complete with two soaring obelisks, one of which was inscribed in hieroglyphs with the name of President Grover Cleveland. Inside the temple were wax models of royal mummies, while sacred music and reenactments of ritual processions added to the Orientalized drama showcased for popular consumption and entertainment.[17] It all rather overshadowed the collection of original antiquities displayed by the University of Pennsylvania (Fig. 2.2). These were more soberly arranged in an exhibit entitled *Objects from the Flinders Petrie Excavations and the Egypt Exploration Fund*. It included more than 160 individual finds from Petrie's expeditions at Kahun, Gurob and Hawara in the late 1880s, as well as his fieldwork at Amarna, and 100 items from the EEF's

Fig. 2.2 Photograph of University of Pennsylvania's exhibit at the 1893 Columbian World Exposition taken by Jas. H. Crockwell, Salt Lake City, Utah. Courtesy of Penn Museum (image #174642).

excavations in the Delta, such as Naukratis, Bubastis and Defennah.[18] The Petrie and EEF displays received an award from the Exposition's international panel of judges, who noted that,

> The scientific importance of the collection can not be overrated, and the clearness and method with which it is labelled and displayed adds much to its value. The University of Pennsylvania, and especially its Department of Archaeology, deserves great credit for the fine exhibit.[19]

Despite the intellectual emphasis here, the Exposition as a whole provided a strong aesthetic and emotional context for the reception of Egyptian archaeology. These two powerful object habits – the aesthetic and emotional on the one hand, and the scientific promise of edification on the other – remained an unsettled impulse for early twentieth-century American museum acquisition.

As a young nation, the United States had faced criticism from abroad that it was devoid of a meaningful cultural heritage (indigenous communities being excluded). The 'great civilizations' of antiquity offered one means of constructing a riposte, and many in the USA articulated the country's position as the vanguard of a new cultural progression from the Old to the New World. In this vein the transfer of antiquities from North Africa to America, via Britain, formed a tangible link to an imagined past and a performance of those sentiments in the present. Egyptian monuments 'served to bind us to antiquity',[20] or so New York City Mayor William Russell Grace declared in 1881, at the event marking the erection of Cleopatra's Needle in Central Park. Other speeches that day conveyed a notably different attitude to Egypt from those articulated in Europe. Mutual friendship, rather than imperial domination, characterized the USA's perceived relationship with Egypt, and the acquisition of the obelisk was presented as a source of national pride rather than imperial might.

There was also a strong religious dimension to this interest, even more so than was the case in Britain. This is perhaps unsurprising, as 'full-blooded Protestant Christianity dominated educated life in nineteenth-century America'.[21] A considerable portion of the American financial backing for the EEF initially came from men of the cloth who, like Winslow, were intent on proving the reality of the Bible. The EEF's second annual report lists 294 Reverends among its American subscribers, constituting 39 per cent of the total number of American donors, far more than are evident in British ledgers. Jewish donors were equally important, as the growth of Zionism offered a means to reflect on the ancient Jewish presence in eastern lands, rather than their marginalized lives in many parts of Europe. Winslow's success in reaching such individuals came from his persistent petitioning of the press for editorial endorsements, or through short, flamboyant articles on the EEF's work. A snapshot of the journalistic world through which Winslow preached the new gospel of scientific exploration is found among the myriad letters he sent Edwards, in which he breathlessly enumerated his labours:

> ...the <u>Literary World</u>, N.Y. Tribune, N.Y. <u>Evening Post</u>, Springfield Republican, N.Y. Observer (Presbyterian), <u>Independent</u> (Congregationalist), Evangelist (N.U. Presby^n), <u>Church Eclectic Magazine</u>, The <u>Presbyterian</u> (Phila), + there are to be articles in the <u>N.Y Times</u>, the Christian Advocate (Cincinnati), + others I hope. The underscored ones I prepared. I sent also to the <u>Examiner</u> N.Y. (Baptist); the <u>Intelligencer</u> (Reformed Dutch) N.Y; to be in I hope (?) this week, + also to these Chicago papers: the <u>Inter-Ocean</u>, daily, the <u>Advance</u>, Congregational, the <u>Interior</u>, Presbyn. The <u>N.Y. Times editor</u> wrote me thanks: so it will be in. What the Whitehouse performance will effect on the Chicago papers, where the Living Church is issued, I cannot say. I sent a short article to the <u>Dominion Churchman</u> of Toronto, for this week. These articles are all temperately + I hope, skilfully drawn.... the editor of the <u>Jewish Messenger</u> (N.Y.) writes me earnestly to have him present the subject to his readers, many of whom are rich. I sent him a circular.[22]

In keeping with this biblical remit, the only other American beneficiaries of finds from EEF work in the 1880s, apart from Boston's Museum of Fine Arts, were two religious institutions: Rochester Theological Seminary, which according to EES distribution lists received 'a selection of minor antiquities' in 1886, and New York's Chautauqua Assembly, a teaching camp for Sunday School teachers founded in 1874, which acquired an estimated 456 items in 1887. Chautauqua's share comprised lamps, bronze figurines of gods and goddesses, coins, scarabs, statuettes, mosaics and bronze latticework. These had been secured for the Assembly's 'Oriental House' by the Reverend Kittredge, regional secretary for the EEF and head of the Chautauqua Archaeological Society. His own vision for the Assembly was that it should illustrate or corroborate the geography of the Middle East, and help to interpret the text of the Bible. The mass of relics was reported dismissively by Rudyard Kipling, who described 'a place called a museum which had evidently been brought together by feminine hands, so jumbled were the exhibits'.[23]

By comparison, Boston's acquisitions were impressive, and between 1885 and 1911 the Museum of Fine Arts obtained some 3000 objects from the Fund. As one of the most active centres of American culture, with a well-defined urban upper class known as the Boston Brahmins, the museum was well provisioned, albeit shaped more by patron interests than by principled research agendas. By the 1890s, however, Boston was facing stiff competition from other US cities for British finds, a situation that draws into relief one of the primary differences between European and American museums. As Stephen Conn has argued, early museum growth in the US was linked more to the decentralized expansion of its urban centres, notably in Boston, New York, Philadelphia and Chicago, than it was to the imperial zeal that characterized much European collecting.[24] As was the case in Boston, museums in these other major US centres were established by a wealthy local elite, with little government funding. Since citizens identified more with their local area than they did with their nation – you would be a Bostonian first and an American second – urban aspiration and individual philanthropy goaded the development of institutions as each attempted to secure cultural authority over one another. It is unsurprising, therefore, that branches of the EEF were quickly established in New York, Chicago and Philadelphia in the 1890s, all aiming 'to aid this English Archaeological Society in its very important excavations now being carried on in Egypt, and to receive for the museums in this country our share of the antiquities discovered by the explorers'.[25] The Art Institute (est. 1879) and the Haskell Oriental Museum (est. 1896) in Chicago, the University of Pennsylvania Museum (est. 1887), the Detroit Museum of Art (est. 1885), New York City's Metropolitan Museum of Art ('the Met', est. 1870), and Pittsburgh's Carnegie Museum (est. 1895) all competed for the EEF's best finds. In response, Winslow's campaigns for Boston grew more determined:

> ...fine sculptures, including the noble palm-leaf shaft from Ahnas (2500 BC), have come to our Museum, which has beyond all question, the best collection, historically and chronologically, of monuments and sculptures from Egypt to be found on this Continent... Candor compels me to say that the work of our Society, so emphatically endorsed by our best minds in every department of learning, is having less practical support in 'the modern Athens' than in some other cities, notably New York and Chicago.[26]

By invoking Athens, Winslow assumed and promoted the idea that the US was heir to the cultural traditions of Western Europe, including its orientalist sleight of hand that identified itself with world history as a 'euphemism for European history'.[27] Winslow, however, could not compete with more influential individuals. These included Charles Dudley Warner, who had the ear of the Metropolitan Museum of Art's Director, General Luigi Cesnola, and was thus able to secure a direct line between the EEF and New York's principal museum.[28]

Coincident with this new topography of US museums was a period of particularly liberal partage agreements in Egypt, during which the EEF had been able to remove a series of spectacular monuments. An estimated 125 tonnes of material was extracted from Bubastis over the course of three seasons, for instance, around two-thirds of which were shipped abroad by the EEF.[29] Unlike distributions to municipal museums in Britain – which were frequently characterized by small concessions of packets of beads, diminutive bronzes or sets of amulets – the American distributions of the late 1880s and early 1890s were, on the whole, more substantial. Boston, for instance, acquired a gold statuette of a ram-headed god, a colossal statue of Ramesses II and an enormous 20-tonne granite column.[30] Chicago's share was diverse, and included large temple reliefs, architectural elements and other fine stone inscriptions (Fig. 2.3). Detroit received part of an altar, sections of stone lintels and several relief slabs of Ptolemaic date from the 1897–8 Dendereh mission.[31] The list for

Fig. 2.3 Photograph of material received by the University of Chicago in 1896 from the Egypt Exploration Fund's work at the Ramesseum. Courtesy of the Oriental Institute, Chicago.

the University of Pennsylvania includes several limestone blocks with the names and images of kings from Tell Basta, a large statue of Ramesses II in red limestone, and a series of well-preserved coffins.[32]

The penchant for large, striking antiquities also characterized the distributions from Flinders Petrie's BSAE to American patrons. In particular, Petrie played to the popularity of excavating biblical remains and, emulating the EEF's initial strategy, sought funding for work in the Delta with a view to tracing evidence of the Israelites. 'There were many Americans,' Petrie felt, 'who would contribute to a biblical excavation, but not to that of a heathen temple'.[33] He canvassed the same set of institutions that financed EEF investigations, as they had far more purchasing power than most European agencies. This included the University of Pennsylvania Museum of Archaeology and Anthropology, which underwrote the full expense of transporting a 12-tonne sphinx of Ramesses II more than 6000 miles across the Mediterranean Sea and the Atlantic Ocean from the 1913 BSAE excavations in Memphis. This was the single largest Egyptian antiquity to make the journey since Cleopatra's Needle was installed in Central Park, an astonishing feat involving hundreds of labourers throughout the route.[34] This acquisition ultimately altered the trajectory of the museum's collecting activities, providing the impetus for the director's ambition to construct a grand Egyptian wing designed to hold monumental sculptures, which was realized less than ten years later.

Given these tendencies, the characterization by influential German art historian Wilhelm Worringer that America and ancient Egypt shared 'a craving for the colossal' seems apt.[35] This American imperative to collect arresting treasures was enabled by philanthropy and civic ambitions, but it can also be attributed to a shift in its museum strategies between the Gilded and Progressive eras. In the former, the South Kensington Museum and its educational mission to train industrial designers was the template for American institutions, but as their own museums came of age, the model of Kulturgeschicte in German-speaking countries became more attractive.[36] Organizations such as the Schweizerisches Landesmuseum in Zurich and the Bayerisches National Museum in Munich represented a new framework in which chronologically ordered material was set in atmospheric settings of period rooms. In the years running up to the First World War, the Boston MFA and then the Met, followed by Midwestern museums, adopted similar concepts and installed dynamic period rooms embellished with architectural fragments to convey the spirit of an era. Although this approach to display was developed primarily for the representation of

American history and decorative arts, in so doing aesthetic concerns were more broadly combined with the historical in museum strategies generally, far more than had been the case in Britain. In comparison, institutions in Britain tended to maintain their dense typologically focused displays into the 1920s, these being better able to accommodate the more mundane archaeological finds that Flinders Petrie's teams and the EEF mostly returned in the early twentieth century.

'When Women Reigned': Amelia Edwards's US Tour

Biblical links and intercity competition gave momentum to the EEF's American cause, but other political undercurrents concomitantly influenced late nineteenth-century American acquisitions. In 1887, Henry White (1850–1927), First Secretary to the American Legation, gave thanks for the gift of antiquities to Boston in person, at the EEF's fifth annual general meeting in London. He applauded the EEF not only for its research into ancient history, but also because 'it formed an invaluable link between the two great English-speaking nations of the modern world'.[37] Anglo-American relations had been steadily improving throughout the latter part of the Victorian era, and by the late nineteenth century a 'Great Rapprochement' grew between the two nations as diplomatic, political, economic and military interests converged. The transfer of antiquities was just one of a number of soft-power gestures that cemented these relationships. White went on to note a second key reason for the EEF's appeal in the United States:

> This rapprochement, moreover, had been largely fostered by the interest which the American nation took in the Society's Honorary Secretary on account of the popularity of her works, and they were naturally attracted to a Society in which that lady occupied so prominent a position.

He was referring, of course, to Amelia Edwards, and to the widespread support the EEF was garnering from the US women's movement. This was clearly evident in 1889–90 when Edwards undertook an arduous five-month lecture tour of the US East Coast and Midwest (Fig. 2.4).[38] During that time she delivered an impressive 120 lectures to an estimated 100,000 people, proselytizing British fieldwork in Egypt as she went. Luncheons were held in her honour, receptions thrown to welcome her and interviews conducted by the regional and national press. Following

Fig. 2.4 Photograph of one of the press cuttings in Amelia Edwards's scrapbook taken from the *Daily Graphic*, 11 January 1890, showing Edwards lecturing in New York. Courtesy of the Principal and Fellows of Somerville College, Oxford.

Edwards's tour the number of women subscribing to the EEF multiplied: in 1887–8 the EEF annual general report lists at least 99 female US subscribers; by 1891–2, that number had risen to 171, while almost half of the local US honorary EEF secretaries were women.[39] Appearing in these lists are the names of several prominent American suffragists: Caroline Healey Dall (1822–1912) a leading nineteenth-century American reformer, feminist and essayist;[40] Mary A. Livermore (1820–1905), a journalist, the first president of the Association for Advancement of Women, and president of the American Woman Suffrage Association;[41] and Julia Ward Howe (1819–1910), co-founder of the New England Woman Suffrage Association, and founder of the suffragist magazine *Woman's Journal*.[42]

The University of Oxford's Somerville College library holds a scrapbook of press clippings that record Edwards's American journey and provide vignettes to these busy months: 'She scores a distinct triumph at the Odeon', cried the *Cincinnati Gazette* on 7 February 1890, 'Honors to a Talented Lady', announced the *Boston Herald* on 30 November 1889, and 'An Intellectual Treat', proclaimed the *Newhaven Morning News* on 12 November 1889. Other captions underscored Edwards's position at the forefront of women's reform: 'A Lecture by a Woman', exclaimed the *Baltimore America* on 4 December 1889, and 'When Women Reigned', stated the 25 February 1890 *Detroit Evening News* report. Most telling of all is the very last small press cutting pasted into this 76-page scrapbook. It is undated and unattributed:

> Those persons who are so much exercised because women are denied their rights should go and hear Amelia B. Edwards on the lecture platform. Here is a woman who has asserted her rights by sheer intellectual force and has secured them too. There was never a time when a woman with brains in her head and a talent for action, instead of mere agitation, could do so much as now.

It is a glowing portfolio, testament to her popularity. Letters in the EEF archive, however, reveal a more fraught picture, in which there was considerable resistance to Edwards as a female scholar, and to the EEF as a scholarly organization.[43] Nevertheless, adulation for Edwards continued to be professed through gifts and honours. She received a bracelet from the women of Boston, as well as honorary degrees from Colombia College, NY Smith College in Northampton and the College of the Sisters of Bethany in Kansas. At Harvard's Peabody Museum she was noted as being the first woman admitted to deliver a lecture.

Edwards spoke additionally at several women's colleges, including Vassar, Wellesley, Smith, Bryn Mawr and Mount Holyoake, all of which by the end of the century were contributing sponsorship money to the EEF and a few years thereafter began to receive small objects in the distributions. The New England Women's Press Association threw a breakfast in Edwards's honour, as did the influential New York Women's Club, the 'Sorosis'. The latter group had been founded in 1868, after the wife of the managing editor of the *New York World*, the noted journalist Jane Cunningham Croly (1829–1900), applied unsuccessfully for a ticket to attend a function hosted to honour Charles Dickens. The ensuing controversy ultimately led to the formation of an independent women's-only body whose object was to 'promote agreeable and useful relations among women of literary and artistic tastes'.[44] Given Edwards's own prominent journalistic background, as well as her contributions of ghost stories to Dickens's periodicals, she was a revered guest.

There was clearly much these women had in common, but attitudes to political and social issues diverged. The Sorosis did not advance the cause of women's suffrage for instance, but it held strong views on temperance. Edwards circumvented the latter by asking her travelling companion, Kate Bradbury, to discreetly arrange for her Chianti to be served in a china teacup at luncheons.[45] On the issue of suffrage, Edwards took other opportunities to make her own political opinions clear. She was quoted in the 21 February 1890 edition of the *Chicago Herald* as saying 'I am one of those suffragists who believe the present condition of affairs is outrageous'. Similarly, in the *Detroit Tribune*, which led with an article on 25 February 1890 entitled 'The Women of Egypt – more than man's equal in pre-historic times', Edwards again made her views known. Her opinion of modern day Egyptians, however, was also laid bare. The comments in the *Detroit Tribune* betrayed her disdain for 'the Arabs', who she claimed were responsible for the destruction and disposal of Egyptian monuments for monetary gain. Her assertions were blind to the fact that foreign interests fuelled the art market, and that tourists were responsible for much of the damage to Egypt's heritage. She was equally ignorant of the concerted attempts by Egyptians themselves to study and to educate the Egyptian public about their past and the world around them.[46] For Edwards, the British protectorate was a necessary civilizing mechanism over what she saw as an untrustworthy population that was totally disconnected from the ancient remains it lived among. Her remarks serve to reinforce Elliot Colla's point that scientific authority over Egyptian antiquities went hand in hand with colonial control of Egypt.[47] In other words, Western intervention was considered a moral necessity in order to protect ancient artefacts from unscientific treatment by local Egyptian populations, and its institutions were felt to be fully entitled to Egypt's heritage. Celebratory accounts of the lives of individuals like Amelia Edwards tend to overlook comments of this kind, which sit uncomfortably with the heroic and progressive tone that infuses traditional disciplinary histories. The archives remind us, though, of the complexity of worldviews, which are informed by an array of intersecting experiences and identities. Edwards's own outlook was ultimately shaped, and indeed enabled, as much by her elite social class, financial independence, English nationality and unmarried status, as it was by her gender.

Edwards presented antiquities during several of her visits to US institutions. In some cases these constituted the very first Egyptian artefacts acquired by organizations, ushering in new foci for collecting initiatives. For instance, she gifted to fledgling American museums such as the Art Institute in Chicago and the Metropolitan Museum of Art in New York a number of fine 2300-year-old shabtis made for the tomb of a priest named Horudja. Flinders Petrie had fished out around 399 of these figurines from a perilously submerged burial chamber in the Fayum at Hawara the previous year. Egyptologists sometimes refer to shabtis as 'answerers', servant figures ready to undertake manual labour on behalf of the deceased. Undoubtedly Edwards hoped that these attractive little relics would now serve the EEF's cause.

Amelia Edwards was an exceptional individual, but in the late nineteenth-century world of museums and Egyptology she was not an exception. Other prominent women and women's groups were likewise driving forward the study of Egypt, including Sara Yorke Stevenson (1847–1921) in Philadelphia, her collaborator and then rival Phoebe Hearst (1842–1919) in California, and the USA's first professionally-trained Egyptologist, Caroline Ransom Williams (1872–1952), who catalogued Egyptology collections in New York, Detroit, Minneapolis, Cleveland and Toledo. Even the EEF's American branch came to be administered and publicized almost single-handedly by Marie Buckman, a wilful, energetic woman with a flair for the dramatic, from the late 1890s through to her retirement in 1935.

In Chicago, the newly appointed Egyptologist at the University of Chicago, James Henry Breasted (1865–1935),[48] encouraged the Chicago's Woman's Club (CWC) and its Philosophy and Science Department to divert its energies towards securing subscriptions for Flinders Petrie's Egyptian Research Account (ERA). The committee they convened became 'the working force of the Chicago Society of Egyptian

Research'.⁴⁹ As a result, Breasted boasted that the University of Chicago 'will receive the subscriptions of any who are interested in unearthing and *bringing to America* the rapidly disappearing remains of this ancient people, among whom the Hebrews dwelt'.⁵⁰ The CWC was founded in 1876 with a stated mission to deal with civic problems, philanthropy and reform issues. The group's efforts included practical social activism, and its ethos was relatively liberal on issues such as race and suffrage. It raised $404 between 1896 and 1897 for the ERA, and on 20 October 1898 the *Chicago Tribune* ran a story celebrating the recent acquisitions by the Field Museum and the University of Chicago. The article ended with the announcement that CWC member and suffrage campaigner Mary Wilmarth would 'lecture on the work of the Chicago Society of Egyptian Research'. The CWC maintained its support for several years, raising a further $1578, thereby securing for the Haskell Museum Predynastic and Early Dynastic finds from the EEF excavations at Hu and Abydos, as well as continuing to attract media attention for women's work.

Caroline Louise Ransom arrived in Chicago around the same time that the CWC was active, in the autumn of 1898.⁵¹ She had studied previously at Mount Holyoke, where her aunt, Louise Fitz Randolph, established the University's museum and procured artefacts from the EEF in order to teach archaeology and art history. Ransom enrolled in Breasted's newly formed Egyptology degree program at the University of Chicago, the first course of its kind in North America, as its first female student. She graduated with an MA in 1900. After an interlude studying with Adolf Erman in Berlin, she returned to Chicago where she successfully completed her doctorate in 1905 on – what might have been considered an appropriately feminine domestic topic – ancient furniture. Despite an offer of marriage, Ransom remained single in order to build her career, beginning with a teaching post at Bryn Mawr.

In 1910 Ransom took up the position of assistant curator in the Department of Egyptian Art at the Metropolitan Museum of Art.⁵² With most of the (male) members of the department engaged in active fieldwork abroad, it fell to Ransom to take responsibility for almost everything else, such as cataloguing the collection⁵³ and managing the annual arrival of material from fieldwork. Her efforts were not merely administrative. Ransom's documentation of the collection demonstrated her 'great knowledge and impeccable scholarship',⁵⁴ while her interventions in the gallery were innovative. In 1912, for instance, she reported to the American Association of Museums on her experiment in mounting an extensive series of photographic illustrations in the main Egyptian galleries, showing the museum's own excavations in progress and the original context for the archaeological discovery of many displayed items.[55] In this way archaeological processes and modern Egypt were made publicly visible almost a century before such strategies would become a more commonplace feature in museums internationally. The initiative also underscored the different directions that American archaeological displays were beginning to take, away from the dense, object-focused arrangement of most British establishments. There is perhaps also a sense here of Ransom's agency in responding to her exclusion from 'masculine' fieldwork, with photographs offering a mediation between different worlds; between the ancient and the modern, the male and female, the field and the museum. Her position gave Ransom the opportunity and the authority to transform knowledge obtained through excavation into new forms of archaeological narrative. Kathleen Sheppard has observed that this work might not have been perceived as glamorous in the way fieldwork was, but it was 'foundational, discipline-building scholarship'.[56] This new means of materially performing knowledge was also perhaps a sign of the increasingly nationalist turn that American archaeology was taking, especially as promoted by Breasted, Ransom's mentor. The display of the scale of US efforts in Egypt within the Metropolitan Museum's galleries signalled its authority over the artefacts shown, in contrast to the British-procured objects it had relied upon previously.

Sara Yorke Stevenson, a shrewd and vigorous lady remembered for her sense of humour and good-tempered realism,[57] established herself in 1870 within Philadelphia's close-knit intellectual elite, the Mitchell-Furness coterie. This group comprised writers, scientists, physicians and scholars who shaped the social and civic life of Philadelphia. In this milieu Stevenson was perfectly comfortable. As an accomplished intellectual she quickly became known as the America's 'only lady Egyptologist',[58] who lectured to great acclaim at the University of Pennsylvania where she received an honorary doctorate in 1894. Throughout the 1890s she served as president of the women's reform organization the Philadelphia Civic Club, and was a founding member of the Archaeological Association of the University of Pennsylvania, the organization that evolved into the current University Museum, where she held the first (honorary) position of curator of Egyptian and Mediterranean collections. Through another organization founded on her initiative, the American Exploration Society, she arranged for a shipment of 42 boxes of material excavated at Dendereh to be sent directly from Petrie to the Penn Museum. She approached Petrie again in 1895 with the offer of financial support in return for objects. Her letter reveals the encyclopaedic vision for the museum that she and her close colleague William Pepper, the provost of the University, passionately shared:

> ... it has occurred to me that we might through you do, in Egypt, what we are doing elsewhere – In Babylon we are conducting as you no doubt know an exploration at ancient Nippur – in South America, I have just arranged with Dr Uhle... to explore for us in the vicinity of Cuzo (Peru) and Tiahuanale (Bolivia) – In Yucatan we have an expedition exploring caves – with the hope of settling certain questions as to the antiquity of the American Civilizations – We are cooperating with Harvard in Honduras – and it has recently occurred to me ... that it might be agreeable to you that we should cooperate with you.[59]

The correspondence between Petrie and Stevenson reveals a 'bond of personal friendship'[60] and mutual respect. He appreciated her for 'her whole-hearted and unselfish dedication to the subject', and she was 'glad to be your [Petrie's] mouthpiece over here'.[61] Her donations led Petrie to joke that she seemed 'to take a naughty pleasure in putting me into difficulties to adequately compensate your generosity'. [62] She could afford to be munificent. The 1893 budget of the University Museum had allotted $80,000 to the Old World Archaeology section. In contrast, the American and Prehistoric department received a paltry $331.20.[63] Stephen Conn has explained this disparity as a result of the desires of wealthy Philadelphians who funded the institution, and who took a greater interest in the Old World than the societies in their own backyard. As he goes on to explain, however, it was also a consequence of intellectual tensions. On the one hand, explorations in the Near East pursued biblical and Classical frameworks, founded upon specific histories and chronologies. On the other, New World fieldwork was situated more within the disciplinary development of anthropology, which emphasized cultural evolutionary frameworks that placed indigenous American groups on a 'natural' timescale. Correspondingly, British finds from Egypt were placed on the first floor of the museum, while archaeological finds from the Americas were situated on the ground floor with natural history specimens.[64]

Almost all of the aforementioned activity was focused in the urban centres of north-eastern America, where the 'new women' of the Progressive Era were clustered. One museum pioneer, however, took the challenge of furthering a professional career southwards, to poverty-stricken South Carolina. Here the feminist movement had not been as strong, and expectations of demure 'Southern ladies' had remained largely unchanged since the Civil War. Laura Bragg (1881–1978), a 'self-proclaimed social missionary and reformer', [65] arrived in Charleston in September 1909 to find a town largely untouched by modernization, with dilapidated mansions spread along mostly dirt-track roads. She was to take up a position in the Department of Public Instruction at the US's oldest museum, the Charleston Museum, founded in 1773. By the twentieth century much of the collection was languishing in store, and it was Bragg's responsibility to install the old museum into a new location in Thompson's Auditorium. She eventually became its Director in 1921, the first woman to be named director of a major museum in the US. Bragg threw herself into these roles, developing the Charleston Museum as a democratic and educational establishment for the whole community (inclusive of African Americans, Chinese and indigenous peoples). If these communities did not come to the museum, then she took it to them in the form of educational 'Bragg Boxes', miniature dioramas with curriculum books, photographs, cultural artefacts and scientific specimens to touch and pass around. A total of 63 were constructed by 1914, to which a further 84 were added over the next twelve years.

It was Bragg who devised the plan for the 'History of Man' exhibit within which 'Egypt is a tale by itself, to be emphasised here... because of the part it played in the building up of other civilizations'.[66] It was at this time that objects from the BSAE concessions at Harageh and Lahun were acquired, most likely via Bragg's personal connections in the Egyptian Departments of the Metropolitan Museum of Art and the Boston MFA, where she had spent brief periods working, or through her friend Caroline Sinker, who had links with Philadelphia museums. Although the rhetoric of these displays was couched in the then familiar terms of 'primitive peoples' and 'civilization', Bragg held 'no brief for the Nordic race theory', and felt rather that museums can 'change our supercilious attitude toward the rest of the world'.[67] In 1920 she wrote to Flinders Petrie directly, outlining the history of the museum, its status as 'the only large, active museum in the South', and her ambitions for exhibiting 'typical forms of civilization and endeavouring to show the origins and migrations of various cultural elements'.[68] In this scheme, she went on to explain, 'you can readily understand that Egypt is the corner stone'. In 1922 the arrival of a second batch of finds from Flinders Petrie, together with material from Eckley B. Coxe, Jr's[69] US expeditions, 'led to the reinstallation of the Egyptian exhibit'.[70] For Bragg, Egyptian antiquities represented her 'deepest interest of making the history of the past live for people of the present',[71] and she was thrilled by the sorts of things that Petrie's excavations could supply: the pottery vessels, stone tools, faience amulets and metal tools. These were not just things for display. Bragg insisted on the value of tactile engagement with objects, and in this context Egyptian 'minor antiquities' became 'a real asset in teaching' in South Carolina.[72] It is even possible that some of the smaller pieces found their way into one of her travelling 'Bragg Boxes'. Whether Egyptian objects were always so revered in the South should, however, be questioned. Slavery was a narrative that was assumed for much of ancient Egyptian history, and this would not have been lost on those of African descent in what had been the largest slave port in the US. Such contemporary voices, however, are absent from currently accessible archives.

These activities are not necessarily evidence that arts at this time were being feminized, because ultimately such cultural institutions were still served by a male policy-making elite.[73] For these reasons it is commonly assumed that museums were shaped by white, male interests.[74] Kathleen McCarthy has nevertheless argued that fundraising and philanthropic efforts enabled politically disadvantaged groups, like diverse women's assemblies, to influence American society in other ways.[75] Their activities offered to its mostly wealthy proponents a parallel cultural world in which social relationships could be negotiated and through which they could make their presence known. Lobbying for Egyptian antiquities fitted this profile, as was the case in Britain. For others, the fluidity of the quickly changing field of higher education and the developing museum world allowed for new professional identities to be forged. And within the latter, partage models empowered women to proximally engage in the sorts of scientific collecting that was usually the preserve of men. It allowed them to directly shape knowledge constructed within institutions, and it involved them establishing terminology and canons of expertise around material objects that future generations would require to advance their careers.

Museum Cartographies

As American museum collections grew, questions began to emerge as to where they should be located. These quandaries formed part of broader negotiations over intellectual boundaries, as the contours of academic practices were realigned between museums and universities at the beginning of the twentieth century. In the US the consequences of collecting policies on Egyptian antiquities and related material were particularly marked in Philadelphia. Here material was exchanged between the Commercial Museum (est. 1893), the University of

Pennsylvania Museum of Archaeology and Anthropology (est. 1887) and the Philadelphia Museum of Art (est. 1877), as has been thoroughly explored by Stephen Conn. Through these transfers Egyptian artefacts troubled the lines between art, industrial art and archaeology.[76] In Chicago there are three venues in which objects acquired from British excavations are housed: the Oriental Institute (formerly the Haskell Museum) of the University of Chicago (est. 1894), the Field Museum (est. 1893) and the Art Institute of Chicago (est. 1879). The histories of these institutions are also closely interrelated, particularly through the intermediation of James Henry Breasted, with Petrie at the periphery.[77]

Collections in Philadelphia and Chicago provoked the support, and occasionally the ire, of the city's university scholars. Other institutions, such as the Brooklyn Museum, faced different sorts of conflicts with its 'twin city', New York, on Manhattan Island. The Brooklyn Institute had hosted Edwards's first and final lectures on her tour, at the Brooklyn Academy of Music Hall on Montague St, with the dual aim of promoting the EEF and generating funds to purchase works of art.[78] When Amelia Edwards first visited in 1889, Brooklyn was still an independent city whose local press lamented its lack of a museum. Newspapers such as the *Brooklyn Standard* used her tour as a platform to continue to call for a cultural institution in which local citizens could take pride. The Brooklyn Museum was eventually opened in 1897, but the following year the city was merged, along with five other boroughs, to form New York City, much to the disappointment of many Brooklynites, who feared losing their civic sense of self. The museum's identity was, as a result, contested. On each side of the newly constructed Brooklyn Bridge opinions clashed as to what should fill the grand Roman Neoclassical building that had been erected. Those in Brooklyn initially had lofty aspirations, identifying themselves with London's South Kensington Museum and its reputation as a prominent centre of learning in the technical and industrial arts.[79] Many New Yorkers, on the other hand, believed that there should be 'only one great museum of art in Central Park', relegating Brooklyn's Museum to the position of a 'great organization for popular study'.[80] By 1905 a letter from the museum to Flinders Petrie, who was then leading excavations in the Sinai, gives away the direction taken by Brooklyn Museum, at least with regard to Egyptian antiquities. The museum authorities requested 'larger showier specimens suitable for display', and they earnestly hoped 'that a good mummy case may turn up the time you next visit Cairo. A mummy case is always an attractive object and regarded with much interest by the public.'[81] As they went on to explain:

Mr Petrie's judgement will be considered as superior to our own in all these matters, provided he understands that there are no Egyptologists in Brooklyn, and that inscriptions or papri [sic] will not be valued from the standpoint of the scholar or hyerglyphic [sic] expert... we do not hope to obtain rare historic pieces. We want to make a popular exhibit. [82]

Brooklyn's appeal came at a time when America's universities and museums were beginning to strike out on their own. Millionaire philanthropists provided investment capital for independent American expeditions to Egypt, filling a niche opened by fractures in the EEF's American branch after Winslow's 1902 dismissal and the discontinuation of the affiliate EEF branches in Philadelphia and Chicago in 1904. The first of these plutocratic patrons was Phoebe Hearst, who sponsored the University of California expedition to Koptos, north of Luxor, in 1899, where George Reisner (1867–1942) was granted a large concession to work. He continued to explore a number of sites on behalf of the Phoebe Hearst Museum over five years, including at Ballas, Naga ed-Deir and Giza, before the funding was rescinded. By that time, Albert Lythgoe (1868–1934) had been appointed as the Boston Museum of Fine Art's first curator in the new Department of Egyptian Art. The museum joined forces with Harvard University to sponsor a continuation of work on the Giza plateau, shifting the spoils to America's north-east coast.

As Boston's Egyptian collection grew, the Metropolitan Museum of Art became worried that New York was losing out. J. P. Morgan, the museum's wealthy president of the Board of Trustees, launched the challenge that the Met's new Department of Egyptian Art (founded 1906) should 'rank permanently as the best in America',[83] and he swiftly lured Lythgoe to New York to head its own 1906–07 expedition to el-Lisht, capital of Middle Kingdom Egypt. From 1910 onwards the Metropolitan Museum of Art based its operations in Luxor, and its collections expanded to occupy ten newly built galleries in the north wing, primarily administered by Caroline Ransom while Lythgoe was away in the field. The Metropolitan Museum also profited from other 'robber barons', such as Theodore Davis (1838–1915), a man who made his millions as a lawyer and sponsored work in the Valley of the Kings before giving up the concession to Lord Carnarvon in 1914. On his death Davis bequeathed his rich collection to the New York institution. Brooklyn Museum commissioned Henri de Morgan (1854–1909) for two winters of excavation in 1906–07 and 1907–08, fieldwork that considerably enlarged its Predynastic collection in the process, while the University of Pennsylvania's expeditions began in 1907 through the support of Eckley B. Coxe, Jr. (1872–1916), a wealthy heir to a fortune made mining coal fields. By 1915 the Coxe endowment allowed for budgets as high as $15,000 per season in Egypt, far in excess of any British project.[84] In Chicago, Breasted's initiatives at the University of Chicago's Oriental Institute were eventually financed by one of America's wealthiest individuals of all time, the oil magnate John D. Rockefeller (1839–1937).

On account of such financing America was able to organize archaeological practice in Egypt on a much more massive scale than had previously been seen, with considerable sums being spent on equipment, dig-houses and libraries. This allowed the US to aggressively advance its influence over Egyptian archaeology in competition with the longer-established claims of Europeans. The material results of these missions were closely linked to the institutional affiliations of the excavators and their philanthropists. As such, they were accountable to a far narrower set of museums than British campaigns.

Given this lavish expenditure and the scale of work it financed, it is understandable why book titles such as *The American Discovery of Ancient Egypt*[85] give the impression of a nationally bounded narrative of heroic exploration. In practice, however, US work moved into the Egyptian archaeological labour market that had been partially restructured by British interests and which enabled increasingly sophisticated excavations.[86] Generating knowledge about ancient Egypt implicated a fluid set of transnational relationships. Some of those involved, like Breasted, received their first archaeological excavation experience directly under Petrie, while for others it was more indirect, with 'Petrie's pups'[87] forming the initial logistical foundation for US-led missions. Theodore Davis's privately financed work, for instance, was undertaken by several British excavators, including John Garstang, James Quibell, Edward Ayrton and Percy Newberry. Meanwhile, individuals such as Frederick Green, James Quibell, Kate Quibell and Arthur Mace, as well as several unnamed Egyptian workmen, who had all gained their first experiences of running archaeological excavations under Petrie, were employed on Phoebe Hearst's expedition specifically because Reisner was 'absolutely inexperienced'[88] during his first seasons between 1899 and 1901. Yet Reisner quickly established his own exacting methods, critiquing 'the search for museum specimens' that had driven British enterprises as 'an offence against historical and archaeological research which is utterly unworthy of any institution which pretends to be dedicated to the advancement of knowledge'.[89] Every tomb was to be recorded, photographed and published, in contrast to Petrie's selective accounts.

This greater emphasis on empirical findings by US-led expeditions was, given the sponsorship, as much a product of political economy as it was of intellectual reform. Nevertheless, the museum was still in the mind's eye of the excavator, and Reisner envisaged that his records would be for public benefit, as well as of research value. In letters to his sponsor, Phoebe Hearst, he outlined his specific plans for an Egyptian museum in California which would utilize photographs *in situ* alongside displayed objects to illustrate archaeological context.[90] Like Ransom's work in the Metropolitan Museum a decade later, these trends in US collecting reveal distinct sets of museum values which were 'worked out at the interface of photograph and object',[91] with photographic collections operating to authenticate and authorize narratives of scientific work.

A second key element in Reisner's management of sites was the introduction of simple index cards, known in archaeological circles as 'tomb cards', to organize observations. This systematization of field documentation instituted on the Hearst campaigns in turn impacted British field-logging methods, which adopted more formal note-taking from at least 1908. On Ayrton and Loat's EEF excavation at Abydos, for instance, pre-printed, bespoke tomb cards were used to record cemetery F. Notably, the large central portion of these cardboard records was reserved for a 'catalogue of objects', rather than as a space to document the broader context of the finds (Fig. 2.5). Object-led knowledge of the past remained the focus of excavation. By 1910 these individual 'context sheets' had been restructured for use by Petrie's BSAE teams,

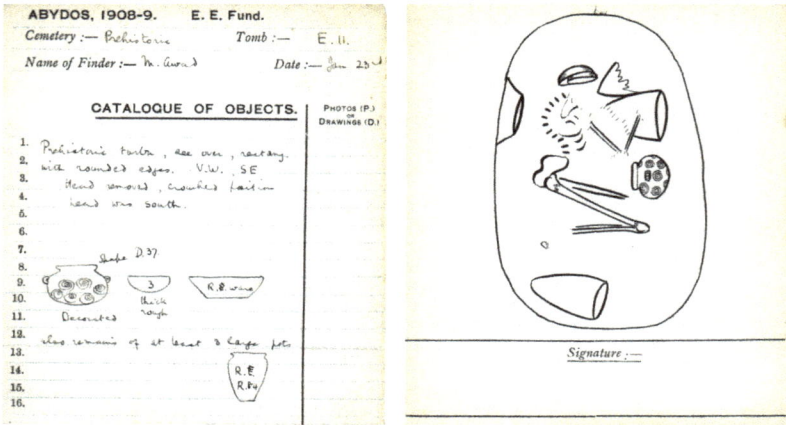

Fig. 2.5a & b Front and back of a 'tomb card' from EES Abydos excavations, 1908–09. Courtesy of the Egypt Exploration Society (AB. TC.E.0011).

with discrete sections for listing different categories of grave goods, as well as for recording the specifics of tomb dimensions and the sex of the occupant. Despite the latter two sections being dedicated to contextual detail for the finds, practitioners rarely used them, and they continued to list object types for the next decade. By this time, the BSAE excavation reports published lists of artefacts sent to museums by reference to tomb number, meaning that such field recording mechanisms could be a means of facilitating the distribution, as much as the archaeological interpretation, of finds.

The circulation of finds between Britain and the US continued during the Progressive Era, albeit in alternative ways. Smaller sets of material from the EEF and BSAE from 1905 onwards continued to trickle into institutions in Boston, Chicago and Philadelphia, but on nothing of the scale of the returns seen in the previous century, nor of the sort that could rival what American institutions were now able to procure independently. It is true that such institutions often still maintained a watchful eye on the spoils that came into Boston's harbour, but they were usually quick to dismiss the type of objects that were arriving. In 1911, for example, the Docent of the Boston Museum of Fine Arts, Louis Earle Rowe (1882–1937), inspected the cargo of antiquities sent by the EEF to the Boston office and noted that 'so many museums were already supplied with much of the material', which was in any case 'of second rate character, yet decidedly of use for students, especially the several varieties of pottery'.[92] He suggested that Rhode Island School of Design might acquire a few pieces for their art museum. They took the opportunity.[93]

Through such mechanisms, ad hoc donations and opportunistic acquisitions began to find their way to a few new American destinations between 1906 and 1915. These included Johns Hopkins University Museum in Baltimore, and Williams College Museum of Art in Williamstown, but in these cases it was the simple happenstance of personal connections, rather than intercity competition, which was the primary motivating factor for acquisition. In Baltimore's case that involved the participation of local attorney James Teackle Dennis (1865–1918) in the EEF Deir el-Bahri excavations. A different sort of personal association led to nearly one hundred archaeological relics ending up in the Iowa Masonic Lodge in Cedar Rapids. This was reportedly on account of the husband of EEF American Branch Secretary, Marie Buckman, who was a Knight Templar and a Scottish Rite Mason.[94] As a result of this initial donation the Grand Secretary of Cedar Rapids Lodge was eventually appointed as EEF Honorary

Secretary for Iowa. The Lodge took particular interest in two ibis mummies and material from Abydos, the centre of the Osiris Cult in Middle Kingdom times. Osiris was a god who 'all Scottish Rite Masons will be interested in', because of the nineteenth- and early twentieth-century belief that freemasonry had its origins in ancient Egypt. These beliefs formed a strong current in American interest in Egypt. They lay behind, for instance, the acquisition of 'Cleopatra's Needle' in New York, through the agency of Henry H. Gorringe (1841–1885), the installation of which was an event attended by several thousand Masons.[95]

By 1910, smaller institutions beyond the metropolises of the East Coast were building up their own Egyptian collections, and in the absence of millionaire philanthropists, appealed to the EEF for concessions to American museums. The timing could not have been worse, however: much of the Old World was set to be engulfed by the First World War.

'Business As Usual': Excavation and Distribution During the War

The initiative for a group of American museums to acquire material through the EEF was led by an elusive and very private professor, Thomas Whittemore (1871–1950).[96] He was well connected with wealthy American patrons, and had long-standing friendships with European and Europe-based artists like Henri Matisse and Gertrude Stein. As a student Whittemore had become fascinated with the ancient world, and in 1911 he abandoned his post at Boston's Tuffs College to excavate for the EEF with Naville at Abydos. From there Whittemore sent 400 undecorated, small brown pottery libation cups back to America, which when distributed to individual subscribers 'proved at that time a wonderful attraction and gained us [the EEF] subscribers'.[97] Encouraged by this response, Whittemore sought to direct his own excavations, funded solely by American donations. He enlisted the support of the Boston Museum of Fine Arts, the University of Pennsylvania, Brooklyn Museum, Cincinnati Museum, Wellesley College, Toledo Museum of Art, the University of Illinois, Yale University, Brattleboro Public Library in Vermont, and Louisville Museum in Kentucky, all of which were to be reimbursed with ancient finds. Sawama and Balabish cemeteries near Abydos were identified for excavating, but no pretence was made to scientific investigation. Ostensibly, this was exclusively an exercise in museum enrichment:

Both [cemeteries] had been previously excavated by the Department of Antiquities, as well as frequently plundered by natives, but it was thought that they might still yield types of pottery much sought by the museums, and, perhaps, other objects of interest.[98]

It seems that where the objects were from was considered less important than where they were going. The asymmetrical colonial power relations underpinning this treasure hunt are represented in a photograph of what is apparently payday at Balabish (Fig. 2.6). Whittemore can be seen seated at a table in tweed trousers, shirt, tie and cloth hat, surrounded by Egyptian workmen standing barefoot on the rocky desert surface, together with dust-covered basket boys seated on the ground. Is this simply another illustration of business as usual, mobilizing and administering the oriental other for Western gain? Perhaps, but not quite. Photographs can disguise more complicated histories of colonial encounter than is readily apparent. As anthropologists have increasingly come to realize, such snapshots are not only images, but also material performances through which complex relationships were negotiated.[99] In this case, the frozen moment captured on a glass plate negative was clearly staged. Whittemore's profile at the left hand edge of the picture is assured as he holds still for the exposure, while the animation of the group jostled around him is apparent from the

Fig. 2.6 Photograph of payday at Balabish, March 1915. Courtesy of the Egypt Exploration Society (BAL.NEG.10).

ghostly expressions that streak across the image. Early twentieth-century photography was a cumbersome business. Unlike the well-financed US expeditions, British fieldwork was less able to invest in the bulky and fragile equipment that such practices relied upon. As a result, which aspects of fieldwork were to be recorded had to be more selective than was the case for American excavations. In this case, the rationale for setting up such a portrait of fieldwork life was a composite of circumstances and conflicting interests, of which archaeology or museum acquisition were the least important considerations.

The photograph was taken around March 1915, a time when trench warfare was tearing Europe apart. Whittemore had witnessed the casualties of the conflict first hand, as a volunteer with the British Red Cross in 1914, serving in France where he attended to 'acres of wounded' amid 'unimaginable suffering'.[100] He had flown to Egypt that season from Germany, where he had been attempting to visit his friend, Matthew S. Prichard, who was being held at a prisoner of war camp near Berlin. Most of his war after leaving Balabish in April 1915 was spent engaged in humanitarian efforts in France, Russia and Bulgaria, using the fundraising skills honed for the EEF to campaign for supplies for refugees and fugitives. It would simplistic to attribute his interlude in Egypt between the horrors of the Western Front and the bleak Balkan war-torn landscape as merely a privileged hiatus. Whittemore was in fact responding to a personal plea from an Egyptian foreman (*rais*), Aly Osman, one of the Egyptian workmen he knew from his previous seasons at Abydos and whose own livelihood was now under threat from Europe's war. He had written personally to Whittemore in broken English at the end of 1914. Of the thousands of archival documents relating to the distribution of finds from Egypt, this is the only one known to represent the voice of an Egyptian worker:

Dear Sir,

I hope that you are quite well please if there is any work tell us because the workers waiting any work this year and if you dont [sic] come and not work tell us to search for work we are much oblige [sic] from your work.[101]

Whittemore forwarded the letter to Marie Buckman at the EEF American branch head office noting that 'you will see by the enclosed what a pity it is not to go on with the work'. The American Committee immediately cabled Whittemore to make arrangements to travel to Egypt and to commence excavations, while Buckman informed the London office that 'Aly Osman's letter is our appeal to you for <u>special</u> support of this expedition'.[102] Any altruism apparently expressed here could be dismissed as a ploy to encourage a reticent British organization to endorse an excavation for American benefit. Notwithstanding this possibility, Osman's intervention remains significant. Egyptian foremen, as Wendy Doyon's work has shown,[103] occupied pivotal positions between indigenous workmen and Western archaeologists, as they played a central role in mediating the economic relations of archaeological fieldwork in Egypt. This is no more evident than here.

The London office consented to the American branch's request, but it did so on its own terms. All official contemporary EEF accounts of the Balabish expedition efface the Egyptian workers' agency and their stake in the archaeological process. Instead the initiative was reframed jingoistically as one of heroic British defiance. The editorial of the April 1915 edition of the *Journal of Egyptian Archaeology* boasts that:

> The action of the American Committee in carrying on our work under the joint Anglo-American leadership of Professor Whittemore and Mr Wainwright, is much appreciated as a ready help in time of difficulty, and as proof that the American public has no belief whatever in the ridiculous German lies about disturbances in Egypt. The fact that Professor Reisner is carrying on 'business as usual' at Gizeh, of course, tells Boston that all is well on the banks of the Nile in spite of the absurd inventions of the egregious Herr Encke and the credulity of 'Tante Voss'. And so Boston keeps the Fund's flag flying in Egypt.

Similarly, Whittemore's colleague, Gerald A. Wainwright's journey to the field site was commended as an act of heroism, his having 'escaped the attentions of German pirates'[104] in order to reach Egypt from England. Against this background, perhaps the purpose of the photograph was, in visual anthropologist Elizabeth Edwards's terms, a 'mode of reassurance',[105] an attempt to present a picture of stability, of 'business as usual', when all else in the world was in a state of flux and uncertainty. Today this image of the individuals around Whittemore also acts as a reminder that the money raised by the EEF did not just enable the dispersal of antiquities, but also went directly towards the creation of a new wage labour economy. In turn this created 'a particular division of labour for the extraction of ancient artefacts whereby the labour of Egyptian peasants was "invested" in Egypt's archaeological development'.[106]

The antiquities wrested from Balabish were the EEF's last consignment of material to make it out of Egypt and Europe before the war depleted finances, diverted manpower and disrupted transport. In November 1915, the steamship *SS Arabic* was sunk by a German torpedo, with the loss of 44 lives together with its cargo of Egyptian antiquities originally destined for the Metropolitan Museum Art. Petrie and his colleagues were horrified, and they did not dare to ship anything else, despite the *Journal of Egyptian Archaeology's* repetition of British war propaganda that 'the Navy has crushed the German submarines in our waters'.[107]

While many archaeologists enlisted for war duty, Petrie was forced begrudgingly by age to remain in London, 'managing the collection there all the winter, and wondering when a bomb might scatter it all'.[108] In the interim he also tried to negotiate a home for one of the most spectacular finds made by his teams over the winter of 1913–14: an exquisite set of 3800-year old jewellery belonging to the Middle Kingdom Princess Sithathoryunet, found concealed in a niche of her underground tomb alongside King Senwosret II's pyramid. The set included a pectoral inlaid with 372 skilfully cut pieces of semi-precious stones (Fig. 2.7), hundreds of gold and amethyst beads (some shaped into lion claws), obsidian and gold cosmetic vessels, travertine canopic jars to hold the deceased's internal organs, and delicate, ivory ornamented wooden caskets. It was

Fig. 2.7 Pectoral and necklace of Queen Sithathoryunet with the name of Senwosret II (c. 1887 BC) (museum number 16.1.3a, b) excavated by the British School of Archaeology in Egypt team at Lahun in 1914. Creative Commons Zero (CC0) The Metropolitan Museum of Art, New York.

heralded in *The Times* on 20 May 1914 as 'The Treasure of Lahun', and the article closed with a reminder that the jewellery that had not been retained by the Cairo Museum was now in London and would shortly be exhibited at University College London that June. The display was still open when war was announced in August, and Petrie rushed back from a lecture tour to dismantle it. The precious assemblage survived the Zeppelin raids and was eventually dispatched to New York after the war. Petrie later alleged in his memoir *Seventy Years in Archaeology* that he accepted an offer from the Metropolitan Museum 'reluctantly', as it was the only institution then capable of providing the appropriate financial recompense for such a sensational find. Britain's war effort, he claimed, had restricted available funds, and South Kensington and the British Museum were apathetic towards accommodating the find.[109] Letters in the archive reveal this to be somewhat disingenuous assertion. Rather, as Petrie confessed to the Head of the Metropolitan Museum's Egyptian Department, 'I should be glad to think of it being in a safe place out of reach of the barbarians.'[110] Missives in the Metropolitan Museum archive further detail the extent of the bargaining that went on, and Petrie's active role in promoting competition to inflate the price further. A bid of £7500 had been made by Berlin Museum by June of 1914, which New York countered with an offer 'to advance as much as nine thousand pounds in case you can purchase the whole material'.[111] Petrie, as Breasted remarked shortly after, had 'become a mere digger after museum pieces and stuff to satisfy his subscribers'.[112]

***

The passing of royal treasures from British to American hands was in another sense symbolic of Britain's post-war displacement from the forefront of Egyptian archaeology. As Breasted boasted, 'far and away the best work done in Egypt is being done by three American expeditions here, Reisner, Lythgoe and Fisher, that is Boston (Harvard), New York and Philadelphia'.[113] Such a statement was typical of the American exceptionalism that pervades much of Breasted's rhetoric, such as that in the widely disseminated high school textbook *Ancient Times* (1916), which emphasizes a 'cultural kinship' between modern America and ancient Egypt, predicated on a shared imperialist quest to conquer the wilderness.[114] He had a point, however. By the early 1920s seven out of eight foreign missions in Egypt were sponsored by American organizations.[115]

The shift was keenly felt back in London. In late 1918 the EEF rallied the support of Lord F. M. Grenfell (1841–1925), President of the

Fund and former Sirdar of the British Army, to push for a British Imperial Institute of Archaeology for Egypt,[116] while Sir John Evans penned an appeal in the 3 March 1919 edition of *The Times*. The issue was also one of the first agenda items of the newly formed Joint Archaeological Committee, assembled by the British Academy and representing all the principal English societies concerned with Archaeology, 'with the object of urging on the Government the proper organization of the control of antiquities of all periods in the lands opened up by the war'.[117] The group laid down a memorandum addressed to the Treasury in January 1919. All to no avail. At the fourth meeting of the Joint Archaeological Committee on 6 March 1919, the Chair of the Committee, British Museum director, Frederic Kenyon, read the Treasury's terse response: 'in the present financial conditions it was not possible to increase any liabilities by endorsing a British Institute in Egypt'.[118] It was a prudent decision, as the following decades would demonstrate.

Notes

1. Twain, M. and Warner, C. D. 1873. *The Gilded Age: A Tale of Today*. Chicago: American Pub. Co., F. G. Gilman.
2. President Theodore Roosevelt became a member of the American Branch of the EEF around 1902/1903 after donating $25. Letter from Charles W. Darling to Theodore Roosevelt, 4 February 1903, Theodore Roosevelt Papers, Library of Congress Manuscript Division.
3. As charted, for instance, in Coleman, L. V. 1939. *The Museum in America: A Critical Study*. Three Volumes. Washington DC: The American Association of Museums.
4. Conn, S. 1998. *Museums and Intellectual Life, 1876–1926*. Chicago and London: The University of Chicago Press, p. 13.
5. Letter from Winslow to Edwards, 8 March 1888, EES.COR.2.d.180; see also Winslow to Edwards, 18 June 1889, EES.COR.2.d.247.
6. This correspondence is housed in the Boston Museum of Fine Arts, Department of Egyptian Art Archives. See also Winslow, W. C. 1903. *The Truth About the Egypt Exploration Society: The Singular Reorganization of the American Branch*. Boston: Self published; D'Auria, S. 2007. The American branch of the Egypt Exploration Fund. In Hawass, Z. A. and Richards, J. (eds.) *The Archaeology and Art of Ancient Egypt: Essays In Honor of David B. O'Connor*. Cairo: American Research Center in Egypt, pp. 185–98.
7. Letter from W. J. Holland to Emily Paterson, 31 December 1901, Boston Museum of Fine Arts, Department of Egyptian Art Archives.
8. EEF 1884. *Report of the Second Annual General Meeting and Balance Sheet*. London: Egypt Exploration Fund, p. 10.
9. One of the oldest collections in the US was the Library Company of Philadelphia, founded in 1731, which acquired an Egyptian mummy hand in 1767. Zytaruk, M. 2017. American's first circulating museum: the object collection of the library company of Philadelphia. *Museums History Journal* 10(1): 68–82.
10. Many local museums sprang up across America in the Antebellum Era. They were often focused on natural history and curios, but these tended to be operated as forms of popular entertainment rather than education, and few were long-term enterprises. See Wallach, A. 1998. *Exhibiting Contradiction: Essays on the Art Museum in the United States*. Amherst: University of Massachusetts Press, p. 24.
11. Thompson, J. 2016. *Wonderful Things: A History of Egyptology 2, The Golden Age 1881–1914*. Cairo: American University Press, pp. 211–14.
12. Wolfe, S. J. 2016. Bringing Egypt to America: George Gliddon and the 'Panorama of the Nile'. *Journal of Ancient Egyptian Interconnections* 8: 1–20.
13. Irwin, J. T. 1980. *American Hieroglyphics: The Symbol of the Egyptian Hieroglyphs in the American Renaissance*. New Haven: Yale University Press, p. 21.
14. Giguere, J. 2014. *Characteristically American: Memorial Architecture, National Identity, and the Egyptian Revival*. Knoxville: University of Tennessee Press.
15. Pratt, M. 2009. *Imperial Egypt: Travel Writing and Transculturation*. London and New York: Routledge, p. 3.
16. Delamaire, M-S. 2003. Searching for Egypt: Egypt in 19th Century American World Exhibitions. In Humbert, J-M. and Price, C. (eds.) *Imhotep Today: Egyptianizing Architecture*. London: UCL Press, pp.123–34.
17. Hinsley, C. M. and Wilcox, D. R. (eds.) 2016. *Coming of Age in Chicago: The 1893 World's Fair and the Coalescence of American Anthropology*. Lincoln and London: University of Nebraska Press.
18. Pezzati, A. 2015. Gold medals and grand prizes. *Expedition Magazine* 57(1): 19–21.
19. Original certificate in the University of Pennsylvania Museum archives (number 249505). With thanks to Alessandro Pezzati for sharing a copy with me.
20. Giguere, *Characteristically American*, p. 202.
21. Kuklick, B. 1996. *Puritans in Babylon: The Ancient Near East and American Intellectual Life, 1880–1930*. Princeton: Princeton University Press.
22. Letter from Winslow to Edwards, 19 May 1884, EES.COR.2.d.5.
23. Rieser, A. C. 2003 *The Chautauqua Moment: Protestants, Progressives and the Culture of Modern Liberalism*. New York: Columbia University Press, p. 155.
24. Conn, S. 2010. *Do Museums Still Need Objects?* Philadelphia: University of Pennsylvania Press, p. 20.

25 Undated EEF flyer in the Boston Museum of Fine Arts archive.
26 Winslow, W. C. nd. *Gifts to the Boston Museum of Fine Arts*. Leaflet in Boston Museum of Fine Art, Department of Egyptian Art archives.
27 Said, E. 1978. *Orientalism*. New York: Pantheon Books, p. 86.
28 Letter from Charles Dudley Warner to General Loring, 19 September 1897, Boston Museum of Fine Art, Department of Egyptian Art archives.
29 Spencer, N. 2007. Naville at Bubastis and other sites. In Spencer, P. (ed.) *The Egypt Exploration Society: The Early Years*. London: Egypt Exploration Society, p. 22.
30 Berman, L. M. 2002. The prehistory of the Egyptian Department of the Museum of Fine Arts, Boston. In Eldamaty, M. and Trad, M. (ed.) *Egyptian Museum Collections Around the World: Volume Two*. Cairo: American University in Cairo Press, pp. 119–32.
31 PMA/WFP1/D/6/1.2.
32 EES.DIST.06.03b.
33 Drower, M. 1985. *Flinders Petrie: A Life in Archaeology*. London: Victor Gollancz, p. 296.
34 Wegner, J. and Wegner, J. H. 2015. *The Sphinx That Travelled to Philadelphia: The Story on the Colossal Sphinx in the Penn Museum*. Philadelphia: University of Pennsylvania Press.
35 Worringer, W. 1928 *Egyptian Art*. London: Putnam, p. 25.
36 Curran, K. 2016. *The Invention of the American Art Museum: From Craft to Kulturgeschichte. 1870–1930*. Los Angeles: Getty Research Institute.
37 EEF 1887. *Report of the Fifth Annual General Meeting*. London: Egypt Exploration Fund, p. 19.
38 For further details on this and what follows, see Moon, B. 2006. *More Usefully Employed: Amelia B. Edwards, Writer, Traveller and Campaigner for Ancient Egypt*. London: Egypt Exploration Society, pp. 221–33.
39 19 out of 40 listed names, as based on salutations Miss or Mrs in the subscription lists. Where 'Dr' or only initials are given it is impossible to make a judgement on an individual's gender.
40 Dall's papers can be consulted in the Massachusetts Historical Society and include several pieces of correspondence with the EEF: http://www.masshist.org/collection-guides/view/fa0270/i-c03_49?terms=civil%20war [accessed 27 October 2017].
41 For example, a donation of $5 is recorded in EEF 1892. *Report of the Sixth Ordinary General Meeting 1891–92*. London: Egypt Exploration Fund, p. 49.
42 For example, a donation of $5 is recorded for in EEF 1891. *Report of the Fifth Ordinary General Meeting 1890–91*, p. 47 and again in the EEF, *Report of the Sixth Ordinary General Meeting 1891–92*, p. 49.
43 Muñoz, R. 2017. Amelia Edwards in America: a quiet revolution in archaeological science. *Bulletin of the History of Archaeology* 27(1): DOI: http://doi.org/10.5334/bha-598.
44 Croly, J. C. 1886. *Sorosis: Its Origin and History*. New York: Press of J. J. Little and Co., p. 8.
45 Griffith Institute Archives, Diary of Mrs Kate Griffith (née Bradbury), made during the journey to America with Amelia Edwards in 1890 (2 volumes).
46 As documented by Reid, D. 2002. *Whose Pharaohs? Archaeology, Museums and Egyptian National Identity from Napoleon to World War I*. Berkeley and Los Angeles: University of California Press.
47 Colla, E. 2007. *Conflicted Antiquities: Egyptology, Egyptomania, Egyptian Modernity*. Durham: Duke University Press, p. 76.
48 Breasted held a doctorate in Egyptology from the University of Berlin, and went on to become Instructor in Egyptology at the University of Chicago. He simultaneously held the post of Assistant Director and curator of the University's Haskell Oriental Museum, which had opened in 1896. See Abt, J. 2012. *American Egyptologist: The Life of James Henry Breasted and the Creation of the Oriental Institute*. Chicago: University of Chicago Press.
49 Breasted, J. H. and Petrie, W. M. F. 1897. Professor Petrie's 'Egyptian Research Account'. *The Biblical World* 9(2): 138–42.
50 Breasted and Petrie, Egypt Research Account. Italics in the original.
51 Sheppard, K. (ed.) 2018. *My Dear Miss Ransom: Letters between Caroline Ransom Williams and James Henry Breasted, 1898–1935*. Oxford: Archaeopress.
52 Lesko, B. S. 2004. Caroline Louise Ransom Williams, 1872–1952. In *Breaking Ground: Women in Old World Archaeology*. Web resource available at: https://www.brown.edu/Research/Breaking_Ground/bios/Ransom%20Williams_Caroline%20Louise.pdf [accessed 24 September 2017].
53 Ransom, C. L. 1911. *Handbook to the Egyptian Rooms*. New York: Metropolitan Museum of Art.
54 Hayes, W. 1990. *The Scepter of Egypt: A Background for the Study of the Egyptian Antiquities of the Metropolitan Museum of Art From the Earliest Times to the End of the Middle Kingdom*. New York: Metropolitan Museum of Art, p. vii.

55 The address was originally made at the session of the American Association of Museums, 10 June 1912 and published as Ransom, C. L. 1912. The value of photographs and transparencies as adjuncts to museum exhibits. *The Metropolitan Museum of Art Bulletin* 7(7): 132–4.
56 Sheppard, *My Dear Miss Ransom*.
57 Lesko, B. S. 2004. Sara Yorke Stevenson. In *Breaking Ground: Women in Old World Archaeology*. Web resource available at: https://www.brown.edu/Research/Breaking_Ground/bios/Stevenson_Sara%20Yorke.pdf [accessed 24 September 2017].
58 Starr, F. 1892. Anthropological work in America. *Popular Science Monthly* 41(22): 297.
59 Letter from Sara Yorke Stevenson to Flinders Petrie, 15 February 1895, University of Pennsylvania, Penn Museum archives, call number 0057. With thanks to John Baines for copies of these letters.
60 Letter from Yorke to Petrie, 15 February 1895.
61 Quoted in O'Connor, D. 1987. The earliest pharaohs and the University Museum. *Expedition* 29(1): 30.
62 O'Connor, The earliest pharaohs, 30.
63 Conn, *Museums and American Intellectual Life*, p. 93.
64 Not everything sent to Stevenson was accommodated in the Penn Museum. As president of the American Exploration Fund, she also mediated the transfer of hundreds of smaller artefacts to places such as Bryn Mawr and the Peabody Museum at Harvard University.
65 Allen, L. A. 2001. *A Bluestocking in Charleston: The Life and Career of Laura Bragg*. Colombia: University of South Carolina Press, p. 35.
66 Anon. 1916. *Charleston Museum Bulletin* 12(6): 48.
67 Quoted in Allen, *A Bluestocking*, p. 95.
68 Letter from Laura Bragg to Flinders Petrie, 16 October 1920, Charleston Museum Archive.
69 Brinton-Coxe was also an Honorary Secretary of the EES in America.
70 Bragg, L. 1922. Exhibit and lecture notes. *Bulletin of the Charleston Museum* 17(3): 22.
71 Allen, *A Bluestocking*, p. 67.
72 Allen, *A Bluestocking*, p. 123.
73 McCarthy, K. 1991. Women's *Culture: American Philanthropy and Art, 1830–1930*. Chicago: University of Chicago Press.
74 For example, comments in MacKenzie, J. M. 2009. *Museums and Empire: Natural History, Human Cultures and Colonial Identities*. Manchester: Manchester University Press, p. 15.
75 McCarthy, *Women's Culture*.
76 Conn, *Museums and American Intellectual Life*, p. 218.
77 Teeter, E. 2010. Egypt in Chicago: A story of three collections. In Hawass, Z. and Wegner, J. (eds.) *Millions of Jubilees: Studies in Honor of David P. Silverman*. Cairo: Conseil Suprême des Antiquitiés de l'Egypt, 303–14.
78 Muñoz, Amelia Edwards in America.
79 Anon 1899. Brooklyn's opportunity. Value of an industrial arts museum. *New York Tribune*, 19 June 1899.
80 Anon. 1897. The Brooklyn Institute. *New York Tribune*, 3 June 1897: 6.
81 Letter from Brooklyn Museum to Petrie, 7 January 1905, PMA.WMP1.115.10.1.13.4.
82 Letter from Brooklyn Museum to Petrie, 7 January 1905, PMA.WMP1.115.10.1.13.4.
83 Tomkins, C. 1970. *Merchants and Masterpieces: The Story of the Metropolitan Museum of Art*. New York: E. P. Dutton, p. 114.
84 Doyon, W. 2018. The history of archaeology through the eyes of Egyptians. In Effros, B. and Lai, G. (eds.) *Unmasking Ideology in Imperial and Colonial Archaeology*. Los Angeles: Cotsen Institute of Archaeology Press, pp. 173–200; Doyon, W. 2013/2014. Egyptology in the shadow of class. *Egyptological Documents, Archives and Libraries* 4: 261–72.
85 Thomas, N., Scott, G. D. and Trigger, B. (eds.) 1996. *The American Discovery of Ancient Egypt*. Los Angeles: Los Angeles County Museum.
86 Doyon, History of archaeology through the eyes of Egyptians.
87 As explained by Olga Tufnell, this 'was a term applied by the hierarchy in the early part of this [the twentieth] century to those people selected by Flinders Petrie to act as his assistants in the field'. See Tufnell, O. 1982. Reminiscences of a 'Petrie Pup'. *Palestine Exploration Quarterly* 114(2): 81.
88 Reisner, G. 1908. *The Early Dynastic Cemeteries of Naga-ed-Der Part I*. Leipzig: J. C. Hinrichs, p. v.
89 Reisner, *The Early Dynastic Cemeteries*, p. vii.

90 Kroenke, K. R. 2010. *The Provincial Cemeteries of Naga-ed-Deir: A Comprehensive Study of Tomb Models Dating from the Late Old Kingdom to the Late Middle Kingdom*. Berkeley: UC Berkeley Electronic Theses and Dissertations, p. 17.
91 Edwards, E. and Morton, C. 2015. Between art and information: towards a collecting history of photographs. In Edwards, E. and Morton, C. (eds.) *Photographs, Museums Collections: Between Art and Information*. London: Bloomsbury Publishing, p. 7.
92 Letters from L. Earle Rowe to Mrs Gustave Radeke, July 1911. L. Earle Rowe Correspondence, Rhode Island School of Design Archive, collection number 213.1.2.
93 EES.DIST.34.24 and EES.DIST.34.26d.
94 Anon. 1912. Museum of masonic library is made depository of valuable pottery. *Quarterly Bulletin Iowa Masonic Library* 13(4): 3–4.
95 Anon 1880. Laying the corner-stone: masons preparing the obelisk's foundation, *New York Times*, 20 October 1880.
96 Holger K. 2011. Tarifi Zor Bay Whittemore: Erken Dönem, 1871–1916. The elusive Mr. Whittemore: The early years 1871–1916. In Holger, K., Ousterhout, R. and Pitarakis, B. (ed.) *The Kariye Camii Reconsidered*. Istanbul: İstanbul Araştırmaları Enstitüsü, pp. 478–9.
97 Letter from Buckman to Jonas, 18 August 1925, EES.USA.COR.
98 Wainwright, G. A. 1920. *Balabish*. London: Egypt Exploration Society, p. v.
99 See for instance Edwards, E. 2009. Photography and the material performance of the past. *History and Theory* 48(4): 130–50.
100 Whittemore, T. 1914. War surgeons work with anaesthetics: Thomas Whittemore of Boston wires of operations without ether. *Boston Journal* 81 (November 5): 7.
101 Letter from Aly Osman to Thomas Whittemore, 27 November 1914, EES.USA.COR.
102 Document titled 'Aly Osman's Letter', included in letter from Buckman to Paterson, January 1915, EES.USA.COR.
103 Doyon, The history of archaeology through the eyes of Egyptians.
104 J. O. 1915. Notes and News. *Journal of Egyptian Archaeology* 2(2): 115.
105 Edwards, E. 2014. Photographic uncertainties: between evidence and reassurance. *History and Anthropology* 25(2): 171–88.
106 Doyon, History of archaeology through the eyes of Egyptians; Doyon, Egyptology in the shadow of class, p. 266.
107 Anon. 1916. Notes and news. *Journal of Egyptian Archaeology* 3(1): 58.
108 Letter from Petrie to Lythgoe 8 May 1915, Metropolitan Museum of Art, Department of Egyptian Art archives.
109 Petrie, W. M. F. 1931. *Seventy Years in Archaeology*. London: Sampson Low, Marston & Co., p. 235.
110 Letter from Petrie to Lythgoe, 8 May 1915, Metropolitan Museum of Art, Department of Egyptian Art archives.
111 Letter from Paris to Lythgoe, 21 June 1914, Metropolitan Museum of Art, Department of Egyptian Art archives.
112 Larson, J. A. 2010 *Letters from James Henry Breasted to His Family: August 1919–July 1920*. Chicago: The Oriental Institute of the University of Chicago, p. 107.
113 Larson, *Letters from James Henry Breasted*, p. 107.
114 Bryant, M. and Eaverly, M. A. 2007. Egypto-Modernism: James Henry Breasted, H.D., and the New Past. *Modernism/Modernity* 14(3): 434–53.
115 Goode, J. F. 2007. *Negotiating for the Past: Archaeology, Nationalism, and Diplomacy in the Middle East, 1919–1941*. Austin: University of Texas Press, p. 93.
116 Anon. 1918. Notes and news. *Journal of Egyptian Archaeology* 5(3): 216–17.
117 Memorandum dated January 1919, British Academy Archives, BAA/SEC/2/4/1(a).
118 AJC Minute Book, 1918–1945, British Academy archives, BAA/SEC/2/4/1.

Chapter 3
International, Colonial and Transnational Connections (1880–1950)

The front matter of the Egypt Exploration Fund's (EEF) late 1880s annual reports lists the names of a dozen local honorary secretaries. Dispersed in locations as far apart as Canada, New South Wales, Switzerland and Mexico, these individuals were responsible for securing donations from their own area's networks for the Fund's cause. For the most part, such fundraising efforts resulted only in the circulation of pamphlets and fieldwork accounts, but for a significant number they also provided the opportunity to acquire Egyptian antiquities for their local institutions directly from the field. International scholarly networks gave British archaeologists the means to promote their discoveries and methodologies globally, as well as to forge and consolidate professional relationships. When, for instance, Flinders Petrie announced the discovery of a 'Great New Race' at the site of Naqada in 1895, the details of the surprising finds were widely reported. Petrie wrote eagerly to noted French prehistorian Emile Cartailhac, enticing him to visit the temporary displays of the finds in London;[1] he promptly dispatched examples of key objects to Adolf Erman at Berlin's Königliche Museen, where 'an exposition of the new race in the Egyptian courtyard of the museum'[2] was hastily constructed; and via Martyn Kennard he sent type specimens of finely flaked flints to the Director of the National Museum in Copenhagen for comparison with the famed Danish Neolithic flint knives. These material offerings became emissaries for new theories that could be tried and tested against the cultural-historical mosaic of world cultures being pieced together internationally. By the First World War, objects from British missions had been shipped to no fewer than nineteen countries in five continents, among them France, Germany, Italy, Denmark, South Africa, India, Canada, Australia, New Zealand and Japan. The EEF and related outfits were clearly not acting simply in British nationalistic interests, but were transnational organizations.[3]

Nationalist endeavours undeniably underpin and inform both archaeological and museum practices in complex ways, and their development alongside the construction of the modern nation-state is the subject of an extensive literature.[4] The study of such endeavours, however, has assumed a primacy at the expense of other contexts that organize how knowledge about the world is created. 'Methodological nationalism', in which the nation or state is the fundamental unit of historical analysis, has increasingly been perceived as problematic, and transnational analyses have been advocated in its place.[5] Transnational history foregrounds the 'interconnectedness of human history as a whole, and while it acknowledges the extraordinary importance of states, empires, and the like, it also pays attention to networks, processes, beliefs, and institutions that transcend these politically defined spaces'.[6] The global sponsorship model adopted by British archaeological expeditions is one area that can benefit from a transnational approach, given that this model created a vast network that allowed objects to move across state boundaries.

As the physical remains of Egypt's past circulated, original interpretations were variously perpetuated, appropriated, transformed or wholly ignored. When these antiquities came to rest – which sometimes they did only briefly – it became clear that they were far more elastic in their meanings than earnest archaeologists or curators claimed. In other words, Egyptian finds acted as what have been called 'boundary objects', 'scientific objects which inhabit several intersecting social worlds... and satisfy the informational requirement of each of them [with] different meanings in different worlds'.[7]

This chapter examines how and why such archaeological objects became grounded in specific places. It also considers how, far from being 'immutable mobiles',[8] in these various sites of encounter the value and status of antiquities was contingent upon relationships with local interests, regional politics and the specific nature of the collections they found themselves alongside. Together, these variables shaped attitudes as to the purpose and significance of the objects. Frequently, Egyptian things were placed into relationships with alternative bodies of knowledge, casting them in a different light and profoundly influencing their future trajectories.

These processes are sketched out here on three supra-regional levels, beginning with Europe, then the peripheries of empire, and finally stepping outside the Western sphere entirely to East Asia. Closest to home were rival European nations which were just as active in Egypt as the British, and had few obvious incentives to defer to British archaeology. Nevertheless, alternative object habits and museum exigencies sparked a chain of connections between Britain and institutions in France,

Germany, Italy, Scandinavia and Eastern Europe. Beyond Europe, the most likely destinations for objects of partage were Britain's colonial outposts. Museums in the 'settler colonies' of South Africa, New Zealand and Canada, for instance, have been portrayed as 'beacons' for British citizens in these regions, although they were often insecure about their status in relation to museums in the metropole, which it is often believed they attempted to emulate.[9] The acquisition of Egyptian antiquities by these countries could therefore be aspirational: a promising means of self-fashioning. Receptions and motivations, however, were far from uniform. The case studies brought together below, while certainly not exhaustive, can begin to challenge monolithic metanarratives of the colonial processes that underlie museum collections. Outside the British Empire, some countries envied its ability to extract cultural capital. The case of Japanese collecting offers a counterpoint to the Western development of museums and archaeology, with Egyptian antiquities drawn into nationalistic narratives, transnational appropriations of museum models and Japanese imperial ambitions.

***

Of the European nationalities engaged in archaeological work in Egypt in the late nineteenth century, it was the French who held the upper hand. In addition to controlling the Service des Antiquités de l'Égypte, the French were the only country that had a physical institutional presence in Egypt in the late nineteenth century: the Institut Français d'Archaéologie Orientale (IFAO), established in 1880. Germany followed suit some thirty years later, when an Imperial German Institute for Egyptian Archaeology was established in 1908 under Ludwig Borchardt (1863–1938), albeit not on the scale of the IFAO, following intermittent but significant German survey work in Egypt under Richard Lepsius (1810–84) and Heinrich Brugsh (1827–94). Italian collecting activities were led by Vitaliano Donati (1717–62) and the French Consular General Bernardino Drovetti (1776–1852), the latter's gains forming the kernel of the now vast Museo Egizio in Turin. The establishment of the Graeco-Roman Museum in Alexandria in 1892 by Italian director Giuseppe Botti and his successor Evaristo Breccia, further cemented Italian interests in Egypt. At the outset of the twentieth century the director of the Egyptian Museum in Turin, Ernesto Schiaparelli (1856–1928), received finance from King Victor Emmanuel III to found an Italian Archaeological Mission, and Turin's collections tripled between 1903 and 1920.

Despite this direct European activity, for political, scholarly and personal reasons, Egyptian antiquities were not infrequently dispatched by Britain to the continent. For example, although British-sourced artefacts were only very rarely distributed to France, the fledgling EEF deemed it prudent in 1885 to forward a selection of minor antiquities to the Louvre '…for it is as well to propitiate the French who can aid or hinder us a good deal'.[10] In 1890, a more substantial shipment of temple columns and relief sculptures was gifted from EEF work at Bubastis to the Louvre, and in 1895 pots and model tools from Deir el-Bahri were dispatched to Paris. Notably, both Bubastis and Deir el-Bahri were sites excavated under the direction of Swiss archaeologist Édouard Naville, suggesting social connections as much as political ones.[11] Elsewhere, a variety of concerns directed the path of antiquities.

Philological Habits: Egypt in Germany

In contrast to the limited contacts cultivated with French museums, relatively large numbers of German institutions received finds in the late nineteenth and early twentieth centuries, chiefly those attached to universities. They included Berlin's Neues Museum (through the intermediary of the Universität Berlin professorship), Universität Bonn, Universität Leipzig and Heidelberg's Antikenmuseum der Universität.[12] Their eagerness to participate in the EEF's network of sponsors stemmed from the very different object habits that had been historically fostered in Germany.

Politically, Germany was not an imperialist power in Egypt. Otto von Bismarck refrained from political engagement in Egypt, promising that if Britain gave Germany concessions regarding its colonial ambitions, it would not side with the French.[13] There was, however, state funding for Egyptology, and academia was professionalized far earlier than had been the case in Britain. Consequently, the British model of private funding, gentlemanly scholarship and personal collecting for museums was relatively less important. This was reflected in Germany's disciplinary attentions. Nineteenth-century German Classical pedagogy emphasized ancient texts, a perspective that infused *Gymnasiums* and universities. The authority of philology was so deeply ingrained within the consciousness of Germany's cultured middle class (*Bildungsbürgertum*) that, in contrast to Britain, it has been claimed that the German public was largely ignorant of Oriental antiquities: the 'artifacts needed to dislocate philhellenist habits were simply not there'.[14] As German

Egyptology was nurtured in its universities and academies, philology became its strongest suit, most notably defined by the Berlin School under Johann Peter Adolf Erman (1854–1937) and his monumental *Wörterbuch der ägyptischen Sprache* project. Germany's Egyptological scholarship was internationally lauded, but its scholars were left somewhat 'underprepared for the new importance material culture took on at the end of the century',[15] despite Egypt's high cultural profile in the country.[16] By 1900 this deficiency was commonly acknowledged, and nationalistic rivalries were amplified as a strategy to gain the attention of 'maßgeblichen Kreise'– the Kaiser and leading entrepreneurs.[17] In 1898 the newly formed Deutsche Orient-Gesellschaft (DOG), for example, expressed concern in the *National-Zeitung* that the British and French were exhuming vast quantities of treasures throughout Egypt and the Orient, to the detriment of German museum collections and the public's prevailing view of them.[18]

These trends stood in contrast to the development of museums outside the universities. In German ethnographic institutions, for instance, intellectuals had already attempted to move away from simply employing Classical artefacts to support ancient textual evidence, towards producing ideas from objects themselves.[19] And, unlike many British object arrangements, in these institutions displays were pioneered to avoid explicit evolutionary narratives and typological arrangements. As a result, nineteenth-century German Egyptology existed within a very different configuration of disciplinary bodies of knowledge than was the case in Britain, where Egyptology was more strongly allied to the development of anthropology, both physically in many collections and intellectually in university courses.[20] It may also have inflected differential access to Egyptology as a subject, since it was more strongly tied to the academy and specific philological training. While Egyptology was beginning to open up to women in the late nineteenth century, it was not as new or as liminal a subject as it was in Britain or the USA at this time. This may be one reason why the share of women in the DOG was substantially lower than British or American EEF membership.[21]

This nationalistic characterization of British Egyptology as fixated by artefacts and German Egyptology as being predicated upon texts may seem reductive. Up until the first decade of the twentieth century, however, this was largely how scholars central to the discipline portrayed themselves. Petrie, in his 1892 inaugural lecture, remarked that England's focus would be on 'material civilization' as opposed to Germany's, where 'the language has its greatest exponents',[22] and Egyptologist Kurt Sethe (1869–1934) noted 'Was Erman für die ägyptische Philogie geleistet hat, hat in gewissem Sinne entsprechend für die ägyptische Archäologie Flinders Petrie geleistet'.[23] As observed by Thomas Gertzen, German Egyptologists were initially more than willing to defer to British pre-eminence in archaeology, albeit with a certain degree of condescension; they considered their British colleagues (with the exception of the linguistically gifted Griffith) to be 'amateurs' or 'dilettantes', since they lacked the credentials that a robust Classical university education provided.[24] German openness to transnational exchanges was further influenced by cosmopolitan trends in cities like Hamburg, Berlin, Leipzig and Munich, which were competing with each other to become *Weltstädte*, a disposition reflected in the high number of foreign students on their university courses. This included Egyptology, where many of the subject's foremost scholars of the late nineteenth and early twentieth centuries, such as Alan Gardiner, George Reisner, Caroline Ransom and James Henry Breasted, trained.[25]

Germans, then, were initially largely reliant upon, and open to, personal and institutional networks for archaeological specimens. The royal museums in Berlin were among the first continental recipients of EEF efforts, with material from the Delta sites of Naukratis and Nebesheh dispatched in 1885. Erman was effusive in his praise for the products of British investigations, which he considered the 'first made in Egypt in a truly scientific way', and which paid 'attention to those small but important relics of ancient civilisation'.[26] For Erman, Petrie's artefacts were a bridge between mute objects and textual history. Writing from Berlin in September 1890, for instance, Erman appealed to Petrie 'to cede some samples of your duplicates to our collection… what we are missing are datable examples because almost all of our jars, tools etc. lack the documentation of provenance'.[27]

Petrie's other contacts facilitated the circulation of things to German colleagues, including Georg Steindorff (1861–1951) in Leipzig, Alfred Wiedemann (1856–1936) in Bonn and Wilhelm Spiegelberg (1870–1930) in Strasbourg. The latter was considered by Petrie to be 'the pleasantest German I know next to Weidemann',[28] perhaps because neither Spiegelberg nor Wiedemann were members of the Berlin philological school. Spiegelberg contributed directly to Petrie's scholarship by providing philological expertise during the 1894–5 season in Thebes. Petrie subsequently arranged for seven crates of finds from the Naqada excavations – mostly pottery vessels, flints and greywacke palettes of the 'New Race' – to be shipped to the University of Strasbourg. In return, Petrie was awarded an honorary doctorate in July 1897. Such antiquities were clearly social transactions as much as scientific specimens; they cemented intellectual and personal networks, legitimized intellectual authority and reinforced obligations to nationalistic disciplinary progress.

Early twentieth-century *Kulturpolitik* was geared more towards direct fieldwork in Egypt, leading British and German teams to eventually come into conflict only a few years before war drove a deeper wedge between the nations, largely bringing to an end material exchanges.[29] Notably, however, the Germans adopted a different strategy to archaeological diplomacy and administration from missions that were initiated by museums in other countries. The General Secretary of the Deutsches Archäologisches Institut (DAI), Alexander Conze (1831–1914), implored the Reich Chancellor for excavations to be administered by the DAI rather than museums to avoid the perception that fieldwork was simply unscientific treasure hunting.[30] Nonetheless, the acquisition of texts remained a primary pursuit of German scholarship. It was not until the Weimar Republic that a substantial shift in its research agenda, from positivist philology towards 'völkische Wissenschaft', was witnessed, underpinned by anthropological evidence and racial concepts, directly inspired by British colleagues such as Petrie.[31] Yet even this renewed engagement with British approaches did little to return material exchanges to their pre-war levels.[32]

At Home in the Landscape: Egypt in Italy

Unlike Germany, Italy had long coveted Egyptian objects. For centuries Egyptian antiquities had formed part of the very fabric of the Italian cultural and intellectual milieu, not to mention being physically embedded within its landscapes. Prominent scholars of the seventeenth century, like Jesuit Priest Father Athanasius Kircher (1601–1680), marvelled at the mysterious hieroglyphs carved onto the obelisks and sphinxes that had been brought back by Imperial Rome and set up in the empire's capital.[33] Egyptian objects removed anciently were also frequently rediscovered through digging activities within Italy itself. Today, numerous prominent Italian museums hold substantial Egyptian collections, such as the Museo Civico Archeologico di Bologna, Museo Egizio in Turin, Museo Gregoriano Egiziano in the Vatican, and Museo Archeologico Nazionale di Napoli. These Italian collections became key reference points for Flinders Petrie's object-centric construction of the past, and he spent considerable time studying and drawing Egyptian collections in Turin, Venice, Rome, Florence and Bologna.[34]

Italian Egyptologists were also a vital enabling link for British fieldwork, most notably Rodolfo Vittorio Lanzone (1834–1907), a member of staff in the Turin Museum between 1872 and 1895. In the winter of 1883, Petrie stopped over in Turin on his way to Egypt, where he was due to commence his first major excavations. While in Turin he engaged in lengthy discussions with Lanzone, and sought 'his opinion of several details of management with workmen in the Delta and he [Lanzone] freely talked over his way of working'.[35] Lanzone advised Petrie on differential pay for Egyptian workmen on site according to ability, and in such a way as to encourage finders to bring material directly to him, rather than to a local dealer. It was a strategy that Petrie adopted, systematized and advocated for the rest of his career.[36] Additionally, Lanzone implored Petrie to work on only one site at a time, recommended methods for managing relationships with the Egyptian Museum, and shared schemes for avoiding conflicts of interest with other excavators. For the young and relatively inexperienced Petrie, it was all sage advice. While Petrie is often viewed as the progenitor of scientific methods in excavating Egypt, these were clearly predicated on transnational discourses and built upon collective experience.

Given Italian expertise in navigating both Egypt's material culture and its labour relations, their institutions had little need to acquire objects from the British. Even the strong connections that existed between British and Italian archaeologists, and which resulted in the exchange of ideas and practices, were not accompanied by material transfers to the main Italian centres of Egyptology.[37] Instead, it was a group of smaller, distinctive institutions that benefited from Britain's partage gains. The Pontificio Istituto Biblico, a Holy See in Rome, administered by Jesuits and founded in 1909 to promote Catholic doctrine, was one. Its first rector, Leopold Fonck (1865–1930), admired Petrie's fieldwork in the Sinai,[38] and the BSAE offerings that came to the new institution between 1912 and 1913 reflected the See's outlook: a selection of votive steles, statuettes of deities and two Coptic crosses.[39] In contrast, the appeal of craftsmanship appears to have been the motivation for the acquisition of objects by Faenza's Museo Internazionale delle Ceramiche (International Museum of Ceramics) from the 1920–2 BSAE excavations at Lahun. The museum was established by Gaetano Ballardini in 1908 as a centre for the comparative study of ancient and modern ceramics; the pottery vessels and 'blue containers' (faience) listed on the BSAE distribution lists were in keeping with this mission.[40] In the Italian Riviera town of Bordighera, an altogether different private museum was built in 1888 by English expatriate Clarence Bicknell (1842–1918). It was one of several buildings (including an Anglican church, a theatre and a tennis club) in a resort where the British upper classes outnumbered the local population. In 1906–07 another British-appropriated export arrived: kohl pots, beads, amulets, mud models and mirrors from the BSAE fieldwork at Gizeh and Rifa.[41]

Chronologies and 'Grand monuments': Egypt in Scandinavia

Norway, Denmark and Sweden were logical allies in Flinders Petrie's intellectual quest to promote the value of material histories. In part this was due to a certain symmetry of archaeological enquiry that existed between Egypt and Scandinavia, which was predicated upon typologies of both regions' rich heritage of prehistoric grave goods and hoards. From the beginning of the nineteenth century, Danish archaeology had achieved European prominence through Christian Jürgensen Thomsen's (1788–1865) influential 'Three Age System' of Stone, Bronze and Iron Ages, assembled in the Royal Museum of Nordic Antiquities[42] and later popularized by Jens Worsaae (1821–85) in the 1840s. British and Scandinavian scholars came to share an intellectual focus on objects and sequences that ultimately facilitated dialogue and the transfer of sundry pottery vessels, beads and flint tools from Flinders Petrie to the National Museum in Copenhagen in the 1890s. Therefore, when Petrie's close friend Flaxman Spurrell (1842–1915) sought to understand the sophisticated flint knives discovered at Naqada, it was Danish Neolithic forms that quickly came to mind.[43] There was also a shared ambition to construct chronologies. Thus when Egyptologist Jens Daniel Carolus Lieblein (1827–1911) first acquired archaeological pieces for the ethnographic collection at the University of Christiania (Oslo) in Norway, it was because he was adamant that Petrie's finds from the 'New Race' were of 'extreme importance' for prehistorians, allowing them 'to determine the approximate chronology' of the period before the First Dynasty.[44]

Although prehistoric archaeology of this sort initially drew objects towards the Nordic territories, it was a wealthy man's passion for Classical art and sculpture, more traditionally valued by the elite, that capitalized to a greater extent upon Britain's openness to transnational transfers. Carl Jacobsen (1842–1914), the son of the founder of Carlsberg breweries, was one of early twentieth-century Denmark's most prominent celebrities, more renowned even than its king.[45] In the 1890s Jacobsen donated his art collection to the nation, with the proviso that the government fund the establishment of a new institution, the Ny Carlsberg Glyptotek, opened in 1897. The name itself signalled a different conception of the museum from Petrie's ideals, as this was a repository for sculpture, like its model, the Glyptotek in Munich; here individual responses to art would be encouraged, rather than be imposed through scientific sequencing. The Danes' understanding of art, Jacobsen preached, would be enhanced by his gift to the nation, inspiring Danish artists to strive for higher standards. His perspective was greatly influenced by a close friend, the Danish art historian Julius Lange (1838–96), who had introduced the notion of 'initial art'.[46] Lange believed that it was only with the development of Greek naturalism in art from around 450 BC that the world's underlying original artistic structures were transformed. Initial art encompassed ancient Egyptian visual culture, admired by Lange as its pinnacle, yet comparable in its core structure to the work of indigenous American groups or Pacific artists. At the same time, because Egypt had been an important influence on Greek repertoires, it was incorporated by Jacobsen into his vision for the Glyptotek to present the finest examples from a tradition stretching back thousands of years.

For the purchase of Egyptian antiquities Jacobsen depended largely upon Valdemar Schmidt (1863–1944), Denmark's first lecturer in Egyptology and Assyriology.[47] As Jacobsen had no interest in the 'fragments and pots' that constituted the majority of finds displayed at the temporary exhibitions staged by Petrie in London and frequented by Schmidt, he insisted that only 'the grand monuments' should be bought.[48] These demands put him in direct competition with American institutions who were also vying for the biggest and most striking pieces of the BSAE's haul. The deep pockets of the Ny Carlsberg foundation ensured the delivery to Denmark of 4.5-ton statues, relief blocks from tomb chapels, and delicate Roman era mummies with painted panel portraits (Fig. 3.1). Two overlapping object habits towards Egypt were thus embodied within the urban fabric of Copenhagen: one more archaeological in the National Museum and, on the opposite side of the street, the art historical, as presented in the Glyptotek.

A Solitary Traveller: Egypt in Eastern Europe

Eastern European countries shared the interest in Egyptian artefacts, but had fewer economic and political means to participate in imperial archaeology. Opportunistic acquisitions of Egyptian material from

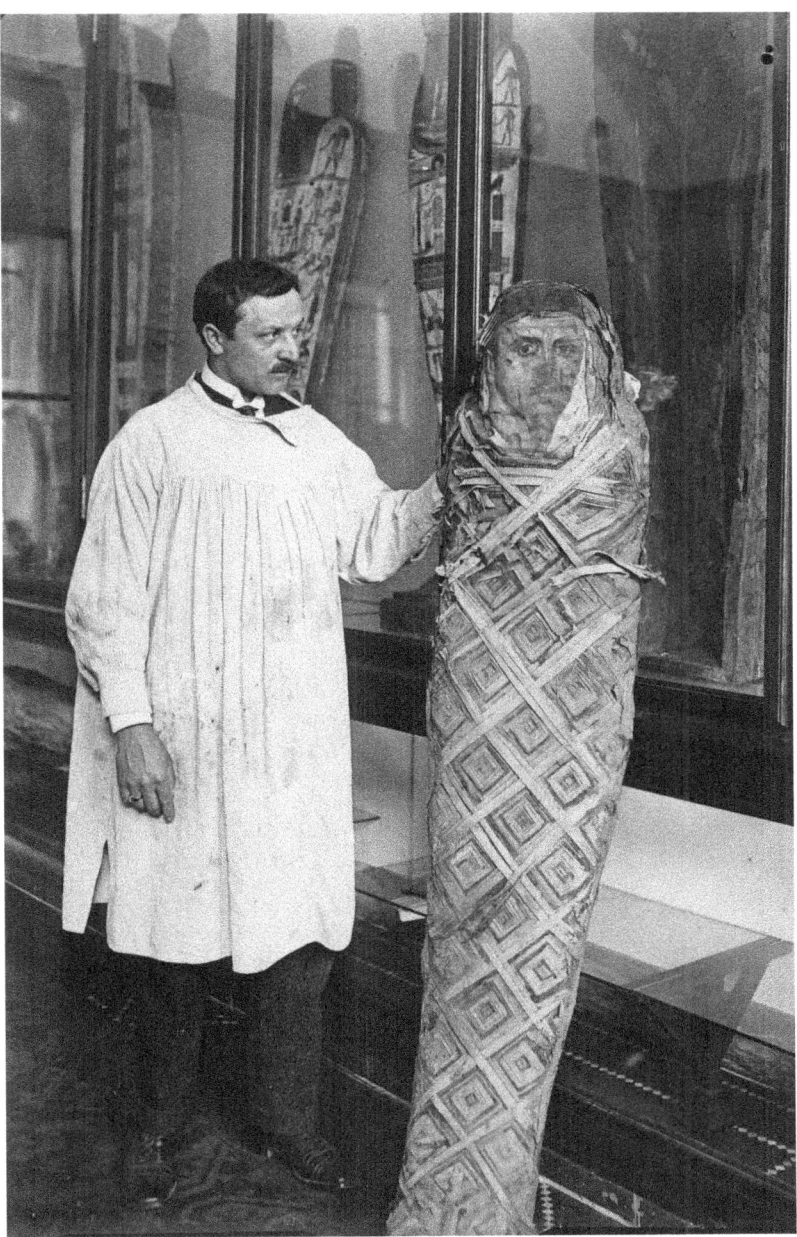

Fig. 3.1 Glyptotek Museum conservator 'Elo' with mummy (museum number AE1425), excavated by the British School of Archaeology in Egypt at Hawara in 1911. Archive photo held by Royal Library and Courtesy of Tine Bagh, Glyptotek Museum.

Britain offered a chance to vicariously engage with international fieldwork. The Opava Museum, in the north of the modern-day Czech Republic, was the fortuitous recipient of one such small collection through the initiative of a Silesian German poet, Marie Stonawská-Scholzová, better known as Maria Stona (1861–1944). In Central Europe Opava was considered something of a 'Silesian Weimar', and Stona used to host salons in her Trebovice Castle for artistes, politicians and other writers. She also made many foreign journeys, including a solo excursion to Egypt in February 1913. As she made her way up the Nile she happened upon one of Flinders Petrie's excavation team – an 'older Englishman' – who invited her to the site of Tarkhan, around 50 km south of Cairo, where the BSAE was conducting fieldwork in an enormous 5000-year-old cemetery.[49] There she met Flinders Petrie in person, took lunch with Hilda Petrie and purchased a small set of finds, including an anthropoid mummy case, pottery vessels, stone containers, bead necklaces and a scarab. These Stona forwarded to one of the regular attendees of her salon, her friend Edmund Wilhelm Braun, director of the Museum of Applied Arts in Opava.[50]

***

Beyond Europe, the distribution of finds to colonial museums was regularly celebrated in the Fund's annual reports. There was, however, limited uniformity in how these institutions came to obtain antiquities, and what their impulses were for seeking such material in the first place. Such heterogeneity aligns with the early twenty-first-century intellectual trend that has moved away from the idea that there existed an overarching, co-ordinated imperial project. In studies of museum histories, this trend has translated into more nuanced accounts of individual institutions in their specific historical contexts.[51] These recognize that although establishments often did act as tools of empire, they were not supported or directed by British Government offices, at least not in the late nineteenth to early twentieth century. Instead, a mixture of local personalities and conditions were responsible for the growth of museums in Britain's colonies. Most studies of colonial museums have taken as their focus the interface between settler institutions, the metropole and local cultures. My focus below, however, is on the cultural juxtapositions around displaced Egyptian finds that were extracted from one imperial context, managed through the empire's centre and transplanted into colonial institutions where finds could be marginalized or fetishized.

'Eienaardighede wat van Egipte af kom':
Egypt in South Africa

During the period roughly between 1890 and 1930 the continental fantasy that a route from the 'Cape to Cairo' could be established was variously promulgated, particularly by Cecil Rhodes. This was both a political and an ideological vision that aligned colonial South African interests with Mediterranean histories, cultures and climate to form a 'geographical metaphor for a constellation of strategic intentions'.[52] The desire to acquire Egyptian antiquities in the Cape was implicated within these worldviews.

By 1910 around ten public museums existed in South Africa, clustered primarily in towns of the Eastern Cape. For the most part, these buildings were filled with natural history specimens, as non-indigenous settlers grappled to make sense of the countryside around them. They were not historical museums instilled with a vision to comprehend or to represent the human story of this landscape, as its original inhabitants were dismissed as existing outside time and history.[53] Instead, the founders of these colonial museums looked towards European models for the material foundations upon which to build a nation. Ancient Egyptian antiquities were one such import from European centres. 'In a young country like ours', the director of Grahamstown's Albany Museum noted on the acquisition of an Egyptian mummy from John Garstang in 1908, 'it is perhaps even more necessary than in a European country to put such links with the past before the public.'[54] A similar sentiment was expressed by Kate Fannin of St Anne's College in Natal's Pietermaritzburg, who responded enthusiastically to the same newspaper advert offering pottery vessels from Beni Hasan that had attracted the attention of Albany Museum: 'in a new country such as ours we have so little opportunity for studying antiquities of this kind'.[55] The purpose and status of South African museums as bastions of white British colonial identity was long lived. Decades later, the 1932 *Report on the Museums and Art Galleries of British Africa* concluded from a demographic profile of South Africa that 'museums are only likely to thrive where there is a large white or other literate population'.[56] Indigenous communities were explicitly excluded.

The principal collection of Egyptian archaeology in the Republic of South Africa is today displayed incongruously on the first floor of Cape Town's Iziko Slave Lodge, an institution whose current purpose is to raise awareness of human rights. Egyptian artefacts, along with a much reduced collection of Classical material from Italy and Greece, remain there in limbo, presented in exhibits with as yet no sense of place within the re-Africanization of the museum. Their inertia is partly a legacy of the collections' history, procured by white British settlers as a rejoinder to their perceived lack of a national past, a shallow colonial worldview that continues to weigh heavily upon it. The collection's origins are linked to the South African Museum, founded in 1825 with a modest, idiosyncratic assortment of natural history specimens and relics from Greece and Egypt, all displayed rather haphazardly in a single room.[57] When a new building opened in 1896 far better provision was made for staff and objects. This included funding for new acquisitions from the EEF in 1898, bringing a more focused collection of Egyptian antiquities to South Africa for the first time.[58] Sponsorship of British work resulted in a more substantial batch of finds from Petrie's excavations at Tarkhan being sent back to Africa in 1912 and 1913, comprising grave assemblages of pottery, stone palettes and jewellery dating to the foundation of the ancient Egyptian state.[59] Further BSAE material was directed to the Cape in the 1920s through the intermediary of 'Petrie pups' Guy and Winifred Brunton, who had family connections to South Africa. The couple eventually retired to the grand and opulently decorated mansion built by Winifred's father at Prynnsberg in the Free State. They brought with them numerous finds from their excavations, which were displayed in gilt rooms adorned with whimsical, Egyptian-inspired murals populated by decidedly European-looking characters, painted by Winifred.[60]

In 1964, in the mid-apartheid era, black and white cultural history were divided further between separate buildings in Cape Town. Natural history – comprising ethnographic black cultural history – remained in the original 1896 museum building, while all the Classical and Egyptian collections were transferred to the old Slave Lodge, then renamed the South African Cultural History Museum. Here visitors could follow the collections 'chronologically' from the ancient world of the Egyptians and Greeks, through to Europe (predominantly Northern Europe) before arriving at colonial Cape Town.[61] Those visitors were white and the museum was rendered a site of exclusivity, with Egyptian collections implicitly trussed to expressions of apartheid and the ideological prejudices that accompanied it.

Numerous other South African settlers also sought Egyptian antiquities. The initiative of Cyprian Rudolf, a history teacher at the Anglican St John's School in Johannesburg, led to the token acquisition in 1923 of 'odds and ends, broken shabti figures, a canopic jar, model boats and mummified animals'[62] from BSAE excavations at Qau. The KwaZulu-Natal Museum in Pietermaritzburg (established in 1904), like Albany Museum, purchased finds directly from John Garstang in 1909, and a reference to four boxes of pottery for 'Natal' in the EEF distribution records for 1899 also indicates South African interest, although the final destination, if indeed material was dispatched, is unknown.[63] Perhaps not coincidentally, the distribution for the year 1899 would have been made in October, after the annual exhibition. The timing coincides with the outbreak of the Second Boer War. A British garrison had existed at Natal since the end of the First Boer War in 1881, but was due to be withdrawn in 1898. The War Intelligence Division, however, concluded in 1899 that it was worth holding on to for reasons of prestige, and in the summer of 1899 the British reinforced the colony with an additional 11,500 men as tensions with Boers grew.[64] Sir Francis Grenfell (1841–1925), an active committee member of the EEF, was one of the military leaders considered to lead the recruits. Perhaps somewhere within these networks, Egyptian antiquities found a route to the tip of the African continent.

None of these collections were well known. In 1946 Huguenot University College in Wellington, a women's educational training centre, received a crate of Egyptian artefacts. These were mainly small glass and faience amulets from the EES's 1930s work at Amarna, and had been obtained through Emily Armistead, the headmistress of a school in Wolverhampton, England, who was a long time friend of the College staff, and a supporter of British excavations in Egypt and the Near East. A report written for the school magazine romanticized the history of the objects, and concluded that 'wealth of an unexpected kind has indeed come to Huguenot and through Huguenot to South Africa for it is believed that this collection is unique in this country.'[65] Similar collections, however, had been sent to Cape Town, Durban and Johannesburg in the 1920s and 1930s, including comparable small finds from Amarna. Nevertheless, for a brief period the artefacts in the school inspired awe. The school magazine noted the following year in its annual bilingual (Afrikaans and English) alphabet of notable events that E was for *'Eienaardighede wat van Egipte af kom:* Oor die oudhede staan die studente verstom' (E is for the Peculiarities coming from Egypt: the students are stunned by the antiquities). The school closed in 1950, and the artefacts eventually found their way to the local Wellington Museum. Once again this Egyptian collection sits awkwardly in an institution with very little else in the way of world archaeology.

Set in Stone: Egypt in Canada

The only Canadian institution to receive finds from British archaeologists in the nineteenth century was Montreal's McGill University.[66] Its museum, the Redpath, was named after the wealthy industrialist who provided funding for its foundation in 1882, but its origins were twenty years in the making, inspired by the zeal of the University's principal and geologist, John William Dawson (1820–99). Built in an imposing Neoclassical style, the Redpath is one of Canada's oldest museums and, in its heyday, one of the most important.[67] It was nevertheless, like most colonial museums, administered not with government finances, but with the far more limited resources of the University. As in the case of South African museums, the Redpath's focus was on local inventory pursuits in natural history and geology, while the University's chief specialism was medicine. The acquisition of Egyptian material from the EEF in 1887 may therefore seem odd at first. Yet in Canada these 'minor antiquities' had a pivotal role to play within Victorian imperial science dialogues emanating from Britain. In this instance, however, their display was not intended to emulate those narratives. On the contrary, Dawson was an outspoken critic of Darwin's theories, and Canadian trends in natural science inflected an alternative set of object habits towards broader evolutionary tenets that had otherwise structured culture-evolutionary museum displays at the empire's heart.

In 1884 Dawson hosted the British Association for the Advancement of Science's (BAAS) annual meeting in Montreal on the McGill University campus and in the galleries of the Redpath Museum. The BAAS had been founded in 1831 to promote dialogue between scientists in different parts of the British Empire and to serve as an enlightening civic movement. Montreal was its first overseas meeting. The decision to move beyond Britain was a controversial one, but given that British towns were by then better served with museums and universities, there were fewer opportunities for this 'parliament of science' to fulfil its civic mission there.[68] Transferring BAAS activities abroad offered a fresh direction. The geographical setting of such gatherings in places like the Redpath, attended by the leading figures of emergent disciplines, again highlights the well-established role of museums as key locations in the late Victorian production of knowledge. At the meeting, for example, was the University of Oxford's recently appointed anthropologist, Edward B. Tylor (1832–1917), one of the foremost proponents of cultural evolution, who addressed a newly constituted section of the University: section H, anthropology, 'now promoted from the lower rank of a department of biology'.[69] This section incorporated an eclectic range of subjects, assembled under the loose heading the 'study of mankind', and it was here that Egyptian archaeology was frequently debated. It was within this configuration of scholarly discourse that Egyptian antiquities found themselves jockeying for a place in the Redpath Museum.

Alongside other cultural materials, the Redpath's small Egyptian collection was subordinate in number and emphasis to the natural history specimens (Fig. 3.2). A guide produced for the BAAS meeting describes the small anthropology room and the nucleus around which the EEF materials was later assembled: 'collections from Pre-historic caves in the Lebanon and stone implements from Egypt (J.W.D.)' and 'collections to illustrate the various rocks and useful ornamental stones employed by the ancient Egyptians and their modes of working these materials (J.W.D)'.[70] Dawson's initials indicate that he was the benefactor and highlights his strong personal interest in Egyptian material. An internal museum report a decade later outlines the ongoing development of the Egyptian collection, which by now integrated artefacts from the EEF's work in the Delta (mostly Naukratis) and a granite monumental doorway fragment of Ramesses II found at Bubastis.[71]

Some insight into how these displays were structured under Dawson's curatorship can be gleaned from looking at his publications.

Fig. 3.2 Photograph of the interior of McGill University's Redpath Museum, circa 1893. Through the open door of the museum hall is the room devoted to archaeological and ethnological material. Courtesy of Notman Photographic Archives, McCord Museum of Canadian History, Montreal (view 2604).

Most telling is his 1888 work, *Modern Science in Bible Lands*, which signalled Dawson's profound commitment to the Bible, emphasized his belief in the unchanging nature of humanity and served as a platform for him to contest humankind's antiquity. Different levels of complexity, he concluded, had existed throughout time, and as Egypt's civilization was among the oldest, its artefacts could serve as a benchmark against which prehistoric finds from elsewhere could be assessed. Throughout *Modern Science in Bible Lands* Dawson cited objects he had personally acquired from Flinders Petrie's work at Naukratis and in the Fayum. Alongside his religious convictions he promoted his vision for the pedagogical potential of museums to cultivate awareness of natural resource development and the 'higher interests of humanity'.[72] It was this combination that set Dawson's agenda in conflict with the thrust of British anthropology, as he denounced human biological and cultural evolution using the same categories of artefacts that were arrayed in British museums by those such as Pitt-Rivers. These differences arose again in Dawson's 1893 article 'Notes on useful and ornamental stones in Egypt'[73] – a title reflected in the Redpath displays cited in the 1885 BAAS catalogues – in which he juxtaposed detailed geological observations of Egyptian stones with a commentary upon Egyptian technical skill and development. He noted with regard to flint, for example, that its continuous use 'should furnish caution against sweeping generalisations as to ages of stone and metal and of progress in the manufacture of flint tools and weapons.'[74]

It is clear that alongside these global debates, Dawson also used Egyptian displays in locally relevant ways, as the transit of artefacts permitted new spatial proximities between materials. For example, he remarked that he had 'placed in the Redpath Museum a specimen of anorthosite from a Canadian locality with the Egyptian specimen to show the resemblance'.[75] Therefore, although the Redpath's collections ostensibly reflected anthropological topics of interest in Britain, they were not derivative. Rather, the intention was to deploy them as a means to resist the pulse of cultural evolutionary rhetoric, and to do so with a stern practical orientation focused on unassailable geological detail relevant to the agenda of Canadian natural history and the mapping of its resources.

Geographer David Livingstone has suggested that Nova Scotia-born Dawson's disdain for Darwin's work had its roots in his Scottish education at Edinburgh University, which had been steeped in the Baconian virtues of patient accumulation of detail and which eschewed sweeping generalizations.[76] Through this lens, Darwin's thesis was considered by Dawson to be a speculative and unwarranted extrapolation from the data. Many of Canada's naturalists were similarly inclined towards this inductive philosophy as they navigated Canada's unfamiliar landscape. These principles and experiences produced an intellectual environment in which Canadian reactions to Darwinism, and by extension cultural evolution, have been characterized as muted at best.[77] Thus while ancient artefacts were valued within the cataloguing tradition inspired by inductive methods, early Canadian museum presentations avoided the structuring principles of archaeological displays in Britain and Scandinavia. The boundary nature of Egyptian objects as symbolic of ancient civilization nevertheless allowed them to remain valuable museum acquisitions of curatorial interest.

In the longer term, Dawson's keen creationist convictions, going against the grain of anthropological development elsewhere, deflected further scholarly attention from the Redpath's collections. A university programme in archaeology was not established at McGill until 1966, and even then never included Egyptology as a discrete subject area, despite the presence of around 2000 Egyptian antiquities in the collection. In the early twentieth century it was other institutions in Canada that benefited from EES and BSAE fieldwork: Vancouver Museum, the New Brunswick Museum, the National Gallery of Canada and the Royal Ontario Museum (ROM).[78] Of these, it is the ROM that now maintains the most significant Egyptian collection, today numbering some 30,000 artefacts. Many of these objects have links to British fieldwork, mostly through the intervention of Charles Trick Currelly (1876–1957), a man described as a buccaneer, maverick and self-styled adventurer whose brazen approach to collecting world cultures was laid bare in his 1956 autobiography, *I Brought the Ages Home*.[79]

By the early twentieth century Toronto had overtaken Montreal as the primary economic centre of Canada, but its museum development lagged behind. The ROM was built between 1910 and 1912 as part of the University of Toronto, and opened to the public in 1914 as a more popular and outward-facing institution than perhaps many of the university's scholars were comfortable with.[80] Currelly was a major driver in its establishment, having been collecting omnivorously for the past decade, beginning with Egyptian material. He excavated alongside Petrie at his EEF mission at Abydos in 1902, and at Ehnasya the following season, and used his own wealth to sponsor many other BSAE activities. As a result, at least a thousand objects in the ROM's collections can be linked back to work directed by Petrie, and are displayed according to his typological principles.[81] Currelly also spent time as part of the Deir el-Bahri missions headed by Naville between 1905 and 1907. In 1909, Currelly mounted a popular exhibition of Egyptian and other antiquities in Toronto, and it was this that marked the departure point for a determined effort to establish a new museum. For the next twenty years Currelly aggressively acquired collections, enlisting financial support from wealthy philanthropists such as Robert Mond, and frequently haranguing the secretaries of the EES for a share of their best finds. In these efforts he was driven as much by personal ego as by the particular situation within North America of Canada, which saw itself as in direct competition with American museums and collectors. Museum development in Toronto was a clear means of establishing Canadian national identity in opposition to American ambitions, and was enabled by voracious imperial hoarding rather than locally focused collecting.

'A magnificent strategical centre': Egypt in Australia

At the end of the nineteenth century, each of Australia's six colonies administered its own museum system independently of the others. Although founded and endowed by the government, these institutions were largely sustained by wealthy individuals, and when that funding was insufficient, museums were at the mercy of the public purse. Another key variable in the development of Australian museums was their links with museums overseas, particularly British institutions, and these links were ultimately far stronger than any collaboration with each other. For the most part, these institutions expressed little interest in Aboriginal material culture.[82]

The activities of museum agent and congregational minister William Roby Fletcher (1833–94), illustrate some of these trends. For him, Egypt was 'a gateway between the north and the south; between India and Australia on this side of the globe, and the dear old motherland on the other… a magnificent strategical centre, [a] keystone in the arch of political destiny.'[83] This zealous imperial rhetoric accompanied Fletcher's popular series of lectures on *The Wonders of Ancient and Modern Egypt* (1891), in which he proudly recounted his commission on behalf of the South Australian Museum to acquire antiquities through distinguished connections, among them General Sir Francis Grenfell and Evelyn Baring. Acquisitions for Melbourne's National Gallery were similarly narrated on their arrival in 1898. The influential daily newspaper, *The Age*, carried the story under the headline 'an antique gift from England',[84] placing the emphasis for acquisitions with the metropole and not the originating country – Egypt. The agent in this case was Norman de Garis Davies (1865–1941), at the time a Unitarian Minister in Melbourne as well as a member of the EEF Archaeological Survey. Davies expressed the hope that 'the gift of these antiquities to the museum will do something to bind the mother and daughter nations in yet another, not the least noble of her enterprises – that of scientific research'.[85] Despite these devotions to the imperial cause, in both cases it is telling that the efforts were ultimately personally, rather than centrally, initiated. By his own admission it was Fletcher's approach to the Governor of South Australia, the Earl of Kintore, that led to his being granted a commission to collect. Notably, however, he was not granted the finances to do so, and instead was left to 'beg' for antiquities.[86] Davies, meanwhile had had to rally the support of half a dozen private subscribers to secure the donation of antiquities in the absence of museum sponsorship.

Museums in Sydney were particularly well provided for, although again this was more a result of private agency rather than of government investment. The Nicholson Museum of the University of Sydney was one of the earliest beneficiaries of the EEF's work. At the Nicholson there was already a strong antiquarian nucleus in the founding collection of Sir Charles Nicholson (1808–1903), who had travelled to Egypt in the 1850s and 1860s and sought by his acquisitions to position Australia within a world-historical frame. The museum subscribed to the Fund's fieldwork in 1887 with the financial backing of Josiah Mullens (1826–1915), one of the founding members of the Sydney Stock Exchange. His generous support of £100 towards the excavations at Tanis in 1884 and 1885, together with regular subscriptions of the EEF, ensured that the Nicholson was awarded a black granite statue head found in 1887 at the temple of Bubastis. A few years later a monumental red granite column, surmounted by a capital of the goddess Hathor, was laboriously shipped from the site. By the First World War the museum had received just over 1100 artefacts from its excavations.

In all of these cases collecting was sanctioned and enabled by imperial structures, but it was certainly not directed thereby. And while it satisfied settler desires to participate in imperial intellectual and collecting activities, it did little to establish Egyptology or archaeological study on the Australian continent.[87]

Pākehā Treasures: Egypt in New Zealand

Despite, or perhaps because of, the fact that New Zealand was the furthest outpost of the British Empire, imperial connections with Britain were strong. This 'Britain of the South' had established museums from the mid-nineteenth century, but it was only two years after New Zealand's colonial status had been upgraded to that of a dominion that Egyptian objects excavated by British teams were sent to the South Pacific in 1909. On that occasion it was the Prime Minister himself, Joseph Ward (1856–1930), who personally sent the thanks 'of the Government and the people of New Zealand' to the EEF London office for the gift of antiquities.[88] For Ward, 'there was no country so British and so loyal in the Empire as New Zealand',[89] and his fervent support found one more expression in his acknowledgement to the EEF. His response, however, is not necessarily representative of the rather more muted reception that the Egyptian antiquities received from local museums and the public.

The timing of the acquisition is significant. Three years earlier, the country's largest international exposition, wholly financed by the government, had been held in Christchurch. The driving force behind it was Ward's predecessor, Premier Richard Seddon (1845–1906), who viewed it as a means of celebrating progress and nationhood following more than fifteen years of Liberal government. It served too as a visible manifestation of nascent colonial settler identity alongside the promotion of industry, trade and tourism. For historians, the event has formed a central case study for critical evaluations of the presentation of Māori culture, ranging from arguments concerning imperial domination of indigenous groups, to accounts that have recognized the active agency of the Māori as co-producers of the exhibits.[90] Others have examined the presentation of national identities – British and New Zealander – through the products of those countries.[91] Yet objects extracted from other parts of the empire were also on display. Antiquities from Egypt are not mentioned in the official exhibition guides, whose focus was principally on contemporary arts and crafts, but their presence was striking enough to elicit comment from Māori visitors. In November 1906, Reweti Kohere, editor for the Māori periodical *Te Pipiwharauroa*, wrote enthusiastically of his experience of the event and 'the kinds of Pākehā treasures that are heaped up there'. He noted that the 'things from England are very numerous', and he was taken by two aspects of this section in particular: the English royal coat of arms, and ancient Egyptian antiquities:

> to the eyes of a stranger the best sight of all is the kings' coats of arms; these belong to kings living in the distant past, and others right down to the present day... Some of the amazing things there are treasures from Egypt. The era to which these things belong is not fully known. They may perhaps be from the days of Abraham – it's really awesome![92]

The existence of Egyptian objects within the British Government exhibit firmly positioned them as domesticated items and taken-for-granted imperial goods.

It is against this background that the newly renamed Dominion Museum (formerly the Colonial Museum and now the Museum of New Zealand Te Papa Tongarewa) in Wellington acquired its first excavated Egyptian finds from Britain: a set of Predynastic pottery vessels and beads from the site of El-Mahasna, obtained through the agency of George Lambert, the EEF's Local Honorary Secretary. When Lambert wrote to Augustus Hamilton, Director of the Dominion Museum, he amplified the political significance of the acquisition: 'the Prime Minister', he reminded Hamilton, had a 'great interest in everything pertaining to the advancement of the Dominion', including links with the EEF.[93] No mention was made in any of the communications between the Fund, Lambert and Hamilton of the material qualities of the artefacts themselves, their scientific value or their historical significance. Rather, Lambert's appeal to their diplomatic importance was the means to leverage support from a Director and an institution who were otherwise more passionate about collecting Māori material culture than what Hamilton referred to fleetingly in his diaries as 'curios'.[94] In turn, Lambert's agency in the transactions was a means of self-fashioning, as he acted between the Prime Minister's Office and cultural institutions in Wellington and in London. In Lambert's own effusive words, the museum's acquisition were 'the means of procuring for me the honour of an introduction to your [Hamilton's] esteemed self the good fortune of whose friendship I shall ever esteem as the privilege of acquaintance'.[95]

Any claims as to the deeper imperial or political significance of these finds is tempered by the muted local reception to their arrival. The *New Zealand Herald* reported on the delivery under the headline 'Curios from Egypt' on 12 November 1909, but informed their readers regretfully that the list of finds did not include any mummies. Wellington's metropolitan daily, the *Evening Post*, was equally derisive in recounting the acquisition in its 10 November 1909 edition, and went on to report, rather sardonically, that

> Speaking this afternoon about the scope of the [Egypt] Exploration Fund's work, Mr Lambert remarked that efforts here to arouse enthusiasm in enterprises calculated to make the past give up its dead for the benefit of the present had not been very successful. New Zealanders, apparently, failed to appreciate the value of archaeological research. He could number on one hand the live local members of the 'Fund'.

Here in New Zealand Egyptian antiquities did not yet fit into any established museum order, nor were they deemed to be objects that required transformation into scientific specimens via typological acts, as the use of the deprecating term 'curio' by both curators and journalists suggests. This is a reminder that while many colonial museums have been portrayed as seeking to organize the world systematically, that did not take place uniformly.

In the inter-war period, museum curators elsewhere in New Zealand did make some efforts to acquire further Egyptian finds. H. D. Skinner (1886–1978) wrote to the EES in 1934 to request Egyptian objects for Otago Museum,[96] as part of his broader agenda to represent 'culture area arrangements' in the institution,[97] while a posting to Cairo during the Second World War for Lieutenant-Colonel Fred Waite (1885–1952) led to antiquities being sent to Auckland through his personal connections.[98] Nevertheless, interest in Egyptian material remained rather marginal, and such collections in New Zealand today are modest in size and composition.

Ajaib Ghar: Egypt in the British Raj

Western collecting practices were anchored in the Indian subcontinent at an early date, and museum development initially followed a typical nineteenth-century imperial profile. The India Museum, for instance, grew out of the Asiatic Society of Bengal that had been established in Calcutta in 1784 by the Englishman Sir William Jones (1746–94). Notably, in conceptualizing the society, Jones declared that since 'Egypt had unquestionably an old connexion with this country [India]... you may not be displeased occasionally to follow the streams of Asiatick learning a little beyond its borders'.[99] This supposition of a link between Egypt and India would re-emerge time and again, particularly in the context of racial speculation regarding a 'Dravidian people', who were variously linked with Sumeria, Egypt and the Indus valley over the decades,[100] and in Flinders Petrie's musings on the racial identification of terracotta heads excavated at Memphis in 1908–09 (Fig. 3.3).[101] The India Museum was inaugurated in 1814 to illustrate 'Oriental manners and history or to elucidate the peculiarities of Art or Nature in the East'.[102] Military officers and high-ranking British officials deposited curiosities there from their travels, with the result that amid the profusion of local antiquities a small ensemble of Egyptian things began to haphazardly coalesce. Further development was facilitated by the nature of the bureaucracy that governed Egypt from 1882, as it

Fig. 3.3 Roman era terracotta figurine excavated in 1908–09 by Flinders Petrie's teams at Memphis. Described by Petrie as 'Indian'. Courtesy of the Petrie Museum of Egyptian Archaeology (UC8932).

was structured in a similar manner to the British Raj, with numerous government officials moving directly between India and Egypt. These included Evelyn Baring, whose administrative acumen was honed in the 1870s as private secretary to Lord Northbrook, Viceroy of India.[103] Other itinerant civil servants who spent time in both countries helped to delineate colonial currents through which more Egyptian 'curios' drifted into the India Museum.

Despite these similar beginnings, John MacKenzie has noted that imperial museums in Asia can be distinguished from those established in other areas of British settlement.[104] Rather than playing a key role in constructing colonial white identities, from the close of the nineteenth century museums in India were absorbed into local Indian culture. The provincial embrace of these institutions was reflected in the profile of museum visitors, as well as the staff, who were predominately Indian.[105] Some Indian princes even took an active interest in acquiring Egyptian art, such as Sayaji Rao III in the late nineteenth century, whose collection is now in Baroda. Nevertheless, India's own wealth of monuments and art ensured that it was native material culture that took precedence in its museums. Egyptian antiquities were of ancillary interest and held a marginal status in collections.

The first Indian institution to petition British organisations for finds was the celebrated museum in Lahore, now in Pakistan. Instituted in 1849, Lahore Museum's growth was spurred on by its most famous curator, John Lockwood Kipling (1837–1911). His son, the author Rudyard Kipling, popularized the red sandstone museum's local and enduring vernacular name in the opening lines of his novel *Kim*: Ajaib Ghar or Wonder House. Kipling's successor at the museum, Percy Brown (1872–1955), had worked congenially alongside the young Howard Carter as an artist at the EEF's Deir el-Bahri excavations, and soon after arriving in India he wrote from Lahore Museum to his colleagues at the EEF to request antiquities. The Fund's Committee was happy to oblige, and resolved to send objects when they next became available. It is unclear if any antiquities were ever sent.[106] Perhaps this appeal to the centre of empire was more significant than any acquisition of the objects themselves.

Lucknow Museum in northern India, however, certainly did obtain a crate of finds around this time. Its Indian curator, Babu Ganga Dhar Ganguli, responded swiftly to John Garstang's February 1904 advertisement of antiquities in the *Athenaeum*, promising to cover all expenses of freight and carriage to ensure that the museum could obtain specimens of Egyptian pottery. Thirty-two vessels were promptly dispatched to join an archaeological collection that was otherwise almost wholly devoted to regional history. The museum's annual reports around this time dutifully list all acquisitions, and the arrival of the Egyptian things stands out as the only example of 'world archaeology' to be incorporated into the institution. Ganguli rationalized the acquisition by asserting that the vessels 'bear a close resemblance to the Indian pottery of today'.[107] Universal histories were thereby localized experimentally as a way of orientating and legitimating Indian collections on a world stage. The collection nevertheless remained small and easily overlooked.[108]

In what was then Bombay, the Prince of Wales Museum of Western India (now the Chhatrapatī Shivaji Mahārāj Vastu Saṅgrahālay (CSMVS)) was designed to display 'art, archaeology, history, economic products and natural history of the Bombay Presidency in particular, and the "Oriental Region" in general'.[109] It was founded to celebrate George V's visit to India in 1905, but drew its founding collection from the longer-established Bombay Branch of the Royal Asiatic Society, which had also acquired Egyptian things passively over the decades.[110] A building to house and display the collections was not completed until 1915, and its inauguration was further delayed until 1922 because of the First World War. The museum's name appears listed against the distribution of finds of textiles from the BSAE's 1920–1 season,[111] perhaps reflecting the institution's attempt to stock up on more antiquities ahead of its official opening. These were possibly displayed in Gallery II, which was devoted to Non-Indian Antiquities, including Egyptian Assyrian, South Arabian and Persian remains.

***

The European genesis of the museum phenomenon is responsible for a tendency to overlook other cultures of collecting that have existed outside Europe's influence. Nevertheless, museums as a product of modernity have had a pervasive global influence that has transcended cultural, political and language borders. The development of Japanese institutions is one example.

Hakubutsukan: Egypt in Japan

In the century-old wooden vitrines of the University of Kyoto's museum there is an assembly of Egyptian and Classical antiquities (Fig 3.4). Scattered between the pots, inscribed figurines and bronze deities lie

Fig. 3.4 Photograph of antiquities displays inside the Exhibition Hall at Kyoto University's Faculty of Letters, circa 1923. Courtesy of the University of Kyoto.

printed English-language tags belonging to the BSAE and the EEF, alongside yellowing labels neatly inked with kanji writing. The juxtaposition of Latin script, kanji characters and ancient hieroglyphs speaks to the complex transnational ways in which Japanese museums functioned as a means of comprehending Western cultural interests and reasserting Japan's own in contradistinction.[112] These well-travelled antiquities, acquired from Egypt by way of British archaeologists, have an additional subtext here, relating to the Anglo-French ability to exploit Egypt's past, which became a model for Japan's own imperial ambitions and colonial heritage practices in the Asia-Pacific region. Egyptian material culture consequently resonated with a very different series of reference points in Japan to the frameworks that shaped their reception elsewhere. Rather than biblical or Classical links, nationalism and imperialism took on far greater significance in the establishment of Egyptian archaeology in Japan than it ever had in Britain.

The Meiji restoration of 1868 ended more than two centuries of isolation, after which Japan commenced a programme of modernization to establish new systems of government, defence and education. These developments were informed by fact-finding excursions to Europe and the USA, most notably the 1871–3 Iwakura Mission,[113] when detailed accounts were compiled about the culture and politics of the countries visited. Victorian Britain's innovative museum practices were of particular interest, and London's South Kensington Museum made a lasting impression upon several high-ranking reformers who were keen for similar Japanese museums to stimulate the country's industrializing economy. However, it was the encyclopaedic cultural-historical gatherings at the British Museum that ultimately came to shape Japanese permutations of the museum idea.[114] Exhibition venues had existed in Japan previously within the confines of temples, for example, but there was nothing comparable to the permanence, breadth or public nature of the organizations that Japanese delegations first encountered in the West. Japan began to experiment with new institutions of its own in Tokyo in the early 1870s. By 1880, numerous publicly accessible collections had been set up in other centres like Kyoto, Osaka and Nagoya.[115] These new buildings of visual edification were categorically Western-inspired entities that came to be called *hakubutsukan*: 'hall of diverse objects'.

On the basis of these international forays, new universities were also founded, including the University of Tokyo in 1877 and Kyoto Imperial University in 1897. It was within these institutions that academic archaeology was established in the early twentieth century. The rise of antiquarianism in Japan is comparable to its development in Europe, whereby educated and wealthy land-owning scholars interested in local history encountered material from prehistory during the seventeenth and eighteenth centuries. No systematic appraisals of such finds were made, however, and it was not until the late nineteenth century that the foundations for a sustained archaeological research structure were laid. Individuals such as the American, Edward Morse (1838–1925), and the Englishman, William Gowland (1842–1922) – 'father of Japanese archaeology' –[116] have been lauded for establishing the study of Japanese archaeology through their explorations of Kofun period tombs and Jomon era shell middens respectively, but they published almost exclusively in English.[117] Perhaps Morse, more than Gowland (whose work did not reach Japanese scholars), should be considered as having spurred the establishment of domestic Japanese archaeology, but this was not necessarily through positive emulation. Indeed, Morse's interpretation of his 1877 exploration of Ōmori shell middens as evidence for prehistoric cannibalism deeply offended native scholars, including Shōgorō Tsuboi (1863–1913), first professor of anthropology at the Tokyo Imperial University. Tsuboi is famed for founding the Japanese Anthropological Society (*Nihon jinrui gakkai*), a body that under his lead also excavated prehistoric shell middens.[118] Incensed by Morse's claims, Tsuboi and his colleagues insisted that the investigation into Japan's origins must be a Japanese undertaking, not a Western one, thereby establishing Japanese archaeology as a nationalistic endeavour, albeit one that was heavily influenced by external methodologies.

Less well known is Tsuboi's keen interest in Egyptology. He regularly lectured on Egyptological topics at the High Normal School, as well as at public events,[119] and he visited Egypt in 1911. Tsuboi had spent three years studying in London between 1889 and 1892, and it was perhaps through the networks he had established during this time that Tokyo University was able to secure seventeen rather humble objects from the EEF's work at Deir el-Bahri. This included a small stone head of the cow-goddess Hathor and specimens of ancient Egyptian bread, wheat, matting and cloth (Fig. 3.5).

Despite Tokyo's acquisition, it was Kyoto University that was to materially benefit the most from British excavations in Egypt, and today there are around 480 artefacts in the University's collection as a result of its patronage.[120] Credit for this rests primarily with Kōsaku Hamada[121] (1881–1938), a history and Classical art graduate from the University of Tokyo who had attended Tsuboi's lectures. In 1909 Hamada was given a position at Kyoto Imperial University to provide the nation's first lecture course in archaeology, for which he relied heavily on Petrie's *Methods and Aims in Archaeology*.[122] That same year Kyoto Imperial University subscribed to the EEF, and a supply of excavated material promptly

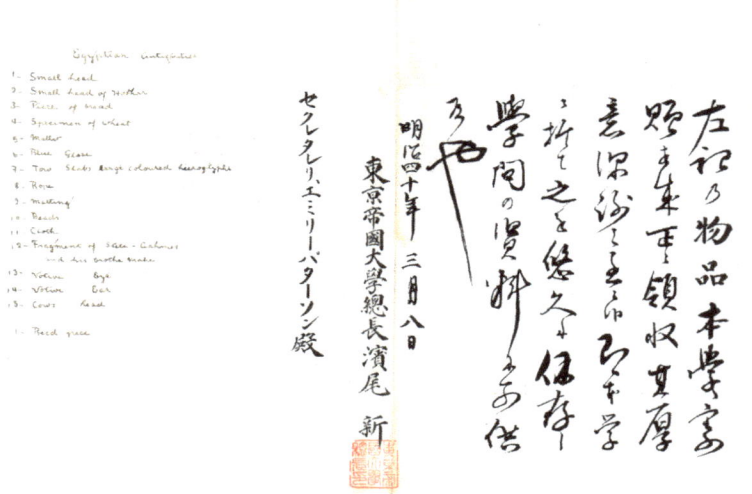

Fig. 3.5 Letter from University of Tokyo acknowledging the donation of antiquities from the Egypt Exploration Fund's 1906–07 excavation seasons. Courtesy of the Egypt Exploration Society (EES.DIST.28.10b).

followed. The EEF selection for Kyoto consisted 'of a representative series of antiquities of all periods from various sites which have been excavated by the Egyptian Exploration Fund during past years'.[123] As a whole it was a generous consignment, noted by the EEF's secretary, Emily Paterson, to be 'greater in number than usual'.[124] Among the offerings was a fragment of stove embellished with the head of a satyr from Naukratis, selected because the EEF committee believed it resembled a Japanese *Tengu*, a form of wild spirit. Such an identification suggests familiarity with Japanese culture. Ties between Britain and Japan had already been strengthened by the 1902 Anglo-Japanese alliance, a treaty that was renewed twice, first in 1905 and then in 1911. This final renewal of the treaty was preceded by the largest international exposition that the Japanese had ever participated in, held at London's White City between 14 May and 29 October 1910. This was widely known in London as the 'Japanese Exhibition', and an estimated 8 million people visited its displays. In this context the generous quantity of antiquities bestowed to Kyoto by the EEF in October that same year is probably no coincidence.

In 1913, Hamada was given leave from Kyoto Imperial University to travel to Europe and familiarize himself with archaeological work and collections there. He spent the majority of his time in England at UCL, perhaps taking heed of the Oxford Assyriologist Archibald Sayce (1846–

1933), who had visited Kyoto in early 1912 and personally advised him to study with Flinders Petrie.[125] Soon after returning to Japan in 1916, Hamada was appointed head of the country's first department of archaeology at Kyoto Imperial University, which now also administered a museum at the Faculty of Letters. Hamada arranged for a subscription to Petrie's BSAE so as to enrich the educational base of his new department. Such a commitment did not necessarily arise out of a specific interest in Egyptology per se, but rather because 'the advanced methods of study in Egyptology will promote the studies of archaeology in Japan and other countries in the Far East'.[126] Hamada recognized that there were limited opportunities for the Japanese to work directly in Egypt and Mesopotamia on account of physical, political and cultural distance. Yet this was of little concern. What was important was that the Egyptian objects acquired from Flinders Petrie represented systematic and scientific archaeology which would fit with Japanese nationalistic agendas. As Angus Lockyer has pointed out,[127] Japanese university programmes were not intended to establish liberal subjects of study, but were ultimately related to the creation of a national aesthetic. By these means, Lockyer argues, the nascent Japanese state sought to attain historical integrity, thereby supporting other institutional and ideological creations that underpinned the state's claim to parity with the West.

After the First World War, Petrie personally arranged for a shipment of nine large crates of Egyptian antiquities to be dispatched to Kyoto. Hamada acknowledged the 'special kindness sending us so many objects, precious and interesting, very much more than we have expected',[128] and he was particularly gratified that they had arrived in time to be shown to Empress Teimei during her tour of the University. The imperative to use the material to stimulate the study of Japanese prehistory was key to Hamada's display strategy for Her Highness; he arranged a 5000-year-old skeleton and grave goods from the excavations at the royal enclosures at Abydos[129] beside Japanese Neolithic human remains and associated burial accoutrements.

Hamada wrote an article for the University journal, *Shirin,* to accompany these new acquisitions, reiterating the point that procuring such antiquities would indirectly provide a stimulus to archaeological study in Japan.[130] 'It is', he wrote in a second article, 'enough if we can just introduce Western researchers' theories to help to study our Eastern history'.[131] This was effected in his *Shirin* article through comparisons between Egyptian finds and those made closer to home. Of a pilaster head and relief decoration found at a theatre at Oxyrhynchus Hamada noted, for instance, that it resembled a Corinthian order used in the Yungang

Grottoes in China, and he went on to make a connection between Six Dynasties China, Suiko Period Japan and Greco-Roman culture.[132] Similarly, Coptic textiles that had caught the eye of the Empress were said to have been stimulated by Persian designs, influences that 'stretched to East Rome in one side and Japan via China in another side', and similarities were also noted 'between the Coptic textiles and textiles preserved in Shōsōin and in Horyuji-temple in Kyoto'.[133]

The Egyptian objects acquired by Kyoto were representatives for particular approaches to understanding the past, as well as a means of negotiating the present. For an influential group of Japanese Government scholars, however, the significance of British archaeological work in Egypt was greater still. The acquisition of antiquities was seen not merely as being of nationalistic benefit, but also as a model of imperial gain. Just three years prior to Hamada's visit to England, Korea had become a Japanese territory, and the new colonial powers were quick to establish a Service of Antiquities together with laws regulating the excavation and preservation of monuments.[134] In his memoirs, Archibald Sayce, who travelled to Korea in early 1912, noted in passing that this new 'Service of Antiquities', together with a law relating to illicit excavation and preservation of monuments, had been based upon those developed for Egypt.[135] One of the key drivers behind this legislation was Kuroita Katsumi (1874–1946), a professor at the University of Tokyo and Head of the Meiji Education Ministry Historical Textbook Compilation Committee. Katsumi's 1912 draft recommendation had been inspired by studying the antiquities, laws and national preservation efforts during visits to Europe and Egypt between 1908 and 1910,[136] including an excursion to the EEF excavations at Abydos, facilitated by Henry Hall of the British Museum.[137] For Katsumi, British explorations in Egypt provided an example of colonial scientific enterprise that the Japanese Government was keen to emulate, given the Japanese Empire's ambitions on the Korean peninsula where, like Britain elsewhere, it administered the country as a protectorate. As argued by historians such as Astrid Swenson, preservationism and imperialism had been ideologically connected ever since the French Revolution, when preservation was likened to civilization and freedom.[138] Although originally formulated to halt military iconoclasm, the sentiment to preserve came to legitimize rather than prevent the looting of heritage by armies across Europe and Egypt. This justification was employed to carry foreign art off to France, where it was thought it would be better appreciated. In a similar fashion, Japanese activities on the Korean peninsula, although conducted within a rhetoric of preservationism, served to validate Japan's efforts to remove Korea's archaeological heritage to museums back home.

Japan's early Egyptian acquisitions were academically circumscribed and not publicly accessible. Hamada's influence was therefore limited to the discipline of archaeology. He published Japan's first archaeology textbook, which was explicitly based upon Flinders Petrie's *Methods and Aims in Archaeology*, a move that aided the project of constructing the nationalistic narratives predicated upon cultural-historical frameworks that would define Japanese archaeology for decades.[139] Hamada's students used the Egyptian antiquities as tangible representations of how to develop a corpus of objects and how to date them in sequence. There was, however, only limited interest in Egyptology itself. A Japanese 'History of Egypt' was finally published in the 1940s by Seitaro Okajima (1895–1948), who had studied in Kyoto. Okajima was at that time credited with being the only Egyptologist in Japan, and it was stated that prior to his work 'Egyptology was totally unknown' as a subject as it was 'beyond the taste of the dilettanti and is not even of interest to students of Western History'.[140] Okajima's volume used images of Kyoto University's collections, thereby embedding them as an essential point of reference for a new generation of Japanese Egyptologists, who themselves went on to undertake the first Japanese archaeological explorations of Egypt during the 1960s.[141] For these reasons, Kyoto University Museum's collection today represents important aspects of the beginnings of modern archaeology and Egyptology in Japan.[142]

***

British activities in Egypt were extensive. There were numerous organizations involved and all of them were in competition with other nation-states for concessions to excavate in Egypt. Yet it was precisely because of the transnational orientation of these British groups – being open to backing from individuals and museums in other countries – that the EEF/EES, the BSAE and Garstang's Liverpool-based operations were able to co-exist and to succeed in gathering sufficient funding to carry out their work.[143] It also meant that the results of these endeavours were widely dispersed, far more than has been possible to convey in this chapter. Museums in Austria, Barbados, Belgium, Greece, Ireland, Jamaica, the Netherlands, Sweden and Switzerland also appear listed in the EES, Garstang Museum and Petrie Museum archives. As in the examples that have been examined, it is highly likely that in these different settings Egyptian antiquities were made to mean different things, conditioned by the environments into which they were introduced.

This chapter has tried to avoid reducing such highly contingent and diverse histories of distribution to monolithic stereotypes. Ultimately, social conflicts, economic forces and personal ambitions created an array of local issues which affected what got collected, when, and why, influencing the extent to which Egyptian things were either foregrounded, overshadowed or regarded with indifference in their new surroundings. What remains, however, is a keen sense of the connectedness enacted through acquisitions. The late nineteenth and early twentieth centuries are commonly characterized as an era of nationalism and imperialism, but they can also be viewed as periods of increasing globalization, particularly in the field of scholarship.[144] Nonetheless, colonial museums did not simply emulate the models at empire's heart,[145] as the example of Canada's Redpath Museum demonstrates. Local factors were always in play, and these were attuned to different facets of Egyptian artefacts, from their geological properties and the presence of accompanying texts, to their symbolism. Where colonial museums engaged more directly with indigenous material culture, as in India and New Zealand, Egypt was largely marginalized; where native culture was deemed to be absent or irrelevant, as in South Africa and Australia, it was celebrated. It is also clear that the expansion of collections was not the only aim of acquisitions. To a large extent exchange itself was the goal, in order to establish or consolidate particular relationships.

In assessing the impact of these objects in these disparate locations, one of the great unknowns is the audience.[146] But snippets from archives and available newspaper accounts hint at challenges to some commonplace assumptions, and suggest alternative attitudes to the Egyptian things. In settler colonies it is often presumed that it was the European colonists who were primarily attracted to Egyptian finds, yet the case of New Zealand shows the interest of Māori individuals in contrast to a seemingly apathetic white community. In India too, local native populations were just as likely to view and collect Egyptian finds as were settlers. The extent to which distribution effected the development of archaeology and museums in these locations was also highly variable. In Germany, the pursuit of material histories became increasingly important, and was key in an exchange economy of intellectual honours. In Australia and South Africa, the arrival of the artefacts was not linked to disciplinary progress, but to inward-looking institutional pride. Arguably, it was outside the sphere of Europe and the Commonwealth, in Japan, that Egyptian antiquities from British excavations had the greatest long-term impact on the production of archaeological knowledge, by instituting particular forms of typological practice and museum display techniques.

Notes

1. Letter from Petrie to Cartailhac, 7 April 1895, la bibliothèque numérique patrimoniale des universités toulousaines, 92Z-300/2.
2. Letter from Erman to Petrie, 19 November 1895, PMA/WFP1/115/10/1/3/3.
3. Iriye, A. and Saunier, P-Y. (eds.) 2009. *The Palgrave Dictionary of Transnational History: From the Mid-19th Century to the Present Day*. Basingstoke: Palgrave; Blunck, L., Savoy, B. and Shalem, A. (eds.) *The Museum is Open: Towards a Transnational History of Museums 1750–1940*. Berlin and Boston: De Gruyter; Adam, T. 2016. *Transnational Philanthropy: The Mond Family's Support for Public Institutions in Western Europe from 1890 to 1938*. Arlington: Palgrave Macmillan.
4. For example, see Diaz-Andreu, M. and Champion, T. (eds.) 1996. *Nationalism and Archaeology in Europe*. Boulder and San Francisco: Westview Press; Kohl, P. L. and Fawcett, C. (eds.) 1995. *Nationalism, Politics and the Practice of Archaeology*. Cambridge: Cambridge University Press; Meskell, L. 1998. *Archaeology* Under Fire: *Nationalism, Politics and Heritage in the Eastern Mediterranean and Middle East*. London and New York: Routledge; Kaplan, F. E. S. (ed.) 1994. *Museums and the Making of Ourselves: The Role of Objects in National Identity*. London and New York: Leicester University Press.
5. Wimmer, A. and Schiller, N. G. 2002. Methodological nationalism and beyond: nation-state building, migration and the social sciences. *Global Networks* 2(4): 301–34.
6. Bayly, C. A., Beckert, S., Connelly, M., Hofmeyr, I., Kozol, W. and Seed, P. 2006. AHR conversation: on transnational history. *The American Historical Review* 111(5): 1446.
7. Star, S. L. and Griesemer, J. R. 1989. Institutional ecology, 'translations', and boundary objects: amateurs and professionals in Berkeley's Museum of Vertebrate Zoology, 1908–39. *Social Studies of Science* 19: 393.
8. C.f. Latour, B. 1986. Visualization and cognition: drawing things together. *Knowledge and Society Studies in the Sociology of Culture Past and Present* 6(1): 1–40.
9. Bhatti, S. 2007. *Translating Museums: A Counterhistory of South Asian Museology*. Walnut Creek: Left Coast Press, p. 80.
10. Letter from Gilbertson to Edwards, 14 July 1885, EES.COR.003.c.54.
11. Subsequent political landscaping has redrawn state boundaries since the objects were dispatched. When artefacts were first sent to Strasbourg it was situated within Germany, prior to the city's annexation by France in 1919. The only other French institution to directly benefit from British excavations was another Parisian establishment, the Musée Guimet, which in 1895 was sent an unspecified number of masks of 'Christian' mummies from Deir el Bahri and 'archaic' figurines from Naukratis. These were subsequently transferred to the Louvre, meaning that today there is only a single institution in France with a small number of objects excavated under the aegis of British organisations. EES.DIST.05.02b and EES.DIST.14.01d.
12. Institutions in Hannover and Hildesheim received material relatively late from the British distribution network. The Museum August Kestner in Hannover acquired a small number of items purchased from Weidermann in the 1930s, while Hildesheim's Roemer-Pelizaeus Museum received Amarna material from 1927 and Qasr Ibrim in the 1990s.
13. Kröger, M. 1991. *Le bâton égyptien – Der ägyptische Knüppel. Die Rolle der ägyptischen Frage in der deutschen Außenpolitik von 1875/76 bis zur 'Entente Cordiale'*. Frankfurt am Main: Peter Lang.
14. Marchand, S. 1998. Orientalism as Kulturpolitik. German archaeology and cultural imperialism in Asia Minor. In Stocking, G. W. (ed.) *Volksgeist as Method and Ethic*. Madison: University of Wisconsin Press, p. 305.
15. Marchand, S. 2000. The end of Egyptomania: German scholarship and the banalization of Egypt, 1830–1914. In Seipel, W. (ed.) *Ägyptomanie Europäische Ägyptenimagination von der Antike bis heute*. Wien: Kunsthistorisches Museum, p. 128.
16. As popularized, for instance, in the best-selling novels of Georg Ebers (1837–1913), Professor of Egyptology at Leipzig.
17. Thomas Gertzen, Personal communication. I am grateful to Thomas Gertzen for his insights into the history of German Egyptology.
18. Cited in Marchand, S. 2003. *Down from Olympus: Archaeology and Philhellenism in Germany, 1750–1970*. Princeton: Princeton University Press, p. 197.
19. Penny, G. 2002. *Objects of Culture: Ethnology and Ethnographic Museums in Imperial Germany*. Chapel Hill: University of North Carolina Press, p. 25.

20   Stevenson, A. 2014. The object of study: Egyptology, anthropology and archaeology at the University of Oxford, 1860–1960. In Carruthers, W. (ed.) *Histories of Egyptology: Interdisciplinary Measures*. London and New York: Routledge, pp. 19–33.
21   Adam notes that in 1910, 29 per cent of EEF membership was female, compared to only 4 per cent of the similarly sized DOG. Adam, *Transnational Philanthropy*, p. 216.
22   Petrie, W. M. F. 1893. Inaugural lecture 14 January 1893. In Janssen, R. 1992. *The First Hundred Years Egyptology at University College London 1892–1992*. London: UCL Press, p. 100.
23   Sethe, K. 1921. Cited in Gertzen, T. 2015. The Anglo-Saxon branch of the Berlin School. In Carruthers, *Histories of Egyptology*, p. 37.
24   Gertzen, The Anglo-Saxon branch.
25   Penny, *Objects of Culture*, pp. 43–4.
26   Letter from Erman to Petrie, 11 November 1888, PMA/Corr/5/ERM/01. See also Gertzen, T. L. 2009. Ägyptologie zwischen Archäeologie und Sprachwissenschaft: die Korrespondenz zwischen A. Erman und W.M. Flinders Petrie. *Zeitschrift fur Ägyptische Sprache und Altertumskunde* 136: 114–69.
27   Letter from Erman to Petrie, 26 September 1890, PMA/Corr/5/ERM/02. Although Erman continued to prefer written evidence. See for instance Erman, A. 1929. *Mein Werden und mein Wirken. Erinnerungen eines alten Berliner Gelehrten*. Leipzig: Quelle and Meyer, p. 211: 'und ich erlaubte mir auch weiterhin im Leben, Bilder, Inschriften und Papyrus für interessanter zu halten als Knochen und Muschelschalen aus dem antiken Kehricht.' With thanks to Thomas Gertzen for drawing this to my attention.
28   Drower, M. 1985. *Flinders Petrie: A Life in Archaeology*. London: Victor Gollancz, p. 220.
29   For instance, in 1911 Ludwig Borchardt was frustrated by Petrie's claims on finds in the Fayum that Borchardt considered had been found on German and Austrian territory. See Bagh, T. 2011. *Finds from W.M.F. Petrie's Excavations in Egypt in the Ny Carlsberg Glyptotek*. Copenhagen: Ny Carlsberg Glyptotek, pp. 20–1.
30   Marchand, Orientalism as Kulturpolitik, p. 300.
31   See Gertzen, T. 2017. *Einführung in die Wissenschaftsgeschichte der Ägyptologie*. Münster: LIT Verlag; Voss, S. 2016. Wissenshintergründe … – Die Ägyptologie als ‚völkische' Wissenschaft entlang des Nachlasses Georg Steindorffs von der Weimarer Republik über die NS- bis zur Nachkriegszeit. In Voss, S. and Raue, D. (eds.) *Georg Steindorff und die deutsche Ägyptologie im 20. Jahrhundert Wissenshintergründe und Forschungstransfers*. Berlin: De Gruyter, pp. 105–332; Voss, S. 2017. *Die Geschichte der Abteilung Kairo des DAI im Spannungsfeld deutscher politischer Interessen. Band 2, 1929 bis 1966*. Rahden/Westf: VML, Verlag Marie Leidorf.
32   For example, some material from BSAE excavations at Matmar and Mostagedda was sent to Museum für Byzantinische Kunst in 1931, but these have been missing since the Second World War. See Fluck, C. 2014. Findspot known: treasures from excavation sites in Egypt in the Museum für Byzantinische Kunst, Berlin. *British Museum Studies in Ancient Egypt and Sudan* 21: 1–30.
33   Curran, B. A. 2007. *The Egyptian Renaissance: The Afterlife of Ancient Egypt in Early Modern Italy*. Chicago: The University of Chicago Press.
34   Drower, *Flinders Petrie*, pp. 183–5.
35   Letter from Flinders Petrie to Reginald Poole, 13 November 1883, EES.COR.16.f.8.
36   For example, Petrie, W. M. F. 1904. *Methods and Aims in Archaeology*. London: Macmillan and Co; also Quirke, S. 2010. *Hidden Hands: Egyptian Workforces in Petrie Excavation Archives, 1880–1924*. London: Duckworth.
37   In addition to the case studies discussed here, a set of 51 objects from EEF work at el-Amrah was sent to Florence through David Randall-MacIver's personal connections. Guidotti, M. C. (ed.) 2006. *Materiale predinastico del Museo Egizio di Firenze*. Firenze: Giunt.
38   Fonck, L. 1908. Review of Nach Petra und zum Sinai. Zwei Reiseberichte nebst Beiträgen zur biblischen Geographie und Geschichte by Ladislaus Szczepański. *Zeitschrift für katholische Theologie* 32(4): 727–29.
39   PMA/WFP1/D/21/15.
40   PMA/WFP1/D/24/5.1.
41   PMA/WFP1/D/15/16.1.
42   First opened in 1819 and continuously redeveloped up to the 1830s when it was relocated to allow for new displays. See Eskildsen, K. R. 2012. The language of objects: Christian Jürgensen Thomsen's Science of the past. *Isis* 103(1): 24–53.
43   Spurrell, F. C. J. 1896. On some flint implements from Egypt and Denmark. *Archaeological Journal* 53(1): 46–55.

44 Letter from Jens Daniel Carolus Lieblein to Flinders Petrie, 5 November 1900, PMA/WMF/C/6/LIE/01. Translated from the French by Chloe Ward. An exception to this pattern is the Swedish professor of Egyptology at Uppsala, Karl Frederk Piehl, who was a philologist. He established a museum largely filled with antiquities purchased on his own travels in Egypt, but supplemented these by taking advantage of Petrie's commercial openness.
45 Jørgensen, M. 2015. *How it All Began: The Story of Carl Jacobsen's Egyptian Collection, 1884–1925*. Copenhagen: Ny Carlsberg Glyptotek.
46 Lange, J. 1892. *Billedkunstens Fremstilling af Menneskeskikkelsen i dens ældste Periode*. Copenhagen: Bianco Lunos Kgl. Hof-Bogtrykkeri (F. Dreyer).
47 Hagen, F. and Ryholt, K. 2016. *The Antiquities Trade in Egypt 1880–1930: The H.O. Lange Papers*. Copenhagen: The Royal Danish Academy of Science and Letters. The possibility of Danish-led excavations was mooted at this time, but largely abandoned because of cost and the perception that people like Petrie were already well placed and amenable to sharing finds.
48 Bagh, *Finds from W.M.F. Petrie's Excavations in Egypt*.
49 Veronika, D. 2015. The lost and forgotten Opava collection of Egyptian finds: The story of objects from digging conducted by famed Flinders Petrie. In Lazar, I. (ed.) *Egypt and Austria VIII: Meeting point Egypt*. Koper: Univerza na Primorskem, pp. 17–31; Pelc, M. 2014. *Maria Stona und ihr Salon in Strzebowitz. Kultur am Rande der Monarchie, der Republik und des Kanons*. Opava: Schleisische Universität.
50 The bulk of the objects sent came from Tarkhan, but at least three items originated from New Kingdom tombs at Riqqa. Only a single stone vessel from the distribution remains in the Archaeological Department of the Silesian Museum, while a Ptolemaic Period coffin is now looked after by the Náprstek Museum. The remainder of the collection is assumed to have been lost during the Second World War. Veronika, The lost and forgotten Opava collection, p. 27.
51 E.g. Longair, S. and McAleer, J. (eds.) 2016. *Curating Empire: Museums and the British Imperial Experience*. Manchester: Manchester University Press.
52 Merrington, P. 2017. The 'Mediterranean' Cape: reconstructing an ethos. In Parker, G. (ed.) *South Africa, Greece and Rome: Classical Confrontations*. Cambridge: Cambridge University Press, p. 131.
53 Gore, J. M. 2004. A lack of nation? The evolution of history in South African Museums, c.1825–1945. *South African Historical Journal* 51(1): 24–46.
54 As noted on the purchase of Egyptian objects from John Garstang's Beni Hasan excavations in 1908. Cited in Gore, A lack of a nation? 36.
55 Letter from K. Fannin to J. Garstang, 4 March 1904, University of Liverpool, Garstang Museum archives, JG/2/2.
56 Miers, H. A. and Markham, S. F. 1932. *A Report on the Museums and Art Galleries of British Africa*. The Museums Association Survey of Empire Museums. Edinburgh: T. and A. Constable.
57 Masters, S. 2017. Museum space and displacement. Collecting classical antiquities in South Africa. In Parker, *South Africa, Greece, Rome*, pp. 293–4.
58 According to the EEF Committee minutes of 7 June 1898 a letter was read from the curator of the Cape Town Museum requesting antiquities. It is not clear if these were sent.
59 E.g. PMA/WMFP/D/21/7.2.
60 The Estate became something of a national gem, but the family's fortunes did not survive the twentieth century and in 1996 a much-anticipated 'sale of the century' took place at the manor. Among the auction lots were numerous Egyptian antiquities excavated by the Bruntons. A few of these lots were acquired by Lambert Vorster, a retired petrochemical mining engineer who now owns a farm at Malmesbury, outside Cape Town. I am grateful to him and his brother for allowing me to see the collection in January 2014, which includes artefacts from the Bruntons' BSAE work in the Badari region, as well as some of their equipment and watercolours by Winifred.
61 Goodnow, K., Lothman, J. and Bredekamp, J. 2006. *Challenge and Transformation: Museums in Cape Town and Sydney*. New York and Oxford: Berghahn Books, pp. 60–1.
62 PMA/WFP1/D/26/25.5.
63 EES.DIST.17.02a.
64 Gooch, J. 2013. *The Boer War: Direction, Experience and Image*. London and New York: Routledge, p. 47.
65 Aitken, E. D. 1948. Egyptian Antiquities at Huguenot University College. *Die Hugenoot*, 1948: 26.
66 Some confusion exists regarding the routes of objects into the Redpath, because Montreal's Natural History Society, which Redpath curator J. W. Dawson was involved with, also sent funds to the EEF and Petrie in the early twentieth century. The Natural History Society's museum was rendered defunct in the 1920s, and in 1925 its collection was turned over to the Redpath.

67 Sheets-Pyenson, S. 1987. Cathedrals of science: the development of colonial natural history museums during the late nineteenth century. *History of Science* 25(3): 282.
68 Miskell, L. 2016. *Meeting Places: Scientific Congresses and Urban Identity in Victorian Britain*. London and New York: Routledge.
69 Tylor, E. B. 1885. Presidential address to the Anthropology Section. *Report of the Fifty-Fourth Meeting of the British Association for the Advancement of Science held at Montreal in August and September 1884*. London: John Murray, p. 899.
70 Lawson, B. 1999. Exhibiting agendas: anthropology at the Redpath Museum (1882–1899). *Anthropologica* 41: 59.
71 Lawson, Exhibiting agendas, p. 60
72 Lawson, Exhibiting agendas, pp. 60–2.
73 Dawson, J. W. 1893. Notes on useful and ornamental stones of ancient Egypt. *Journal of the Transactions of the Victoria Institute* 26: 265–82.
74 Dawson, Notes on useful and ornamental stones, 288.
75 Dawson, Notes on useful and ornamental stones, 268–9. Later in this publication Dawson listed further stones and gems in the museum donated by the EEF that were arranged in a similar manner (p. 288).
76 Livingstone, D. 2014. *Dealing with Darwin: Place, Politics, and Rhetoric in Religious Engagements with Evolution*. Baltimore: Johns Hopkins University Press, pp. 91–107.
77 Berger, C. 1983. *Science, God, and Nature in Victorian Canada*. Toronto: University of Toronto Press, p. 69.
78 Trumpour, M. and Schultz, T. 2008. The 'Father of Egyptology' in Canada. *Journal of the American Research Center in Egypt* 44: 159–67.
79 For example, MacKenzie, *Museums and Empire*.
80 MacKenzie, *Museums and Empire*, pp. 44–58.
81 Trumpour and Schultz, The 'Father of Egyptology' in Canada: 166.
82 Anderson, M. and Reeves, A. 1994. Contested identities: museums and the nation in Australia. In Kaplan, *Museums and the Making of Ourselves*, pp. 79–124.
83 Fletcher, W. M. R. 1892. *Egyptian Sketches*. Adelaide: E. A. Petherick and Co., p. 4.
84 Davies, N. 1898. An antique gift from England. *The Age* 28 November 1898: 5.
85 Davies, An antique gift, 5.
86 On his return, Fletcher presented a series of casts and a single original antiquity to the South Australian Museum: an inscribed lintel with the cartouche of Thutmose III excavated during Petrie's excavations at Gurob and passed to Fletcher via one of Petrie's assistants, Hughes Hughes.
87 Merrillees, R. S. 1990. *Living with Egypt's Past in Australia*. Victoria: Museum of Victoria.
88 Letter from Joseph Ward to George Lambert, 16 November 1909, EES.DIST.29.42a.
89 Anon. 1909. *Evening Post,* 26 October 1909.
90 Henare, A. 2005. *Museums, Anthropology and Imperial Exchange*. Cambridge: Cambridge University Press, pp. 220–7; Thomson, J. M. (ed.) *Farewell Colonialism: The New Zealand International Exhibition*. Palmerston North: Dunmore Press; McCarthy, C. 2009. 'Our works of ancient times': History, colonisation and agency at the 1906–07 New Zealand International Exhibition. *Museum History Journal* 2(2): 119–42.
91 Dibley, B. 1997. Telling times: narrating the nation at the New Zealand International Exhibition 1906–07. *Sites* 34 (Autumn 1997): 1–17.
92 Reproduced in Orbell, M. 1998. Maori writing about the exhibition. In Thomson, *Farewell Colonialism,* p. 149.
93 Letter from George Lambert to Augustus Hamilton, 26 November 1909. In O'Rourke, R. B. 1998. *The Dominion Museum and the Egypt Exploration Fund, London, 1909–1938*. Wellington: Museum of New Zealand Te Papa Tongerewa (unpublished manuscript). With thanks to Andrea Hearfield for sending me a copy.
94 Hamilton, A. 1909. Diary entry for Thursday 11 November 1909. In O'Rourke, *The Dominion Museum and the Egypt Exploration Fund*.
95 Letter from George Lambert to Augustus Hamilton, 26 November 1909. In O'Rourke, *The Dominion Museum and the Egypt Exploration Fund*.
96 Letter from H. D. Skinner to the EES Secretary, 7 April 1934, EES.DIST.58.08.
97 Cameron, F. R. 2014. From 'dead things' to immutable, combinable mobiles: H.D. Skinner, the Otago Museum and University and the Governance of Māori populations. *History and Anthropology* 25(2): 208–26.

98 Emmitt, J. and Hellum, J. 2015. A Predynastic vessel with a potmark in the Auckland War Memorial Museum. *Records of the Auckland Museum* 50: 33–7.
99 William Jones 1788, cited in Guha, S. 2015. *Artefacts of History: Archaeology, Historiography and Indian Pasts*. New Dehli: Sage, p. 68.
100 Guha, *Artefacts of History*, p. 154.
101 Petrie, W. M. F. 1909. *Memphis I*. London: British School of Archaeology in Egypt, p. 16; Challis, D. 2013. *The Archaeology of Race: The Eugenic Ideas of Francis Galton and Flinders Petrie*. London: Bloomsbury, pp. 217–18.
102 Betrò, M. 2004. History of the collections. In Bresciani, E. and Betrò, M. (eds.) *Egypt in India: Egyptian Antiquities in Indian Museums*. Pisa: Pisa University Press, p. 63.
103 Nominated in 1872 to the Secretary of the Viceroy of India, sent to Egypt as Commissioner of National Debt 1877–9, returning to India in 1879 and appointed British agent and consul general in Egypt 1883.
104 MacKenzie, *Museums and Empire*, pp. 234–43.
105 MacKenzie, *Museums and Empire*, pp. 234–43.
106 Salima Ikram enquired at the museum in July 2016, and despite recent documentation efforts no Egyptian artefacts are known, so it may be the case that none were ever sent.
107 Anon. 1905. *Annual Report On The Working Of The Provincial Museum for the Year Ending 31 March 1905, Lucknow*. Allahabad: United Provinces Government Press, p. 2.
108 No Egyptian material is mentioned. Markham, S. F. and Hargreaves, H. 1936. *The Museums of India*. London: The Museums Association. It is otherwise remarked upon for a few other institutions.
109 Markham and Hargreaves, *The Museums of India*, p. 111.
110 Betrò, *History of the Collections*, p. 66.
111 PMA/WFP1/D/26/25/2.
112 Tseng, A. 2008. *The Imperial Museums of Meiji: Architecture and Art of the Nation*. University of Washington Press: Washington, p. 10.
113 Kume, K. 2009. *Japan Rising: The Iwakura Embassy to the USA and Europe*. Edited by Tsuzuki, C. and Young, R. J. Cambridge: Cambridge University Press.
114 Huang, P. 2016. Early museological development within the Japanese Empire. *Journal of the History of Collections* 28(1): 125–35.
115 Anon. 1881. Museums and exhibitions in Japan. *Nature* Oct 13: 562–63.
116 Harris, V. and Goto, K. (eds.). 2003. *William Gowland: The Father of Japanese Archaeology*. Tokyo: Asahi Shinbunsha and London: British Museum Press.
117 The only exception being a Japanese version of Morse's excavation report by Yatabe, R. 1879. *Omori Kaikyo Kobutsu Hen*. Tokyo: University of Tokyo.
118 Yamashita, S. 2006. Reshaping anthropology: a view from Japan. In Ribeiro, G. L. and Escobar, A. (eds.) *World Anthropologies: Disciplinary Transformations within Systems of Power*. London: Bloomsbury, pp. 29–48.
119 Hamada, K. and Chiba, T. 1914. The late Professor Tsuboi and Egyptology in Japan. *Ancient Egypt* 1914: 59–60.
120 Nakano, T. (ed.) 2016. *Catalogue of the Egyptian collection in the Kyoto University Museum / 京都大学総合博物館考古学資料目録エジプト出土資料*. Kyoto: Kyoto University Press.
121 S.E. 1938. Hamada Kosaku (1881–1938) *Harvard Journal of Asiatic Studies* 3(3/4): 407–29.
122 Nakano, T. 2016. Small pieces can tell: the richness and diversity of the Kyoto university museum's Egyptian collection. *Proceedings of the International Symposium on From Petrie to Hamada. Egyptian Antiquities of Kyoto University*. Kyoto: Kyoto University, pp. 28–31.
123 Undated draft of letter from Emily Paterson, EES.COR, probably dated February 1911.
124 Undated draft of letter from Emily Paterson, EES.COR, probably dated February 1911.
125 Sayce, A. 1923. *Reminiscences*. London: Macmillan.
126 Hamada and Chiba, The late Professor Tsuboi.
127 Lockyer, A. 2008 National Museums and other cultures in modern Japan. In Sherman, D. J. (ed.) *Museums and Difference*. Bloomington: Indiana University Press, p. 104.
128 Letter from Hamada to Petrie, 9 November 1922, PMA/WFP1/D/24/57/2.
129 From subsidiary grave 387, see Petrie, W. M. F. 1922. *Tombs of the Courtiers*. London: British School of Archaeology in Egypt.
130 Hamada, K. 1923. Egyptian archaeological objects that has recently arrived at the Kyoto Imperial University. *Shirin* 8(1): 131 [in Japanese].
131 Hamada, K. 1923. Excavations in Egypt and their archaeological results. *Taiyo* 29(5) [in Japanese].

132 Hamada, Egyptian archaeological objects, p. 39.
133 Hamada, Egyptian archaeological objects, p. 39.
134 The Japan-Korea Annexation Treaty was signed in 1910.
135 Sayce, A. *Reminiscences*, p. 383.
136 Il Pai, H. 2010. Resurrecting the ruins of Japan's mythical homelands: colonial archaeological surveys in the Korean Peninsula and heritage tourism. In Lydon, J. and Rizvi, U. Z. (eds.) *Handbook of Postcolonial Archaeology*. London and New York: Routledge, pp. 93–112.
137 Kawai, N. 2017. Egyptological landscape in Japan: past, present, and future. *CiPEG Journal* 1: 51–9. These visits to Egypt were written up in a series of articles for the Japanese *Journal of Archaeology* (考古学雑誌), which at the time of writing were not available for consultation. With thanks to Tomoaki Nakono for the information.
138 Swenson, A. 2013. The heritage of Empire. In Swenson, A. and Mandler, P. (eds.) *From Plunder to Preservation: Britain and the Heritage of Empire, c.1800–1940*. Oxford: Oxford University Press, pp. 12–15.
139 Mizoguchi, K. 2004. Identity, modernity, and archaeology: the case of Japan. In Meskell, L. and Preucel, R. W. (eds.) *A Companion to Social Archaeology*. Oxford: Blackwell Publishing, p. 403.
140 From a postscript to Okajima's last article, published after his death in 1949 and written by Kazunosuke Murata. Cited in Nishimura, Y. and Miyagawa, N. 2017. An early history of Egyptology in Japan with a focus on philological studies. In Langer, C. (ed.) *Global Egyptology: Negotiations in the Production of Knowledges on Ancient Egypt in Global Context*. London: Golden House Publications, p. 150.
141 Okajima, S. 1940. *A History of Egypt*. Tokyo: Heibonsya [in Japanese].
142 Kyoto University 2016. *Proceedings of the International Symposium on From Petrie to Hamada*. University of Kyoto: Kyoto.
143 Adam, *Transnational Philanthropy*, p. 240.
144 Ellis, H. 2017. Collaboration and knowledge exchange between scholars in Britain and the Empire, 1830–1914. In Jöns, H., Meusbruger, P. and Heffernan, M. (eds.) *Mobilities of Knowledge*. Dordrecht: Springer, pp. 141–55.
145 contra. Mackenzie, *Museums and Empire*, p. 266.
146 Hill, K. 2005. *Cultural and Class in English Public Museums, 1850–1914*. London: Ashgate, p. 125.

Chapter 4
A Golden Age? (1922–1939): Collecting in the Shadow of Tutankhamun

'Gold – everywhere the glint of gold'.[1] That was how the awestruck Howard Carter theatrically described the moment he first caught a glimpse of Tutankhamun's treasures. The things he saw were a far cry from the little faience shabtis, the infinitesimal sets of beads and the bulky ceramic vessels that had previously formed the mainstay of British archaeological finds from Egypt. These spectacular discoveries in the Valley of the Kings created new expectations of what constituted archaeological objects, and the public's appetite grew for the sorts of 'wonderful things' Carter's team were documenting. Yet 'minor antiquities', field documents and plaster copies of art works were increasingly all that was available to foreign excavators for export following post-war geopolitical shifts.

Nine months before Carter opened the boy king's tomb, the British Government issued a unilateral declaration of Egyptian independence. The coincidence of the discovery of Tutankhamun's tomb with these developments was profound. A Pharaonist vision of the past in literature and the arts, *al-firawniya*, now converged with a national liberation movement led by the non-sectarian Wafd Party under Saad Zaghloul (1859–1927). With the protectorate abolished, the Director-General of Egypt's Antiquities Service, Pierre Lacau (1873–1963), began tightening previously existing antiquities laws, aligning them more strongly with the nationalist sensibilities of Egyptian politicians who demanded that Egyptians control the administration of antiquities. Lacau's amendments included addressing the provision relating to the division of finds, and in place of a fifty-fifty split between the Cairo Museum and the excavator, it was announced that the Service would claim everything found. Any concessions of material to foreign expeditions would be discretionary. Carter's financial sponsor, Lord Carnarvon, initially believed that the partage agreements that had existed between the British and Egyptian authorities would continue to apply as they always had done. He wrote excitedly to Alan Gardiner in the wake of the discovery of Tutankhamun's tomb, declaring that 'there is enough stuff to fill the whole Egyptian section upstairs of the B.M. [British Museum].'[2] In the end, Egypt retained title to all of the tomb's contents, and nothing left Egypt, at least not legally.[3]

An American front vociferously contested Lacau's plans,[4] and the British Joint Archaeological Committee portentously issued a series of memorandums challenging it.[5] Flinders Petrie, decrying the new situation as 'farcical',[6] eventually quit working in Egypt altogether and moved to Palestine, where he believed British Mandate authorities would be more accommodating. Diplomatic correspondence circulated furiously between offices, societies and museums in London and Cairo, exposing a wider range of views on the situation.[7] These included those of a minority, such as Cecil Firth (1878–1931), who were sympathetic to 'Egypt's legitimate claim to resist undue spoliation by the Museums of America and Europe',[8] but also many, such as Sir Alan Gardiner, who were more rarely in Egypt but who were vocal in their desire to see its antiquities remain closer to home.[9] Generally speaking, this period was one of growing ambivalence towards the idea that it was primarily Western specialists who were entitled to Egyptian antiquities.[10]

In the midst of these debates, the renamed Egypt Exploration Society (EES) attempted to forge ahead with excavations at the site of Tell el-Amarna. More than 3000 years previously the site had been the setting for the short-lived capital of the so-called 'heretical king' Akhenaten, his queen Nefertiti and a royal child known then as Tutankhaten. Worldwide media attention had generated new audiences and fresh opportunities for sponsoring this work, but in lieu of the quantities of exportable finds previously taken for granted by missions, the EES had to find alternative strategies for satisfying museum demand. The deliberations on how to manage this situation emerge more clearly from the EES's archives than do administrative matters before the war, being laid bare in a richer and more varied series of documents that reveal the huge network of people that the practice of distribution necessitated. These archives are a reminder of the quotidian administrative burden that characterized large-scale expeditions – expense receipts, packing labels, telegrams and customs documents – all of which appear, at first glance, to be historically banal. It is here, however, that Steven Shapin's 'invisible technicians' give pause for thought.[11] Shapin's call for historians of science to pay attention to the skilled artisans who collaborated closely with scholars raises the possibility that studying the interventions of people other than archaeologists and curators is not only relevant, but also vital for understanding how knowledge about the past is created. Taking account of this wider network of actors provides a means of understanding relationships among different sorts of work, the socially organized ways of comprehending the status of antiquities, and the distinctive interests of particular professional groups, such as secretaries and museum restorers, who had a significant impact on archaeological practices and values. It also, more simply, stands as a corrective to media features typical of the period which celebrated 'the men who do the spadework of history',[12] but gave little credit to anyone else.

The 1920s and 1930s are often referred to as a 'Golden Age' for archaeology. This was a period of heightened interest, not just in ancient Egypt, but also in other regions within colonial reach, such as at Ur of the Chaldees and at Mohenjo-Daro in the Indus Valley, where archaeological revelations were being announced to worldwide acclaim. In the Middle East, much of this was facilitated by the League of Nations grant of Class A mandates of Iraq[13] and Palestine to Great Britain, where partage principles were eagerly extended and rewarded. Yet, as Stephanie Moser has argued, it was not major discoveries in isolation that led to particularly intensive engagements with archaeological finds.[14] Rather, these were further enabled by the interaction between existing visual traditions of representation, developing academic discourse and currents in popular culture. It is notable, then, that coincident with such discoveries was a new generation of popularizers who capitalized on archaeology's increasing profile[15] among a public that was itself responding to, and being transformed by, modern ways of consuming culture during the roaring twenties and depressed thirties. The threads of consumerism and modernism affected the ways in which Egyptian antiquities and archaeological materials were framed, both in museum practice and in wider society. One of the repercussions of these popular receptions of the past was a more concerted effort by an emerging community of professional archaeologists – largely prehistorians – to set themselves apart. As academic identities became more firmly rooted in universities, museums were cast adrift from the business of producing new knowledge about the world as they sought to engage more with the public. By focusing on aspects of these decades that have historically been neglected – the invisible technicians, administrative documents and replica objects – this chapter charts some of the conceptual fault lines that ran through the inter-war years, and the new sorts of labour that had to be invested in order to 'make things talk'.[16]

Amarna: Between Expectation and Reality

The EES was quick to take advantage of the press frenzy surrounding discoveries in the Valley of the Kings to market its newest concession: Tell el-Amarna, the centre of Akhenaten's cult of the sun disc, or Aten. They did so with the promise to supply museums with 'treasures', as in this funding campaign launched in *The Times* on 22 February 1923:

> Those of your readers who are impressed by the magnitude of the splendour of the discovery at Thebes and by the beauty of the German finds at Amarna, are asked to help in discovering similar treasures, if it be possible, for our national and local museums in Britain and America.[17]

It was a site with enormous public appeal, enhanced further by the fact that Britain had reclaimed the concession from 'our enemies in the late war':

> The shifting of the concession for the excavation of the site of Tell el-Amarna from the German Orient Society to our Anglo-American organization enables this important work to proceed without delay and assures to British and American Museums antiquities of an important and interesting class that have hitherto gone to Berlin.[18]

The characters who populated the ancient urban landscape of Amarna have been subject to some of the most intense speculation in world history. The pharaoh Akhenaten, who founded the town of Amarna around 1348 BC, is an ambiguous and compelling historical figure who has had an expansive cultural afterlife since the late nineteenth century.[19] He has been variously identified as a heretic, a visionary, a false prophet, a revolutionary, an icon and a madman. His chief wife, Queen Nefertiti, became iconic in the 1920s with the controversial display of her famous bust in Berlin. Amarna art was captivating, and a striking departure from many pharaonic canons of representation. It was perceived to be more naturalistic than other periods of Egyptian visual culture, and many of the most characteristic pieces are scenes of the natural world or of the daily life of the royal family, themselves shown with exaggerated, elongated features (Fig 4.1).

The EEF undertook fifteen seasons of excavations at Amarna from 1921 until 1937, under the leadership of several directors, distributing at least 7500 artefacts to around 74 institutions.[20] The mission was at

Fig. 4.1 Relief carving showing Akhenaten and Nefertiti, found during the Egypt Explorations Society's 1926–7 excavations at Amarna. Courtesy of the Egypt Exploration Society (TA.NEG.26-27-073).

first buoyed by press coverage in the months following the discovery of Tutankhamun's tomb and more than 100 new individuals subscribed to the EES in that first year, bringing membership up to it highest pre-Second World War level. However, in contrast to the jubilant and optimistic 1923 report, which basked in the widespread interest in Egypt occasioned by the discovery of the tomb of Tutankhamun, the subsequent annual general meeting was downbeat. The Amarna campaign was described as 'tragic', and following changes to antiquities legislation imminent it was asserted that

> …it would obviously be impossible to maintain public interest in excavations without antiquities to show for them and to present to museums, so that we were faced with the alarming possibility that we might have to close down excavations altogether.[21]

Such a response seems histrionic in hindsight, but the phrasing underscores the deep seated belief that a co-dependency existed between museums and archaeological fieldwork.

In addition to the political uncertainties surrounding the excavation, the dig director, Francis G. Newton (1878–1924), had died mid-season after a short illness. The finds that had been recovered were described in the annual report as disappointing, and the 1925–26 season was cancelled. Not that the finds from the previous year were felt to have been any better. The curator of Bristol Museum and Art Gallery, Herbert Bolton (1863–1936), grumbled that he was 'disappointed, not only in the quality, but also in the general character of the things which we received', and he asked the EES to help him acquire additional antiquities through local dealers in order to fill gaps in Bristol's collection.[22] American institutions were similarly quick to express derision over their allotted share. The City Art Museum in St Louis moaned that the objects were 'of such a character that we do not care to exhibit most of them',[23] while the Director of Penn Museum stated quite frankly that:

> ...with regard to the smaller objects, namely, the faience amulets, beads, etc. I feel that it is right that I should say that we hope we shall never receive another allotment of this kind. The accumulation of these objects in the Museum has been so great for many years that we have been trying unsuccessfully to give large quantities of them away to smaller museums who may not be already provided. You will realise, therefore, that to add to our stock is only an embarrassment for us.[24]

The 1925–26 season led to even more objections. The EES, in its annual report for that year, confessed that it had 'fared badly' in the division, with the Egyptian Department of Antiquities 'seizing' the majority of the finds. The importance of delivering on the promise of finds was becoming ever more apparent, because despite the spread of 'Egyptomania' in fashion, art and cinema, interest in the Society was waning. The Secretary for the American Branch of the EES, Marie Buckman, reported just three years after the opening of Tutankhamun's tomb that, 'there is falling off in subscriptions… Museums will not contribute to such a "dig" as represents a Governmental task of scientific and historical value only'.[25]

The starkest dissonance of all between expectation and reality, however, was in Australia. On New Year's Eve 1923, Sydney's *Sunday Times* newspaper threw a lavish luncheon, sponsored by its editor, the colourful Hugh 'Huge Deal' McIntosh (1876–1942) – former boxing promoter, theatre owner and now state official. The feast was attended by a number of influential men who had expressed their interest in the formation of an Australian branch of the Egypt Exploration Society. On the guest list was William A. Holman (1871–1934), the former premier of New South Wales, together with a group of managing directors and chairmen of prominent Australian businesses. Various speeches loftily pronounced the 'enlightenment which archaeological exploration and research afforded to modern education and science', how 'Australia would from now on assist in a small way in helping this magnificent work', and that the 'establishment of an Australian Branch of the parent Society was an epoch in the history of Australia'.[26] Five days later, McIntosh sent a telegram from Melbourne to London declaring that he was forming a branch society and that it was receiving enthusiastic support.[27] The managing directors of Albert's Music Warehouse, Henderson's Hat company and Australia's Kodak Limited were all on board, and their cheque books were being held at the ready. By July there were seventy-odd members, and McIntosh promised £500 a year for the next seven years on the condition that a third of all 'treasures' discovered by the EES were to be given to Australia to distribute among various museums. Clearly enamoured by the discovery of Tutankhamun's tomb in the Valley of the Kings, the group held inflated expectations that their support of the EES was a relationship that could guarantee for Australia equivalent riches through which their own wealth and status would be reflected in hues of glittering gold and lapis lazuli blue. They would be sorely disappointed.

Amid all of the giddy excitement at the prospect of securing ancient treasures, worries began to surface as political realities set in. A telegram sent from Melbourne to London on 15 January 1924 expressed

> uneasiness here amongst subscribers to our fund over Egypt Government attitude stop unless we can some definite statement that Australias [sic] proportion of discoveries will be permitted leave Egypt will most seriously affect our future subscriptions. Can society cable me some authorities statement for publication?[28]

The EES committee could not. It reassured McIntosh that 'so long as this law stands we can guarantee a fair division to all subscribing parties, and should the law be altered, and no finds be allowed to leave the country the Committee feels that the only course open might be to abandon excavations'.[29] The newest branch of the EES seemed to be satisfied by this response, and the group waited in anticipation of their rewards. McIntosh's *Sunday Times* had been running stories since 1923, stoking hopes with headlines such as 'Treasures of Egypt' (3 Feb 1924), and a front page splash 'Treasures for our Museums' (20 May 1923, Figure 4.2).

The second annual meeting of the EES's Australian branch was held on 12 March 1925. Two cases of antiquities from London were 'solemnly opened' in front of an excited, well-heeled crowd. Inside was a profusion of material: the sole of a sandal, a bronze needle, a fragment of blue glazed pottery, a mould for a rosette and a faience cluster of grapes. The next morning a letter was dispatched to London:

Fig. 4.2 Report in the Australian *Sunday Times* of Lord Carnarvon's death and treasure for museums, 20 May 1923. Reproduced with permission of the Griffith Institute, University of Oxford.

We had visions of carved slabs, whole specimens of painting and pottery, and had in anticipation some preliminary steps had been taken with a view of holding a public exhibition... the actual contents of the cases, it was felt, made such exhibition quite out of the question and disappointment and dissatisfaction were expressed without disguise.[30]

Resignations from the EES Australian Branch followed, and McIntosh failed to make good on his promise of further financial support. The *Sunday Times* published a perfunctory note, 'Relics of old Egypt', in its 22 March 1925 edition, which made no reference to any objects. It simply informed readers that two cases had been opened and that the contents 'will in due course be distributed amongst the contributing museums'. The EES secretary, Mary Jonas, wrote with concern the following year, enquiring after the lack of communications from the Australian branch. Nevertheless, she dutifully dispatched five further cases of antiquities filled with objects from the EES's other mission at Abydos. The Australian branch, Jonas counselled, had 'been extremely generously treated'.[31] The damage, however, had been done, and the Australian branch was quietly disbanded.

Contemporary Antiquities

Even if the Australian branch did not anticipate exceptional golden treasures of the sort the Tutankhamun excavation team was extracting, they had certainly expected something more aesthetically arresting than what they received. As Dominic Montserrat has shown, Akhenaten and Nefertiti's world had by the 1920s come to symbolize wealth, luxury and an extravagant lifestyle.[32] 'Tutmania' appropriated Amarna motifs to market a range of aspirational commodities, from sumptuous evening bags to ornate cigarette cases. Egyptian patterns and themes infused Art Deco-styled architectural embellishments. The cinematic ambience of Egypt in Hollywood blockbusters was replete with set dressings dripping with golden jewellery and fine costumes. They were at odds with the dusty pottery, crumpled leather sandals and chipped faience goods that had arrived in Australia.

Further fuelling anticipation of Egyptian glamour was the media, through which the public consumed archaeological details. While *The Times* newspaper initially had exclusive rights to publishing accounts from Tutankhamun's tomb, it was the *Illustrated London News (ILN)* that acted as the primary media agent for the dissemination of images from the work.

The *ILN* also helped to popularize the EES's work at Amarna. The *ILN* was one of the few general weekly periodicals, targeted towards the middle classes and circulated throughout the empire, that consistently reported archaeological discoveries. It framed its accounts within a rich collage of illustrations and display ads promoting consumer products such as silverware, tea, jewellery, furnishings, tobacco, alcohol and travel packages. The reading experience within which archaeological finds were shown domesticated, glamourized and contemporized them, a process that Eleanor Robson has described for the coverage of Layard's discoveries at Nimrud in the previous century.[33] In a similar manner, these representations of Amarna were placed into a cultural dialogue with fragments of the modern consumer world that vied for readers' attention. Australia's business leaders undoubtedly hoped to tap into this ecology of images.

There were other social trends that altered object habits towards antiquities at this time, most notably the modernist movement and an international art market that had turned more decisively toward non-European things in the aftermath of the First World War.[34] Whereas in Berlin Nefertiti's bust had been set firmly within the canon of European art, modernists now sought to disrupt the received wisdom of elite art education that had elevated Classical works above all others, by experimenting with a range of cultural representations from Oceania, Asia and Africa. Many pioneer modernists, from Pablo Picasso to Jacob Epstein, largely ignored context in favour of direct artistic appreciation. It was a position that contrasted with those museum and archaeological efforts which tried to anchor archaeological finds scientifically within particular settings or typological sequences. For many modernists, the removal of context was a prerequisite for forging deeper, unmediated connections to artworks. Such a sentiment is evident in a 1924, two-verse work by modernist poet Marianne Moore (1887–1972) entitled 'An Egyptian Pulled Glass Bottle in the Shape of a Fish', a poem celebrating art itself. It had been inspired by the *ILN*'s account of a newly excavated polychrome glass vessel from Amarna in the EES's annual London exhibition, and opens with the verse:[35]

> Here we have thirst
> and patience, from the first
> and art, as in a wave held up for us to see[36]

The sculptor Henry Moore (1898–1986) was similarly captivated by Egyptian material. During the 1920s he was a frequent visitor to the British Museum, where he admired 'the monumentality of vision' and the 'timelessness' of Egyptian sculpture.[37] Objects like the Old Kingdom painted limestone statue of Nenkheftka (2450 BC), recovered during Petrie's 1897 excavations at Deshasheh, and a New Kingdom cow head made of calcite (c. 1450 BC), found by EEF-sponsored teams at Deir el-Bahri in 1905, were direct inspirations for his own creations.[38] Henry Moore's friend, Jacob Epstein, was equally attentive to Egyptian art, and he is known to have visited the EES's Amarna exhibition held at the Wellcome Historical Medical Museum in 1933.[39] Jamaican artist Ronald Moody (1900–1984) was, like Henry Moore, 'transfixed' by the Egyptian sculptures he encountered in the British Museum. This influence can be observed in Moody's wooden carving *Johanaan*, which was included in the 1935 Pall Mall exhibition 'Negro Art', and again at the 1939 show in Baltimore.[40] Here Moody's work resonated with the modernist African American Harlem Renaissance, an artistic and intellectual movement that fostered new black cultural identities in the 1920s and 1930s. It too embraced ancient Egyptian themes as part of a broader endeavour to reclaim histories of African civilizations.[41] In turn, this cultural milieu informed how ancient finds were visualized. When, for instance, the EES publicized temple reliefs at Armant, it was reported by *New York Times* correspondent Joseph M. Levy, with the headline 'fine carvings excavated at Erment [sic] show negroes in Harlem Dance attitudes.'[42]

Detached from the archaeological field, these 'timeless' Egyptian forms circulated freely in other contexts where they were mixed within a wider contemporary aesthetic made up of medieval, pre-Columbian, Oceanian and other African sculptures 'apart from time and space'.[43] Yet because of these extrications, artistic interest in aspects of ancient Egypt rarely translated back into a substantial engagement with archaeological practice, nor into sizeable support for enterprises like the EES. A fascination with Egyptian-inspired themes was a sign of being modern, not an indicator of archaeological interest.

***

By the 1930s, Tutankhamun and Nefertiti were household names, fully enmeshed in twentieth-century popular culture. So much so that when the EES announced its discovery in 1933 of an unfinished quartzite sculpture at Amarna, it was reported in a special two-page spread of the 25 June 1933 edition of *The New York Times* under the headline 'Nefertiti: A Modern Woman of 1375 BC'. Almost nothing of what was found in the field was accounted for in the article, which relied instead upon a selection of tropes that fuelled hyperrealist representations of Egypt.

Such public enthusiasm was, however, fundamentally important to the EES, and throughout its history the organization was confronted by a sometimes contradictory need both to capitalize on and distance itself from variously well- or poorly-informed public perceptions of its work, and ancient Egypt more broadly. In the 1920s and 1930s the society, despite campaigning in sensationalist terms, continued to defend its scientific record to museum curators, pleading with them that it

> … must not be judged by the return in objects only… the digging for treasure only would be a simple work, and entail less expense and less educated labour, but such is not the object of our society, we have always prided ourselves on systematic work, clearing and planning each piece uncovered as work proceeds and not scampering from point to point in the search for special treasures.[44]

Try as it might, however, the pressure to satisfy public demand did affect the Society's activities in the field. The search for museum-quality objects led to numerous archaeological finds being left unrecorded on site, as became clear during the 1980s when the waste heaps left by the teams that had been excavated sixty years previously were examined. Other objects which were recorded at the time, but for which no museum destination is now known, are likely to have been reburied on site.[45]

By retaining a focus on the retrieval of museum-quality objects, the EES was able to attract some fresh audiences and new organizations, who ultimately kept its operations afloat despite 'alarmingly low' membership numbers and a steadily declining base.[46] The East Anglia Egypt Society was one such organization whose support benefited Norwich Castle Museum, while Paisley Museum in Scotland also appears on the distribution ledgers for the first time. In the US, the wealthy American philanthropist Ellen Browning Scripps (1836–1932) emerged as a prominent sponsor whose charitable giving extended to schools, hospitals and zoological organizations. She began donating to the EEF in 1911, and her commitment to the Society throughout the 1920s ensured that San Diego's Museum was rewarded with substantial donations for the first time, amounting to some 450 artefacts over the years. Scripps contributed more than $9,000 directly to the Society during her lifetime and after her death through a bequest.[47] Indeed, when the economic crisis of the late 1920s led to the suspension of archaeological work at Amarna, it was Scripps's bequest to the EES, with its annual interest from a $10,000 endowment, that ensured that the excavations could continue into the 1930s.

The EES now also entertained subscriptions from non-educational groups and private bodies. One of the more unusual requests came from the Indiana Limestone Quarryman's Association, which asked for 'several blocks of the various kinds of limestone used for the rough building work, as well as for exterior finish; and a couple specimens of the carved exterior work'.[48] The Society likewise could not refuse the opportunity to take private funding with the promise of personal recompense for individuals rather than museums, despite its long-standing principle that work would not reward people directly in this way. For instance, the name John Jacob Astor, owner of *The Times* newspaper, appears on a 1925 document headed 'Tell el Amarna distributions', his having donated £50.[49] What he received, and where those objects are now, if indeed they were sent, is unknown.

Nevertheless, the EES was still faced with overwhelming dissatisfaction from sponsors, and so the Society turned to alternative strategies to placate them. One solution was to raid their stores for material left over from excavations conducted up to twenty years previously, such as Naville's missions at Deir el-Bahri. Regrettably, information on archaeological context had frequently been lost by this time. A second course of action was to employ restorers to salvage what they could from the broken things that continued to seep past the tussles with Egypt's Antiquities Service over finer artefacts. Alternatively, reproductions could be commissioned. Following Shapin, the individuals involved in these processes of restoration, administration and reproduction need not be viewed simply as labourers whose activities were ancillary to scientific practice. Their intercessions could ultimately be decisive in the processes of creating object value and ensuring the onward trajectories of original objects and their replicas.

Restoration

Archaeology and restoration developed in tandem, but how these practices sit alongside intellectual developments and the formation of professional identities has attracted little comment. In the field there was an immediate need for excavators to intervene, since artefacts extracted from the ground and exposed to modern environments could deteriorate rapidly. Petrie was well aware of the dangers. He developed his own set of techniques to deal with the small finds that had previously been ignored by museums, techniques which he advocated in a paper presented to the Royal Archaeological Institute in 1888 and in a dedicated chapter of his 1904 manual, *Methods and Aims in Archaeology*.[50] Such publications describe his use of paraffin wax, tapioca and shellac for the preservation of delicate and fragmentary objects. That these interventions could be crucial for the conceptualization and construction of archaeological objects was recognized by chemist Alfred Lucas (1867–1945), who worked on material from Tutankhamun's tomb. Lucas noted that efforts to conserve finds scientifically 'enable[d] objects to be photographed, described, and more particularly packed and transported in safety'.[51] In other words, these techniques were often vital for the viability of the distribution project, with restoration the prerequisite for furthering other material, professional and social relationships.

General Pitt-Rivers, the famous museum founder, collector and field archaeologist, had similarly sought to place 'practical knowledge' at the heart of a new degree programme in anthropology (then including archaeology) at the University of Oxford. He advised in 1882, for instance, that students

> Should have a practical knowledge of the mode of preserving bone in various stages of decomposition, as well as iron, and soft wet wooden objects so as to prevent their cracking in the process of drying.[52]

The protean nature of subjects like archaeology allowed such options to be trialled as possible components of disciplinary knowledge and expertize, but ultimately restoration did not fully develop as a staple part of archaeological training. This may have been because there was in large institutions already a niche for restorers and copyists, whose work was placed into a different set of relationships to those who operated in the field. At this time, the work of such specialists was not simply equivalent to what is now known as conservation, the professionalization of which began in the 1930s and which has preventative care at its heart, rather than restoration. Instead, nationally styled museums in the mid-to-late nineteenth century employed men simply to clean, mend and mount objects for immediate display. Several generations of the Ready family were employed to these ends at the British Museum. William Talbot Ready (1857–1914), in addition to being a restorer, was also a collector and dealer, meaning that taste and connoisseurship were as key to his trade as handiwork.[53] This role blurred his relationship with the museum, and when he left their employment to concentrate on his business, the British Museum acquired objects through him, while his brother, Augustus P. Ready, took over restoration duties. Nevertheless, these roles were distinctive enough from curation in large organizations, and perhaps also circumscribed by class prejudice and assumptions concerning manual versus intellectual labour, that they form a parallel track in the institutionalization of professional identities.

William H. Young,[54] formator, electrotypist and restorer at the Ashmolean Museum, was one of the technicians enlisted by the EES. He started his career at the British Museum with the Ready family in the late nineteenth century, but was brought to Oxford in 1900 to clean and mend objects, as well as to form plaster casts of seals and gems. As a new Ashmolean employee he undertook considerable restoration work on finds from Knossos for Sir Arthur Evans, in a specially designed laboratory set up at great expense in the museum's basement. He reconstructed several iconic and unique artefacts in the Ashmolean, which in the Egyptian section notably included the princess fresco from Amarna, recovered by Petrie's teams in 1892, and the Hierakonpolis ceremonial maceheads (Fig. 4.3), found during an ERA-funded mission in the late 1890s. Young's name turns up in several academic papers where he is

Fig. 4.3 Predynastic ceremonial mace-head excavated at Hierakonpolis in 1897–8 (museum number AN.1896-1908/E3632-a), reconstructed by Ashmolean restorer W. H. Young. Image © Ashmolean Museum, University of Oxford.

credited with restoring various artefacts, and in at least one instance there is an indication that archaeologists relied, not only upon his practical skills, but also upon his knowledge and judgement for interpretation.[55] His interventions are not just visible in the published literature, but also clearly detectable on the objects he worked on. Many of the artefacts he reassembled or reproduced can today be identified by the notation 'ΝΕΟΣ', pencilled or etched discreetly onto them (Fig. 4.4).[56] The imposition of Young's own identity upon these ancient artefacts, alongside marks made by others, such as the excavators, suggests that he took great pride in his work. It additionally stakes a claim for his labour in the laboratory being on a par with that undertaken in the field. The excavator's marks made fragments archaeological, while Young's made them museological. There were various styles of restoration in the nineteenth century, much of it excessive where art was concerned, but compulsions instigated by the Arts and Crafts movement had encouraged lighter touch approaches in order to respect the work of original craftsmen.[57] In contrast, Young's inscriptions can be seen as a form of resistance to the anonymizing character of restoration, which for him was not simply about reversing damage, but about becoming part of the object's history. He was also not averse to the extensive use of plaster to reconstitute extremely fragmentary relics into complete artworks for display, often on the basis of only a single sherd.[58] In these ways his work was creative and imaginative.

Fig. 4.4 (i) Plaster cast of a Badarian ivory figurine made by Ashmolean restorer W. H. Young now in the Petrie Museum of Egyptian Archaeology (museum number UC19638); (ii) a second copy of the same figurine from the National Museum of Scotland, shown here with Young's trademark signature, NEOS, inscribed on base (museum number A.1926.722). The original is in the British Museum (museum number EA59648).

In the 1920s, Young was particularly active for both Petrie's British School of Archaeology (BSAE) [59] and the EES, perhaps with help from his son William, who followed him into the business. In 1925, the EES asked him to piece together twelve painted pottery vessels from Amarna to improve the lots assigned to the British Museum, Chadwick Museum (Bolton), Bristol Museum and Art Gallery, Glasgow Kelvingrove Museum, the Auckland Institute, Wellington's Dominion Museum, the Brooklyn Museum and the Australian branch of the EES (Fig. 4.5).[60] In addition

Fig. 4.5 Amarna vase (museum number AN.1926.109-a) restored by the Ashmolean Museum's restorer W. H. Young. Image ©Ashmolean Museum, University of Oxford.

to mending the objects, Young was tasked with commissioning crates and administering all of the international export paperwork. He needed to negotiate with timber merchants and crate construction firms, whose charges, he once commented, were excessive.[61] That his role was pivotal rather than incidental becomes clearer in a series of missives concerning a vase for Manchester Museum. The EES conveyed to Young the desire of Assistant Keeper of Egyptology, Winifred Crompton, for 'very first class specimens';[62] anything less was pointless and should not be sent. If any pieces could not be mended satisfactorily, Young was to destroy the remaining fragments.[63] The exchange indicates the EES's confidence not just in Young's manual labour, but in his ability to discern between what constituted a first class object and what was waste.

The status of these fragments as either antiquities, archaeological specimens, museum objects, commodities or waste should be seen in a broader context. In the field, the sherds had been deemed potential museum specimens, with the excavation team perhaps erring on the side of optimism that these sorts of finds were more likely to be granted an export licence than unique pieces, given new state restrictions. In contrast, on their arrival into Britain, the value of these fragmentary finds was set against a series of other considerations. These included balancing expectations of the aesthetic display of striking artefacts against the costs of restoration, timber, transport and bureaucracy. Young was the decisive node in evaluating the status of these finds as they passed through his laboratory. Any decision he then made initiated a chain of further logistical interventions from the packers, shippers, secretaries and museum administrators in London and beyond.

Administration

On the other side of the correspondence with Young was the EES secretary, Mary C. Jonas (1874–1950). She had taken over the position from the long-serving Emily Paterson in 1919, and remained dedicated to the role for twenty years. Her efficient, typewritten dispatches could easily be dismissed as basic administrative work. She organized meetings, managed project budgets and liaised with museums, subscribers and field directors. Her interventions merit greater recognition, however, for she was the diplomatic pivot around which competing views on the significance and nature of archaeological finds for museum acquisition were balanced. While museum curators berated her for the objects dispatched and implored her for better returns, she emphasized the serendipitous nature of archaeological fieldwork and the significance of scientific efforts. A more attentive reading of the archive also reveals that through these activities Jonas developed a keen sensitivity to the needs of not just the archaeological record, but also of museum practice.

Amid the lively correspondence Jonas maintained with her more flamboyant North American counterpart, Marie Buckman, she described her efforts in managing the distribution of antiquities. In one letter she explains how she was keen 'to make my record as complete as possible, even to the tiny beads etc. so that if any question ever arose we can at once say where each specimen is now located'.[64] Her American colleague was deeply appreciative of Jonas's labels and her lists of objects 'which had not been previously sent with consignments'.[65] Jonas therefore instigated more conscientious archival practices, focused on records rather than, for example, accountability to sponsors. These initiatives have also had a longer term impact, because archaeology does not simply rely on immediate discoveries. Like other forms of scientific practice, it involves creating the foundations for ongoing interpretive work and passing on to the future evidence that can be scrutinized at a later date. Jonas's records permit that ongoing project of archaeological contextualization to be fulfilled in ways that would not have been possible otherwise. Her work also provided institutions with the documentation needed to produce robust museum objects, aligning in this way with the future-making practices of curators.

Jonas's efforts can also be read against a background in which antiquities laws were redefining cultural property, resulting in a new emphasis on empirical data over archaeological specimens that were harder to acquire. The British might no longer have been able to export finds in the way that they wanted, but they had full control over the intellectual products of excavation, namely the field notes and photographs that were organized back at the metropole, often in the London office of the EES. The object cards created at Amarna, for instance, were later annotated with additional information, most probably by Jonas. Codes were applied to indicate any known museum destinations, and cross-referenced with other archival records (Fig. 4.6). This new focus on field records translated further into novel display methods, as most publicly visible at the EES's annual exhibitions that Jonas helped to set up (with occasional help from Emily Paterson, who continued to support the EES after her formal retirement). These exhibitions had, by the late 1920s and early 30s, become more dependent upon the use of models, photographs and watercolours, rather than ancient objects, to visualize archaeological fieldwork. For instance, at the 1931 EES

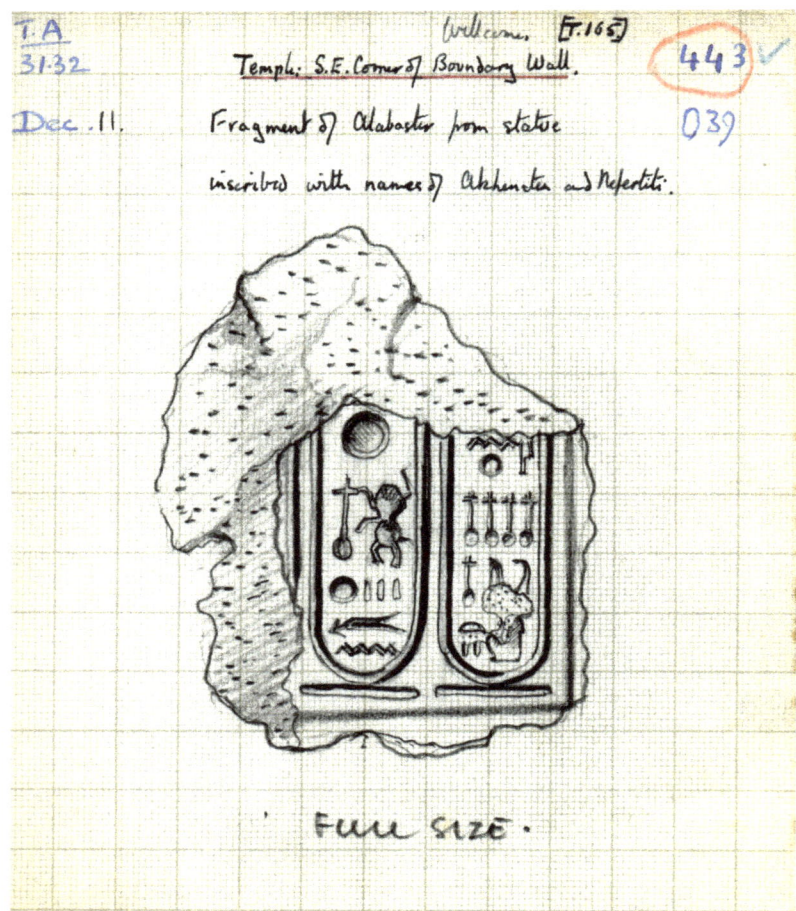

Fig. 4.6 Object card from Egypt Exploration Society's 1931–2 Tell el-Amarna excavations showing an object selected for the Wellcome Historical Medical Museum. Courtesy of the Egypt Exploration Society (TA.OC.31-32.443).

exhibition, hosted in the Wellcome Historical Medical Museum, the first exhibits encountered by visitors were three large maps, beyond which a cast of a carved and painted lintel had been erected, while in the centre of the exhibition space a model of an Amarna House was reconstructed to a scale of three centimetres to the metre.[66] These modes of representation in temporary exhibits pre-empted the post-war shift in public expectations of permanent museum display, in which there were fewer objects and more interpretation.[67]

The American branch secretary, Marie Buckman, intervened more directly with the products of fieldwork. On account of being at a greater remove from the central London Committee, she held a greater degree of autonomy than Jonas. And unlike Jonas she felt more indebted to demanding American museums, who she eagerly sought to appease. Reacting against the impoverished returns from the field sent to her in October 1923, Buckman resorted to taking matters into her own hands by undertaking restoration work on ancient textiles left over from an 1885 excavation of a Roman tomb, in this way attempting to improve the appeal of museum offerings. Crumpled in a box sent from London lay an array of exceptionally dusty and mouldy textiles that she brushed, painted with egg white and ironed between sheets of paper before dispatching to museums. Ten days later, a rash appeared, attributed to the effort of clearing the box of textiles, which spread across her face, neck and arms, while an inflamed throat led to difficulty swallowing. Walking was difficult for many months.[68] Her ill health continued into January 1925, when it was reported to the London office that she needed sustained medical treatment and special care.[69]

Reproduction

Mary Jonas experienced Egyptian archaeology from her office desk in London, Marie Buckman from her home in Boston. One EES secretary, however, took her administrative acumen to the field itself. Mary Chubb (1903–2003) had no previous aspirations to be an archaeologist, and had only taken employment as an assistant secretary with the EES as a means to pay for a course in sculpture. On a wet and cold London morning, while Chubb was rooting around in a box of antiquities in the Society's office basement, she was stopped in her tracks by a vibrant turquoise tile fragment encrusted with desert sand. Entranced, Chubb felt an overwhelming impulse to visit Egypt, and she suggested to 'the nice boss lady', Mary Jonas, that perhaps one member of each fieldwork team could take charge of 'the office work which obviously has to be done on a dig, but which is an entire waste of time for the Egyptologists themselves to have to stop and do'.[70] The EES Committee agreed, and in November 1930 Chubb joined the expedition under the leadership of its charismatic director, John Pendlebury (1904–1941). She made herself an indispensable part of the cadre of archaeologists at Amarna, taking responsibility for field accounts and reports, as well as undertaking registration of the objects discovered. Chubb vividly recounted her time at Amarna in a short book entitled *Nefertiti Lived Here*, the 1998 reprint of which includes a fresh introduction that credits her with 'setting new standards in archaeological publication' as a result of 'the organisation and clarity' that she brought to the expedition's records.[71] This is perhaps an overstatement. As the field records show, Chubb merely continued a well-established tradition of documentation under the guidance of Egyptologist H.W. Fairman (1907–82), albeit one that she had more time to commit to than others in previous seasons, and she did so competently. Where she certainly did have an innovative impact was in the material profile of the expedition's results.

Towards the end of the 1930–31 season, a rare find was made. Beneath the courtyard of an anciently abandoned house was a sealed pottery jar filled with a hoard of unworked ingots, bars of silver and gold, silver rings and a small figurine of Hittite design. Conscious that the little Hittite amulet would be 'swiped' by the Egyptian Museum, Chubb offered a novel solution. She had brought with her several dried cuttlefish obtained from her local London jeweller. These, she suggested, could be used to make a cast. By pressing the figurine between the halves of the soft insides of a dried cuttlefish an impression was formed, providing a mould that was then filled with melted-down gun cartridges to create a replica. When the original was selected by the Cairo Museum, it was Chubb's little duplicate that was exported to London and displayed at the annual exhibition. The ingots found with the figurine were also eventually transformed into casts. Egypt's Antiquities Service had permitted the EES to retain half of the precious metals from the hoard for export. The silver found its way into the British Museum, but most of the gold was sold to the Bank of England for £200 as bullion, and melted down.[72] All that remains of these ingots are some poor-quality painted plaster copies presented to the Petrie Museum of Egyptian Archaeology in London. [73] The existence and biographies of these replicas raises several questions. With the destruction of the originals, can such casts transcend their status as copies? Having been assimilated into the museum through formal acts of registration, were they now on par with the antiquities?

Casts have long held an ambivalent status within museums. As modern facsimiles they seemingly lack that elusive quality of authenticity and timelessness that antiquity confers. The tension between representing the absent and unobtainable through reproduction, on the one hand, and the desire to secure ownership of original works, on the other, was at the heart of heated early-twentieth-century disputes at several institutions, including London's South Kensington Museum[74] and the Boston Museum of Fine Arts (MFA). In a provocative 1904 article, Matthew Prichard (1865–

1936), Assistant Director of the Boston MFA, advocated a fresh approach to the arrangement of museums of art, one that would include expunging all 'mechanical vulgarities' – namely casts.[75] These 'trite reproductions', he argued, should not be displayed next to 'objects of inspiration'.[76] The MFA's Director, Edward Robinson (1858–1931), disagreed, suggesting rather that the cast collections needed to be enhanced as they were vital pedagogical tools. Boston's so-called 'Battle of the Casts' ultimately resulted in Robinson's resignation. He accepted the position of Assistant Director of the Metropolitan Museum of Art, but arrived just when the position of Curator of Casts was abolished. Reviews of this episode have taken the clash as a turning point in museums' use of reproductions.[77] It has been claimed that by 1910 'cast collections no longer had a role to play in museums',[78] and that 'cast collections held their "fine art" status well during most of the nineteenth century but began steadily to lose place through the twentieth'.[79] Such comments over-generalize from a literature focused almost exclusively on Classical collections or from a few prominent American museums or universities. In reviewing the histories of facsimiles of Egyptian and archaeological material, it is clear that museum relationships with cast collections were uneven but enduring.

In the 1920s and 1930s, a large number of plaster reproductions were included in the EES distributions. Archival correspondence confirms that these were warmly welcomed by museums in Canada, America, Britain and New Zealand.[80] In a letter to Charles Currelly at the Toronto Museum, for instance, Mary Jonas observed that

> Now that most museums are not averse to having casts of specially beautiful or interesting objects we feel sure that these will be acceptable, even though not antikas.[81]

These comments resonate with what might be considered something of a resurgence in the value and role of casts in museums in the late 1920s. In 1928, the Royal Commission on National Museums and Galleries proposed the establishment of a 'Museum of Casts', a suggestion that had been in circulation since the 1851 Great Exhibition at Crystal Palace, but was again attracting positive comment in some corners of the British press.[82] The following year, an exhibition of casts of works of art was arranged by the International Museums Office, a body formed by the International Committee on Intellectual Cooperation (ICIC) at the League of Nations in 1926. The show toured Cologne and Brussels, with some 400 specimens being sent by museums and casting workshops in Athens, Berlin, Brussels, Florence, London and Paris, including representations of Egyptian sculpture.[83] The purpose of the show was to demonstrate for 'educational bodies, in towns which have no original collections of works of art, what may be done in this field', and thereby enable them 'to form collections of casts which are necessary for the education and formation of public taste'.[84]

Education was also cited as a reason for the status of casts in London's Science Museum, although their functional emphasis here was different. The foregrounding of technical progress through object series meant that for the Science Museum, like in the Pitt Rivers, Wellcome Historical Medical and Petrie Museums, it was 'not necessary that all the exhibits should contain original specimens.'[85] Copies were perfectly acceptable until originals could be procured, and 'in the meantime, they fill important gaps'.[86] Throughout the 1920s and early 1930s, the director of the Science Museum, Henry Lyons (1864–1944), sent several requests to the EES for material to complete the 'early and primitive' portions of his expanding series of technological groups, with the appeal that 'if originals are not to be had good copies content me!'.[87] Moreover, he argued that, since 'I only want copies I shall not be competing with the regular Archaeological Museums.'[88] Whether the artefacts were original or not was irrelevant, because the concept of authenticity operated very differently in the Science Museum than in the art world. Fine art museums like Boston might have prized what Walter Benjamin famously termed the 'aura' of the ancient original, but for the Science Museum the standard of authenticity resided in the perceived capacity of an artefact to act as objective evidence. Casts were able to fulfil this capacity precisely because they were mechanically reproduced from the originals, not artistically rendered. Plaster copies, then, can be seen as emblematic of the different object habits that informed alternative museum ideologies in science and art.

Facsimiles afforded further benefits to museums. They could, for instance, allow institutions to respond quickly to transformations in public taste. This may have been why the British Museum acquired a copy of the Nefertiti bust very shortly after its unveiling in Berlin in 1924. Its display was said by *The Sphere* to be 'charming London' in November of that same year, 'drawing thousands to the British Museum'.[89] Institutions like the Free Public Museum in Liverpool and the Hancock Museum in Newcastle were keen to follow suit, and both promptly wrote to the British Museum to request casts of their own.[90] Bolton Museum informed Jonas that it also had a reproduction of Nefertiti from Berlin on display, and was keen for a 'small cast of the profile of Akhenaten' from the EES to place alongside it, to 'emphasise the peculiar physiognomy of this family'.

This would have been only one of many casts on show, it seems, since the curator, Thomas Midgely, commented that 'not only in the Egyptian collection, but throughout the museum we use reproductions'.[91]

Replicas were also a way of establishing and standardizing what constituted key pieces of art historical knowledge. To this end, Liverpool Museum spent a not insignificant 79 pounds and 16 shillings on twelve casts of sculptures from the V&A for instructive display, at least twenty of which were present in the galleries before the Second World War.[92] Twelve are described in a dedicated section on casts in the museum's 1932 guidebook.[93] At the Ashmolean Museum, William H. Young manufactured numerous duplicates of its holdings, including one of an obsidian head of King Amenemhat III commissioned by the British Museum,[94] while Egyptologist and epigrapher Myrtle Broome (1888–1978) fabricated and painted plaster copies of a statuette of Akhenaten's daughter in the Petrie Museum collection for the Manchester Museum, among others.[95] American institutions also continued to maintain cast collections. The Chicago Arts Institute in 1923, for example, acknowledged that while the 'chief emphasis has, of course, been laid upon the originals', in its Egyptian collection casts were considered 'essential to discussion of statuary and reliefs'.[96] In these ways, as Latour and Love have argued, works of art could actually grow in their originality through the quality and abundance of their copies; reproductions enhanced the fame of originals by extending their reach and giving them a composite biography.[97] Moreover, the status of the institute that held the genuine antiquity could be bolstered by such transactions, reinforcing networks of patronage through the ability to exchange their collections. For all of these reasons, casts were a regular feature of inter-war museum practice.

There were certainly concerns about reproductions, as there always had been, but this needs to be qualified. For instance, Buckman responded cynically to Chubb's offer of reproductions of amulets and ring bezels from ancient Amarna to sell in America,[98] with the comment that

> only the genuine objects have any carrying interest – for the mystic influence of antiquity, the psycometry [sic] of the long past among our American members particularly enhances the individual regard.[99]

At the forefront of Buckman's mind may have been the attitudes to things embodied by the Antiquus Mysticus Ordo Rosae Crucis (AMORC) first established by Harvey Spencer Lewis (1883–1939) in 1915, and which, by the time of his death in 1939, had several hundred thousand members.[100] Lewis viewed the New Kingdom Pharaohs Tuthmose III and Akhenaten as Rosicrucians, with the latter being 'the last Great Master in the family of founders'.[101] AMORC's success was not only due to its amalgamation of the strategies of other esoteric groups, but also its validation of its history and beliefs with genuine material evidence. That evidence was obtained through the EES, and from 1928 through the finds displayed in the Rosicrucian Egyptian Oriental Museum, San Jose. This sort of collection permitted the AMORC to identify as both an esoteric entity and a reputable scholarly organization grounded in ancient Egyptian knowledge and material testaments.

A general distinction, however, can be drawn between things considered to be archaeological specimens – those 'minor antiquities' – and other objects that were categorized more firmly within art historical canons. Copies of things like amulets were never intended for museum display, and Chubb clearly viewed them as a merchandizing opportunity. They were, for instance, a source of revenue for the EES at the annual exhibition at the Wellcome Museum. Museums were more interested in good quality reproductions of 'masterpieces' of Amarna art: a sculptor's unfinished portrait in quartzite of what is often considered to be Nefertiti, one of the most striking discoveries of the 1932–33 season; a stone head of a daughter of Akhenaten, recovered in 1927; and a small inlay head of Akhenaten, found in 1925. Nonetheless, the distinction between museum object and commercial product remained ambiguous. Efforts to elevate the casts towards the standing of 'masterpieces' could, to some extent, be achieved through backstage museum operations that tend to be overlooked in institutional histories.[102] The formal registration of casts into collections (accessioning), and their incorporation into vitrines, for instance, subjected those objects to a 'museum effect', a rite of passage that detached objects from the outside world and sacralized them with the realm of the museum. In effect these rites constituted processes of cultural authentication.[103] Nevertheless, those efforts were easily undermined by the commercial side of cast production. As Mary Jonas explained to curator Winifred Crompton at Manchester Museum, numerous other copies of the stone head of a daughter of Akhenaten, reproduced for the museum's display, were to be put on public sale at 10/6 each. This offered individuals the opportunity for private possession alongside museum contemplation, and allowed more people to become active participants in the collection and distribution of the EES's fieldwork.[104] Even the presentation of casts lay somewhere in between a packaged product and display technology: copies of the small inlay head of Akhenaten were 'put up in small boxes with glass lids', and offered at five shillings to any museum or private individual who cared to purchase them.[105]

Whether partitioned in museums or left to circulate freely in the market, there was a final, crucial significance to the production of casts at this time. They constituted an alternative technology of collecting that allowed the British to challenge the Egyptian nationalism that asserted ownership over treasures foreigners were otherwise denied permission to remove. Casts performed the role of material testaments to the EES's discoveries. They were simulacra that allowed British archaeologists and curators to claim irrefutable knowledge about those artefacts, to deploy them within their own classificatory schemes and to use them for their own disciplinary self fashioning.

***

Display Tastes and Academic Values

Despite its offers of reconstructed or reproduced finds, the EES continued to struggle to attract interest from museums throughout the inter-war years. The tension between the artistic and archaeological merits of Egyptian material was a long-standing one. However, the renewed attention paid to casts of Egyptian sculptures, together with competing Modernist and Art Deco sensibilities, underscores how aesthetic considerations were becoming a more pressing rationale for museum collecting at this time. This was especially apparent in America, where the museum trends of the Progressive Era towards period rooms and aesthetic taste continued. When the Cleveland Museum of Art in America's Midwest took a renewed interest in subscribing to the Society in 1930, it did so explicitly on the understanding that 'the collection is not at all archaeological but is part of the aesthetic purpose of the whole museum'.[106] In December 1935, the Metropolitan Museum of Art's Egyptian Department director, Herbert Winlock, curtly informed Jonas back in London that 'I do not believe that the Trustees of this Museum could authorize the acceptance of the objects destined for us'.[107] None of the objects, he judged, 'could possibly find a place in our exhibition galleries, and they would not add anything of importance to our study collection'.[108] The gift was formally refused, Winlock requested a refund on shipping costs, and the museum urged the EES to find an alternative home for the unwanted finds. Throughout this correspondence, Winlock continually made reference to the size of the Metropolitan Museum of Art's collection and, like the Cleveland Museum, emphasized the aesthetic needs of display. Both institutions were undoubtedly acutely aware of the public's declining engagement with museums and the competition for the public's attention from other 'taste-makers'.

Until the First World War, argues Neil Harris, American museums stood on a par with world expositions and department stores in setting art and other valuables in dialogue with the past, and in manipulating large numbers of objects within typically dark mahogany wood vitrines.[109] In the inter-war years, however, the major art museums in America fell out of step with these other institutions, as transformations in the building and display techniques of expositions and retailers rendered museum efforts dull by comparison. The department stores of the 1930s were modernized by installing new lighting technologies, increasing attention to customer comforts and services, and employing interior designers and architects to improve show windows and internal shopping arrangements. In New York, the Metropolitan Museum of Art had to compete with the novel displays employed by Saks Fifth Avenue, Macy's, Jay-Thorpe and Bonwit Teller. Not only were exhibits of consumer goods being overhauled, but so too were associated cultural activities through programmes of art classes, cookery shows and furniture demonstrations. The President of the Metropolitan, Robert de Forest (1876–1954), even admitted to a group of department store executives that that their influence exceeded that of museums.[110] As these department stores progressively became the arbiters of taste, critics berated overstuffed museums for their lack of progress.

Similar criticisms were levelled in Britain. A group of influential Museums Association representatives, commissioned by the Carnegie United Kingdom Trust (CUKT), undertook damning surveys of provision outside the national museums. These were the Miers Report (1928) and the Markham Report (1938).[111] Both raised the concern that the public image of museums was of dusty repositories full of dead things. 'To put it bluntly,' Miers stated in 1928, 'most people in this country do not really care for museums… this is not surprising when one considers how dull many of them have become.'[112] For Egyptian archaeological displays specifically, this comment is perhaps corroborated by the poor attendance at EES annual exhibitions reported for the summers of 1934 and 1938.[113]

In both Britain and America, the intellectual prestige of museums was waning. Museums in the nineteenth century had assumed academic leadership through the ways in which they systematized objects. By the end of the first quarter of the twentieth century, it was universities that had gained ascendancy in the production of knowledge across a range of disciplines, archaeology and Egyptology included.[114] Thus, while in the 1920s and 1930s there emerged a clear preference in museums for complete 'timeless' display pieces of art, whether authentic or reproduced, the latest set of fragmentary archaeological finds was less in demand.

In one sense this shift was symptomatic of a growing rift between popular receptions of the past and academic specialization. From the 1920s, a new generation of British-based archaeologists – the so-called 'Young Turks'[115] – began institutionalizing prehistoric archaeology within universities through new positions and formal courses; these included Miles Burkitt (1890–1971), Dorothy Garrod (1892–1968), Mortimer Wheeler (1890–1976) and Gordon Childe (1892–1957). This influential group had new means of practising and communicating archaeology in the form of a dedicated journal, *Antiquity*, established in 1927 to give a voice to the profession in the face of 'newspaper stunts' and books written by 'quacks'.[116] The emergence of *Antiquity* serves as a good example of how the public reception of archaeology in the inter-war years reflected back on the development of the discipline by creating a platform on which a distinctive sense of disciplinary community could form. The EES had also established a flagship academic journal in 1914, *The Journal of Egyptian Archaeology*, edited by Thomas E. Peet (1882–1934), who was similarly jaded by 'pirated popular books' and was more than 'willing to help to kill them'.[117] However, the dry, scholarly content of the journal had the opposite effect. In the USA, Buckman reported, 'the journal has proved disappointing and has killed off a host of would be subscribers'.[118] Consequently, although these endeavours were attempts to control messages about archaeology, the establishment of distinctive academic arenas for disciplinary discourse had the effect of both creating distance from more public forums of communication and of compartmentalizing scholarly study.

A glimpse into the frictions and fortunes of Egyptology and archaeology, their relative public profiles and museum relationships can be gleaned from a comparison of the inter-war levels of support given to the EES and the BSAE respectively. The EES's concessions at Amarna, and to some extent its work in the temples at Abydos and Armant, may have attracted the media limelight, but other substantial advances in the archaeological understanding of Egypt being produced by the BSAE occurred largely without fanfare, and with even more limited financial support. In the region of Badari, teams led by Guy and Winifred Brunton throughout the 1920s recovered prehistoric grave assemblages that were distinctive enough from the assemblages Petrie recognized as 'Predynastic' that they coined a new cultural designation: 'Badarian'. Meanwhile,

Gertrude Caton-Thompson's investigations in the associated habitation area of Hemamieh produced one of the first clear stratigraphic sections in Egyptian archaeology.[119] Her subsequent work in the Fayum proved equally vital for understanding prehistoric Egypt by producing evidence for some of the earliest cereal cultivation on the African continent: fifth-millennium BC baskets, grains, pottery fragments and lithics.[120] These discoveries were quickly taken up in academic literature and key archaeological texts, such as in the syntheses being written by Gordon Childe.[121] Funding for the BSAE, however, was severely curtailed by the late 1920s. Caton-Thompson had to turn to the Royal Anthropological Society for a special grant in 1927,[122] while work in the Badari region at Matmar and Mostagedda was administered by the British Museum after no public support through the BSAE was forthcoming. The lack of general interest could have been due to the unimpressive physical nature of the finds, or because Flinders Petrie was absent from the team after 1925 – his name still courted the attention of a media enamoured of celebrity fieldworkers. Longer standing tensions between prehistory and history in archaeology might also have had a part to play, as well as a lack of interest in other aspects of Egyptian history; it should be remembered that work in the region of Qau and Badari was productive for multiple periods, with particularly rich returns for late Roman, Byzantine and Islamic eras. Whatever the reason, *Antiquity* took up the cause, believing that the full extent of the Bruntons' work on the prehistoric eras was 'known only to a few', and that it deserved wider recognition and support.[123]

The status of these prehistoric finds within museums, against the backdrop of interest in ancient Egyptian society, is also telling. On its arrival in the Metropolitan Museum the prehistoric material from Badari was announced in the Museum's Bulletin as being of special interest.[124] In display, however, these items held a more precarious position. In 1939, the number of galleries available to the Department of Egyptian Antiquities at the Metropolitan Museum expanded, and Herbert Winlock took the opportunity to rearrange the displays. It was now 'possible to devote the entire first room to prehistoric antiquities', but only 'so long as the Museum is not actively excavating in Egypt and space for an annual showing of new acquisitions is not needed'.[125] Clearly in the hierarchy of displays, prehistory held a subordinate position to other parts of the collection.

The distribution of finds from Middle Egypt and the Fayum was nevertheless widespread, as British regional museums still hankered after universalist displays, a tendency that was robustly criticized in both the Miers and Markham reports. The BSAE was well equipped to provide provincial museums with material, because cemetery work returned great volumes of finds. Moreover, prehistoric remains seem not to have been subject to the more stringent control of the Egyptian Antiquities Service, which allowed the BSAE to export far greater numbers of objects in the 1920s than the EES, which was working on pharaonic sites and built structures like temples and settlements. This is most clearly attested by the permitted export to Britain of all known Badarian period human figurines, a rare category of find now only present in London.[126] A large number of objects from the earliest periods of Badari were also dispatched to the newly formed (1928) Egyptiska Museet in Stockholm,[127] following a donation from the then Swedish Minister in Cairo, Baron Harald Bildt. In this case, the impetus was a royal one. The Crown Prince and later King of Sweden, Gustaf VI Adolf (1882–1973), was passionately interested in archaeology. He had personally expressed a desire that the future collection of the Egyptian Museum should be focused on the Predynastic period, so as to connect it with the country's long-standing interest in prehistoric Scandinavian archaeology.[128] It was a rare royal interest in archaeology when the rest of the world remained enthralled with past royalty.

***

The discovery of Tutankhamun is frequently accorded a place in what has been referred to as a 'Golden Age' for archaeology, and it is hyped as one of the greatest discoveries of all time. In terms of disciplinary developments and public engagement with archaeological or Egyptological practices, however, such accolades are superficial at best. More often than not, the term 'golden age' is shorthand for colonial nostalgia for unbridled access to sites, as in G.E. Wright's designation of the 1920s as a 'golden age' for explorations of the Near East, where the Western-controlled territories of Palestine, Syria, Lebanon, Iraq and Cyprus were 'wide open territory for archaeology'.[129] This was clearly not the case for Egypt. Its 'golden age' has been set between 1881 and 1914, when partage was liberal and imperially controlled by Western authorities.[130] The apparent public enthusiasm for archaeology in the 1920s, as expressed in 'Tutmania' or in modernism, was not directed at, nor drawn from, archaeology as a practice or with museums as institutions. Rather, it signalled a societal receptiveness to particular aesthetics and narratives. And as the craze dissipated in the 1930s it left archaeology, Egyptology and museums vulnerable to the further social and political upheavals of the post-war period.

Notes

1. Carter, H. 1976. *Wonderful Things: The Discovery of Tutankhamun's Tomb*. Metropolitan Museum of Art: New York, p. 27.
2. Letter from Lord Carnarvon to Alan Gardiner, 28 November 1922, Gardiner correspondence, Griffith Institute Archives.
3. Nineteen artefacts from the tomb were later discovered in Howard Carter's possession after his death. These were acquired by the Metropolitan Museum of Art, before being repatriated to Egypt in 2010. TNA/FO/371/23355/198.
4. Goode, J. F. 2007. *Negotiating for the Past: Archaeology, Nationalism and Diplomacy in the Middle East*. Austin: University of Texas Press, pp. 67–97.
5. BAA/SEC/2/4/1(a).
6. Anon. 1926. Petrie forced to quit excavating in Egypt. *The New York Times* 7 July 1926: 15.
7. TNA/FO/141/487. In December 1928 the EES mooted raising the 'unsatisfactory condition of affairs that now prevails in Egypt with regard to the export of antiquities discovered during the course of scientific excavations' with the British Foreign Office, but was advised by anthropologist Charles Seligman that such a move was likely to be unproductive. EES archives, uncatalogued file.
8. 'Mr Lacau is absolutely loyal to Egypt's legitimate claim to resist undue spoliation by the Museums of America and Europe'. Letter from Cecil Firth to the High Commissioner of Egypt, 29 January 1926, TNA/FO/141/487.
9. Letter from Alan Gardiner to Prime Minister Stanley Baldwin, 24 November 1924, TNA/FO/141/487.
10. Riggs, C. 2013. Colonial visions: Egyptian antiquities and contested histories in the Cairo Museum. *Museum Worlds: Advances in Research* 1: 65–84.
11. Shapin, S. 1989. The invisible technician. *American Scientist* 77(6): 554–63.
12. Anon. 1923. Men who perform the 'spade work' of history: British names famous in the field archaeology. *Illustrated London News* 10 March 1923.
13. The Class A mandate for Iraq (Mesopotamia) was never enacted, but instead replaced by the 1922 Anglo-Iraqi Treaty, designed to allow for local self-government, but giving control of military and foreign affairs to the UK.
14. Moser, S. 2015. Reconstructing ancient worlds: reception studies, archaeological representation and the interpretation of ancient Egypt. *Journal of Archaeological Method and Theory* 22(4): 1290.
15. For example, the Egyptologist Arthur Weigall (1880–1934) whose career spanned stints as a set-designer, song-writer, film critic and popular writer on modern and ancient Egypt.
16. Daston, L. 2004. Introduction: speechless. In Daston, L. (ed.) *Things That Talk: Object Lessons from Art and Science*. London and Cambridge: The MIT Press, pp. 9–24.
17. EES 1920. *The Proposed Excavations at Tell el-Amarna*. London: Egypt Exploration Society.
18. EES, *The Proposed Excavations*.
19. Montserrat, D. 2000. *Akhenaten: History, Fantasy and Ancient Egypt*. London and New York: Routledge.
20. This is the estimate given by Anna Stevens based on the John Ruffle and Elizabeth Moignard City of Akhenaten Object index originally compiled in 1970, later augmented with information from the original registration cards and the index of photographic negatives in the EES Amarna Archive. See Ruffle, J. and Moignard, E. 1972. *City of Akhenaten: Object Index*. Birmingham: City Museum and Art Gallery. A database of these small finds is available at the Amarna Project website. Available at: http://www.amarnaproject.com/pages/recent_projects/material_culture/small_finds/database.shtml [accessed 8 July 2017].
21. EES 1922. *Report of the Thirty-Sixth Ordinary General Meeting (Fortieth Annual General Meeting)*. London: J. W. Arrowsmith Ltd, p. 13.
22. Letter from Herbert Bolton to Mary Jonas, 1 August 1924, EES.DIST.34.
23. Letter from Samuel Sherek, City Art Museum to Buckman, 22 March 1923, EES.USA.COR.
24. Letter from Gordon to Jonas, 10 September 1924, EES.USA.COR.
25. Letter from Buckman to Jonas, 1 November 1925, EES.USA.COR.
26. Undated document circa 1923. Report regarding the activities of the Australian Division of the Egypt Exploration Society. EES.AUS.COR.

27 EES.AUS.COR.
28 EES.AUS.COR.
29 Letter from Jonas to McIntosh, 19 January 1924, EES.AUS.COR.
30 Letter from W. Woodhouse to Mary Jonas, 13 March 1925, EES.AUS.COR.
31 Letter from Jonas to W. G. Saxon, 9 August 1926, EES.AUS.COR.
32 Montserrat. *Akhenaten*, pp. 84–91.
33 Robson, E. 2017. Old habits die hard: writing the excavation and dispersal history of Nimrud. *Museum History Journal* 10(2): 217–32.
34 Arrowsmith, R. R. 2011. *Modernism and the Museum: Asian, African, and Pacific Art and the London Avant-Garde*. Oxford: Oxford University Press.
35 The original article Moore saw was Peet, T. E. 1921. Home life in ancient Egypt 3000 years ago. *Illustrated London News,* 6 August 1921: 182–5. For more see Swigg, R. 2012. *Quick, Said the Bird: Williams, Eliot, Moore, and the Spoken Word*. Iowa City: University of Iowa Press, p. 128, note 3. Moore drew an image of the vessel in her friend, Scofield Thayer's, copy of her book, *Observations*. The book is in the American Literature collection at the Beinecke Library at Yale. The fish vessel is now in the British Museum (EA55193). Available at: https://moore123.com/2010/06/04/egyptian-fish-for-scofield-thayer/ [accessed 3 January 2018].
36 Moore, M. 1924. *Observations*. New York: Dial Press, p. 20.
37 Moore, H. 1982. *Henry Moore at the British Museum*. London: H. N. Abrams, p. 8.
38 Moore, *Henry Moore at the British Museum*. These are registered as EA1239 and EA42179 respectively.
39 Grundon, I. 2007. *The Rash Adventurer: A Life of John Pendlebury*. London: Libri Publications Limited, p. 167.
40 Challis, D. and Romain, G. 2015. Ronald Moody: Sculpture and interwar Britain. Available at: https://www.ucl.ac.uk/equianocentre/education/a-fusion-of-worlds/artists/moody [accessed 26 July 2017]. Johaan is now part of the Tate collection in London (TA6591).
41 See also Riggs, C. 2017. *Egypt. Lost Civilizations*. London: Reaktion Books, pp. 152–5.
42 Levy, J. M. 1936. Pylon of victory dug up in Egypt. *New York Times* 24 May 1936: 30.
43 This was the title of the 1932 exhibition catalogue of dealer Sydney Burney. For a discussion of his role in acquiring Egyptian material and influencing taste see Hardwick, T. 2011. Five months before Tut. Purchasers and prices at the MacGregor sale, 1922. *Journal of the History of Collections* 32(1): 189.
44 Letter from Jonas to W. G. Saxon, 25 May 1925, EES.COR. Secretary's correspondence files.
45 Frankfort, H. and Pendlebury, J. 1933. *The City of Akhenaten II: The North Suburb and the Desert Altars*. London: Egypt Exploration Society, p. 118.
46 EES 1932 *Report for the Year 1932*. London: Egypt Exploration Society, p. 10.
47 Kamerling, B. 1992. How Ellen Scripps brought ancient Egypt to San Diego. *The Journal of San Diego History* 38(2): 73–91.
48 Letter from Buckman to Jonas, 1 August 1923, EES.USA.COR.
49 EES.DIST.46.22a.
50 Petrie, W. M. F. 1888. The treatment of small antiquities. *The Archaeological Journal* 45: 85–9; See also Odegaard, N. and O'Grady, C. R. 2016. The conservation practices for archaeological ceramics of Sir Flinders Petrie and others between 1880–1930. In Roemich, H. and Fair, L. (eds.) *Recent Advances in Glass and Ceramics Conservation 2016*. Paris: International Council of Museums – Committee for Conservation, pp. 85–95.
51 Lucas, A. 1924. *Antiquities. Their Restoration and Preservations*. London: Arnold & Co, p. 4.
52 Bodleian Library, Acland papers, MS Acland d. 92, fols. 79–90, dated May 1882.
53 Wilson, D. M. 2002. *The British Museum: A History*. London: British Museum Press, p. 357, n.128.
54 Young's dates of birth and death are currently unknown. Mark Norman, former conservator for the Ashmolean, notes (personal communication) that a census places Young in 1881 at nine years old. He worked at the Ashmolean until his retirement in 1937.
55 'Mr W.H. Young, by whose skill and patience the coins have been separated and cleaned, reports that their condition before cleaning was consistent with their having been subject for a considerable period to the chemical action of their soil'. Sutherland, C. H. 1936. A late Roman coin-hoard from Kiddington, Oxon. *Oxoiensia* I: 70–80.
56 Norman, M. 2001. 'It is surprising that things can be preserved as well as they are'. In Oddy, A. and Smith, S. (eds.) *Past Practice-Future Prospects*. London: British Museum, pp. 159–66.
57 Rozeik, C. 2012 .'A maddening temptation': the Ricketts and Shannon collection of Greek and Roman antiquities. *Journal of the History of Collections* 24(3): 369–78.

58 Mark Norman, personal communication. As Dan Potter, National Museums of Scotland, has reported (personal communication) such reconstruction is particularly evident from the pottery corpus distributed by John Garstang from the royal Sudanese site of Meroe.
59 For example, see Brunton, G. 1937. *Mostagedda and the Tasian Culture*. London: British School of Archaeology in Egypt.
60 Letter from Jonas to Hogarth, 28 November 1925, EES.DIST.46.47.
61 Letter from Young to Paterson, 26 January 1926, EES.DIST.40.50.
62 Letter from Jonas to Hogarth, 28 November 1925, EES.DIST.46.47.
63 Letter from Jonas to Young, 13 February 1926, EES.DIST 46.55.
64 Letter from Jonas to Buckman, 26 July 1921, EES.USA.COR.
65 Letter from Buckman to Jonas, 19 August 1921, EES.USA.COR.
66 Anon. 1931. *Catalogue of the Egypt Exploration Society's Exhibition of the Results of the Recent Excavations at Amarna and Armant and of a Loan Exhibition of Egyptian Jewellery: Wellcome Historical Medical Museum 8th September to 3rd October 1931*. London: Egypt Exploration Society.
67 The relationship between temporary exhibitions and permanent displays is more nuanced than is implied here, and is not fully addressed in this account. It is the subject of a DPhil thesis linked to the *Artefacts of Excavation* research project: Williams, A. 2019. *Exhibiting Archaeology: Constructing Knowledge of Egypt at Temporary Exhibitions in London, 1884–1939*. DPhil Thesis. Oxford: University of Oxford.
68 Letter from George E. Smith (Osteopathic physician) to H. R. Hall, 28 April 1924, EES.USA.COR.
69 Letter from Chester Campbell to W. R. Dawson, 29 January 1925, EES.USA.COR.
70 Chubb, M. 1998. *Nefertiti Lived Here*. London: Libri Publications, p. 16.
71 Lacovara, P. 1998. Introduction. In Chubb, *Nefertiti Lived Here*, p. 3.
72 Some of the silver was retained by the EES and was eventually purchased by the British Museum in 1974. It is accessioned under number EA68503, while a gold ingot was presented to the Science Museum.
73 Accessioned under museum number UC72491.
74 Bilbey, D. and Trusted, M. 2010. 'The question of casts': collecting and later reassessment of the cast collections at South Kensington. In Frederiksen, R. and Marchand, E. (eds.) *Plaster Casts: Making, Collecting and Display from Classical Antiquity to the Present*. Berlin and New York: De Gruyter, pp. 465–84.
75 Cited in Born, P. 2002. The canon is cast: plaster casts in American museum and university collections. *Art Documentation: Journal of the Art Libraries Society of North America* 21(2): 10.
76 Born, The canon is cast.
77 For example, Siapkas, J. and Sjogren, L. 2014. *Displaying the Ideals of Antiquity: The Petrified Gaze*. London: Routledge, p. 101–11.
78 Wallach, A. 1998. *Exhibiting Contradiction: Essays on the Art Museum in the United States*. Amherst: University of Massachusetts Press, p. 56.
79 Pearce, S. 1995. *On Collecting: An Investigation into Collecting in the European Tradition*. London and New York: Routledge, p. 363.
80 EES archive distribution files 51 and 57. For example, EES.DIST.51.20 lists 13 international destinations for 'casts of the Akhenaten head' and EES.DIST 51.21 lists 20 for casts 'of the head of the princesses, daughter of Akhenaten, the original having been found at Tell-el-Amarna, 1926–1927'.
81 Letter from Jonas to Charles Currelly, 27 September 1933, EES.COR.
82 Anon. 1929. A gallery of casts. *The Times* 24 October 1929: 17; Anon 1928. A museum of casts. *Museums Journal* 27(4): 320–1.
83 Anon. 1929. An international exhibition of casts of works of art. *Museums Journal* 28(3): 290–1. Anon. 1930. News. *Museums Journal* 29(6): 434–5.
84 Anon. 1930. General note. *Journal of the Royal Society of Arts* 87: 806.
85 Anon. 1926. The Science Museum. *Museums Journal* 25(2): 271.
86 Anon. The Science Museum, 271.
87 Letter from Henry Lyons to Percy Newberry, 23 July 1931, Griffith Institute archive, Newberry correspondence NEWB2/483.
88 Letter from Henry Lyons to Percy Newberry, 5 September 1923, Griffith Institute archive, Newberry correspondence NEWB2/483.
89 Anon. 1924. A new statuette which is charming London. *The Sphere*, 22 November 1924, 213. With thanks to Christina Riggs for drawing this article to my attention.

90 Letter from Joseph Clubb, Curator of Museums Free Public Museums Liverpool, to C. J. Gadd Egyptian Department British Museum, 3 December 1924, British Museum, Department of Middle East Correspondence archives; Letter from J. Russell Goddard, Hancock Museum, to Mr Hall, Egyptian Department, 17 November 1924, British Museum Department of Middle East Correspondence archives.
91 Letter from Thomas Midgely to Jonas, 1 March 1926, EES.DIST.41.44.
92 Ashley Cooke, personal communication.
93 Peet, T. E. and Newberry, P. 1932. *Handbook and Guide to the Egyptian Collection on Exhibition in The Public Museums Liverpool*. Liverpool: Public Museums Liverpool, pp. 40–2. With thanks to Ashley Cooke for making this available to me.
94 Egyptian and Assyrian Antiquities Department Minutes, 8 November 1924, p. 137.
95 Letter from Myrtle Broome to Winifred Crompton, 12 January 1925, Manchester Museum Egypt Archive correspondence ID 70.
96 Allen, T. G. 1923. *A Handbook of the Egyptian Collection*. Chicago: University of Chicago Press, p. vii.
97 Latour, B. and Love, A. 2010. The migration of the aura or how to explore the original through its facsimiles. In Bartscherer, T. (ed.) *Switching Codes: Thinking Through Digital Technology in the Humanities and the Arts*. Chicago: University of Chicago Press, pp. 275–97.
98 Letter from Chubb to Buckman, 22 May 1931, EES.USA.COR.
99 Letter from Chubb to Buckman, 6 June 1931, EES.USA.COR.
100 Ellwood, R. S. 1973. *Religious and Spiritual Groups in Modern America*. Englewood Cliffs: Prentice-Hall.
101 Lewis, H. S. 1929. *Rosicrucian Questions and Answers*. San Jose: Rosicrucian Press, p. 29.
102 Riggs, C. 2017. The body in the box: archiving the Egyptian mummy. *Archival Science* 17(2): 125–50.
103 Varutti, M. 2018. 'Authentic reproductions': museum collection practices as authentication. *Museum Management and Curatorship* 33(1): 42–56.
104 Letter from Jonas to Winifred Crompton, 8 November 1927, Manchester Museum Egypt Archive Correspondence ID 453.
105 Letter from Jonas to Winifred Crompton, 24 February 1926, Manchester Museum Egypt Archive Correspondence ID 437.
106 Letter from Cleveland Museum of Art Curator, Rossiter Howard, to Buckman, 26 November 1930, EES.USA.COR.
107 Letter from H. Winlock to Jonas, 10 December 1935, Metropolitan Museum of Art, Department of Egyptian Art archives.
108 Letter from H. Winlock to Jonas, 10 December 1935, Metropolitan Museum of Art, Department of Egyptian Art archives.
109 Harris, N. 1990. *Cultural Excursions: Marketing Appetites and Cultural Tastes in Modern America*. Chicago and London: University of Chicago Press.
110 Harris, *Cultural Excursions*, pp. 71–2.
111 Miers, H. A. 1928. *A Report on the Public Museums of the British Isles (Other Than the National Museums)*. Dunfermline: Carnegie United Kingdom Trust; Markham, S. F. 1938. *A Report on the Museums and Art Galleries of the British Isles (other than National Museums)*. Edinburgh: Constable.
112 Miers, *A Report on the Public Museums*, p. 80.
113 Letter from Jonas to Guy Brunton, 2 November 1934: 'we don't get as many people as I would like to see, and so many are cranks, play-writers or Akhenatenites, or something weird'. EES. COR.BRUNTON.
114 Conn, *Museums and Intellectual Life*.
115 See Diaz-Andreu, M. 2012. *Archaeological Encounters: Building Networks of Spanish and British Archaeologists in the 20th Century*. Newcastle upon Tyne: Cambridge Scholars Publishing, p. 26.
116 Crawford, O.G.S. 1927. Editorial notes. *Antiquity* 1: 2.
117 Letter from T. E. Peet to H. R. H Hall, 20 May 1924, British Museum, Department of the Middle East correspondence archives.
118 Letter from Buckman to J. Hall, 8 December 1921, EES.USA.COR.
119 Both published in Brunton, G. and Caton-Thompson, G. 1928. *The Badarian Civilisation*. London: British School of Archaeology in Egypt.
120 Caton-Thompson, G. and Gardiner, E. 1934. *The Desert Fayum*. London: Royal Anthropological Institute of Great Britain and Ireland.

121 E.g. Childe, G. V. 1929. *The Most Ancient East: The Oriental Prelude to European Prehistory*. New York: Alfred A. Knopf.
122 Since Flinders Petrie did not agree with her interpretations, there was also an element of personal antagonism that led to Caton-Thompson terminating her BSAE association.
123 Crawford, O. G. S. 1929. Editorial notes. *Antiquity* 3(12): 387.
124 Bull, L. 1933. Two groups of prehistoric Egyptian objects. *The Metropolitan Museum of Art Bulletin* 28(7): 119–20.
125 Winlock, H. E. 1939. New galleries of Egyptian art. *The Metropolitan Museum of Art Bulletin* 34(5): 119.
126 The only known Badarian ivory figurine is in the British Museum together with a red painted pottery statuette, while mud and ceramic examples are looked after by the Petrie Museum at University College London UC9080 and UC9795a.
127 Larsen, H. 1961. Finds from Badarian and Tasian Civilizations. *Medelhavsmuseet Bulletin* 1: 9–19.
128 Warner, N. 2016. *Collecting for Eternity: R. G. Gayer-Anderson and the Egyptian Museum in Stockholm*. Stockholm: National Museum of World Culture.
129 Davies, T. W. 2003. Levantine Archaeology. In Richard, S. (ed.) *Near Eastern Archaeology Reader*. Winona Lake: Eisenbrauns, p. 55.
130 Thompson, J. 2016. *Wonderful Things: A History of Egyptology 2: The Golden Age: 1881–1914*. Cairo: The American University in Cairo Press.

Chapter 5
Ghosts, Orphans and the Dispossessed: Post-war Object Habits (1945–1969)

Sekhmet, the feline-headed ancient Egyptian goddess of war and destruction, sat watching with a stony gaze as the museum erupted into flame. Coffin panels curled and crackled in the heat, copper implements melted and mummies turned to ash. It was 3 May 1941, and an incendiary device, one of more than 112,000 that were dropped on Liverpool that month, had directly struck the city's museum. When daylight broke, the smouldering and sodden remains of the displays emerged. There were no human casualties in the museum itself, but among the gutted galleries were those devoted to Egyptology (Fig. 5.1). More than 3000 objects were obliterated.[1] Two years later, Hull Museum suffered a similar fate. Its curator, Thomas Sheppard (1878–1945), wilfully ignored warnings to evacuate the collection, and the museum was destroyed by fire following a direct hit in the early hours of 24 June 1943. Inside had been numerous objects excavated by the EEF and BSAE, including a bronze jackal-standard from Tell Nebesheh and a small Horus figure from Tanis, on loan from the British Museum.[2] The site where the museum had stood was levelled later in the 1940s, eventually becoming a car park. It was only in 1988, when workers were digging a drainage ditch across the area, that it was realized that some of what had been in the museum's basement was salvable. The Phoenix Excavation Project turned the former institution into an archaeological field site, recovering a few of the artefacts thought to have been lost decades before, albeit now charred and unrecognizable.[3]

In London, hundreds of skulls that had been donated to the Royal College of Surgeons by Petrie and the EES were crushed under the rubble following a bombardment by Germany's *Luftwaffe*, while the curator of Leeds Museum had to dig out the collection after a bomb shattered the archaeology section that housed Egyptian finds. Bombs battered Bristol Museum and Art Gallery, as well as Glasgow's Kelvingrove Museum, but the archaeological collections were unharmed, despite the museum

Fig. 5.1 Bomb damage in Liverpool Museum. A member of the auxiliary fire service carrying a ceramic coffin lid from Garstang's 1906 excavations at Esna on 4 May 1941. A seated statue of the lioness-headed goddess Sekhmet is visible in the background. Courtesy of National Museums Liverpool, World Museum (16.11.06.403).

buildings and other collections being badly damaged. Collections at University College London and in Birmingham City Museum and Art Gallery narrowly escaped destruction after being evacuated before the bombs smashed their display cases, only for the objects to then languish in storage for decades after. German collections were also severely affected, and large numbers of antiquities in Berlin, Bonn, Leipzig and Munich were either destroyed by bombs, lost during the conflict or removed by the Russian army as trophies, including some of the things presented by Petrie and his colleagues. Italian museums equally suffered, among them the Museo Internazionale delle Ceramiche in Faenza, which had been the recipient of pottery and faience pieces recovered during the 1920s BSAE work at Lahun, Gurob and Sedment.

There has been – and continues to be today in some quarters – a misplaced rationale that the removal of Egypt's heritage abroad is a benevolent act of salvation from *in situ* threats. Some of the EEF's early proponents had gone as far as to argue that 'in Egypt, sculptures when uncovered were doomed to certain destruction at the hands of the arab and the traveller, and were never safe until placed within the walls of a museum'.[4] The events of the Second World War stand as violent warning that nowhere is safe in the long term. In this regard, the dispersal of artefacts has merit in diffusing risk, as Flinders Petrie himself once recognized.[5] Some form of loss however, always characterizes archaeology. Despite being hailed for its discoveries, excavation is essentially a form of destruction. It is the records that archaeologists create and the objects that they procure which form the basis for making inferences about the past. For Liverpool Museum, all that remains today of much of its Egyptian holdings are documents and photographs of things that no longer exist. It is, as its curator Ashley Cooke describes it, a ghost collection.

The physical devastation wrought by the war was not the only threat faced by collections in the mid-twentieth century. More insidious was a widespread societal change in attitudes towards objects. When, crate by crate, the mass of material laboriously sequestered away during the war was slowly unpacked, museum practitioners of the late 1940s and early 1950s were confronted with collections in their entirety. These were now reviewed with war-weary eyes. Collecting tastes had become ever more circumscribed, and post-war austerity had tightened budgets. Was there any need to keep everything? Divestment, as much as acquisition, came to define post-war museum spaces, as a large scale re-landscaping of assemblages was set in motion; things were loaned, sold, even deliberately destroyed. Most at risk were 'orphaned' collections, artefacts that had 'either lost curatorial support or were never curated in the first place, and … were never fully analysed or reported'.[6] Yet amid this dwindling faith in the value and power of things were opportunities. Dispossessed objects were ideologically elastic and found new leases of life as the British Empire fractured, generating new contexts for the reception of repurposed Egyptian collections in countries such as newly independent Ghana.

This chapter explores these shifts in British and American museum practice, and the wider changes in society that informed the way institutions assessed objects in the decades around the Second World War. In so doing, this account fills an interpretive gap in historical studies of museums between the acknowledgement that the age of the object had ended by the 1930s and the renewed academic interest in museum collections as sites of knowledge production at the end of the twentieth century. This was far from being a static period in museum history, as many have assumed:[7] objects endured, and their circulation and treatment at this time are as revealing of social, political and intellectual histories as they are in any decade.

The BSAE's Last Distributions: Dwindling Interests in the UK

In December 1948, 77-year-old Lady Hilda Petrie settled down to the familiar task of penning dozens of letters to drum up financial support for the British School of Archaeology in Egypt (BSAE). As Honorary Secretary she had spent much of her life engaged in campaigning, and was adept in such matters. Flinders had passed away five years earlier in Palestine, and the British School was no longer sponsoring any active fieldwork, but there was still an outstanding backlog of reports to be printed before the organization could be finally wound up. There also remained the legacy of previous expeditions concealed in several crates in the basement of UCL's Department of Zoology. Amongst the Palestinian lots from the Petries' later years of excavation was a sizeable number of artefacts from the 1920s BSAE seasons at the Egyptian sites of Lahun, Gurob and Abydos. Pottery, amulets and plenty of the ubiquitous shabtis had all being sitting in reserve for almost three decades. Hilda Petrie was hopeful that these might now attract renewed interest from museums.

Hilda wrote to establishments in Rochdale, Norwich, Halifax, Glasgow, Dewsbury, Cardiff, Brighton, Birmingham and Bristol, all places that for years had keenly sought relics for their galleries. Every single one now declined. The curators replied that local supporters who had once sponsored the BSAE were long dead, regional Egyptian societies were defunct and public interest in Egyptology had waned. The curator of Norwich Castle Museum informed Hilda that there was no more money from the Egyptian Society of East Anglia, which had closed in 1942, and that there was 'no-one locally sufficiently interested to keep the Society alive' following the death of the most active member, Alice Geldart.[8] Similarly, the Glasgow Egyptian Research Students Association (ERSA), founded by Janet May Buchanan in 1912 to support the BSAE, was discontinued with the acknowledgement that membership had been steadily dwindling since 1931, and that the possibility of recruiting new members was small.[9]

For other curators, there was simply no longer the space within their museums for anything more, either because of what were now perceived as overcrowded cases, or because exhibition halls had been lost to the Blitz. Liverpool Museum, for example, lay derelict for some twenty years before rebuilding efforts could commence. Most telling, however, were statements that Egyptian material no longer matched collecting remits, as regional and provincial institutions sought to define themselves more closely vis-à-vis British history or local interests. This included Newcastle Museum, whose curator informed Hilda that:

> Our society has confined its attention to British Antiquities, particularly those of the Northern Counties, for many years now, and I feel that the Egyptian Antiquities you mention would now be quite out of place in either of our museums.[10]

Curators in Dewsbury, Halifax and Cardiff appealed to similar, more restrictive collecting criteria in their letters of refusal.

This refocus on regional collections led to a widespread reconfiguration of the geography of collections.[11] In Edinburgh a disposal board had existed at the Royal Museum since 1910, but it was particularly active in the 1950s, dispersing 'duplicates' and expelling broken or fragmentary objects. Poor storage conditions during the war had been responsible for some damage to artefacts, but there were also other factors in play. One of these was the reinstallation of the displays, which provided the chance to overhaul the interpretive scheme in order to reduce 'very considerably the amount of material to be displayed'.[12] The Royal Museum transferred Egyptian artefacts to institutions in Paisley, Durham and even Sydney, Australia, while other objects were sold and small number destroyed. Behind this drive was museum director Douglas A. Allan (director 1945–61), who sought to refocus the museum's purpose with a more restrictive attitude to collecting and a fresh approach to display that emphasized aesthetic considerations of colour and careful object selection. He outlined his ideas in a lecture given to the Royal Society of Arts in London in 1949, during which he noted that 'the best assemblage of real things requires the use of words to describe their significance, and is enhanced by diagrams, models and photographs in driving its lesson home'.[13] His ideas picked up on the calls for museum modernization promoted in the Miers (1928) and the Markham reports (1938).[14] Both reports advocated that, rather than an inward-looking emphasis on collecting and research, museums should develop a more educationalist approach. In this vein, Allan and many of his colleagues believed that objects were no longer considered able to speak for themselves within display cases, as had been thought in the late nineteenth century. Instead, they required a *mis-en-scène* of visual and textual supports to validate and make apparent their claims to knowledge. 'Museums, like human beings', Allan argued, 'are the better for restricting their diet to what can be digested; both readily display the effects of gluttony'.[15] Fewer objects and more interpretation were the order of the day.

Norwich Castle Museum, which had been the recipient of a considerable volume of finds from EES work in the 1920s and 1930s at Amarna, Armant and Abydos, likewise departed from what were now considered old fashioned museum practices. In 1953, the Museum Committee resolved that the collection policy for archaeological and ethnographic material would be 'confined to Norfolk with the addition of Lothingland in NE Suffolk'.[16] Existing collections unrelated to this new locally focused policy were to be disposed of, and 'foreign archaeological material to be drastically reduced'.[17] A large consignment of material was consequently sold to Liverpool Museum in 1956 to help the beleaguered institution recover from the wreckage left by the *Luftwaffe*. Bankfield Museum transferred the majority of its collection to Manchester, and Shropshire Museum Services assigned most of its Egyptian material to Birmingham Museum between 1958 and the 1970s. Between 1957 and 1971 Bristol Museum destroyed 56 excavated objects donated by the EEF and BSAE, on the grounds that they were either in too poor a condition or 'of no interest'.[18] This was quite a turnaround for an institution that in 1904 had boasted that 'Egyptology has long been made a special feature in this museum'; by the 1950s and 1960s, Bristol too had been prevented from adding to its Egyptian collection because of 'priorities in local archaeology'.[19] Greenock's McLean Museum and Art Gallery sold 23 objects at Spink in 1965 to raise funds for a new building, among which were Predynastic pottery and palettes from el-Amrah, tomb reliefs from Dendereh and a door lintel from Sedment. Reading Museum first disposed of objects in 1939 to Dartford College in New Hampshire, and following the war sent objects to Barbados in 1949. On 5 September 1952, a special meeting of Reading's Museum and Art Gallery Committee convened to address 'economies in local government services' prompted by the Chancellor of the Exchequer's recent speech insisting on the need for local governments to curtail expenditure. Upon consideration of the Town Clerk's report, Reading Museum's director decided on the 'sale of certain surplus object and display cases'.[20] Egyptian objects, among others, were promptly disposed of to Ghana and Birmingham.

This upheaval did, however, raise some voices of unease. At the Museums Association's 1955 conference in Birmingham, the Assistant Keeper of the Ashmolean Museum's Antiquities Department, Donald H. Harden (1901–94), expressed concern over the spate of disposals among which 'Egyptian antiquities have fared equally ill'.[21] He went on to bemoan how 'finds made by Sir Flinders Petrie and others in Egypt, which were distributed to museums in this country and their whereabouts mentioned in print, have similarly been alienated without trace – sold no doubt, to dealers and thence into private collections, or for export'.[22]

Notwithstanding these concerns, Harden also oversaw disposals of Egyptian material from the Ashmolean to other institutions, employing the rationale that these were only 'duplicates'. The question of what constitutes a museum duplicate, however, is far from straightforward. The majority of objects acquired during excavation are original, underscoring how the status of 'unique' or 'duplicate' is ultimately a relational and subjective concept that shifts depending on an artefact's juxtaposition with other objects. For Harden, the decision as to which artefacts should be retained and which disposed of was predicated on the likelihood of their display. Little consideration was given to their value as archaeological record. Whether something was provenanced or unprovenanced was a moot point. The British Museum's Egyptian Department also contemplated disposing of 17 Predynastic pottery vessels in the 1950s, this time as part of an exchange with the Boston Museum of Fine Arts. However, the contentious issue of the 'duplicate' surfaced, with Keeper I. E. S. Edwards having to apologize profusely to the MFA's Dows Dunham that certain pottery vessels excavated at Badari and Mostagedda were no longer options for export, as the museum's technical assistant had observed features – such as the presence of pottery slip on the base – that rendered apparently 'duplicate' items unique in the context of the British Museum's collection.[23] Faced with 'inferior' substitutes, Dunham retorted that he could not justify the exchange. Some artefacts it seems, had become stubbornly inalienable.

Operation 'Weedout': US Institutions and Mid-Century Deaccessioning

Deaccessioning is the polite term museums employ today to describe the processes by which objects that had been formally accepted into a collection are actively removed and disposed of legally and permanently.[24] It is a word that only came into common parlance in the 1970s in the aftermath of *The New York Times* exposé that the Metropolitan Museum of Art was planning to dispose of several high profile works of art, including a Redon, a Manet and an early Picasso.[25] The practice of disposal, however, had been a concerted policy for the Metropolitan Museum since 1955, under the direction of James Rorimer (1905–66), the man who was the inspiration for the *Monuments Men* film character portrayed by Hollywood actor Matt Damon. Like the heroic framing of Rorimer's heritage work in the movie, the history of his tenure as director is celebrated as one in which many significant acquisitions were made for the museum.[26] Yet such narratives are remarkably silent about the large scale deaccessioning that he instigated, which is referred to in internal Metropolitan Museum memos as 'operation weedout'.[27]

Artefacts from excavations had always occupied a precarious position within the expressly fine art Metropolitan Museum. In 1899, EEF Secretary Emily Paterson received an irate letter from New York following the delivery of what the Met considered to be a poor batch of material from the Fund's most recent excavations. There was 'no object of any artistic significance, no inscription, no ornamentation, most of the objects were rude pottery bowls, repetitions of each other'.[28] It was also not the first time the museum had taken drastic action to rationalize its holdings. A fire sale in 1929, authorized by Robert W. De Forest (1848–1931),[29] had sold 159 paintings and 675 objects from the museum's permanent collection, and was a harbinger of the much more aggressive deaccessioning policies of the 1950s. Rorimer's brash successor, Thomas Hoving (1931–2009), estimated that around 30,000 objects – or 'junk' as he referred to it[30] – had been disposed of by the time of his appointment in 1967, and he continued to deaccession vigorously:

> To hell with the dribs and drabs—the little Egyptian pieces, the fragments… I'd acquire only the big, rare, fantastic pieces, the expensive ones, the ones that would cause a splash.[31]

On his appointment to the office of Director in 1955, Rorimer set each department the task of reviewing its holdings. By October that same year, the Egyptian department had fully appraised its collection and earmarked some 3453 objects for disposal, together with 'hundreds of textiles and Egyptian artifacts which are not regarded as saleable'.[32] The mechanisms for the disposals appear various, although not altogether transparent. One offer from an auction house in Switzerland, still kept in the Metropolitan Museum's archives, hints at the covert approaches to disposal that existed:

> Nobody would know that your Museum is selling art objects and we would grant you special conditions… of special interest for us would be European art up to 19th cent. Egyptian, Greek and Roman art Near and far Eastern art Paintings by old and modern masters.[33]

Some things were sold to other institutions, such as the University of Melbourne which purchased a Ptolemaic stela originally acquired by the Metropolitan Museum in 1897 from the EEF work at Oxyrhynchus.[34] Other objects were simply retailed in the Museum's bookshop:

> …the Egyptian artifacts accompanying this note were selected and prices were agreed upon. Each represents a category of which we have numerous examples, making possible a standardization of prices. There will be no attempt to provide catalogue info about these items except for those few which may be in the upper price brackets. It was decided to limit the initial presentation of this material to three categories: scarabs, shawabtis and strings of beads.[35]

When the news of the disposals was made public, the local media were supportive, identifying 'moral in museum's weedout'.[36] *The New York Times* reported that around 2500 sales slips had been taken, testifying to a 'thriving trade in paleolithic and neolithic flints, scarabs, jars found in tombs, fragments of stone and pottery with paintings or inscriptions, bronzes and wood sculptures'.[37] Excavated assemblages were scattered like confetti, carried away in the hands of curious children for a few cents and by beady-eyed adult punters who had never sought to acquire ancient relics but who now seized the opportunity after parting with a few hundred dollars.

The Metropolitan Museum was not alone. The Brooklyn Museum had followed a similar course of action and sold Egyptian objects from the collection through its Museum Gallery shop in 1957–8, while other pieces were transferred to places such as the Denver Museum of Nature and Science.[38] The museum's annual report for 1959 proudly noted how the shop, in its first five years of existence, had extended the 'cultural-educational program as represented by the Museum's collection' and introduced children and adults 'to originals instead of reproductions'.[39] Over in Minnesota, the director of the Minneapolis Institute of Fine Arts was quietly deaccessioning Egyptian, Greek and Roman antiquities,[40] Wellesley College's Davis Museum sold at least 120 acquisitions previously donated by the EEF, and Pasadena's Art Museum marketed the remainder of its Egyptian collections from the EES's Tell el-Amarna campaigns at a Sotheby Parke-Bernet sale on 4 November 1969. The final destinations for these things frequently remains unknown.

At the same time that American museums were breaking up collections, interest in the acquisition of new material from British fieldwork weakened. The Great Depression had by 1935 reduced subscribing US members to a mere 35 individuals, and the American branch of the EES was finally disbanded in 1947.[41] The EES's role as a transnational organization never recovered, and few international distributions occurred after the Second World War.[42]

Lost Museums

Museums are revered as bastions that protect objects against the passage of time. Yet it is clear from the above that, by the mid-twentieth century, museums were in fact far more porous than the salvage philosophies of previous generations had imagined. Even Petrie foresaw this, arguing in 1904 that a 'museum is only a temporary place'.[43] In the most extreme cases of post-war downsizing, whole institutions vanished. Against the grain of commonplace understandings of their functions, museums are not always the guarantors of posterity, so much so that the term 'museum taphonomy' has been coined to recognize the phenomenon of museum loss.[44] Museums could be dismantled by sudden acts, or else be simply forgotten as institutional memory gradually faded and collections lay stagnant.

New York's Chautauqua Assembly had been one of the very first American institutions to acquire finds from the EEF in the 1880s, and these had been displayed for decades in Newton Hall in upstate New York. That building, however, was torn down in 1929, and no record exists as to the fate of the majority of the 456 EEF objects it once housed. Eager efforts to relocate the artefacts were undertaken by Chautauqua Institute's archivist Jon Schmitz in 2014, when the British Museum enquired after material excavated by Flinders Petrie's teams at Naukratis. Schmitz ran a short article in the Institute's newspaper, in response to which a long-time Chautauquan informed him that there had once been several boxes of antiquities stored in a crawl-space under the Hall of Christ where she played as a child in the 1950s and early 1960s. Groups of children, she recalled, would amuse themselves with the jewellery, and invent games using the statues and other items that they happened upon. When a new foundation was added to the building in the mid-1960s, all of what was stored in crawl space was taken to the dump.

Chautauqua's was not the only collection to be so discarded. Brown University's Jenks Museum hauled 92 truckloads of specimens to the University's landfill site on Seekonk River in 1945, in what was a novel interpretation of the perceived obligation to store the collection on University property.[45] It is possible that this included some of the substantial number of finds recovered during the 1899–1900 season at Abydos, which had been shipped to Brown's Professor of Zoology and Geology, Alpheus Spring Packard, Jr. A few pieces, however, found reprieve in the Haffenreffer Museum (Brown's anthropology collection), or in the Rhode Island School of Design. Other US educational establishments similarly discontinued their museum collections. Among them was Colorado College, whose once 16,000-object collection – among which was an extensive series of small finds from the EES Graeco-Roman Branch's explorations in the Fayum, and a series of bronze statuettes of Egyptian gods from Naville's Bubastis seasons – was dispersed in 1977.

British museums were also unceremoniously closing. The 1948 *Directory of Museums*, compiled by the Museums Association, reveals that one third of the 160 museums that closed during the war were unable to reopen. One of these was London's Whitechapel Museum,[46] an institution once distinguished as being the smallest in Britain and the first to be supported by local taxation.[47] Its collections were originally spread throughout the borough's libraries, as well as a disused mausoleum in St George in the East's churchyard, where a Nature Study Museum provided children of the overcrowded inner city area of Stepney with a space to discover the outside world. The curator, Kate Marion Hall (1861–1918), was the first woman in Britain to hold a paid professional role in the museum sector,[48] and she maintained Whitechapel Museum's leather-bound, hand-written registers that list the many thousands of things once present, everything from South African dried geckos to Guyanese weaponry.[49] These ledgers also record a small consignment of twenty amulets and pottery fragments from the 1904 EEF excavations at Deir el-Bahri, probably acquired via Kate's nephew, Henry Hall (1873–

1930), an Egyptologist and Assistant Keeper in the British Museum. Another dispatch of Egyptian material came after her death, this time from the excavations at Amarna in 1934, to complement a growing Egyptology section. But the Second World War changed all that. First, the small Nature Study Museum closed its doors as its primary audience was evacuated to the country. It never reopened. Then, in February 1954, a small advert was placed in the *Museums Journal* announcing brusquely that 'by order of the Stepney Borough Council, the collections of the Whitechapel Museum are now to be dispersed'. Archive papers reveal that, while it would 'undoubtedly retain any items that are purely local interest', the committee was anxious that material be disposed of as quickly as possible.[50] Today, all that remains of the Whitechapel Museum is a forlorn and dilapidated redbrick building, surrounded by gravestones, in St George in the East (Fig. 5.2). Its Egyptian collections were, fortunately, transferred to the Horniman Museum and the Higgins Art Gallery and Museum in Bedford.

Small, local authority institutions were clearly vulnerable. In Falmouth, Cornwall, the Borough Council had maintained a modest museum since the early twentieth century, and from 1931 it was managed and housed by the Royal Cornwall Polytechnic Society. Funding was withdrawn by the council in 1939, rents rose and in 1948 it was reported to the Town Council that

> The Museum has had no curatorial assistance for many years and the present custodian is solely an attendant-cleaner who, although he has charge of keys etc., has no curatorial knowledge. Any systematic arrangement that may at one time have existed is completely obliterated. Confusion exists and the general appearance of the Museum is a jumble of heterogeneous cases with equally heterogeneous and dusty contents that must bewilder rather than educate or give pleasure to the visitor.[51]

In response to this report it was suggested that the collection be reduced to items of Cornish interest, and that a qualified curator be employed. Instead, the council resolved to auction off the whole collection in a local sale. Townsfolk and regional dealers flocked to the Polytechnic Society's premises, where lots of material, including its Egyptian collection, had been drawn up.[52]

The whereabouts of many such disbanded museum collections are hard to ascertain. The fate of the collection at London's Sunday-School Teachers' Institute on Fleet Street, following the institution's relocation in

Fig. 5.2 The former Stepney Borough Natural History Study Museum in London's St George in the East cemetry. Photograph © Alice Stevenson, 2017.

the 1920s, seems not even to have been worthy of mention in any of the Church of England's Minute Books.[53] In the absence of the charismatic authority of its curator, Reverend Kitchin, the collection seems to have become moribund. The personal zeal of such individuals in the foundation of collections is a common theme in museum histories, but so too is the vulnerability of the museums reliant upon them. Although museums may aspire to permanence, as one scholar reflected on the fate of the Jenks Museum, it is only mortal beings that manage them.[54] In the Netherlands of the 1920s, for instance, the banker and ambitious dilettante C. W. Lunsingh Scheurleer (1881–1941) founded a museum in his name, Museum Scheurleer. Ever keen to ingratiate himself within scholarly circles, Scheurleer personally secured sizeable quantities of Egyptian antiquities directly from Flinders Petrie and the BSAE, to display according to his own aesthetic tastes and in order to secure cultural legitimacy.[55] When he was declared bankrupt in 1934 his museum was closed. Although much of the collection was readily adopted by the University of Amsterdam's Allard Pierson Museum, somewhere in the transfer at least forty BSAE-excavated objects simply vanished.[56]

The most dramatic example of charismatic authority and lost museums, however, is undoubtedly the fate of the astonishing collection amassed by pharmaceutical magnate Sir Henry Wellcome (1853–1936). His assemblage was so vast that it was measured in metric tonnes. Frances Larson has referred to this collection as an 'infinity of things',[57] a quixotic attempt to complete a panoramic Historical Medical Museum that would marshal the whole history of humankind. Wellcome's ambition was never realized, and he never saw the majority of his acquisitions, most of which remained in unopened storage crates in warehouses across London. When he died in 1936 it took forty years for these materials to be rehomed, among which were significant quantities of finds made by British organizations in Egypt. Pottery from the prehistoric cemeteries of the Badari region, fragments of 5000-year-old life-sized stone lions from Koptos, and amulets from Akhenaten's and Nefertiti's home at Amarna were all on the move again. In total, more than 300 crates of ancient Egyptian material alone were distributed from Wellcome's hoard in the 1960s and 1970s via the Petrie Museum. Liverpool Museum benefited from at least 90 of these cases, while the University of Wales in Swansea received 92 and the University of Durham's Oriental Museum, founded in 1952, received around 4000 Egyptian objects.

Orphaned Collections

In contrast to the collections that were actively being moved, many simply stayed put. Institutional memory around them, however, receded. In the absence of formal documentation, and with the death of previous generations of curators like the Reverend Kitchin who so passionately animated them, many objects were rendered mute. The scale of the problem became clear to Professor H. W. Fairman, an Egyptologist at the University of Liverpool who, together with a young graduate student named Barry Kemp, attempted to locate material from John Garstang's early twentieth-century excavations in 1963. Fairman and Kemp typed dozens of letters to institutions enquiring after the dispersed assemblages. Several of the replies in the Garstang Museum's archives are confessions that no record of Egyptian artefacts could be found. Yet these were institutions that had eagerly coveted ancient artefacts decades before. The juxtaposition of these 1960s admissions with earlier enthusiastic communications from the same institutions throws into relief the short-term reality of museum lives, despite the long-term ambitions made for them. The curator of Leicester Museum, for instance, wrote enthusiastically to John Garstang in 1904 stating that 'I can assure you that they will be highly appreciated by us when received'.[58] Sixty years later, his successor could find no trace of them.[59] Ipswich Museum received several cases of finds from John Garstang's excavations at Beni Hassan in 1904, but these were reportedly untraceable in 1963.[60]

In some cases, such as Ipswich's, it has since become clear that the objects were there all along, and what was lost was the original documentation. On dispatch from the BSAE and EEF, objects were usually accompanied by cardboard labels containing information about the origin of the object on one side, and a pre-printed instruction in bold letters on the other: 'keep with the objects'. Too often, label and object became separated, any knowledge of the artefact's significance and history remaining only in the mind of the all-too-mortal curator. The objects were obstinately silent to the untrained eye, as it was the label that conferred value. Documentation practices in museums are often perceived as somewhat dull and routine aspects of daily business, but they are the very soul of institutional potential.

Museum Developments

The rather dramatic shift in attitudes to the integrity of museum collections in the mid-twentieth century can be explained by the loss of curatorial expertise, post-war austerity and the logistical challenges of rebuilding galleries damaged during wartime. But death, debt and destruction were not the only factors at play. The war enabled the museum profession to develop new approaches to display, building upon pre-war recommendations in the Miers and Markham's reports,[61] as spaces were vacated by the mass evacuation of objects, in turn forcing curators to adopt new means of narrating themes within galleries. British-based curators also found themselves subject to the demands of mounting high-turnover war propaganda in their displays, which shaped attitudes to permanent galleries when collections began to be returned to their showcases.[62] Nevertheless, efforts to reform receded with the return of curators from their wartime postings, with many retreating initially into the comfort of more traditional modes of practice. It was not really until the 1950s and 1960s that the mantra of decluttering was further promoted by museum reformers through the publication of a series of handbooks encouraging new aesthetic considerations and educational requirements. UNESCO, for example, produced exhibition advice that commended the virtues of orderly displays in which each object 'can be enjoyed on its own with out the intrusion of another', would be placed in an exhibit that might 'catch the eye of the passer-by', and should be set in a gallery that 'must have a pleasing appearance with an artistic colour scheme'.[63]

These trends in the deconstruction of 'salon' style dense displays (Fig. 5.3) were accompanied by the proliferation of dioramas and a new pictoralism[64] that emphasized experience to the detriment of the number of objects on display.[65] Dioramas had first taken root in museums in the late 1920s in natural history museums in Sweden and America, where blank empty spaces and dramatic lighting were mobilized to encourage more selective and focused visitor attention. In Edinburgh, while the museum's disposal board was busily expunging unwanted material, the Keeper of Art and Archaeology, Egyptologist Cyril Aldred (1914–91), was commissioning a series of four large dioramas from artists Raphael Roussel and Dunstan Mortimer for the galleries 'in an attempt to reconstruct notable monuments of different periods in Ancient Egypt and to people them with suitable figures which will illustrate some aspects of their daily life'.[66] These remained on display until the early 2000s, and have more recently been accessioned into the collection as objects in their own right (Fig. 5.4).

Intellectual currents in the USA reflected different tensions. Stephen Conn has suggested that the disappearance of objects from American museum displays coincided with the rise of other kinds of activities inside the museum, including a renewed emphasis on school education, public recreation and popular commercialism.[67] In particular, in thinning out their galleries, many institutions in the US museum sector aligned with a commodity culture fostered by inter-war department stores that emphasized the modernist ideals of discretion over accumulation.[68] American museums were also more vulnerable to the boom and bust cycle of the early twentieth century, given that many were tied to wealthy patrons. The period after the Second World War has been considered something of a 'dark age',[69] one which left museums 'stranded in an institutional, methodological, and theoretical backwater'.[70] Nevertheless, the intercity competitiveness of previous decades maintained pressure on collection management strategies. Many of the aggressive sales in places like Minneapolis, New York and Philadelphia during the 1950s, for instance, have been attributed to a perceived need for such institutions to rid themselves of unfashionable objects and invest in improving their permanent collections.[71] This gear-shift coincided with a more widespread acceptance of abstract modern art, for which New York, rather than Paris, had by the 1960s become the main cultural centre, and the Museum of Modern Art (MoMA) its hugely successful and influential arbiter. Cultural authority was now sought through modern, rather than ancient, art.[72] This accounts for the dismissal of antiquities from Minneapolis Institute of Fine Arts,

Fig. 5.3 Example of a pre-war display at the Ashmolean Museum, 1939. Image © Ashmolean Museum, University of Oxford.

Fig. 5.4 Diorama commissioned by Cyril Aldred to illustrate late Predynastic king Scorpion performing an agricultural ceremony © National Museums Scotland (V.2013.68).

where the director had a personal interest in modern art.[73] In Pasadena, the Art Institute received a bequest of around 500 artworks in 1953 that tipped the collection's balance decisively towards modern art. It began to develop its new focus, acquiring works from Larry Bell to Andy Warhol, and was ultimately renamed the Pasadena Museum of Modern Art in 1973, before its management was assumed by Norton Simon. These new directions made the museum's collection of Amarna art from the EES increasingly irrelevant, leading to the 1969 sale of its Egyptian antiquities.

Alongside these changes in museum practice there were additional longer-term social trends at work that had already begun to undermine the physical collecting of antiquities in the field, and their acquisition by museums. These included changes in the disciplinary frameworks through which objects were understood, and in the value that society at large placed upon tangible goods. In Britain, many of these object habits had begun to shift years before the first bombs fell.

Post-war Fieldwork and Disciplinary Practice

Most directly affecting collecting in Egypt itself were political circumstances that severely curtailed British archaeological activities abroad. Britain's military presence in Egypt had been shaky prior to the Second World War, with continuing dissatisfaction among Egyptian nationalists over the 1936 Anglo-Egyptian Treaty. Nonetheless, when new antiquities laws were mooted during the war, familiar protests were voiced by British Egyptologists. The Keeper of Egyptian Antiquities at the British Museum, I. E. S. Edwards (1909–96), pleaded for 'more generous treatment' in the division of finds, and requested that foreign excavators be allowed only 'a limited number of artistic masterpieces and objects of historical and religious interest to be displayed in foreign museums'.[74] The plea was accompanied by a derogatory characterization of 'the native Egyptologist'. Colonial biases were alive and well.

Initially, post-war multilateralism paved the way for the resumption of British-led work in the 1954–55 season at Saqqara. On the surface, this enterprise was to be conducted 'on behalf of, and in collaboration with, the Department of Antiquities', but behind the internationalist language, as William Carruthers has documented, there remained hopes that antiquities for export might be forthcoming in order to distribute among the EES's supporters.[75] The 1956 Suez Canal Crisis rendered those hopes short-lived, and no objects from that season of fieldwork left Egypt. Between 1938 and 1964, other than a few epigraphic seasons and limited survey work, the EES was unable to undertake any large-scale excavations in most of Egypt itself, and instead turned its attentions to Nubia and Sudan. Italian and German fieldwork was similarly reduced, and only the French were able to vigorously pursue investigations.

In the intervening period, the British Academy did begin to provide state funded grants to the EES for the first time from 1947, although this was less a liberal investment in archaeology as a disciplinary enterprise than it was an exercise in ensuring that Britain remained a soft power within the region. During the war there had been renewed calls for a British Institute of Archaeology in Cairo, a move supported by both the British Embassy and the Foreign Office. In early October 1951, Egyptian prime minister, Mostafa al-Nahhas, repudiated the 1936 Anglo-Egyptian Treaty, and anti-British demonstrations erupted.[76] By the end of the month, Law No. 215 dealing with antiquities was passed (Appendix A). In this deteriorating international context the Treasury finally rejected the application for a British Institute. The British Academy grant was nevertheless maintained, which eased the pressure on the EES to leverage public funding through a harvest of archaeological finds. As a result, the accompanying programme of promotion that the Society had pursued for some seventy years was reduced, the annual exhibition abandoned and the widespread distribution of finds significantly curtailed.

In the late 1950s and 1960s excavations came to be situated in the context of Egyptian modernization efforts, which included the building of the Aswan High Dam (1960–71) in order to increase the country's agricultural productivity. The plan would result in extensive flooding of Egypt's southern Nubian Nile, creating Lake Nasser. Preparations for addressing the heritage of the affected region were begun in the mid-1950s, with agencies such as Centre d'Étude et de Documentation sur l'Ancienne Égypte (CEDAE) established prior to the salvage campaign that was launched under the aegis of UNESCO in March 1960 with an international appeal for help. Carruthers has described the CEDAE as a 'revolutionary ordering mission' that gave Egyptians leverage, as their government encouraged foreign institutions to embark on excavation and preservation work in Nubia.[77] Many new parties were also able to commence work, including those from Poland and India; these parties were now also able to benefit from partage. In the case of Poland, this was the beginning of a long-term commitment to the study of Egyptology through active fieldwork, in what was an ever more crowded mosaic of foreign concessions that Britain now competed with.

The UNESCO appeal came at an opportune moment for the EES. The Society, being unable to work in Egypt, had already commenced excavations in northern Sudan in 1957 at the Middle Kingdom fort site of Buhen, and was thus well placed to benefit from the British Government's gift of £75,000 to save the temples of Abu Simbel. The dig director, Walter B. Emery (1902–71), suggested that the EES could additionally contribute to the salvage efforts by excavating at Qasr Ibrim in Nubia, 'where there were cemeteries containing rich graves'.[78] The lure of antiquities remained, and Emery, who maintained many of Petrie's by now outdated methods and ideas about the 'dynastic race', noted with optimism that 'in the case of sites in Egyptian Nubia which were not productive of antiquities but were otherwise important, the Egyptian Government had undertaken to recompense excavators from the antiquities in their magazines'.[79] The UNESCO campaign did result in what proved to be the final temporary exhibition of EES finds from a recent expedition, and a subsequent distribution of finds to twenty institutions in the Britain, the USA and Canada, but this was exceptional. It was merely recompense for the British Government's financial support of the salvage operation. Nevertheless, it was not lost on the British media that the amount of material displayed was still 'small enough to be contained in the fifth room at the museum', and was 'modest'.[80]

In terms of archaeological practice more broadly, fieldwork methodologies had altered significantly by the war, and the disciplinary boundaries between the related fields of archaeology, anthropology and Egyptology were more sharply defined by their proponents. Most notably, from the 1930s onwards all three disciplines became less fixated upon the recovery of artefacts and on the use of objects for the production of knowledge. In anthropology, fieldwork now privileged the generation of field notes for the production of original forms of ethnographic monograph that moved 'away from the physical and material towards the psychological and social aspects of the life of Mankind'.[81] At the London School of Economics, anthropologist Bronislaw Malinowski (1884–42) had led the charge, and he implored his colleagues to discard 'the purely Antiquarian association with Archaeology and even pre-history'.[82] In the USA, the anthropological vision of Franz Boas cast an increasingly long shadow over evolutionary assumptions. His view that museum displays should be contextual rather than evolutionary had not been accepted overnight, but by the late 1930s was recounted as general wisdom.[83] As an experienced museum curator,[84] as well as a German-born and educated citizen steeped in German Kulturgeschicte approaches, Boas had a dim view of the series of objects that had been the mainstay of late Victorian exhibition arrangements in Britain. He instead advocated culture as the organizing principle of human difference, one manifested through the more abstract ideational world of symbolic meaning.[85]

In archaeology, earlier descriptive studies of objects, like those of Petrie and his colleagues, began to be replaced by a new emphasis upon site features and depositional sequences. This change is typified by the practice of the widely influential Mortimer Wheeler (1890–1976), whose work in several countries from the 1920s, and particularly from the 1930s onwards, employed box grids, encouraging far greater attention to site formation histories.[86] Wheeler and his colleagues were vocal in their criticism of Petrie, and they actively instilled in the new generation the idea that archaeologists were responsible for 'digging up, not things, but people'.[87] As anthropology and archaeology both sought self-definition through specific fieldwork methodologies that were actively taught as part of the professionalization of the disciplines, Egyptology, faced with more restricted opportunities for new fieldwork, looked increasingly inwards towards its most uniquely distinguishing feature: the ancient language. It is perhaps no coincidence that Eric Peet (1882–1934) had remarked in his inaugural University of Oxford lecture of 'the present position of Egyptological studies', that 'we are not very likely to learn very much more Egyptian history from excavation in Egypt itself.'[88] This constituted for Egyptology what the American archaeologist, W. Y. Adams, has referred to as a disciplinary 'divorce' from anthropology.[89] These trends were all part of a gradual, albeit uneven, diminution of the status of objects within the formation of knowledge.

Despite these divergent disciplinary paths, what was shared across these subjects more generally was implicit agreement about the diminishing role of the narrative of 'civilization'. For much of the nineteenth century this ideology had propelled the assured intellectual discourses of Western civilization's continuing progression and, in equal measure, concern about its degeneration. As Chris Wingfield has noted, the post-war shift away from these frameworks can be linked to ideological changes that accompanied Britain's move from an expansionist imperialistic power in the nineteenth century, towards an actively decolonizing nation in the later twentieth century.[90] This observation highlights again the need to situate museum and disciplinary practice within the wider world. In this vein, a series of cultural shifts that also had a profound impact on attitudes towards archaeological practices, antiquities and their place in the museum can be identified: developments in home-building and interior design, and the post-war future boom.

Post-war Object Habits

In Britain, the aesthetic modernism that had first taken root on the continent earlier in the twentieth century finally came ashore after the Second World War. Le Corbusier's architectural 'machine for living in' eschewed ornament, while English art historians and philosophers such as Herbert Read (1893–1968) argued for industrial art that was stripped down in its aesthetic appeal, would perform a utilitarian function, and would retain value regardless of its cultural or historical context.[91] Cultural commentators looked back on the Victorian era's bric-a-brac consumption with disdain. In the late 1920s, materialist critic Walter Benjamin argued that the busy interiors of the 1860s to 1890s were profoundly soulless and lifeless.[92] Britain lagged behind its continental neighbours in the uptake of modernism in the home, but Second World War rationing and post-war restrictions cemented a distaste for pretentious display and encouraged a wider embrace of continental trends. Sleek, simple designs that were unencumbered by the weight of the trinkets of the Victorian and Edwardian Ages were extolled by magazines such as *Ideal Home*, which catered to a burgeoning middle class. As Britain embarked upon an exuberant period of home-building (up to 300,000 houses a year in the early 1950s under Housing Minister Harold Macmillan),[93] architects progressively imposed open plan interiors that lacked the mantelpieces and parlours that had previously provided platforms for material display.[94] With rising numbers of families becoming homeowners, there emerged a greater concern for fitting in as opposed to standing out.[95] Tastes were being gradually homogenized, and after the bleakness of war, were optimistically infused with the promise of a fresh aesthetic. Decluttering, and the concomitant turn away from object fixations, was as much a general shift in society as it was a result of the internal dynamics of museum practice or the disciplinary focus of archaeology.

The contrast of worldviews was manifest in London's Bloomsbury district. Heal's department store on Tottenham Court Road, an active promoter of modern design, put the spotlight on simple, modernistic steel and timber frames, while a short walk away, UCL's Petrie Museum of Egyptian Archaeology was reinstalling thousands of objects into a cramped set of early twentieth century vitrines in University College London. Despite the Petrie Museum's return to pre-war aesthetics, Britain's Museums Association was echoing the modernizing rhetoric of home improvement magazines, and its official diploma guidance advocated that professionals should 'clear out the clutteration of your collections and make your museums bright and cheerful!'.[96]

This period of home-building in Britain was not just a physical restructuring of domestic and social space: it was equally an ideological reconfiguration. The dominant post-war attitudes regarding the traditional role of women in the home – the 'back-to-the-kitchen' movement – reverberated through educational policy,[97] heavily gendering a workforce that was itself becoming more professionalized. In a searing critique of the gender politics and the history of women in archaeology, Rachel Pope has documented the shift from the relatively intense involvement of women in archaeology during the 1920s and 1930s – albeit along privileged class lines – towards the exodus of older professional female archaeologists from the country as the popular image of women in the home took hold in the 1950s.[98] With the next generation less able to develop active participation in archaeology or museum work, a vacuum emerged. This may go some way towards explaining the dissolution of so many local Egyptology societies at this time, which had been largely administered by women. The Egyptian Research Student Association, which had supported the EEF and BSAE in previous decades, was one such society that became a victim of the times.

A second broad trend undermining the status of antiquities within museums was the post-war 'future-boom'. Nuclear science, the Cold War space race and other such 'Big Science' enterprises were catalysts to a widespread interest in the future and its modern, high-tech visual iconography. As the economic historian David Staley has recognized, these industries depended upon scientifically minded futurists – engineers, systems analysts and economists – who found employment in government agencies and think-tanks.[99] They were the 'advice establishment', tasked with creating predictions for public policy decision-makers, thereby ensuring the diffusion of futurism throughout society. Such modernist idealism found its way into futurist architectural designs for museums, including an unrealized glass and concrete rotunda, the 'Climatron', for the University of Oxford that was proposed in 1967 to replace the Victorian atrium space that the Pitt Rivers collections had occupied since 1884 (Fig. 5.5).[100]

A scientific mindset and an interest in the future was of course nothing new, but this futurist industry was fundamentally different to Victorian conceptualizations, which had been more strongly grounded in the historical field. Under the influence of cultural evolutionism, late Victorian visions of the future, including those popularized by H. G. Wells and Jules Verne, were tied to trends extending from the past through to the present and into the future. Flinders Petrie's material histories, like those of Pitt-Rivers' typologies, were predicated upon an ardent

Fig. 5.5 Photograph of an architect's model showing part of a proposed new building for the Pitt Rivers Museum, designed by Pier Luigi Nervi, Powell and Moya, circa 1967. Courtesy of the Pitt Rivers Museum, University of Oxford (photograph number 2008.74.5).

conservative belief in evolutionary gradualism, in which changes were linear, incremental and could be mapped out along the axis of primitive to civilized with the aid of well-ordered museum collections of antiquities and ethnological specimens. Cross-cultural methods of this nature permitted curators to collapse spatial and temporal distance by bringing together objects for comparative study to create coherent universalist narratives of societal advance or decline. The science boom of the 1950s and 1960s broke away from these nineteenth-century forms of knowledge. Instead of collection and enumeration, experiment and theory were now considered to be foundational to understanding.[101] One further effect of these trends was a widening of the conceptual distance between past and future, as French historian Pierre Nora has observed. The rapid social, political and economic transformations of the 1960s, Nora contends, radically altered the perception of history rendering 'the past totally foreign'.[102]

The relative impacts of these various post-war trends can be illustrated by London's Science Museum, which acquired finds from the EES's work at Amarna and Armant in the 1920s and 1930s. The Museum's inter-war director, Sir Henry Lyons, had played a key role in securing objects based on a long-standing professional interest in Egypt, where he had lived for almost two decades since his 1890 Royal Engineers posting to Cairo. During that time he led clearances of the temples of Buhen, and directed the first Archaeological Survey of Nubia in 1907. As a close acquaintance of several Egyptologists, including Flinders Petrie and Percy Newberry, and as an EES Committee member, Lyon was in a position to ensure that finds distribution came to include the Science Museum once he was appointed its Director in 1919.[103] For Lyons, the museum's 'key-note is development and it aims at illustrating man's striving after a greater efficiency from the earliest stages of his civilization'.[104] Such a position subordinated pure history to the purposes of culture, and was deemed vital to the Science Museum's ongoing cultural relevance.[105]

After the Second World War, the number of antiquities on display was vastly reduced. A report to the Minister of Education in 1951 advised that 'even before the war most collections had been overcrowded', and that 'with even less space, the great developments in science and engineering during the war had to be provided for as well'.[106] The decision was therefore taken to allow no more than a third of what had previously been displayed back into the galleries. In 1952 it was reported that the number of objects in the possession of the museum but not on display before 1939 was around 5 per cent. Just over a decade later that estimate was 50 per cent.[107] Nevertheless, Egypt, now an embedded Western cultural touchstone, still had currency as a generic reference for antiquity. Therefore, although when the new agricultural galleries opened in 1951 dioramas took centre stage to demonstrate the modern development of rural industries, the gallery was framed overhead by large vignettes of ancient Egyptian agricultural scenes, despite few genuine antiquities being present.[108] By the 1960s, however, there was increasing anxiety about the institution's purpose. Museum directors maintained that conveying progress was of primary importance to the institution, and although temporary exhibitions did occasionally include ancient Egyptian material, the post-war media counselled that the museum's focus should be new science, not old technology.[109] By the 1970s, Egypt's visible presence in the institution was minimal, and the Egyptian objects acquired during Lyon's tenure came to be regarded as 'relics'[110] of old museum practices.[111]

***

A dismal picture of the museum world can easily be painted for the decades either side of the Second World War. To do so, however, is to ignore the opportunities that arose in other places as institutions divested. A simplistic portrayal of these decades as ones of stagnation and disengagement for the museum sector misrepresents a more nuanced period of institutional activity. Claire Wintle, for instance, has identified more collaborative, egalitarian museum practices in this period, in which national and university museums cooperated with, and provided placements for, museum professionals from decolonizing nations, as well as pathways through which collections moved in and out of Britain.[112] An artefact's value and status was negotiable, being dependent upon the context in which it found itself.[113] Many could be repurposed, as a group of Egyptian objects sent back to Africa in the 1950s highlights.

A Return to Africa: Egypt in Ghana

Ghana was the first sub-Saharan African country to attain independence from colonial rule. In March 1957, on the eve of independence, the newly built National Museum of Ghana opened it doors to the public in Adabraka, Accra. It had been designed by a British architect and inaugurated by a British royal, yet this Eurocentric construction was intended to valorize a more ancient pre-colonial Ghanaian past (Fig. 5.6). And in order to do so, Egyptian artefacts, dispossessed from British museums, including Reading Museum and Art Gallery, the Ashmolean Museum, the Pitt Rivers Museum,

Fig. 5.6 Outside the National Museum of Ghana. Photograph © Alice Stevenson, 2017.

the Wellcome Historical Medical Museum and Tunbridge Wells Museum,[114] became caught up in a complex West African dialogue between new cultural institutions, symbolic nationalism and pan-African ideologies.

A Department of Archaeology was first founded in 1951 at the University College of the Gold Coast, Legon. It encompassed Achimota College's teaching collection, an eclectic assemblage developed initially by colonial administrators and systematized by Cambridge-educated archaeologist Charles Thursten Shaw (1914–2013). Unlike the establishment of colonial museums in the nineteenth and early twentieth centuries, the post-war British Government now took a more active interest in such institutions, with attempts made to found museums in West Africa under the auspices of the British Colonial Office between 1938 and 1948. These activities were envisaged as a paternalistic partnership through which the metropole sought to guide the colonies towards self-government, civil society and educational progress. These sorts of sporadic initiatives in Nigeria, Sierra Leone and the Gold Coast never reached fruition, with British officials remaining circumspect about the cost and value of the exercise.[115] In 1951, the Government of the Gold Coast independently approached Arnold W. Lawrence (1900–91), a Professor of Archaeology at the University College – and younger brother of T. E. Lawrence – to form a national museum.[116] It was at this point that Achimota's collection became the nucleus around which the new institution developed, with Lawrence the man responsible for bringing a diverse collection to hot and humid Legon. A few years after the inauguration of the new museum building, Richard Nunoo (1922–2007) – who had previously studied at London's Institute of Archaeology and at the British Museum – took over the role. He oversaw the transfer of about half of the objects at the university to the modern museum.[117]

The creation of a new nation, and a national museum, was a daunting prospect. The former Gold Coast Colony encompassed a diversity of ethnic and elite groups, resulting in complex tensions between national identities, regional loyalties and its new leader, Kwame Nkrumah's (1909–72), radical post-colonial politics. One strategy adopted to transcend these differences was to appeal to a pre-colonial identity. Joseph B. Danquah's *The Akan Doctrine of God* (1944), whose 'Ghana hypothesis' sought deep historical roots for a common 'Empire of Ghana' on the fringes of the Sahara Desert, was one source.[118] At Achimota College, the anthropologist Eva Meyerowitz took this theory even further. Ghana's origins (more specifically, those of the Akan ethno-linguistic groups), she argued, were to be found in Egypt's pharaonic past.[119] Lawrence agreed, defending the rationale that in the new National Museum 'Ancient Egypt had to be treated rather amply, in view of known or suspect relations with West Africa'.[120] This became a common refrain in the 1950s and 1960s in West Africa, with the respected Senegalese historian and physicist, Cheikh Anta Diop (1923–86), publishing a number of influential works fuelling origin myths based on migration from Egypt.[121] Therefore, although it might be expected that West Africa would be the sole focus for Accra's newest museum displays, additional relics from Nigeria and Southern Africa, the Greek, Carthaginian and Roman periods in North Africa, as well as ancient Egyptian finds, were prominent. As stated in the museum's first annual report, the scope of the museum 'has been defined, for the time being, as: to represent the culture of the Gold Coast from the earliest times to the present day, against the background of what Man has achieved throughout the rest of Africa; material from other continents is excluded unless relevant to African studies.'[122] To this end, Lawrence used his personal connections to procure for the nascent National Museum a large group of Egyptian artefacts, including a black-topped Predynastic pot, excavated at Naqada in 1894, from the Ashmolean, and four Predynastic palettes, recovered at Hu in 1899, from Reading Museum, as well as original watercolour copies of tomb paintings made by Norman de Garis Davies on behalf of the EES's Archaeological Survey.

In accommodating these things, the museum's first 'Man in Africa' exhibition partly aligned with Nkrumah's Pan-Africanist ambitions that accepted and admired other African countries' heritage as belonging to the entire continent, especially that of Egypt.[123] The original layout of the museum materialized these various cross-cutting rationales by dividing the 'cumbersome'[124] circular display area in two; the first section was dedicated to local and regional collections of Ghana, and the second to wider relations which 'inevitably begins with Ancient Egypt, that great source of civilization whose influence still seems to be recognizable in West African culture'.[125]

Unfortunately, most of these connections were tenuous. Ghanaian archaeology was still in its infancy in the 1950s, and few absolute dates were available to tether local finds to a clear chronology. As a result, there was a tendency for anthropologists to 'derive anything of skill, culture or interest in sub-Saharan Africa from Egypt'.[126] Such deference to Egyptian archaeology also regrettably continued to give credence in the West to the scientific racism inherent in related theories such as the Hamitic hypothesis. These paradigms credited the major achievements of more 'advanced' African people below the Sahara (such as Ghana or Great Zimbabwe) to their 'Hamitic' ancestors, who many scholars considered to be, on entirely spurious grounds, 'Mediterranean' rather than 'Negroid'.[127]

Other connections represented by these collections had more immediate political goals. The appeal to ancient Egypt, for instance, resonated with the post-colonial political and social orders created during the 1950s and 1960s, including the Non-Aligned Movement.[128] South-to-south gift exchanges between President Nkrumah and Egypt's Gamal Abdel Nasser (1918–70), together with Nkrumah's marriage to an Egyptian, Fathia Halim Ritzk (1932–2007), ensured that additional ancient Egyptian objects percolated into Africa's newest museum.[129] When Peter Shinnie, Head of the Department of Archaeology at the University of Ghana from 1958, proposed that he and his students should contribute to the international efforts to save the monuments of Nubia, it 'was well received in Ghana at the highest level of government and special funds were provided'.[130] This made possible three seasons of excavation, from 1961 to 1964, at the medieval Nubian town of Debeira West. The country's involvement in the UNESCO Aswan Dam campaign was portrayed on new Ghanaian postage stamps, one of the most common pictorial devices in Africa. Postage stamps had previously been a tool of colonial authority, but after independence were used to proclaim and legitimize African statesmanship, and were issued under direct mandate from Nkrumah's Cabinet. In November 1963, a series of 'Save the Monuments of Nubia' stamps was issued, including images of Pharaoh Ramesses II at Abu Simbel, and Queen Nefertari. These images of ancient Egyptian royalty and monuments were juxtaposed with the Ghanaian flag, in effect equating the glories of ancient Egypt with Ghanaian history.[131]

On the National Museum's opening, Nkrumah opined that the space available for the displays was too small and would require extensions. He further expressed a personal interest in designing fresh displays and facilities.[132] Whether he did so is unknown, but the initial extension plans announced in a 1965 issue of the UNESCO quarterly journal, *Museum*, included a Department of Egyptology with a greatly enlarged Egyptological collection.[133] It was never to be. The year after UNESCO published its optimistic and confident account, Nkramah was deposed in a military coup and fled into exile. After the early fluorescence of activity,

Fig. 5.7 'Save the monuments of Nubia':
Ghanaian stamps dated 1963. Photograph © Alice Stevenson 2017.

the Egyptian collection was largely disregarded and, when displayed, was set in a little-frequented and easily overlooked mezzanine level.[134] Only a few original pieces were included, with the majority of displays comprising plaster casts of more substantial works of art. Just over a decade after assertions that Egypt would have a key role in the museum, the National Museum's handbook made no mention of it,[135] although Nile Valley archaeology continued to be taught at the University in the 1970s and 1980s by Shinnie's first student, James Anquandah (1938–2017).

The museum's initial aims have ultimately been considered ineffective, and it has played a marginal role in Ghanaian life.[136] Most Ghanaian citizens deem the National Museum to be a tourist destination for foreigners, or else the preserve of a small educated middle-class, not a locally relevant symbol. Its failure might also be attributable to West African object habits that did not support centralized accumulation. As Malcolm McLeod has remarked, artefacts severed from their cultural context are thought by many Ghanaians to have lost their meaning, and are thus considered unworthy of keeping.[137] This is a philosophy that challenges what is often considered the standard museum functions of active collecting and preservation of cultural heritage.

***

In the post-war period, archaeological artefacts became increasingly nomadic, tracking circuitous routes from their original destinations to fresh settings where they were evaluated with alternative sensibilities. In terms of the development of archaeology, Egyptology and museums, it is a period that has attracted far less scrutiny than the Victorian, Edwardian and inter-war eras, but developments in these areas was clearly just as dynamic and changeable as had been the case earlier. The realities of managing large collections were starkly apparent, on occasion being quietly managed by transferring objects to other institutions or else aggressively marketed by selling artefacts openly to the public. The result, for some institutions, was decisive, and museums emerge not as the final resting place for objects, as is so often assumed, but as just one of many potential stopping points in their lives. Even if artefacts escaped damage in wartime conflict or emergency storage conditions, meaning that their material qualities had not changed, many nevertheless lost the allure that they had once held for previous generations whose objects habits they more closely resonated with. None were immune from post-war politics that directly and indirectly affected their futures.

Notes

1. Anon 1941. Liverpool museums destroyed. *The Museums Journal* 41(6): 55.
2. Accession numbers EA 18680 and EA 22149, respectively. In total there were 63 objects on loan from the British Museum to Hull at the time of the bombing. With thanks to John Taylor for drawing these to my attention.
3. The Phoenix project was never published, but some information is given on Hull Museum's website: Available at: http://museums.hullcc.gov.uk/collections/storydetail.php?irn=439 [accessed 10 May 2017].
4. EEF 1888. *Report of the Sixth Annual General Meeting*. London: Egypt Exploration Fund, pp. 22–3.
5. Petrie noted that that the 'risks due to many peaceful causes – to say nothing of the greater risks of warfare – render any one museum at least liable to serious injury'. Petrie, W. M. F. 1903. Report. *Egypt Exploration Fund Report of the Seventeenth Ordinary General Meeting*. Egypt Exploration Fund: London, p. 22.
6. Voss, B. 2012. Curation as research: a case study in orphaned and underreported archaeological collections. *Archaeological Dialogues* 19(2): 14.
7. For example, Macdonald, S. 1998. Exhibitions of power and powers of exhibition. In MacDonald, S. (ed.) *The Politics of Display: Museums, Science, Culture*. New York: Routledge, pp. 9–15; Kavanagh, G. 1990. *History Curatorship*. Leicester and London: Leicester University Press, p. 32; Karp, I. 1991. Other cultures in museum perspective. In Karp, I. and Lavine, S. D. (eds.) *Exhibiting Cultures: The Poetics and Politics of Museum Display*. Washington: Smithsonian Institution Press, p. 378.
8. Letter from the Curator of Norwich Castle Museum to Hilda Petrie, 18 December 1948, PMA/WFP1/D32. I am grateful to Faye Kalloniatis and Maarten Horn for information on the Egyptian Society of East Anglia.
9. Committee Meeting minutes, 15 May 1951, Glasgow Egypt Society Minutes Book 3, Kelvingrove Museum archives.
10. Letter from W. Bulmer of the Society of Antiquities of Newcastle Upon Tyne to Lady Flinders Petrie, 13 December 1948, PMA/WFP1/D32.4.
11. These trends were not limited to Egyptology, but were equally felt in other areas of the museum world. A report in the 1952 May edition of Britain's *Museum Journal* lamented that 'many museums are quietly destroying or dumping large mammals, are sending back ethnological collections to their countries of origin, and are speeding up the gradual disintegration of exotic insects'. Owen, D. 1952. The changing outlook. *Museums Journal* 52(5): 51–3.
12. Knowles, C. 2014. Negative space: tracing absent images in the National Museums Scotland's collections. In Edwards, E. and Lien, S. (eds.) *Uncertain Images: Museums and the Work of Photographs*. Farnham; Ashgate, pp. 73–91.
13. Allan, D. A. 1949. Museums and education. *Journal of the Royal Society of Arts* 97: 964.
14. Miers, H. A. 1928. *A Report on the Public Museums of the British Isles (Other Than the National Museums)*. Dunfermline: Carnegie United Kingdom Trust, p. 40; Markham, S. F. 1938. *A Report on the Museums and Art Galleries of the British Isles (other than National Museums)*. Edinburgh: Constable, p. 84.
15. Allan, Museums and education, p. 962.
16. Norwich Record Office, N/TC 20/8, Museum Committee minutes 1950–6, folio 178 (Jan 1953). With thanks to Faye Kalloniatis for bringing this to my attention.
17. Norwich Record Office, Museum Committee minutes 1950–6.
18. Sue Giles, Bristol Museum and Art Gallery, personal communication.
19. Letter from L. V. Grinsell to Prof. Fairman, 1 July 1963, University of Liverpool, Garstang Museum archives.
20. Museum and Art Gallery Committee Minutes, 5 September 1952, p. 4. Offprint in Reading Museum and Art Gallery.
21. Harden, D. B. 1955. The cult of the known. *Museums Journal* 55(6): 152.
22. Similar threats also led to ethnographic and fine art collections being disposed of carelessly at this time, for more see Robertson, I. 1995. Infamous deaccessions. In Fahy, A. (ed.) *Collections Management*. London and New York: Routledge, pp. 168–71.
23. Letter from I. E. S. Edwards to D. Dunham, 15 November 1954, British Museum, Department of Egypt and Sudan archives. With thanks to John Taylor for drawing these letters to my attention.

24 A good overview of the debates that emerged at this time is collected together in Weil, S. E. (ed.) 1997. *A Deaccession Reader*. American Association of Museums: Washington.
25 Canaday, J. 1972. Very quiet and very dangerous. *The New York Times*, 27 February 1972.
26 Husband, T. 2013. *Creating the Cloisters*. New York: Metropolitan Museum of Art, p. 43.
27 Metropolitan Museum Archives, Rorimer Box 3, Folder 3.
28 Letter from Metropolitan Museum of Art to the Kate Bradbury, 27 November 1899, EES. DIST.17.16.
29 Forest, R. W. 1929. How museums can most wisely dispose of surplus material. *The Metropolitan Museum of Art Bulletin* 24(6): 158–60.
30 Hoving, T. 1993. *Making the Mummies Dance: Inside the Metropolitan Museum of Art*. New York: Simon and Schuster, p. 290.
31 Hoving, *Making the Mummies Dance*, p. 102.
32 Inter-departmental memo, 30 September 1955, Metropolitan Museum archives, Rorimer Box 3, Folder 3. Objects from British excavations, as well as the MMA's own excavations in Egypt, were included.
33 Letter from Arthur Fischer, Lucerne 'Galerie Fischer', to Mr Rorimer, 3 March 1955, Metropolitan Museum archives, Rorimer Box 3, Folder 3.
34 Elias, C. 2012. Discovering Egypt: Egyptian antiquities at the University of Melbourne. *University of Melbourne Collections* 10: 12.
35 Document entitled 'Re. sale of disposable property at the Museum bookshop', 3 August 1956, Metropolitan Museum archives, Rorimer Box 3, Folder 3.
36 Anon, 1956. *New York Herald-Tribune* Sunday 19 February 1956, press cutting in Metropolitan Museum archives, Rorimer Box 3, Folder 3.
37 Knox, S. 1958. 2500 eagerly buy museum surplus: Egyptian antiquities on sale in lobby for 5 cents to $300 attract many. *New York Times* 13 August 1958: 29.
38 Carey, T. 1978. Bringing museum ethics into focus. *ARTnews*, April: 93.
39 Fox, C. 1959. The gallery shop. *The Brooklyn Museum Bulletin Annual Report 1957–58*: 27–8. During the 1950s, the Egyptian Classical and Ancient Near Eastern Art (ECANEA) department deaccessioned 302 objects, primarily Roman glass, most of which was sold through the Museum's Gallery Shop. Deaccessioned objects from the Arts of the Americas and Decorative Arts collections were similarly treated. None of the objects acquired by Brooklyn from the EEF or EES were deaccessioned between 1950–70. With thanks to Yekaterina Barbash, ECANEA, for the information.
40 Harer, W. B. 2008. The Drexel collection: from Egypt to the diaspora. In D'Auria, S. (ed.) *Servant of Mut: Studies in Honor of Richard A. Fazzini*. Leiden and Boston: Brill, p. 115.
41 Letter from Buckman to H. M. Last, 5 July 1935, EES.USA.COR.
42 As discussed more fully later in this chapter, political circumstances constrained the ability of the EES to excavate in Egypt after the war. When excavations resumed at Saqqara the only international distributions were to Toronto, the Metropolitan Museum of Art and Leiden.
43 Petrie, W. M. F. 1904. *Methods and Aims in Archaeology*. London: Macmillan and Co., p. 180.
44 Lubar, S., Rieppel, L., Daly, A. and Duffy, K. 2017. Lost museums. *Museum History Journal* 10(1): 1–14.
45 Duffy, K. 2017. The dead curator: education and the rise of bureaucratic authority in natural history museums, 1870–1915. *Museum History Journal* 10(1): 29–49.
46 Later known as the Stepney Borough Museum.
47 Hall, K. M. 1901. The smallest museum. *Museums Journal* 1(1): 38–40.
48 Hill, K. 2016. *Women and Museums, 1850–1914: Modernity and the Gendering of Knowledge*. Manchester: Manchester University Press, pp. 23–5.
49 Now in Tower Hamlet Archives: Stepney Borough Museum donations books and accessions books 1896–1940 L/SMB/E/51–3.
50 Letters from Borough Librarian and Supervisor of Museums to South Midlands Museums Federation, 9 July 1953 and 1 January 1954, Stepney Borough Museum correspondence file L/SMB/E/5/4.
51 Falmouth History Archive 1948, courtesy of Michael Carver.
52 For information on the former Falmouth Museum I am very grateful to Michael Carver of the Falmouth History Archive.
53 Held in the Church of England Record Centre, Lambeth, London.
54 Duffy, The dead curator.

55 van Rheeden, H. 2001. The rise and fall of the plaster-cast collection at the Hague Academy of Fine Arts (1920–1960): a personal enterprise of the Dutch dilettante and classicist, Constant Lunsingh Scheurleer (1881–1941). *Journal of the History of Collections* 13(2): 215–29.
56 The Lunsingh Scheurleer museum history is complicated because it also hosted part of the private collection of von Bissing (which itself contained items from Petrie). Some material was sent to Brooklyn, and some to Brussels, and it is possible that the BSAE items went to institutions there.
57 Larson, F. 2009. *An Infinity of Things: How Sir Henry Wellcome Collected the World*. Oxford: Oxford University Press.
58 Letter from curator of Leicester Museum to John Garstang, 11 March 1904, University of Liverpool, Garstang Museum archives.
59 Letter from Leicester Museum to Fairman, 17 July 1963, University of Liverpool, Garstang Museum archives.
60 Letter from Elizabeth Owks, to H. W. Fairman, 9 July 1963, University of Liverpool, Garstang Museum Archives.
61 Miers, *A Report*; Markham, *A Report*. In addition to sparser, more discerning displays, Markham had also recommended a refocus on local collections, and criticized provincial museums for attempting to emulate the universalist displays of the national museums.
62 Svedberg, E. 1949. Museum display. *Journal of the Royal Society of Arts* 97: 850–65. New handbooks and guides on mounting temporary and circulating exhibitions also began to be published post-war, such as Wakefield, H. and White. G. 1959. *Handbook for Museum Curators: Part F Section I: Circulating Exhibitions*. London: Museums Association.
63 Allan, D. A. 1960. The museum and its functions. In UNESCO (ed.) *The Organization of Museums*. Paris: United Nations, pp. 22–3.
64 For example, see Rader, K. A. and Cain, V. E. 2014. *Life on Display: Revolutionizing U.S. Museums of Science and Natural History in the Twentieth Century*. Chicago: Chicago University Press, pp. 52–90; Nahum, A. 2010. Exhibiting Science: changing conceptions of Science Museum display. In Morris, P. J. T. (ed.) *Science for the Nation: Perspectives on the History of the Science Museum*. London: Palgrave Macmillan, pp. 178–86.
65 With the exception perhaps of independent museums that arose in the 1980s and 1990s during the 'heritage boom'. See Candlin, F. 2016. *Micromuseuology: An Analysis of Small Independent Museums*. London: Bloomsbury, chapter 5. For a discussion about the shrinkage of objects on display see Conn, S. 2010. *Do Museums Still Need Objects?* Philadelphia: University of Pennsylvania Press.
66 Aldred, C. 1979. *Scenes from Ancient Egypt in the Royal Scottish Museum Edinburgh*. Edinburgh: Royal Scottish Museum, p. 1.
67 Conn, S. *Do Museums Still Need Objects*? p. 26.
68 Henning, M. 2005. *Museums, Media and Cultural Theory*. Maidenhead: Open University Press, p. 34.
69 Jacknis, I. 2006. A new thing? The NMAI in historical and institutional perspective. *American Indian Quarterly* 30(3/4): 521.
70 Stocking, G. W. 1985. *Objects and Others: Essays on Museums and Material Culture*. Madison: University of Wisconsin Press, p. 8.
71 Conforti, M. 1997. Deaccessioning in American Museums: II – some thoughts for England. In Weil, S. E. (ed.) *A Deaccession Reader*. Washington: American Association of Museums, p. 74.
72 Trask, J. 2012. *Things American: Art Museums and Civic Culture in the Progressive Era*. Philadelphia: University of Pennsylvania Press, p. 234.
73 Harer. The Drexel collection, p. 115.
74 Note from I. E. S. Edwards to the Foreign Office, British Embassy Cairo, 9 April 1943, TNA/FO/371/23355.
75 Carruthers, W. 2016. Multilateral possibilities: decolonization, preservation, and the case of Egypt. *Future Anterior: Journal of Historic Preservation, History, Theory, and Criticism* 13(1): 37–48.
76 Reid, D. 2015. *Contesting Antiquity in Egypt: Archaeologies, Museums and the Struggle for Identities from World War I to Nasser*. Cairo: The American University in Cairo Press, p. 353.
77 Carruthers, Multilateral possibilities.
78 EES Committee Minutes, 17 March 1960.
79 EES Committee Minutes, 17 March 1960.

80 Waterhouse, R. 1968. Touch of Egyptian beauty. EES newspaper cutting n.d. but around October 1968.
81 Rivers, W. H. R. 1917. The government of subject peoples. In Seward, A. C. (ed.) *Science and the Nation: Essays by Cambridge Graduates*. Cambridge: Cambridge University Press, pp. 306–7.
82 Stocking, G. 1996. *After Tylor: British Social Anthropology, 1888–1951*. Madison: University of Wisconsin Press, p. 291.
83 Bennett, T., Cameron, F., Dias, N., Dibley, B, Harrison, R., Jacknis, I. and McCarthy, C. 2017. *Collecting, Ordering, Governing: Anthropology, Museums, and Liberal Government*. Durham, NC: Duke University Press, p.131–2.
84 Boas assisted F. W. Putnam of the Peabody Museum in preparing exhibits for the 1893 Chicago World Fair, then went on to be Curator of Anthropology at the Chicago Field Museum 1893–94 and Assistant Curator of Ethnology and Somatology at the American Museum of Natural History 1896–1905.
85 Boas, F. 1907. Some principles of museum administration. *Science* n.s. 25(650): 921–33.
86 Trigger, B. G. 2006. *A History of Archaeological Thought*. 2nd ed. Cambridge: Cambridge University Press, p. 294.
87 Wheeler, M. R. E. 1954. *Archaeology from the Earth*. Oxford: Oxford University Press, p. v.
88 Peet, E. T. 1934. *The Present Position of Egyptological Studies: An Inaugural Lecture Delivered Before the University of Oxford on 17 January 1934*. Oxford: Clarendon Press.
89 Adams, W. Y. 1997. Anthropology and Egyptology: divorce and remarriage? In Lustig, J. (ed.) *Anthropology and Egyptology: A Developing Dialogue*. Sheffield: Sheffield Academic Press, pp. 25–32.
90 Wingfield, C. 2011. From Greater Britain to Little England: The Pitt Rivers Museum, the Museum of English Life, and their six degrees of separation. *Museum History Journal* 4(2): 245–66.
91 Read, H. 1934. *Art and Industry*. London: Faber and Faber.
92 Benjamin, W. 1985 [1928]. Manorially furnished ten-room apartment. In Benjamin, W. *One Way Street and Other Writings*, translated by Jephcott, E. and Shorter, K. London: Verso, pp. 48–9.
93 For an overview of Macmillan's efforts and British politics at this time see Hennessy, P. 2006. *Having It So Good: Britain in the Fifties*. London: Allen Lane.
94 Attfield, J. 1999. Bringing modernity home. Open plan in the British domestic interior. In Ciearaad, I. (ed.) *At Home: An Anthropology of Domestic Space*. New York: Syracuse University Press, pp. 73–82.
95 Cohen, D. 2006. *Household Gods: The British and their Possessions*. New Haven: Yale University Press, p. 198.
96 P. Storer Peberdy, comments on Harden, The cult of the known, 156. The Museums Association diploma was established in 1934.
97 For example, Newsom, J. 1948. *The Education of Girls*. London: Faber.
98 Pope, R. 2011. Processual archaeology and gender politics: the loss of innocence. *Archaeological Dialogues* 18(1): 59–86.
99 Staley, D. J. 2010. *History and Future: Using Historical Thinking to Imagine the Future*. Lanham: Lexington Books, p. 29.
100 Hicks, D. 2016. Pitt Rivers AD2065: the future of museums, past and present. *Museum iD* 19: 31–7.
101 This contrast has been demonstrated in Allison-Bunnell, S. W. 1998. Making nature 'real' again. Natural history exhibits and public rhetorics of science at the Smithsonian Institution in the early 1960s. In MacDonald, S. (ed.) *The Politics of Display: Museums, Science, Culture*. London and New York: Routledge, pp. 77–83.
102 Nora, P. 2001. *Rethinking France: Les Lieux de memoire, Vol. 1. The State*. Translated by Jordan, D. P. Chicago: University of Chicago Press, pp. xvii–xviii.
103 See Bierbrier, M. L. 2012. *Who Was Who in Egyptology*. London: Egypt Exploration Society, p. 344.
104 Lyons, H. [1933] cited in Scheinfeldt, T. 2016. The first years: the Science Museum at war and peace. In Morris, *Science for the Nation*, p. 52.
105 Scheinfeldt, The first years, p. 51.
106 Science Museum 1940–51. *Report of the Advisory Council Covering the Years 1940–51*, p. 2.
107 Science Museum 1952. *Report on the Policy of the Science Museum 1952*, p. 32.

108 Nahum, Exhibiting Science, p. 181. The exception here was in the weights and measures section, curated by F.G. Skinner who had joined the museum service in 1922. He arranged for a loan of Islamic weights from the Petrie Museum, which arrived in the early 1950s.
109 Anthony, S. 2016. The Science Museum 1950–1983. In Morris, *Science for the Nation*, p. 98.
110 Bud, R. 2016. Infected by the bacillus of science. In Morris, *Science for the Nation*, p. 35.
111 Peter Morris, personal communication. When the Science Museum took over management of the remainder of the Wellcome Collection, further Egyptian items did once again enter the Science Museum as much by accident as design as they were swept up among the many tens of thousands of artefacts were moved to the museum's store at Blythe House.
112 Wintle, C. 2017. De-colonising UK world art institutions, 1945–80. *On Curating* 35. Available at: http://www.on-curating.org/issue-35-reader/decolonising-uk-world-art-institutions-1945-1980-371.html#.Wm2i6pOFhPM [accessed 28 January 2018].
113 Nichols, C. A. 2016. Exchanging anthropological duplicates at the Smithsonian Institute. *Museum Anthropology* 39(2): 130–46.
114 The nucleus of the ancient Egyptian collection was 47 objects purchased from Reading Museum and Art Gallery in 1951, together with material presented by Professor A. B. Cook of the University of Cambridge and watercolours of tomb paintings made by Nina de Garis Davies. The Ashmolean dispatched six Egyptian artefacts in 1953 (along with Sudanese and Medieval English pottery) and the Pitt Rivers sent at least twenty-one flint artefacts from the work led by Gertrude Caton-Thompson in the Fayum. Information from the Annual Reports of the National Museum of Ghana TNA/CO/605/19 and the National Museum of Ghana's Accession registers 1951–7.
115 The British Colonial Office's attempts at administering plans for West African Museums has been outlined in detail by Basu, P. 2012. A museum for Sierra Leone? Amateur enthusiasms and colonial museum policy in British West Africa. In Longair, S. and McAleer, J. (eds.) *Curating Empire: Museums and the British Imperial Experience*. Manchester: Manchester University Press, pp. 145–67.
116 Department of Archaeology and National Museum of the Gold Coast; correspondence and annual reports, Lawrence, A. W. 28 January 1951, National Museum of the Gold Coast, TNA/BW 90/439.
117 Crinson, M. 2001. Nation-building, collecting and display: The National Museum, Ghana. *Journal of the History of Collections* 13(2): 231–50.
118 Danquah was a historian and lawyer that became one leading figure of the United Gold Coast Convention, from which Nkruma's Convention People's Party split in 1949.
119 Meyerowitz, A. 1960. *The Divine Kingship in Ghana and Ancient Egypt*. London: Faber and Faber.
120 Lawrence, A. W. and Merrifield, R. 1957. The National Museum of Ghana. *Museums Journal* 57(7): 89.
121 In English translation: Diop, C. A. 1974. *The African Origin of Civilization: Myth or Reality*. New York: Lawrence Hill and Company.
122 Lawrence, A. W. 1952. *First Annual Report of the Nation Museum of the Gold Coast. For the Year Ending 31 December 1951*. Unpublished manuscript dated 23 February 1952, TNA/CO/605/19.
123 Fuller, H. 2014. *Building the Ghanaian Nation-State: Kwame Nkrumah's Symbolic Nationalism*. New York: Palgrave Macmillan.
124 Nunoo, R. cited in Mew, S. 2016. Managing the cultural past in the newly independent state of Mali and Ghana. In Craggs, R. and Wintle, C. (eds.) *Cultures of Decolonisation: Transnational productions and practices, 1945–70*. Manchester: Manchester University Press, p.181.
125 Lawrence and Merrifield, The National Museum of Ghana, p. 92.
126 Shaw, T. 1990. A personal memoir. In Robertshaw, P. (ed.) *A History of African Archaeology*. London: James Currey Ltd, p. 210.
127 Seligman, C. G. 1930. *Races of Africa*. Oxford: Clarendon Press; see critical overview of this hypothesis in Wengrow, D. 2003. Landscapes of knowledge, idioms of power: the African foundations of ancient Egyptian civilization reconsidered. In O'Connor, D. and Reid, A. (eds.) *Ancient Egypt in Africa*. London: UCL Press, pp. 123–4.
128 The founding countries included Yugoslavia, India, Indonesia, Egypt and Ghana.
129 For example, a Late Period-Ptolemaic anthropoid coffin now in the National Museum collection was reported to be one wedding gift from Nasser to Nkrumah. See Morfini, I. 2016. An Egyptian collection held in the National Museum in Accra. *Göttinger Miszellen* 249: 125–9.

130 Shinnie, P. L. 1990. A personal memoir. In Robertshaw, P. (ed.) *A History of African Archaeology*. London: James Currey Ltd, p. 229.
131 Fuller, H. 2015. Father of the nation: Ghanaian nationalism, internationalism and the political iconography of Kwame Nkrumah, 1957–2010. *African Studies Quarterly* 16(1): 39–75.
132 Nunoo, R. 1965. The National Museum of Ghana, Accra. *Museum. Quarterly Review Published by UNESCO*, 18(3): 155–9.
133 Nunoo, The National Museum, 156. Crinson has suggested that Nkrumah regarded the National Museum with some equivocation due to the director, Lawrence's, association with one of his political rivals and as such may not have actively followed through on these statements. Crinson, Nation-building, 240.
134 Mew, S. 2012. *Rethinking Heritage and Display in National Museums in Ghana and Mali*, PhD thesis. SOAS, University of London, p. 324.
135 National Museum of Ghana 1970. *National Museum of Ghana Handbook: Ethnographical, historical and art collections*. Accra: Ghana Publishing Corporation.
136 Fuller, *Building the Ghanaian Nation-State*, pp. 92–4.
137 McLeod, M. 2004. Museums without collections. Museum philosophy in West Africa. In Knell, S. (ed.) *Museums and the Future of Collecting*. Ashgate: Farnham, pp. 52–61; see also Fogelman, A. 2008. Colonial legacy in African museology: the case of the Ghana National Museum. *Museum Anthropology* 31(1): 19–27.

Chapter 6
Legacies and Futures (1970–)

'Is it worth this to the museums which now hold the scattered fragments?'[1]

In November 2002, a 'Declaration on the Importance and Value of Universal Museums' was issued by the directors of eighteen European and American museums.[2] Their statement stressed that 'objects acquired in earlier times must be viewed in the light of different sensitivities and values, reflective of that earlier era', and highlighted that such artefacts were 'acquired under conditions that are not comparable with current ones'. The proclamation was a counter-challenge to claims from countries seeking the repatriation of their heritage from Western institutions. It has also been read as an implicit call for continued acquisitions from foreign territories,[3] justified on the basis that 'museums serve not just the citizens of one nation but the people of every nation'.[4] The irony of such a statement coming exclusively from wealthy Western institutions was not lost on the worldwide museum community, which largely condemned it as exclusionary and essentialist.[5]

These critiques of the 2002 Declaration form the departure point for a reflection on the history of partage and an evaluation of its legacy in the present. It is a history that is frequently unknown, misunderstood or over-simplified. During my time as the curator of an Egyptian collection, I regularly heard it commented in the galleries that the material on display was stolen, and that it should be returned to Egypt. Such remarks could be dismissed as sweeping, ill-informed generalizations. But underlying them are uncomfortable truths regarding the inequalities on which legal collecting was predicated, as well as the complexities of acquisition, which are frequently not tackled effectively in public exhibitions. Equally, they raise valid questions around ownership (or rather, cultural authority), access and social responsibility that should be addressed. In attempting a critical examination of these issues, and in preparing the ground for a moral argument, the mutable status of antiquities can be a challenge. Despite public museums being the stated final destination for objects that were subject to partage, the realities of dispersal saw antiquities regularly oscillate between the categories of gift and commodity. These competing object habits persist, and artefacts extracted from late nineteenth and early twentieth century excavations continue to enter and exit institutions in a variety of ways. The contemporary object habits of capitalism, commodification and fetishization, like the habits of all other periods in this account, require scrutiny.

In order to navigate these competing values I argue that museums and archaeology should not adopt an instrumentalist approach to managing the past, but follow instead a more contingent model of ethical practice. This is an appeal, too, for more creativity in how museums and archaeology engage with this material, so that a greater variety of narratives around antiquities might be embraced. In this model, a return to partage is completely unnecessary. Instead, I recommend a turn to 'bricolage' in order to animate and layer the myriad meanings that have been sedimented in collections over the passing decades.

Colonial Doubts and International Realignments

The opening rationale of the 'Universal Museum' declaration, that contemporary conditions are not comparable to historic ones, seems at first sight to be a benign truism. Times change. But this is a reductive argument of historicism that glosses over many complex dialectical and unequal relationships that have existed, and continue to exist, between archaeological practices, museum activities and wider society. In its deliberate attempt to relegate the past to a dimension where it is not seen to impinge on the present, the declaration seeks to sanitize the objects inherited from those times. It implies that one set of values existed back then, and a separate, more enlightened, set of values pertains now. Yet, as the past few chapters have shown, attitudes to antiquities have always been ambivalent. As long as excavators and museums have been acquiring things, anxieties over the morals and ethics of doing so have existed.

Take, for instance, the opening quote of this chapter. It speaks to the present, but it comes from a written account of a visit to Bubastis in 1890. Bubastis was an urban and temple site that functioned as a major religious centre for the cult of the cat-headed goddess Bastet in Egypt's Eastern Delta. The Egypt Exploration Fund (EEF) had been excavating there since 1887, furnishing at least twenty-one foreign institutions in seven countries with a record haul of finds in the process. When the author of the 1890 article described what he saw at the site, he professed horror: nearly everything of interest had been removed. 'Egypt', he lamented 'is not all there'.[6] This article serves as an effective reminder that the line between preservation and destruction is a fine one.

His was not the first voice of alarm. Apprehensions had been expressed decades before partage arrangements expedited the export of antiquities. In 1835, Khedive Muhammed Ali (1769–1849) decried that 'foreigners are destroying ancient edifices, extracting stones and other worked objects and exporting them to foreign countries'.[7] George Gliddon (1809–57), an English-born American, published *An Appeal to the Antiquaries of Europe and the Destruction of the Monuments of Egypt* in 1841, decrying the exodus of antiquities from the country. By the early twentieth century the Service of Antiquities itself recognized the damage being done to Egypt's sites and monuments because of scholarly interest from the West.[8] Within archaeological circles there were concerns that the freedom of export had been the source of 'evil to Egyptian archaeology'.[9] This was the view of the University of Liverpool's Classical archaeologist, John Droop. In particular he reprimanded his colleagues for their activities:

> ...with the power of getting what he found for himself or his employers the excavator's attention was in the past too often focused exclusively on the objects, with neglect of the conditions of the finding.

These anxieties also manifested themselves in other domains, such as in fictional tales of unfortunate curators who succumbed to the wrath of re-animated mummies or cursed relics now housed in Western museums.[10] By the late 1940s, there were professional quandaries over the merits of satisfying the apparently insatiable appetites of museums, with Egyptologist Stephen Glanville stating in his 1947 inaugural address at the University of Cambridge, that the acquisition of antiquities 'chiefly for the enhancement of the large European museums and the satisfaction of an uninstructed public curiosity, destroyed almost as much evidence as it garnered.'[11] In 1969, the director of Ulster Museum scoffed that the 'distribution of excavation material by previous generations of Egyptologists has always struck me as a monstrous practice'.[12]

Remonstrations aside, is this not all water under the bridge? Hundreds of thousands of objects were distributed by British organizations from fieldwork in Egypt to museums the world over. It can be reasoned that the model of partage was in fact perfectly legal. Export licenses were issued, and antiquities personnel in Egypt were given opportunities to retain the best material in the country. That does not mean, however, that there were not inequities inherent in the scheme. It was a practice initiated and controlled by colonial powers. Even some of the anxieties cited above stem more from a concern with a lack of provenance for objects that would otherwise better inform Western knowledge, than for the voids left in the Egyptian landscape. Gazing upon richly furnished collections across the Western world should at least give us some pause for thought.

What has certainly changed over the last century is the legislative environment (Appendix A). In 1970, the UNESCO Convention on the Means of Prohibiting and Preventing the Illicit Import, Export and Transfer of Ownership of Cultural Property treaty was formulated, stipulating that no items of cultural heritage could be excavated or exported from a source nation without elaborate permissions from the national government. In essence, this granted artefacts excavated and exported before that year a certain degree of amnesty, but thereafter this international standard was to be upheld. Many market countries remained sceptical. The USA did not join until 1983, Britain not until 2002. Underlying the hesitations were concerns that Western museums would be frustrated in their attempts to acquire materials at a time when they, and the antiquities trade, were once again prospering after post-war stagnation.[13] Britain claimed that the convention was too onerous, overly bureaucratic and would harm its art market. Its eventual decision to join after thirty years of prevarication was motivated not by any concern for foreign antiquities, but by worries over metal detecting and thefts from heritage sites within Britain.[14] The UNESCO Convention was seen as a means to recover objects illegally removed from Britain, not as a framework for monitoring material entering it.[15]

The museum world experienced vigorous growth throughout the 1970s, both in terms of the number of museums and the size and scope of professional museum staff. Modernization of galleries and storerooms in the 1960s, together with widespread professional dialogue around exhibitions, collections management and the needs of visitors, was reflected in a renewed enthusiasm for museum-going among the public.[16] This interest was further energized by blockbuster exhibitions, the first of which catapulted Tutankhamun to the forefront of the British public imagination once more, following shows in the USA, France and Japan in the late 1960s. The 1972 *Treasures of Tutankhamun* exhibition, featuring 45 objects from the tomb, was jointly hosted by the British Museum and Egyptian Ministry of Culture to coincide with the fiftieth anniversary of the discovery. Ostensibly a celebration of archaeological productivity, it was in reality a key element in the re-establishment of diplomatic relationships and cultural exchange between Britain and Egypt following the Suez Canal Crisis, as per the Cultural Convention between Britain and the United Arab Republic, signed in Cairo in September 1965.[17] The exhibition's political caché is apparent from the two years of painstaking diplomacy and extensive bureaucratic machinations that were required to secure the loan, administered through numerous government departments and via the intercession of senior officials.[18] Over the nine months it was on display, it was visited by an estimated 1,694,117 people.[19] After leaving London, the exhibition was hosted at three museums in the USSR, before returning to the United States in 1977–8, where it was vigorously championed by Metropolitan Museum Director Thomas Hoving, who sought to bring a new element of populism to a cultural sector charged with elitism.

The Tutmania of the 1920s had been mediated by the press. These exhibitions, on the other hand, allowed a museum-going public to confront the gold and the wealth of the find for the first time outside Egypt. Personal recollections of the spectacle in London affirm that the finds were received primarily as 'art' rather than history, while archaeology was firmly aligned with the drama of 'discovery' rather than the processes of interpretation.[20] Similarly, the show's stint in America has been credited with dramatically expanding the appeal and reach of the aestheticization of art through the commodification and mass marketing of Tutankhamun's objects. Melani McAlister, for instance, has commented that these transformations in museum display were firmly set within a capitalist and nationalist model: the great nations were not necessarily defined as those that produced great art, but as those who had the taste and the resources to collect and display it.[21] The imperialism and inequalities that suffused the *Tutankhamun* show were apparent to at least some contemporary observers, who linked it to 'colonial brigandage' and noted how, at the expense of modern Egypt, the objects in the exhibition:

> …were stripped of their particular historical dimension and turned instead into vehicles for the romantic dreams and emotional dramas of Western bourgeois art and literature.[22]

Despite the renewed prominence of ancient Egyptian material culture in the West, access to artefacts fresh from the field was curtailed. One hundred years after finds from the EEF's first dig in Egypt had arrived in the British Museum, Egypt passed Law 117 'Protection of Antiquities'

(1983), establishing that all monuments and artefacts uncovered in Egypt were the property of the Egyptian Government. The intention was that all exports would be brought to a halt. The Egyptian Antiquities Organization, 'feeling compelled by the importance of the Egyptian cultural heritage, and desiring to enlarge and enrich the Egyptian museolocial [sic] offer to both Egyptian and the foreign public', now hoped to create a new National Museum of Egyptian Civilization in Cairo (on the Gezira Island Fairgrounds) and a Nubia Museum in Aswan.[23] Formal repatriation requests for items in the British Museum's collection were also issued for the first time, including a plea for the return of a piece of the sphinx's beard held by the British Museum.[24]

Notwithstanding the far greater degree of control exercised by Egypt over its antiquities from 1983, the EES was nevertheless able to negotiate dispensations for limited partage, but under strict conditions (Appendix A). Thus, when the Boston Museum of Fine Arts formally acquired from the EES a Third Intermediate Period wooden coffin in 1994 (from a 1986 distribution of material excavated at Saqqara), a flurry of correspondence attempted to accommodate the museum's *modus operandi* that entailed the signing of a 'Deed of Gift' stating that objects were to be accepted as an 'unrestricted gift'. As the EES pointed out, however, its contract with the Egyptian Higher Council for Antiquities required it to ensure that all exported objects were kept for study in institutes or for exhibition in museums. The transfer of the coffin could not therefore constitute an 'unrestricted gift' – which might be disposed of in the future – unless it was passed directly to another institute or museum.[25]

By the 1990s even these limited divisions had largely ceased. The 2002 Declaration on Universal Museums provoked a strong response in Egypt, and in April 2004 the then Head of the Antiquities Service, Zahi Hawass, organized a convention in Cairo. It was attended by 22 countries and concluded with the 2004 Cairo Declaration on the Protection of Cultural Property. It outlined four general principles:

> Cultural heritage belongs to the country of origin, and is essential to its culture, development and identity. Ownership of cultural heritage by the country of origin does not expire, nor does it face prescription. Cultural property is irrevocably identified with the cultural context in which it was created. It is this original context that gives it its authenticity and unique value. The combating of illicit trade in cultural heritage is the shared responsibility of market countries and countries of origin.[26]

Six years later, Egypt passed an amendment to Law 113, making it absolutely clear that no finds whatsoever were permitted to leave the country, not even a single seed for radiocarbon dating. There are, however, still opportunities to acquire antiquities, as objects excavated by previous generations of archaeologists continue to circulate through the art market.

Selling the Past

From the outset of partage in 1883, there was a single stated justification for permitting it, namely that a public good would be served by enriching public museums and educational establishments. Commercial sales of excavated finds to private individuals were frowned upon. In 1888, for instance, the travel agent Thomas Cook wrote to Flinders Petrie, having been 'informed that the bulk of things' displayed at the annual exhibition of finds were available for purchase, and claimed that 'the object of excavating was to obtain things for sale'.[27] Petrie was furious. He wrote back immediately informing Cook curtly that he was 'completely wrong' and that he was 'anxious to contradict such misstatements'.[28] The EEF regularly proclaimed that it 'must be clearly understood that the principal object of the Fund is that of research… subscriptions, therefore, must not be looked upon as mere purchase money'.[29] The BSAE regulations, first written in 1905, explicitly stated that antiquities not claimed by the Egyptian Government should be divided entirely among public museums. Hilda Petrie was still obliged to stress this point to the Australian Institute of Archaeology in 1949; the objects that she was sending from the BSAE were the result of 'a grant + not a sale or purchase'. If the material was to be passed on, then 'it should be to a public museum + not a private or personal collection'.[30]

These sentiments were unfortunately neither absolute nor equally applied. John Garstang's approach to dispersal was unabashedly business orientated, and he courted wealthy patrons with the promise of substantial recompense. For Flinders Petrie, 'duplicate' objects were considered feasible tokens for private gifts or incentives to garner further financial support. Excavation participants, from Reverend Garrow Duncan in the early 1890s to Margaret Drower in the 1960s,[31] were permitted to take souvenirs home with them, and subscribers to the EEF occasionally received small finds, such as the shabtis sent out in 1901. Buckinghamshire Museum holds evidence that small antiquities were for sale at Petrie's annual exhibitions: a formal BSAE printed card on which had been stuck examples of first millennium BC Persian scale armour found during the 1909 Memphis seasons at the palace of Apries.[32] The EES archives also demonstrate that, on at least one occasion, members of the Committee were direct benefactors. A 1904 letter from John Ward to the then president of the EEF, Sir John Evans, expressed concern over the 'sale of the gold' to members of the Committee, which Ward felt would 'imperil our interest at the Cairo Department of Antiquities'.[33] Meanwhile, objects that remained in Cairo following partage were not always retained in the Cairo Museum, the *Salle de Vente* of which was used to sell excavated objects until the mid-1970s, including those acquired through Petrie, the EEF/S or BSAE.[34] In sum, archaeological finds have always circulated through both private hands and public institutions.

Even for those objects that were dispatched to specific institutions for posterity, secondary routes of dispersal sometimes led to the commercial auction house. Take for instance the lost collection of Chautauqua, discussed in Chapter Five. In fact, one object from this collection did eventually turn up in 1979: a 1500-pound, 3½ foot tall, granite block statue of a royal scribe and charioteer from the reign of Ramesses II. It was rediscovered by a student, crated up in the corner of an unused room and sold at a Christie's auction in June 1983 for a record $341,000, which was at the time the highest price ever reached at auction for an Egyptian artefact. Charterhouse School in England sold its collection via Sotheby's in 2002, including antiquities procured via the EEF. There were protests in various media outlets, and pressure from local archaeologists led to the removal of British prehistoric material, but the other items disappeared from the sales room into private ownership.[35] On 2 October 2014, Bonham's in London offered two lots of Egyptian antiquities for sale on behalf of the Archaeological Institute of America (AIA), St Louis Chapter. The first (lot 160), billed as 'the treasure of Harageh', consisted of a group of travertine vessels and inlaid silver jewellery; the second (lot 162) was a stone headrest.[36] These artefacts had all been excavated in 1913–14 by teams working for the BSAE.[37] Lot 160 was removed from auction following the Metropolitan Museum of Art's intercession and a private sale to the Met for an undisclosed sum. The second, lot 162, was sold for three times the asking price and disappeared into private hands.

Material does not only surface in the physical auction house. Increasingly, online bidding forums like eBay have played host to antiquities sales, and here too artefacts from excavation have surfaced.[38] A small collection of rough, plain pottery vessels, excavated by the EEF at Abydos, and said to have been formerly part of a small US liberal arts college collection at Muhlenberg, was offered through a number of online auction platforms, including eBay.³⁹ The collection had been disposed of in the early 1990s.⁴⁰ These items, like much of what is sold online, are generally of a type that is not traditionally favoured by high-end merchants or auction houses, which might consider them trinkets, trifles and oddments. Consequently, the internet market has opened up new means of viewing a wider range of archaeological materials in more lucrative terms than was previously the case.

Disposal via the commercial market is more common in the United States than in Britain. This is especially the case among museums that promote their 'fine art' credentials, a legacy of America's Progressive Era museum sensibilities and civic competitiveness. The rationale has been that the art market is a democratic arena, giving multiple parties an equal opportunity to acquire pieces, rather than favouring one particular institution. Given sales prices, such justifications seem disingenuous today. The Toledo Museum of Art is one of the more recent institutions to put Egyptian artefacts from its collection on the auction block. In October 2016, 68 objects were offered for sale through Christie's in New York. Twenty-four of them were Egyptian, including Predynastic pottery acquired through Caroline Ransom, and several shabtis, one of which was acquired through EEF field director Thomas Whittemore in 1917. In the interests of transparency, the museum released an open letter justifying its decision in terms of professional sector practice.⁴¹ The proceeds of the sale, it confirmed, would be used solely to improve its collections through the purchase of new art, a move compliant with the Association of Art Museum Directors Professional Practice in Art Museums, the American Alliance of Museums Code of Ethics and the International Council of Museums Code of Ethics. The objects selected for disposal had been measured for their 'quality' and assessed as to whether they constituted 'singular artworks by singular artists'. The objects being sold, the museum concluded, were 'not of the quality of our permanent display collection; have been on display rarely; have not been sought out by scholars; or have not been published in recent decades'. The artefacts were not deemed to be 'working to fulfil our mission'.

In each of these cases, the decisions to sell antiquities from collections were entirely legal, they abided by ethical codes and they did not contravene the 1970 UNESCO Convention or Egypt's Antiquities laws. While their auction might violate the intent of the original agreements, those distributions were not documented in ways that stand up to legal scrutiny today. Most recent sales have been defended by institutions, like Toledo Museum, as demonstrating best practice because the sector's main concern has been unprovenanced antiquities with opaque collection histories, not those objects with rich documentation. In archaeology, the rallying cry has been 'culture without context',[42] with efforts focused on mobilizing a collective voice to petition against auctions in which artefacts with no clear histories, and which are very possibly a result of destructive and criminal looting, are offered. As archaeologists are at pains to point out, objects orphaned from their find-spots offer limited insight into the ancient world. Art historical analysis might permit the dating of items, or could identify an artefact in typological terms. Ultimately, however, those frameworks tell us more about our own classifications and aesthetic values than about the object's history or its role in the past. Such approaches cannot tell us who or what a specific object may have been associated with in its life (other than an artist perhaps), the settings within which it was made meaningful or the environment within which it existed. The destruction of context also limits the opportunity for local communities to gain any longer-term benefits of site association, both culturally and economically. Considerable effort has, therefore, been put into developing codes of conduct that enshrine the need for due diligence in acquiring material from the art market. Against this backdrop, artefacts documented through official pre-1970 archaeological excavations can emerge as the most legitimate items that can be bought and sold.

The 2002 Declaration on the Importance and Value of Universal Museums strongly aligned itself with this position on undocumented antiquities in its opening statement: 'the international museum community shares the conviction that illegal traffic in archaeological, artistic, and ethnic objects must be firmly discouraged'.[43] This line acts to dissociate museums from the indiscriminate purchases of the past and the trade in 'illicit antiquities'. In other words, the museum signatories of the declaration identified a black market in illegitimate artefacts on the one hand and, by implication, a white, legitimate market on the other.[44] More recent thinking on the antiquities market has questioned whether such a decoupling is possible. Research into auction lots has consistently demonstrated that it remains a 'grey trade', in which antiquities lacking detailed ownership biographies are just as likely to be offered at the same sales as those with transparent provenance.[45] Neil Brodie's painstaking analyses, for example, concluded that the majority of antiquities handled by dealers and auction houses since 1970 have lacked detailed provenance.[46] For Egyptian material specifically, it has been noted that at Sotheby's, between 1998 and 2007, 95% of lots had no stated find-spot, while some 68% were first known after 1973.[47] The result is that museums who sell or buy antiquities at public auction legitimize what are often obscure auction house practices in which the identities of sellers and buyers usually remain concealed. On account of the esteem in which many museums are held in the general public's eyes, their participation in the trade gives the impression that the whole art market is beyond reproach and is adequately self-regulating. This is simply not the case.[48]

It is not just participation in the grey market that is problematic. Auctions do not occur in a vacuum, and sales act back upon museum practices and the integrity of field sites. Auction houses constantly inflate the prices paid for antiquities, generating problems for museums trying to insure collections and, by extension, limiting the ability of museums to manage international loans. Moreover, the high prices that these auctions achieve[49] can become attractive sources of revenue in times of austerity. In 2015 the British Museums Association's 'Cuts Survey' revealed that 11% of 115 museums surveyed said they would consider financially motivated disposal.[50] Whereas previously there was pressure on curators to ensure that museums did not acquire 'culture without context', there is now a concern that museums might look to dispose of artefacts with strong collections histories or archaeological context, as these are seen to be the most legitimate items to sell. Yet doing this would destabilize confidence in museums as long-term repositories. It fundamentally threatens public trust in them. For museums to be seen to profit financially from the sale of objects additionally undermines their role in promoting cultural values, and social meanings above commercial ones.

Most troubling of all, however, is how the steep premiums of auctions, and the media profile of high performing sales, catalyse market demand in the developed world for the cultural property of the developing world. And demand has been rising. The twenty-first century has seen new markets emerge in the Gulf Region and Asia, alongside longer-standing interests in North America and Europe.[51] What is worrying is that such demand fuels the pillage of archaeologically rich sites through a variety of mechanisms, from opportunistic subsistence digging to organized looting by sophisticated and well-connected criminal gangs.[52] Looting has been a perennial issue for Egyptian authorities, but it became a more acute concern during the Arab Spring. Most visible during the protests themselves was the Cairo Museum in Tahrir (Liberation) Square, which was subject to theft and vandalism on the night of 28 January 2011. A total of 54 artefacts were confirmed missing following the incident, among them four items of statuary from the EES's fieldwork at Amarna.[53] It has been demonstrated, however, that the increase in archaeological site looting, regularly linked by commentators to lack of policing after Arab Spring, in fact dates back at least to 2009 with the onset of the global financial crisis. Yet throughout this global financial crisis, the

American market for Egyptian antiquities increased, as charted in the value of Sotheby's New York sales between 1998 and 2010.[54] External incentives, therefore, are as much a factor in driving looting as economic pressure and conflict.[55] Crucially, such factors are just as evident outside Egypt. Several examples of ancient Egyptian jewellery were stolen from Leicester's New Walk Museum in May 2012, for instance.[56] Four items had been gifts of the BSAE from excavations just prior to the First World War.[57] All were selected by the thieves on the basis of their material – gold wire, bronze and copper alloy – and it is likely that they have since been melted down.

The concern over the legal sale of archaeological heritage might be seen as a overreaction to what is currently a small-scale problem in comparison to the flourishing trade in undocumented antiquities. There remains, however, a moral argument. These are objects excavated by colonial nations in a country whose own more limited resources are frequently overstretched by the attempt to tackle looting that is itself being undertaken for the first world market. Donna Yates has pointed out that much of the international regulatory framework for the prevention of antiquities trafficking focuses on source countries, rather than on domestic contexts.[58] The 1970 UNESCO Convention puts the onus on source countries to protect themselves from external threats that originate in rich states. More could be done to tackle demand outside Egypt, and given mounting evidence of the manifest problems of the art market, a re-evaluation of museum ethics towards participation in the commercial market would be timely.

The good intentions of institutions to abide by ethical codes are laudable, but the existence of standards does not absolve the sector from ongoing scrutiny. Archaeologist Yannis Hamilakis has argued that there is a danger that such codes become instrumentalized as purely technical devices that enable 'business as usual'.[59] More recent conceptualizations of museum ethics, however, have been defined in terms of their contingency and dependence upon constantly shifting social, political, technological and economic factors. They have also been framed with reference to 'radical transparency', a 'mode of communication that admits accountability'.[60] Such formulations situate ethics as a form of dialogue that can make plain past attitudes towards objects, while also negotiating their status in the present. As contingent practice, it should therefore be queried whether museums and institutions in the developed world have the moral right to sell for profit the heritage of developing countries, and to reinvest the proceeds according to their own priorities. The AIA Harageh sale proceeds were intended for community excavations in the

USA, while for Charterhouse it was a fundraising exercise for their library. Understandably, Egyptians see this as exploitation of their heritage, a far cry from 'universal value' when the benefits are so far removed from source nations.

The argument against the commercial sale of museum collections does not equate to a wholesale condemnation of the ability of museums to dispose of objects from their collections. Collection reviews may identify material that is no longer of benefit to any of a museum's activities, and in such cases disposal is an option that can be carefully considered. There are many ways to achieve this, but financial sale on the open market should only ever be an exceptional last resort after other routes of disposal have been investigated. In the case of antiquities, it should be specifically avoided. If antiquities are identified for disposal they should be offered first to other accredited museums, via either transfer or sale, and thus remain in the public realm, or alternatively to curatorially-responsible educational establishments for use in teaching and research. Use of objects beyond display could also be considered, such as in school loans boxes or in handling collections. Returning material to Egypt is also preferable to any commercial disposal.

Deaccessioning linked to repatriation claims remains exceptionally rare for Egyptian objects. There have been the high profile cases of requests for iconic objects, such as the long-running dispute concerning the Nefertiti bust in Berlin and the more recent claims on the Rosetta Stone as reported in the media. There have also been demands for objects that are suspected of having been stolen since 1970, as in the case of the funerary mask of Ka-Nefer-Nefer, bought by St Louis Museum in 1998.[61] Arguably, for exceptional objects, their status as the cultural property of Egypt might be strengthened on the grounds that they hold significance for the country today, rather than simply because they happened to have been found within the modern state of Egypt.[62]

No objects from excavation acquired through partage with Britain have ever been subject to repatriation requests, nor are they likely to be. The vast majority of artefacts was removed prior to current patrimony laws and the UNESCO Convention.[63] Most are 'minor antiquities' of lesser cultural significance to Egypt today. Zahi Hawass, the former head of the Ministry of Antiquities, and ardent pursuer of repatriation claims, has himself said that where there is no reason to doubt an object's export prior to 1970, then Egyptians are happy to see their heritage promoted by responsible institutions.[64] As such, if museums were to concede a few iconic objects to Egypt, it simply does not follow that the floodgates would open for requests for the millions of other objects still in worldwide collections. That would be logistically and economically impossible. It does imply, however, that Western powers have a responsibility to manage materials they removed respectfully and transparently.[65]

The Future of Collecting: A Return to Partage?

Despite the huge numbers of Egyptian antiquities in museums worldwide, there remains a prestige associated with ongoing acts of acquisition. Active collecting is deemed to be a key curatorial prerogative, and central to a museum's organizational health. As the first director of the US National Museum famously stated in an address to the British Museums Association, 'a finished museum is dead museum, and a dead museum is a useless museum'.[66] The keen eye many curators keep on the antiquities market is driven by this consideration. Other professionals have sought even more direct access to material, with prominent advocates of the universal museum principle arguing for a return to partage.[67] James Cuno, former Director of the Art Institute of Chicago, has been the most vocal. In his provocative book, *Who Owns Antiquity?*, institutions like the Louvre and the British Museum are presented as stewards of global heritage, dependent upon transnational cosmopolitanism.[68] Patrimony laws, Cuno fervently argues, are a barrier to this ideal, and grant certain nations too much control over ancient objects that by accident of geography and history just happen to fall within their modern national boundaries. In many cases, he claims, contemporary groups have no historical relation to the ancient material they administer. This latter assertion is a common refrain with regard to Egypt, stemming from Enlightenment distrust of Islamic culture, and deeply rooted in the appropriation of ancient Egypt to perpetuate narratives of European modernity. It is predicated on a set of sharp Orientalist oppositions in which, Elliott Colla has noted, ancient Egypt is associated with the modern West and present-day Egypt, the East.[69] Such a dichotomy overlooks the realities of the centuries and millennia in which diverse groups have inhabited the landscape of northeastern Africa, imbuing and drawing meaning from its environment through the creation, modification and use of material. The antiquities that speak to these interactions are not so easily divorced from these settings, and modern communities continue to elicit meaning in their presence.[70] Even if relations with the land that the modern Egyptian state now occupies are somehow discounted, this still leaves the known facts about ancient beliefs concerning the place of bodies and artefacts within it. The Vermillion Accord on Human Remains, adopted in 1989 by the World Archaeological Congress, for instance, states that 'respect for the wishes of the dead concerning disposition shall be accorded whenever possible, reasonable, and lawful, when they are known or can be reasonably inferred'.[71] For Egypt, the broad beliefs that structured ancient burial rituals for many periods are known. The iconic, 4000-year-old Egyptian *Tale of Sinuhe*, for instance, provides a vivid and emotional story of an Egyptian man who fled abroad. Near the end of Sinuhe's life he began to long for a return home so that he could receive a proper burial. The extraordinary provisions made by the Egyptians for death were grounded in this desire to be placed within the physical environs of the Nile Valley and Delta regions. Immortality was intimately connected to place.[72] There is no absolute moral right to remove these objects to other parts of the world.

Cuno's stance can be criticized as a form of neo-colonialism and as demonstrating ignorance of the inherent inequalities it is dependent upon. Who, for example, is able to share in this common humanity if it has been removed to cities out of reach economically, culturally and socially for much of the world? The historically uneven relationships between centres and peripheries, together with issues of power, which authorize access and inclusion, remain. Cuno counters that such obstacles can be mitigated through museum loans, by taking Kwame Appiah's cosmopolitanism as a model of cultural circulation. More porous borders, he contends, would permit the free flow of valuable antiquities. But who could afford the expenses for such enterprises? Rising insurance costs are just the tip of a bureaucratic and political iceberg militating against such activities.

There is little need, however, for yet more of Egypt's heritage to leave its borders, and Cuno's assertions should also be challenged by the material legacy that more than a century of partage has already created. The British Museum and Petrie Museum alone hold nearly 200,000 Egyptian artefacts, while elsewhere in the city the V&A, the Horniman Museum, the Science Museum, Sir John Soane's Museum, the Freud Museum and Kew Gardens all hold Egyptian collections. Manchester Museum manages 18,000 Egyptian antiquities, while in Scotland, Edinburgh's National Museum holds 6,000 pieces. A 2006 survey estimated that across Britain there are at the very least 112 collections of Egyptian antiquities.[73] The actual number is likely to be much higher. In the USA, the Metropolitan Museum of Art's Department of Egyptian Art curates 26,000 items and Boston Museum of Fine Art's collection contains an estimated 45,000 artefacts. Do museums still need to acquire ever more Egyptian artefacts, when their collections are already bloated and widespread?

Another argument that can be made against the need to return to partage is that there *are* still ways to collect material relating to Egypt, albeit not antiquities. Opportunities to collect antiquities may also, of course, still surface. In 2014, a pottery vessel from the Petrie-led excavations at Naqada reappeared in a garage in Cornwall, inherited from a taxi driver who had received it in return for unpaid fares in the 1950s.[74] Two years later, some of the ancient Egyptian objects once housed in the long defunct Falmouth Museum were reported; they had been bought by a local dealer, inherited by a nearby family, transported to New Zealand and are now being acquired by the British Museum. If, however, it is proactive collecting that is desired, undertaken with a sense of institutional mission and curatorial acumen, then curators might look elsewhere for objects that can help to interpret existing collections and which can broaden the range of stories that they can tell. Modern reproductions, Egyptian material culture from the last century and contemporary art are all areas under-represented in modern collections, but which can provide valuable research tools, helpful interpretative aids and illuminating juxtapositions.

Products of experimental archaeology, for instance, are worthy of collection. Cases in point are two beads crafted from meteoric iron, acquired by the Petrie Museum in 2013, which had been created to provide an insight into fourth millennium BC Egyptian metallurgic technologies. The original meteoric beads were recovered from Predynastic graves at the site of Gerzeh, excavated by BSAE teams in 1911. In their present condition these beads appear as small, grey, corroded lumps, rendering them uninspiring exhibits for the general public. The modern examples made by Diane Johnson, on the other hand, are vibrant articles of iridescent blue and metallic pink (Fig. 6.1). When set beside the ancient specimens, their contrast enables a deeper appreciation of the capabilities of the people who made the originals 5000 years ago, and provides a view on how striking these artefacts would have once had been. It is also a potential demonstration of the ongoing work of archaeological interpretation.

Similarly, examples of modern archaeological practice itself might be actively acquired and managed in the museum. That could include, for instance, thin sections of pottery from destructive sampling, which would, if retained as official parts of collections available for re-examination by future generations, mean that further sampling might not be necessary. What, though, of other sorts of material now considered archaeological finds? Are they worthy of collection by museums, or is that the responsibility of research institutions? If the

Fig. 6.1 Beads made of meteoric iron by Diane Johnson. Courtesy of the Petrie Museum of Egyptian Archaeology, UCL (museum number UC80628–9).

oddments, trinkets and trifles brought back by Petrie and the EEF were hard to visualize as museum objects in the nineteenth century, much of what archaeologists value can be even trickier to elicit public enthusiasm for – the soil samples, microscopic residues and pottery chips. At the very least, any such materials exported in the past with permits, if managed in public collections, might be easier for future researchers to locate than if they are held by research organizations with no public face. Moreover, innovative display techniques can be employed to enliven such material, as has been done for 2000 glass slides of microscopic creatures in the Grant Museum of Zoology at UCL, which were mounted, wall-to-wall, on a backlit alcove, creating the feel of an installation and acting as a hook to engagement. Such collecting might also open a window into the methodologies through which disciplinary knowledge is filtered. Most museums present the results of archaeology, and more recently the history of discovery, but few provide insights into contemporary fieldwork or other knowledge practices through which inferences about the past are made. Collaboration with science museums might offer new models of practice, allowing curators to collect around archaeologists themselves and the social context of their work, if not the archaeological archive they create. For instance, calls for a concerted effort to collect the material culture of science were made from the 1980s and have been taken up by museums in order to demystify science and challenge stereotypes about its practitioners.[75] This is a model that museum archaeologists would do well to explore.

What is conspicuously absent in the majority of museums is the modern country of Egypt, a pernicious oversight given Western assumptions about the East that allow 'potentially contradictory images of past glory and present barbarity to coexist.'[76] Consequently, Egyptians are frequently segregated within a hermetically sealed present that militates against autochthonous commentary on the past. In this context, the British Museum Department of Egypt and Sudan's new programme of collecting, established in 2013, is a welcome initiative. Its 'Modern Egypt' project aims to bring the Department's collections into the twenty-first century through the acquisition of homewares, everyday items, ephemera and photographs. Project curator, Mohamed Elshahed, has sought out artefacts capable of relating stories about Egypt's historic, economic and cultural developments over the course of the last century, including objects like a Nefertiti sewing machine from the 1960s (Fig. 6.2).[77] As a form of visibly engaged collecting, a series of events in Cairo and London have set these new collections within a series of discourses around art, design, modernity and history. It has included, for instance, an art installation in Cairo's Kodak Passageway, featuring a series of talks and presentations about the exhibit's theme by participating artists and parties, including the project's curator Mohamed El Shahed, artist Huda Lutfi and collector Amgad Naguib, as well as the Women's Museum Project led by the Women and Memory Forum, and the Downtown Museum. Nevertheless, there remains in Egypt an uneasiness around the collection of objects for a Western institution, a tension that is unlikely to ever be fully resolved.[78]

Dialogues across time and space also feature extensively in contemporary arts and crafts. These offer further avenues for enriching collections physically and intellectually. Gemma Tully, for instance, has argued that the promotion of contemporary Egyptian art, which incorporates elements of ancient Egyptian visual language with a modern context, could be a strategy for bridging cultural and temporal divides within Egyptological displays.[79] In 2013 she collaborated with contemporary artist Khaled Hafez to produce the temporary exhibition 'Re-imagining Egypt' at Saffron Waldon Museum. The creative, transcultured objects displayed in such exhibitions need not be seen as simply derivative. Collecting can foreground local contexts of production,

Fig. 6.2 Modern Egypt project display in the British Museum, 2017. Courtesy of the Trustees of the British Museum.

in which engagement with the past in the present, from perspectives outside of the museum, injects new life, and lives, into otherwise static museum assemblages that are constrained from growth. The work of Syrian artist Zahed Taj-Eddin offers a second demonstration of the possibilities of such an approach. Using archaeometric experiments, Taj-Eddin explored the production of ancient Egyptian faience, in turn using the findings to create dozens of 'nu-shabtis' to inhabit the present day and engage with its issues. His creations have, since 2013, been placed in dialogue with Egyptian collections in the Petrie Museum, Manchester Museum and the V&A. In developing new collecting and display strategies, there are therefore numerous opportunities to bridge the artificial divides between ancient and modern Egypt. These activities may further enable questions around curatorial authority to be embedded within exhibitions, events and public programmes. In turn, these should, ideally, have a transformative effect on museum mission statements and collections management strategies, all with the aim of being as transparent as possible about collections histories.[80]

For all of these positives, however, curators still need to remain wary of the modernist tendency to valorize form over context. Like ethnographic display, contemporary art should be considered as historically and culturally constituted, as Haidy Geismar has cautioned.[81] Its presentation equally embodies particular object habits that have ramifications for modern Egyptian identity politics, which are as complex an intersection of class, gender, religious and ethnic differences as anywhere. For many, sculpture and painting, for instance, retain connotations of elite high culture, and an exclusive focus on these arts overlooks the opportunities for other forms of locally relevant cultural production and commentary that might find spaces in museum dialogues. It has also been argued that using artists merely shifts the responsibility for developing counter-narratives from the museum to external practitioners, undermining an institution's resolve to address change itself.[82]

There is a second argument that can be made against the need to return to partage: museums need not be judged by the quantity of their collecting. Instead, it is the quality of their care for their collections – how they re-situate and make them accessible – that provides a real measure of a museum's worth. Some might counter that the majority of collections, even when managed professionally within institutions, are inaccessible if not on display. This assumes, however, that museums are solely a form of exhibitionary media, when in fact their function is far broader. Museum collections are a valuable resource for ongoing research, and they may be deployed in a variety of innovative public programmes. Nor should these activities be limited to providing visual insights into the ancient past or the histories of recovery, as they might additionally become a point of departure for health and wellbeing initiatives, social commentary or artistic inspiration.

If prestige-building is what institutions seek, then they might consider diverting their energies and budgets away from collecting antiquities and into high-profile methods of recontextualizing, animating and making accessible the vast reserves of material they already have. With the advent of online arenas for the dissemination of information and content, it is now possible to make collections far more visible, offering a vehicle for experimentation in radical transparency. This also counters the perception that collections management activities are mundane, behind-the-scenes administrative tasks, necessary but not in themselves intellectually stimulating or publicly visible. Databases enable object biographies to be made visible when fields that allow multiple interpretations and commentary are utilized online in a public-facing way. Two and three dimensional imaging are also possibilities ripe for critical expansion and discourse.[83] The difficulty is often in resourcing these activities, in terms of time, staff and funding.[84] Why, then, spend thousands, hundreds of thousands, even millions of pounds or dollars on acquiring a few objects, when that capital might make so many artefacts more meaningful and accessible?

Old Collections, New Research

There is a insidious assumption that the longer something exists out of sight, inert within a museum store, the more irrelevant it becomes. Yet the flip-side to inertia is latency, and while the term 'hidden' has often been used in a pejorative sense with regard to museum storerooms, its correlate is the more invigorating possibility of 'discovery'. Are there still discoveries to be made among collections distributed decades ago, now in storage? Do such legacy collections have the potential to provide new insights into past societies? The short answer is yes, but with caveats. Excavated material is a resource that has been spread exceptionally thin, that often retains the excavation biases of yesteryear, that has been subject to the vagaries of institutional processes or neglect, and which can be arduous, and sometimes impossible, to recontextualize adequately. Nevertheless, archaeologists should be adept at navigating this terrain. The profession, after all, is predicated upon the critical interpretation of fragmentary remains. Re-evaluation of historic collections can and does inform fieldwork at specific sites, with museum assemblages and excavation activities set into dialogue with each other. Moreover, when mixed with material from other sites, different periods and diverse cultures, Egyptian legacy collections have the potential to creatively disrupt assumptions that might arise from the study of a single site. No one excavation can reveal the complex story of the past.

A good example of the problems and possibilities implicated in using older archaeological collections for contemporary research is provided by the British Museum's Naukratis project. From 2011, the project set out to examine objects from this famous 'Greek' port city which had been spread across some seventy museums worldwide. The site was first identified by Flinders Petrie in 1884, and he led excavations there for the EEF the following year. It was subsequently investigated under the leadership of Alan Gardiner and then by David Hogarth for the British School at Athens. Thousands of small finds were recovered across these four seasons of British-led work. Amelia Edwards was one of the first to study recovered Naukratis material, and she wrote a paper in 1885, 'Terracottas of Naukratis', taking the opportunity to review the ensemble before individual artefacts were 'distributed among various museums, and, scattered far and wide'. 'Never again', she thought, would 'it be possible to compare them with one another, except in photographs or engravings'.[85] The British Museum's ambitious undertaking proved her wrong by surveying the entire distribution of nearly 17,000 individual pieces and assembling an online catalogue bringing together objects and archives. By these means, the project team was able to develop new conclusions about the history of Naukratis, the people who lived there and what their relationships were with sites across Egypt and the Mediterranean.

The Naukratis project revealed the highly selective retention of certain categories of finds for museums, which had skewed the material profile of Naukratis and subsequent interpretations of it.[86] While 17,000 artefacts may sound like a lot, records of the original excavations reference several hundred thousand more that remained on site. In particular, Alexandra Villing has noted that undecorated ceramics, though documented as plentiful, were generally not kept, studied or published, meaning that most of the once large corpus of Egyptian pottery from the site is lost. Equally absent in collections are household pottery and trade amphorae of all periods and types, with the exception of stamped amphora handles. In contrast, other classes of finds, such as Egyptian bronzes and amulets, and Ptolemaic and Roman terracotta figurines, are plentiful in many museum collections, but they have remained largely unpublished and therefore outside scholarly discourse. Critical re-examination of this material, together with fresh fieldwork, has provided a corrective to the previous picture of a 'Greek' town, leading to more nuanced insights into the dynamics of what was a multi-ethnic trading community. Tacking back and forth between old collections and new fieldwork has further value in these contexts: it can heighten awareness of recovery strategies, increase critical reflection on how current fieldwork, curation and documentation stands up to historical scrutiny, and allow alternative research questions to be formulated.

Many of these recontextualization projects are reliant upon archaeological archives – photographs, site plans, distribution lists and field notes – through which the discipline took shape. These types of collections have historically ranked low in hierarchies of museum objects, but they equally require curatorial management as distinctive but integral parts of a museum collection. The importance of archival research in animating legacy collections is highlighted by the recent discovery by Campbell Price, curator for Egypt and Sudan at the Manchester Museum, of an Eighteenth Dynasty statue of Senenmut, a famous courtier of Queen Hatshepsut, in that collection.[87] The anonymous statue had arrived in 1907, and was originally dispatched to the north of England through the EEF division of finds from Deir el-Bahri. Establishing this fact, and where in the temple it had been recovered from, necessitated archival consultation, which when combined with a fresh review of the inscriptions on the battered base of the statue led to its identification as belonging to Senenmut. Born a commoner, Senenmut, rose to be the chief architect of Queen Hatshepsut's Deir el-Bahri complex, her confidant (some say lover), and tutor to her daughter Princess Neferure. Price's discovery is by no means the only recent example of the potential of archival research to yield surprises. Tony Leahy of the University of Birmingham has established that an EEF-excavated Abydos relief fragment in the collection of the National Museum of Scotland is the only known artefact from the tomb of a twenty-fifth dynasty Kushite prince.[88]

New scientific techniques, such as isotope analyses and the extraction of ancient DNA, vastly improved approaches in radiocarbon and related absolute dating methods, as well as novel developments in the imaging of objects, such as Reflectance Transformation Imaging (RTI),[89] equally hold great promise for eliciting new information from old finds. As a consequence, it has been claimed that archaeology is experiencing a 'third science revolution', permitting the micro-archaeology of material investigations to be meshed with broader theorizing of macro-archaeological problems.[90] Such a revolution, it has been said, could mean that 'old collections will suddenly take pole position as the primary source material in archaeology'.[91] Given the difficulties of undertaking fieldwork in many parts of the world, this could well be true.

Despite the promise of these technological developments, however, they cannot be applied to museum collections indiscriminately. Many require destructive sampling of small portions of ancient artefacts, creating tensions between the commitment of museums to preserve, display and make accessible objects on the one hand, and the benefits to be gained from scientific investigations on the other. For Egyptian artefacts, in particular, there are additional factors to take into consideration. In many parts of the world a 'curation crisis' has been identified as a result of ongoing archaeological fieldwork, rescue operations and development interventions that have continued to generate archaeological assemblages, but which have not invested in long term plans for their care.[92] This has created new pressures on the storage and accessibility of archaeologically procured material, raising questions about the future of collecting from the field. This is not the case for Egyptian material outside Egypt. These collections are unlikely to grow in the near future, nor, as argued above, do they need to. But because of this, they are a finite resource in great demand. Often it is museum objects that provide the only available samples for the application of cutting-edge techniques that are otherwise unavailable in Egypt.

Thankfully, the sample sizes required for many approaches are nowadays very small. For example, in the area of radiocarbon dating one of the most notable advances has been the introduction of Accelerator Mass Spectrometry (AMS), which converts samples to graphite prior to dating, allowing more precise readings from significantly smaller samples. To put that into perspective, a sample of human skin from Naqada excavated by Petrie's teams in 1894–5, tested in 1952, weighed 57 grams and was dated with a margin of error of 300 years;[93] human skin from the same site examined with AMS in 2012[94] weighed less than 0.1 grams, and produced a date with a margin of error of 32 years. Furthermore, new modelling techniques using Bayesian statistics have allowed the construction of ever more precise chronologies, like that published by a team of scientists and archaeologists based at the University of Oxford in 2010.[95] Through the acquisition of 211 dates from short-lived plant remains from museum collections (seeds, basketry, plant-based textiles, plant stems, fruits) the team was able to produce a robust absolute chronology for the Pharaonic Era.

The ability to obtain a date from small sample sizes is vital for exceptional objects, such as a tunic in the care of the Petrie Museum. The garment itself was only discovered in 1977 when a dirty bundle of linen that had been brought back from the 1911–12 BSAE season at Tarkhan was sent to the V&A for conservation. The pile of cloth had originally been located outside a large mudbrick tomb (a mastaba) dated to the First Dynasty, but because this was a plundered context, the garment's dating was uncertain. Moreover, on account of the textile's delicacy, only associated linen was able to be analysed in the 1980s, when AMS was in its infancy, and it was then thought to date to the late third millennium BC. In 2015, a single, two-centimetre piece of thread from the garment itself, weighing just 0.002 grammes, was analysed by the University of Oxford's radiocarbon unit. It confirmed not only the First Dynasty date, but also that the item was the world's oldest known piece of tailored clothing.[96]

Notwithstanding these advances, issues remain. Take, for instance, many types of pottery analysis in which only a centimetre or so of a ceramic is needed for thin sectioning. In contrast to many areas of world archaeology, museum collections rarely have large Egyptian sherd collections. Instead, intact vessels for display purposes are the norm, which are often unsuitable for destructive analysis. Those sherds that were exported were usually acquired because of a distinctive feature, be that a certain type of decoration, a potmark or a characteristic rim. While it is unlikely that single sherds can be reconnected with others, it is nevertheless also the case that joins can be identified. The Deutsches Archäologisches Institut has been working at Abydos in the region excavated by Petrie's teams, and their archaeologists, such as Andreas Effland, have recovered pottery sherds that connect with fragments in museums recovered a century previously.[97] Choosing an area of a pottery sherd to slice through without compromising the integrity of specimens and their contours is therefore not always straightforward, and needs to be subject to considered curatorial research and judgement. Other limitations are the result of unknown conservation treatments applied in earlier periods of museum practice. A recent effort to investigate the lipid content of Badarian era sherds held in the Petrie, for example, was thwarted when it was realized that most of the sherds contained high amounts of plasticizers, a compound called anthraquinone found in synthetic dyes and indicators of petroleum. Their modern museum lives had left an indelible signature rendering their ancient ones elusive for the time being.[98]

Similar issues surround sampling for the purposes of radiocarbon dating, although these can be mitigated. Nevertheless, the mechanism for modelling chronologies is dependent upon the 'certainty of association' between the object and the event it is aiming to date. An organic sample in a grave could be a later intrusion, and previous generations of fieldworkers rarely provided the kind of documentary resolution needed to determine its contemporaneity with associated objects. Ideally, controlled sampling in the field is needed for robust studies, but there are currently no AMS facilities in Egypt and no legal channels for the export of samples. Such a situation highlights the inherent structural inequalities of practice. There is a continuing disparity between the archaeologically rich nation of Egypt, on the one hand, and the wealthy international institutions through which disciplinary advancement is impelled, on the other. Studying objects outside Egypt's borders can constitute 'scientific colonialism' or 'vestigial colonialism'.[99] Training, facilities, language barriers and costs all inhibit equal opportunities for Egyptians to partake in the generation of new knowledge about their country's heritage, while the distribution of research benefits most frequently favours Western scholars. Museum training for international partners has created useful bridges, although the 'best practices' established for European institutions are not necessarily directly transferrable to Egyptian contexts, while international projects can generate rivalries for opportunities and status that undermine the good intentions of sharing expertise. The realities of collaborative work, however, should not detract from efforts to empower disenfranchised groups or individuals. But it takes time, critical awareness, effective communication and ongoing reflection.

Old Collections, New Displays

More than a century of partage has ensured that Egyptian antiquities are today considered a staple part of the museum visiting experience, so much so that their tropes – mummies, death, elite culture – are frequently rendered more real than the reality the displays are supposedly meant to illustrate. In other words, these displays constitute a sort of hyperreality[100] in which the Egypt that is encountered is conceptual, detached in time and space from the modern country.[101] Egypt's self-contained and homogenized representation in the museum is, in part, a product of the disciplinary and social histories that have privileged Pharaonic Egypt (3000 BC–30 BC) above other pasts. It is also a product of deep-seated universalist claims on representing other cultures that disenfranchise counter-claims and complex realities. This has been especially apparent in audience research studies conducted in anticipation of new galleries, which have exposed the lack of public interest in alternative topics beyond very set ideas of what Egypt should look like.[102] There have been concerted efforts in the last decade to counter the assumptions on which the popularity of Egyptian displays are based in a series of gallery refurbishment projects and innovative temporary displays. But, as has always been the case, balancing the range of demands on Egypt across intellectual, political and popular imaginations is challenging. Fortunately, that is what the twenty-first century museum platform can offer: a space for contested histories.

Given public expectations, many institutions with small collections may feel discouraged when reviewing the unassuming archaeological finds that comprise their holdings. Yet Egypt's rich history of reception presents extensive opportunities for lateral thinking that can provide engaging additions to the essential label components that describe an object and identify its ancient use. The concept of object biographies has been an especially productive one for the museum sector, facilitating the incorporation of multi-layered histories into online collections management systems that can map out their relational aspects, and museum displays that may be shaped from several perspectives.[103] Combined with the 'narrative turn' in the social sciences, a stronger storytelling approach in museum exhibition design has been encouraged.[104] Concomitant developments in curatorial thinking challenge subjective codes of connoisseurship that privilege exceptional pieces. The Toledo Art Museum, for example, has aligned itself more with the principles of the art market than with developing museum practice. The narrative turn enables museums to transcend the narrow confines of art history that assess objects purely on their aesthetic qualities, towards collecting, enabling and sharing meaning. Multi-disciplinary exhibitions are notably geared towards these ends by blending science and art to appeal to a broader range of interests.

This sort of museum work can be characterized as 'bricolage', a term used by Claude Lévi-Strauss and more recently applied to museology by Anwar Tlili.[105] Bricolage, as formulated by Lévi-Strauss, constitutes a theory of production that does not privilege the author, artist or artisan, but instead embraces ad hoc combinations and recombinations that create meaning from a diverse range of sources. The bricoleur must navigate heterogeneous assemblages – 'whatever is at hand' – to construct new narratives, rather than generate material afresh. This is not tantamount to suggesting an unbridled bricolage, however, that would dislocate an object's history and cultural contexts. In any such undertaking, the present continues to weigh on dialogues with the past, and interventions are never neutral acts. Bricolage does, however, allow for new forms of re-assemblage, that are not necessarily predicated on fieldwork, but on a broader range of experimental creative acts that facilitate new understandings.[106]

The exhibition *Origins of the Afro Comb*, developed at the Fitzwilliam Museum in Cambridge in 2013 (Fig. 6.3), is an example of the way in which a simple type of ancient Egyptian object can resonate powerfully with modern times through the alliance of anthropological scholarship, contemporary design and community engagement. The exhibition opened with a striking juxtaposition: a prehistoric Egyptian bone comb decorated with a pair of bull's horns, excavated during Petrie's EEF 1900 mission at Abydos, set beside a black plastic Afro comb with the clenched fist symbol of the Black Power Movement, made in 1972. These alternative associations offered opportunities to explore themes of social identities and beliefs through the symbol of the comb.[107] The project built upon previous experience of curating the 2011–12 exhibition, *Triumph, Protection and Dreams, East African Headrests in Context,* which looked

Fig. 6.3 Poster advertising the 2013 'Afro-combs' exhibition. Reproduced with the kind permission of The Fitzwilliam Museum and the Museum of Archaeology and Anthropology, Cambridge.

at the function, design and development of headrests across cultural and chronological boundaries, including ancient Egypt. More direct still was the travelling *Digging for Dreams* exhibition, curated by Dominic Montserrat in 2000, that explicitly questioned stereotypes of ancient

Egypt, foregrounded colonial histories and tackled issues of race and the ethics of human remains display. The agency of Egyptians themselves in the recovery of their past was recognized explicitly in the exhibition *Beyond Beauty: Transforming the Body in Ancient Egypt*, held at London's Two Temple Place in 2015.[108]

The strategies of these exhibitions uproot Egyptian artefacts from the genealogies that had allied them exclusively with Western modernity, and disrupt universalist claims of representation. Such displays, however, are only temporary interventions. More permanent, longer-term presentations of Egyptian finds are staged in the main galleries only infrequently. Anthropologically styled institutions, such as the Pitt Rivers Museum in Oxford, have long maintained eclectic displays of cross-cultural comparisons, often as much by accident as by design. Nevertheless, in contrast to popular assumptions, the displays of the Pitt Rivers Museum are not 'frozen in time', and the culture-evolutionary underpinnings of the Victorian era have not been retained. They have been replaced by an arrangement scheme that looks at how similar problems across the world's societies have been addressed in a multitude of ways. For galleries devoted exclusively to ancient Egypt, recent museological trends in documenting collecting histories have led to a diversification of the stories that are presented. Since 2008 there have been numerous Egyptian gallery redevelopment programmes in Britain: at the Ashmolean in Oxford (2011), Manchester Museum (2012), World Museum Liverpool (2017) and Edinburgh's National Museum (2019). Several of these renovated displays include introductory panels that acknowledge the activities of archaeologists like Flinders Petrie and curatorial interventions by Margaret Murray and Winifred Compton, albeit often still in one-dimensional heroic terms.

What of collections of Egyptian antiquities in Britain's former colonies? Are these mere relics of colonialism, or can they be deployed for fresh explorations of the present in ways that might be of local relevance? Post-colonial museum initiatives have rightly focused on the self-representation of indigenous stories, regional histories and local artefacts, but where does that leave collections that fall outside this remit? There has been very little cross-cultural dialogue about how collections of 'world culture' in the global south might find new significance. Expertise on the histories and ancient meanings of these objects resides primarily in the Western sphere, and even with the best intentions, how might top-down influences be mitigated given that economic circumstances often dictate and perpetuate unequal relationships? In these instances, future long-term dialogues might be established, encouraging the two-way exchange of ideas rather than the didactic provision of information. Through these means, it may be possible to find ways in which knowledge can benefit local professionals and empower them to develop locally meaningful narratives.

Take, for instance, the archaeological assemblage acquired through Flinders Petrie's BSAE, now in Cape Town in the Iziko Museum. The name 'Iziko' is a Xhosa term for 'centre of cultural activity' or 'hearth', and was adopted as a representation of the re-Africanization of the museum organization. The current dislocation of Egyptian material from this initiative could be addressed within the organization's remit, revealing and liberating Egyptian antiquities from colonial taxonomies. Nelson Mandela, in his 1994 *The Long Walk to Freedom,* himself fantasized about visiting Egypt, and this might be one departure point for future discourse. 'This was not amateur archaeological interest', he said, 'it is important for African nationalists to be armed with evidence to dispute the fictitious claims of whites that Africans are without a civilized past that compares with that of the West'.[109] At the time of writing there are ongoing discussions about the future of this material and its display, with much at stake in the choice of what to exhibit. There are also opportunities for the Egyptian collection of the National Museum of Ghana, as its central building undergoes renovation throughout 2015 to 2019, with plans for a reinstallation of its objects.

In India, the last few years have seen an upturn in concern for Egyptian Antiquities. Staff of the Chhatrapatī Shivaji Mahārāj Vastu Saṅgrahālay (CSMVS) in Mumbai, in partnership with the British Museum, curated a show around the mummy in its collections: *Mummy– An Unsolved Mystery: Conserving Mumbai's Egyptian Treasures* from October 2016 to January 2017. The show built on interest generated by the British Museum's touring exhibition *Mummy – the inside story* that was hosted in the city a few years earlier. For CSMVS Museum Director, Sabyasachi Mukherjee, the temporary display of the mummy, together with 21 small Egyptian artefacts (shabtis, amulets and scarabs) was a significant opportunity to challenge the cultural hegemony of Western institutions:

> World museums or museums of world culture are a concept mostly associated with the West. It is our endeavour to evolve as a 'world cultures' museum in the East. While we have been realising this motto through collaborative exhibitions with museums across the world, we now want to utilise our own small but significant collection of world artefacts to this effect.[110]

In these ways Egyptian heritage's prominent status as a touchstone for debates over cultural progress and authority has found new contexts in twenty-first century global discourses. And, as in the nineteenth century, these grand aspirations are frequently still predicated on only a handful of trinkets, trifles and oddments.

***

Archaeology's popular reputation is of a profession through which discoveries are made. But it constitutes just one set of interventions in longer-term cycles of loss and recovery, assembly and re-assembly, that are socially embedded and historically produced. The old rejoinder, '*autres temps, autres moeurs*', cannot be a rationale for claiming uncritical authority over Egypt's cultural heritage. Certainly, there are far greater sensitivities around collection histories than was the case a hundred years ago; a sale of genuine antiquities in museum shops as happened in the 1950s, for instance, would be unthinkable today. Nevertheless, demand for antiquities continues to have a destructive effect on sites in Egypt, just as was the case in the nineteenth century. The beguiling promise of obtaining Egyptian artefacts remains intense, but it is a desire that sits uneasily alongside what is frequently a more prosaic reality. Whether the objects are threadbare textiles or robust statues, the facts of their existence necessitate long-term care, curatorship and interpretation. These are opportunities as much as responsibilities.

Notes

1. Ellsworth, W. W. 1891. Spoiling the Egyptians. *Century Magazine* 41: 152.
2. Signed in December 2002, but published in 2004: The Art Institute of Chicago; Bavarian State Museum, Munich (Alte Pinakothek, Neue Pinakothek); State Museums, Berlin; Cleveland Museum of Art; J. Paul Getty Museum, Los Angeles; Solomon R. Guggenheim Museum, New York; Los Angeles County Museum of Art Louvre Museum, Paris; The Metropolitan Museum of Art, New York; The Museum of Fine Arts, Boston; The Museum of Modern Art, New York; Opificio delle Pietre Dure, Florence; Philadelphia Museum of Art; Prado Museum, Madrid; Rijksmuseum, Amsterdam; State Hermitage Museum, St. Petersburg; Thyssen-Bornemisza Museum, Madrid; Whitney Museum of American Art, New York; The British Museum, London, 2014. Declaration on the importance an value of universal museums. *ICOM News* 1 (2004): 4.
3. E.g. Abungu, G. 2004. The declaration: a contested issue. *ICOM News* 1: 5; Fiskesjo, M. 2010. Commentary: The global repatriation debate and the new 'universal museums'. In Lydon, J. and Rizvi, U. Z. (eds.) *Handbook of Postcolonial Archaeology*. London and New York: Routledge, pp. 303–10.
4. The Art Institute of Chicago et al. Declaration on the importance an value of universal museums: 4.
5. Curtis, N. 2006. Universal museums, museum objects and repatriation: the tangled stories of things. *Museum Management and Curatorship* 21(2): 117–27; Gorman, J. M. 2011. Universalism and the new museology: impacts on the ethics of authority and ownership. *Museum Management and Curatorship* 26(2): 153; Abunga, The declaration; Fiskesjo, The global repatriation debate.
6. Ellsworth, Spoiling the Egyptians, 152.
7. Cited in Reid, D. 2002. *Whose Pharaohs? Archaeology, Museums and Egyptian National Identity from Napoleon to World War I*. Berkeley and Los Angeles: University of California Press, p. 21.
8. Goode, J. F. 2007. *Negotiating for the Past: Archaeology, Nationalism, and Diplomacy in the Middle East, 1919–41*. Austin: University of Texas Press, p. 70 .
9. Droop, J. P. 1915. *Archaeological Excavation*. Cambridge: Cambridge University Press, pp. 74–5.
10. Luckhurst, R. 2012. Counter-narrative in the Egyptian rooms of the British Museum. *History and Anthropology* 23(2): 257–69.
11. Glanville, S. R. K. 1947. *The Growth and Nature of Egyptology: An Inaugural Lecture*. Cambridge: Cambridge University Press, p. 16.
12. Letter from Laurence N. W. Flanagan, Ulster Museum to H. Fairman, University of Liverpool, 27 June 1963, Garstang Museum archives.
13. In the USA, relevant legislation to implement the convention was passed in the House of Representatives during the late 1970s, but stymied in the Senate by Senator Daniel Patrick Moynihan of New York, who represented the heart of the United States art and antiquities market, as well as the Metropolitan Museum, and was himself involved in the antiquities collecting world. See Gerstenblith, P. 2017. Implementation of the 1970 UNESCO Convention by the United States and other market nations. In Anderson, J. and Geismar, H. (eds.) *The Routledge Companion to Cultural Property*. London and New York: Routledge Press, pp. 70–88.
14. Efrat, A. 2016. Thieves: art law, war and policy. In Charney, N. (ed.) *Art Crime: Terrorists, Tomb Raiders, Forgers and Thieves*. New York: Palgrave Macmillan, pp. 339–40.
15. Efrat, Thieves, p. 354
16. Redman, S. J. 2015. Museum tours and the origins of museums studies: Edward W. Gifford, William R. Bascom, and the remaking of an anthropology museum. *Museum Management and Curatorship* 30(5): 444–61.
17. Signed in Cairo, 26 September 1965. See also Francis, D. 2015. 'An arena where meaning and identity are debated and contested on a global scale': narrative discourses in British Museum exhibitions, 1972–2013. *Curator: The Museum Journal* 58(1):41–58.
18. TNA files: FCO/13/455; FCO/39/570; FCO/39/749; FCO/39/997–9; FCO/39/1238–42; FCO/93/32/110; MEPO/26/3.
19. Barker, E. 1999. Exhibiting the canon: the blockbuster show. In Barker, E. (ed.) *Contemporary Cultures of Display*. New Haven and London: Yale University Press, p. 128.
20. Various. 2007. Memories of the Tutankhamun Exhibition at the British Museum. *The Telegraph* 20 October 2007. Available at: http://www.telegraph.co.uk/culture/3668643/Memories-of-the-Tutankhamun-Exhibition-at-the-British-Museum-1972.html. [accessed 12 December 2017].

21 McAlister, M. 1996. 'The common heritage of mankind': race, nation, and masculinity in the King Tut exhibit. *Representations* 54: 85.
22 Gidiri, A. 1974. Imperialism and archaeology. *Race* 15(4): 434.
23 Letter from Ahmed Kadry to Robert Anderson, 23 December 1982, EES archive, uncatalogued papers.
24 Walker, C. 1982. Egypt asks for return of Sphinx's beard. *The Times* 9 February 1982: 6. The request was rejected and the beard remains in the British Museum collection to this day.
25 EES.DIST.74.
26 Available online at: https://www.icrc.org/en/document/cairo-declaration-protection-cultural-property [accessed 17 February 2018]. With thanks to Heba Abd El Gawad for drawing this to my attention.
27 Letter from Flinders Petrie to Thomas Cook, 19 October 1888, Thomas Cook Archives.
28 Letter from Flinders Petrie to Thomas Cook, 19 October 1888, Thomas Cook Archives.
29 Letter from Emily Paterson to EEF Hon. Treasurer America, circa 1890, EES.COR.3.j.57.
30 Letter from Hilda Petrie to Mr McKay, 20 September 1949, Australian Institute of Archaeology archives, 4902. Emphasis in the original. With thanks to Chris Naunton and Chris Davey for drawing this letter to my attention.
31 See for instance, the distribution list recorded in Mond, R. 1937. *Cemeteries of Armant*. London: Egypt Exploration Society.
32 Serpico, M. 2013/2014. Re-excavating Egypt: unlocking the potential in ancient Egyptian collections in the UK. *Egyptian and Egyptological Documents Archives Libraries* 4: 136.
33 Letter from John Ward to John Evans, 5 July 1904, Ashmolean Museum, Department of Antiquities, John Evans archive.
34 Piacentini, P. 2011. The dawn of museums and photography in Egypt. In Piacentini, P. (ed.) *Egypt and the Pharaohs. From Conservation to Enjoyment*. Milan: Skira, pp. 26–8.
35 Kennedy, M. 2002. Charterhouse treasures go to auction as academics rail. *The Guardian*, 27 July 2002: 9.
36 Bonhams 2014. *Antiquities, 2 October 2014*. London: Bonhams, pp. 144–9, p. 151.
37 Engelbach, R. and Gunn, B. 1923. *Harageh*. London: British School of Archaeology in Egypt.
38 Brodie, N. 2015. The internet market in antiquities. In Desmarais, F. (ed.) *Countering Illicit Traffic in Cultural Goods: The Global Challenge of Protecting the World's Heritage*. Paris: ICOM, pp. 11–20.
39 https://www.worthpoint.com/worthopedia/egyptian-nile-siltware-grain-vessel-old-kingdom [accessed 21 November 2017].
40 With thanks to Susan Falciani, Special Collections and Archives Librarian at Muhlenberg College, for confirming the disposal of this collection.
41 http://www.toledomuseum.org/collection/provenance-and-tma/deaccessioning/ [accessed 21 November 2017].
42 Renfrew, C. 2000. *Loot, Legitimacy and Ownership*. London: Duckworth; Renfrew, C. 2006. Museum acquisitions. Responsibilities for the illicit traffic in antiquities. In Brodie, N., Kersel, M. M., Luke, C. and Tubb, K. W. (eds.) *Archaeology, Cultural Heritage and the Antiquities Trade*. Gainesville: University Press of Florida, pp. 245–57.
43 The Art Institute of Chicago et al., The universal declaration.
44 Mackenzie, S. and Yates, D. 2016. What is grey about the 'grey market' in antiquities. In Beckert, J. and Dewey, M. (eds.) *The Architecture of Illegal Markets: Towards an Economic Sociology of Illegality in the Economy*. Oxford: Oxford University Press, pp. 70–86.
45 Bowman, B. 2008. Transnational crimes against culture: looting at archaeological sites and the 'grey' market in antiquities. *Journal of Contemporary Criminal Justice* 24(3): 225–42; Brodie, N. 2014. Auction houses and the antiquities trade. In Choulia-Kapeloni, S. (ed.) *Third International Conference of Experts on the Return of Cultural Property*. Athens: Archaeological Receipts Fund, pp. 71–82; Tsirogiannis, C. 2016a. Mapping the supply: usual suspects and identified antiquities in 'reputable' auction houses in 2013. *Cuadernos de Prehistoria y Arqueología* 25: 107–44; Tsirogiannis, C. 2016b. Reasons to doubt: misleading assertions in the London antiquities market. *Journal of Art Crime* Spring: 67–72; Tsirogiannis, C. 2015. 'Due diligence'? Christies' antiquities auction, London, October 2015. *Journal of Art Crime* Fall: 27–37; Yates, D. 2016. The global traffic in looted cultural objects. In Rafter, N. and Carribine, E. (eds.) *The Oxford Encyclopedia of Crime, Media, and Popular Culture*. Oxford: Oxford University Press. Available at: DOI: 10.1093/acrefore/9780190264079.013.124 [accessed 19 January 2018].

46 Brodie, N. 2012. Uncovering the antiquities market. In Skeates, R., McDavid, C. and Carman, J. (eds.) *The Oxford Handbook of Public Archaeology*. Oxford: Oxford University Press, pp. 230–52.
47 See Gill, D. 2008. The sale of Egyptian antiquities at Sotheby's: a reflection. *Looting Matters Blogspot*. Available at: http://lootingmatters.blogspot.co.uk/2007/12/sale-of-egyptian-antiquities-at.html [accessed 17 December 2017].
48 Dietzler, J. 2013. On 'organized crime' in the illicit antiquities trade: moving beyond the definitional debate. *Trends in Organized Crime* 16(3): 329–42.
49 Some 16 per cent of antiquities at Sotheby's between 1998 and 2007, for instance, were Egyptian, fetching around US$42,826,000. See Gill, D. 2008. The sale of Egyptian antiquities at Sotheby's: a reflection. *Looting Matters Blogspot*. Available at: http://lootingmatters.blogspot.co.uk/2007/12/sale-of-egyptian-antiquities-at.html [accessed 17 December 2017].
50 Museums Association 2015b. *Cuts Survey 2015*. Available at: https://www.museumsassociation.org/download?id=1155642 [accessed 26 June 2017].
51 Yates, The global traffic in looted cultural objects.
52 Hanna, M. 2013. Looting heritage: losing identity. *Al Rawi* 5: 22–5; Hanna, M. 2016. Documenting looting activities in Post-2011 Egypt. In Desmarais, F. (ed.) *Countering Illicit Traffic in Cultural Goods. The Global Challenge of Protecting the World's Heritage*. Paris: International Council of Museums, pp. 47–64.
53 Following a statement made by Zahi Hawass to the *Al Arabya* news channel on 13 February 2011. A painted limestone statue of seated man (JE52976/JE53249); a steatite figure of Bes on a calcite base (JE 53250); a steatite statue of scribe with the God Thoth as a baboon (JE59291); and a quartzite head of an Amarna princess (JE 65040).
54 Gill, D. W. J. 2015. Egyptian antiquities on the market. In Hassan, F. A., Tassie, G., Owens, L. S., de Trafford, A., van Wetering, J. and el Daly, O. (eds.) *The Management of Egypt's Cultural Heritage, Volume 2*. London: ECHO and Golden House Publications, pp. 67–77.
55 Parcak, S., Gathings, D., Childs, C., Mumford, G. and Cline, E. 2016. Satellite evidence of archaeological site looting in Egypt: 2002–2013. *Antiquity* 90: 188–205.
56 Martin, D. 2017. From Rhino horns to Egyptian jewels – these are the items that have been stolen from Leicester's museums. *Leicester Mercury* 4 October 2017. Available at: www.leicestermercury.co.uk/news/leicester-news/rhino-horns-egyptian-jewels-items-578208 [accessed 10 January 2018].
57 With thanks to Stephanie Boonstra, and New Walk Museum, for confirming the archaeological context of lost items. New security and fresh investment in the Egyptian displays have since been instituted.
58 Yates, The global traffic in looted cultural objects.
59 Hamilakis, Y. 2016. From ethics to politics. In Hamilakis, Y. and Duke, P. (eds.) *Archaeology and Capitalism: From Ethics to Politics*. London and New York: Routledge, p. 24.
60 Marstine, J. 2011. The contingent nature of the new museum ethics. In Marstine, J. (ed.) *The Routledge Companion To Museum Ethics: Redefining Ethics Of The Twenty-First Century Museum*. London and New York: Routledge, p. 14.
61 See Ikram, S. 2010. Collecting and repatriating Egypt's past: toward a new nationalism. In Silverman, H. (ed.) *Contested Cultural Heritage: Religion, Nationalism, Erasure and Exclusion*. New York: Springer, p. 145.
62 For example, Young, J. 2007. Cultures and cultural property. *Journal of Applied Philosophy* 24(2): 111–24.
63 Ikram, Collecting and repatriating Egypt's past, p. 153.
64 Letter from Zahi Hawass, Secretary General Supreme Council of Antiquities, to Nick Dodd, Director Sheffield Museums, 3 April 2009. Copy held in the Petrie Museum of Egyptian Archaeology.
65 See for instance Kamel, N. 2016. Foreword. In Serpico, M. and El Gawad, H. 2016. *Beyond Beauty. Transforming the Body in Ancient Egypt*. London: Two Temple Place, p. 4.
66 Goode, G. B. 1895. *The Principles of Museum Administration*. York: Coultas and Volans, p. 10.
67 E.g. Montebello, P. 2009. And what do you propose should be done with those objects? In Cuno, J. (ed.) *Whose Culture? The Promise of Museums and the Debate Over Antiquities*. Princeton: Princeton University Press, pp. 55–77.
68 Cuno, J. 2008. *Who Owns Antiquity? Museums and the Battle Over Our Ancient Heritage*. Princeton: Princeton University Press.
69 Colla, E. 2007. *Conflicted Antiquities: Egyptology, Egyptomania, Egyptian Modernity*. Durham: Duke University Press, p. 103.

70 See Ingold, T. 2000. Ancestry, generation, substance, memory, land. In Ingold, T. (ed.) *The Perception of the Environment: Essays in Livelihood, Dwelling and Skill*. London and New York: Routledge, pp. 132–51.
71 Zimmerman, L. J. 2002. A decade after the Vermillion Accord: what has changed and what has not. In Fford, C., Hubert, J. and Turnbull, P. (eds.) *The Dead and Their Possessions: Repatriation in Principle, Policy and Practice*. London and New York: Routledge, p. 92.
72 See, for example, Hubert, J. 1989. A proper place for the dead: a critical review of the 'reburial' issue. In Layton, R. (ed.) *Conflict in the Archaeology of Living Traditions*. London and New York: Routledge, pp. 131–66.
73 Serpico, M. 2006. *Past, Present and Future: An Overview of Ancient Egyptian and Sudanese Collections in the UK*. London: Museums, Libraries and Archives.
74 Kennedy, M. 2014. Battered pot found in Cornish garage unlocks Egypt excavation secrets. *The Guardian* 26 May 2014.
75 Gauvin, J-F. 2016. Functionless: science museums and the display of 'pure objects'. *Science Museum Group Journal* 5. Available at: http://dx.doi.org/10.15180/160506 [accessed 7 August 2017].
76 Motawi and Merriman cited in MacDonald, S. 2003. Lost in time and space: ancient Egypt in museums. In MacDonald, S. and Rice, M. (eds.), *Consuming Ancient Egypt*. London: UCL Press, p. 98.
77 Elshahed, M. 2017. Collecting modern Egypt. http://blog.britishmuseum.org/collecting-modern-egypt/ [accessed 10 December 2017].
78 Hassan, M. S. 2016. Modern Egypt: on objects that represent the world. *Mada Masr* 17 November 2016. Available at: https://www.madamasr.com/en/2016/11/17/feature/culture/modern-egypt-on-objects-that-represent-the-world/ [accessed 17 February 2018].
79 Tully, G. 2011. Re-presenting ancient Egypt: re-engaging communities through collaborative archaeological methodologies for museum displays. *Archaeological Review from Cambridge* 26(2): 149.
80 Bell, L. 2009. Engaging the public in public policy. *Museum and Social Issues. A Journal of Reflective Discourse* 4(1): 21–36.
81 Geismar, H. 2015. The art of anthropology. Questioning contemporary art in ethnographic display. In Message, K. and Witcomb, A. (eds.) *The International Handbook of Museum Studies: Museum Theory*. Malden: Blackwell Publishing, pp. 183–210.
82 Whitehead, C. 2009. *Museums and the Construction of Disciplines: Art and Archaeology in Nineteenth-Century Britain*. London: Duckworth, p. 24.
83 E.g. Many 3D models of Egyptian artefacts in the British Museum are available in Sketchfab. Available at: https://sketchfab.com/britishmuseum [accessed 28 January 2018].
84 For further discussion see Watrall, E. 2018. Public heritage at scale: building tools for authoring mobile digital heritage and archaeology experience. *Journal of Community Archaeology and Heritage* 5(2): 114–27.
85 Cited in Thomas, R. 2015. Naukratis: Stone and terracotta figures – an introduction. In Villing, A. Bergeron, M., Bourogiannis, G., Johnston, A., Leclère, F., Masson, A. and Thomas, R. *Naukratis: Greeks in Egypt. The British Museum, Online Research Catalogue*. London: British Museum, p. 2.
86 Villing, A. Reconstructing a 19th-century excavation: problems and perspectives. In Villing et al. *Naukratis*.
87 Accession number 4624. See Price, C. 2014. Object biography #15: A previously unidentified statue of Seneut (ACC. No. 4624). Available at: https://egyptmanchester.wordpress.com/2014/01/29/object-biography-15-a-previously-unidentified-statue-of-senenmut-acc-no-4624/ [accessed 6 November 2017].
88 Object number A.1901.429.11. Leahy, T. 2014. Kushites at Abydos: the royal family and beyond. In Pischikova, E., Budka, J. and Griffin, K. (eds.) *Thebes in the First Millennium BC*. Cambridge: Cambridge Scholars Publishing, pp. 62–70. With thanks to Margaret Maitland for drawing this to my attention.
89 For example, see Piquette, K. E. 2016. Documenting Early Egyptian imagery: analyzing past technologies and materialities with the aid of Reflectance Transformation Imaging. In Graff, G. and Serrano, A. J. (eds.) *Prehistories of Writing: Iconography, Graphic Practices and Emergence of Writing in Predynastic Egypt*. Marseille: Presses Universitaires de Provence, pp. 87–112.
90 Kristiansen, K. 2014. Toward a new paradigm? The third science revolution and its possible consequences in archaeology. *Current Swedish Archaeology* 22: 11–34.

91 Ytterberg, N. 2016. Analysing museum collections in Scandinavia. *Museum Worlds* 4(1): 133.
92 Kersel, M. M. 2015. Storage wars: solving the archaeological curation crisis? *Journal of Eastern Mediterranean Archaeology and Heritage Studies* 3(1): 42–54.
93 Laboratory number C-814, see Libby, W. F. 1954. Chicago radiocarbon dates, IV. *Science* 119: 135–40.
94 Laboratory number OxA-X-2485-26, see Bronk Ramsey, C., Higham, T., Brock, F., Baker, D., Ditchfield, P. and Staff, R. 2015. Radiocarbon dates from the Oxford AMS system: Archaeometry datelist 35. *Archaeometry*, 57(1): 177–216.
95 Bronk Ramsey, C., Dee, M. W., Rowland, J. M., Higham, T. F. G., Harris, S. A., Brock, F., Quiles, A., Wild, E. M., Marcus, E. S., and Shortland, A. J. 2010. Radiocarbon-based chronology for dynastic Egypt. *Science* 328 (5985): 1554–59.
96 Stevenson, A. and Dee, M. 2016. Confirmation of the world's oldest woven garment: the Tarkhan dress. *Antiquity* 90, Project gallery. Available at: http://antiquity.ac.uk/projgall/stevenson349 [accessed 22 July 2017].
97 Stevenson, A. 2015. Connecting across the centuries: fragments from Abydos. In Stevenson, A. (ed.) *The Petrie Museum of Egyptian Archaeology: Characters and Collections*. London: UCL Press, p. 64.
98 Email from Julie Dunn to Alice Stevenson, 28 September 2016. The project was initially an extension of investigations into evidence for the first dairying in Africa based on the following study: Dunne, J., Evershed, R. P., Salque, M., Cramp, L, Bruni, S., Ryan, K., Biagetti, S. and di Lernia, S. 2012. First dairying in green Saharan Africa in the fifth millennium BC. *Nature* 485: 390–4.
99 See overview in Nicholas, G. and Hollowell, J. 2007. Ethical challenges to a postcolonial archaeology: the legacy of scientific colonialism. In Hamilakis, Y. and Duke, P. (eds.) *Archaeology and Capitalism: From Ethics to Politics*. Walnut Creek: Left Coast Press, pp. 59–82.
100 Urry, J. 1990. *The Tourist Gaze*. London: Sage Publications; Meskell, L. 2005. Pharaonic legacies: postcolonialism, heritage and hyperreality. In Kane, S. (ed.) *The Politics of Archaeology and Identity in a Global Context*. Los Angeles: AIA Monographs/Cotsen Institute, pp. 149–71.
101 MacDonald, Lost in time and space.
102 Exell, K. 2015. Innovation and reaction: a discussion of the proposed re-display of the Egyptian galleries at the Manchester Museum. In Kousoulis, P. and Lazaridis, N. (eds.) *Proceedings of the Tenth International Congress of Egyptologists*. Leuven: Peeters Publishers, pp. 2187–97.
103 Gosden, C. and Marshall, Y. 1999. The cultural biography of objects. *World Archaeology* 31(2): 169–78; Gosden, C. and Larson, F. 2007. *Knowing Things: Exploring the Collections at the Pitt Rivers Museum 1884–1945*. Oxford: Oxford University Press; Hill, K. (ed.) 2012. *Museums and Biographies: Stories, Objects, Identities*. Woodbridge: Boydell Press.
104 Macleod, S., Hanks, L. H. and Hale, J. (eds.) 2012. *Museum Making: Narratives, Architectures, Exhibitions*. London and New York: Routledge.
105 Tlili, A. 2016. Encountering the creative museum: museographic creativeness and the bricolage of time materials. *Educational Philosophy and Theory* 48 (5): 443–58.
106 Wingfield, C. 2018. Collection as (re)assemblage: refreshing museum archaeology. *World Archaeology*. 49(5): 594–607.
107 Ashton, S. A. 2013. *Origins of the Afro Comb: 6,000 Years of Culture, Politics and Identity*. Cambridge: Fitzwilliam Museum.
108 Serpico and El Gawad 2016. *Beyond Beauty*.
109 Mandela, N. 1994. *Long Walk to Freedom*. New York: Back Bay Books, pp. 296–7.
110 As reported to Fernandez, F. 2016. Mid-day exclusive: Mumbai's own mummy on display for the first time in History. 23 October 2016 *Mid-day.com*. Available at: http://www.mid-day.com/articles/mid-day-exclusive-mumbai-egyptian-mummy-display-first-time-mumbai-news-csmvs-museum-exhibition/17705179 [accessed 1 October 2017].

Conclusion

On reaching the third floor of the Liverpool World Museum visitors are confronted with a sign offering two choices: go left to the new Ancient Egypt gallery (opened in 2017), or turn right for the World Cultures gallery. This division neatly captures the exceptionalism that characterizes Egypt's place in world archaeology and in many museum displays globally. It is a product of a range of object habits cultivated over some two centuries. Beyond the geographies explored in the previous chapters, it is clear that emergent axes of wealth and influence are still today seeking cultural authority through an appeal to ancient Egypt. The power of Egyptian artefacts to symbolize early twenty-first century global modernity is evident in their prominence in newly established museums and exhibitions in the Gulf and in Asia. In the Louvre Abu Dhabi, opened in 2017 as 'the first universal museum in the Arab world', one of the primary gateway objects visitors encounter in the introductory Great Vestibule is a bronze figurine of the ancient Egyptian goddess Isis nursing Horus. Meanwhile in China, intense interest in ancient Egypt has been fostered through a flurry of international loans to Chinese museums.[1] In both countries, these high profile acts of transculturation have been almost wholly shaped by foreign expertise, and it would be easy to assume that these are largely derivative exhibits, drawing on the tropes of mummies, monuments and royalty constructed in the West. Yet the idea of the object habit, as explored throughout this book, suggests that understanding these ongoing movements of antiquities still requires a sensitivity towards the conditions that enable and shape cultural mediations, and which influence the types of things chosen, the mechanisms of diplomacy, the styles of engagement with artefacts and attitudes to their reception. That these regions are also seeking new fieldwork opportunities in Egypt for themselves further underscores the need to consider how these representations translate into the ongoing construction of archaeological knowledge.

While much of this book has been concerned with the object habits of the past, this concept should not merely encourage museum histories of greater texture and insight. I would suggest that it might additionally facilitate the integration of those histories into contemporary debates, not just those relating to the antiquities trade, as was the focus of Chapter Six. As Murray and Spriggs have argued,[2] histories of archaeology assist the formulation and assessment of present day theories, as well as provide insights into the functioning of disciplines. For Egyptology particularly, they offer the prospect of challenging the commonly held view that there exists an ordered set of practices constituting a stable discipline, predicated on the heroic achievements of a few individuals, and the establishment of secure, bounded intellectual tenets.[3] Consideration of object habits can provide counter-narratives to such standard display or disciplinary accounts that have become canonical. Chapter One, for instance, addressed an axiomatic principle in archaeology: that small and everyday artefacts are valuable for archaeological inference if finds are well contextualized. This was not a self-evident principle, however, nor one that was simply recognized through an inspired intellectual feat by a man like Flinders Petrie. Establishing archaeological value was a longer-term, historically situated project, an ontological issue as to the status of objects in the politics of collections that was neither essential nor stable, but repeatedly constructed and deconstructed. And because of this, categories continue to be questioned and remain relative. Therefore, while Chapters One to Four charted some of the variegated motivations for collecting 'trinkets', 'trifles' or 'oddments', Chapters Five and Six revealed the shifts in attitudes to those same categories of 'minor antiquities' that were now likely to be disposed of for the very reason that they were, under particular circumstances, deemed to be of 'minor' importance. In the case of material sent to the United States, Chapter Two's discussion of the development of a distinctive fine art museum ethos is instructive today for the increased likelihood of disposing of archaeological finds in the USA, where judgements often continue to be made on art-historical and aesthetics grounds, rather than contextual ones. Egyptian antiquities also clearly still act as significant boundary objects in transnational acts of soft diplomacy and national interest, such as those explored in Chapter Three. The aforementioned Gulf and Chinese attentions are a case in point. For contemporary heritage discourses, the post-Second World War shift in attitudes to foreign objects discussed in Chapter Five has never been more relevant. At the time of writing, in Britain, economic austerity and the decision to leave the European Union (Brexit) are once again fostering more parochial attitudes to transnational acquisitions like those last seen in the 1950s, exerting new pressures on the integrity of museum collections acquired in previous centuries. The widely condemned sale of the ancient Egyptian statue of Sekhemkha in 2014 by Northampton Borough Council from the local museum is just one example. The borough's councillors claimed that the object was irrelevant to local communities. Social histories that demonstrate how entangled Egyptian things are with such towns would argue otherwise, and contingent ethics would foreground the international implications of the inward-looking concerns of British local government.[4]

These sorts of multi-sited histories connect the field and the museum, meaning that contemporary actions in one space can have consequences for another. Ongoing antiquities looting, conflict and environmental degradation all directly impact field sites around the world, placing greater responsibility on the stewards of collections from those places to reveal the multi-layered histories behind things, connecting past, present and future through the prism of current attitudes. How objects are treated in and by museums affects in turn how objects are valued in other arenas, such as the art market, which itself exerts a pressure on field sites. If, as argued in Chapter Six, ethics are a matter of contingent practice, then these historical currents require future reckoning. More importantly, such appraisals need to be accountable and transparent to a broader range of stakeholders than has previously been the case, something which might be achieved by integrating critical voices and more probing questions about museum displays and disciplinary dialogues. The resources for doing such work are rich, especially if it is remembered that the material subject to dispersal was not simply ancient finds, but, as discussed in several chapters, was part of a larger mixed assemblage of documents, photographs and reproductions that travelled with and among them. Often ranking low in hierarchies of museum collections, these other forms of material culture need not operate simply to authenticate and authorize antiquities, but can work to construct or challenge received wisdom. They are worthy of attention in their own right. Reading 'against the archival grain'[5] can allow for a reassessment of the broader agencies behind collections and the vital roles (be they physical or intellectual) played by 'invisible technicians', like those discussed in Chapter Four, such as Egyptians, copyists or women. Encouragingly, important new discoveries are being made in Egypt. This includes the Abydos Temple Paper Archive project,[6] which offers the promise of new insights from Egyptian perspectives and which can provide a more nuanced commentary on foreign archaeological activities, their treatment of finds, and local involvement in international processes.

Museums outside Egypt can no longer procure artefacts from the field for their collections. Consequently, most of their holdings represent the archaeological products of particular historical moments, principally the nineteenth and early twentieth centuries when excavation was empowered by modernist, imperialist and colonial agendas. A century on it is imperative that there is reflection on the extent to which these continue to frame Egypt's archaeology, and what sorts of object habits they provoke. Inertia too easily envelops museums, either confining material to static, hyperreal epochs branded as 'ancient Egyptian' or else cushioning it within nostalgia for a so-called 'golden age of discovery'. For twenty-first century museums, the challenge is to re-animate Egyptian heritage within fresh narratives that draw from and make transparent a broader range of histories. And given how scattered finds from Egypt are, there is the opportunity to do so within an extraordinary range of spaces and communities worldwide. Yet if there is anything that the examination of these histories reveals, it is that whichever stories are selected, they are likely to provide just as much insight into more recent and contemporary worlds as they are into any ancient reality.

Notes

1. In 2016, the Royal Ontario Museum loaned more than 150 ancient Egyptian objects to the *Pharaohs and Kings: Treasures of Ancient Egypt and China's Han Dynasty* exhibition, displayed first at the Nanjing Museum (Jiangsu Province) and then at the Jinsha Site Museum (Sichuan Province) from January to May 2017. More recent is the loan of 235 Egyptian artefacts by Turin's Museo Egizio for the touring *Egypt House of Eternity* exhibition that, between 2017 and 2018, travelled to Sahxi Museum, before heading to institutions in the provinces of Lianing, Hunan and Guangdong.
2. Murray, T. and Spriggs, M. 2017. The historiography of archaeology: exploring theory, contingency and rationality. *World Archaeology* 49(2): 151–7.
3. See discussion in Carruthers, W. 2015. Introduction: thinking about histories of Egyptology. In Carruthers, W. (ed.) *Histories of Egyptology. Interdisciplinary Measures*. London and New York: Routledge, pp. 1–18.
4. Quirke, S. and Stevenson, A. 2015. The Sekhemka sale and other threats to antiquities. *British Archaeology* 145: 30–4.
5. Stoler, A. L. 2010. *Along the Archival Grain: Epistemic Anxieties and Colonial Common Sense*. Princeton: Princeton University Press.
6. A paper archive found at Abydos containing documents from the Egyptian Antiquities' Service related to the heritage management of the site of Abydos and surrounding areas, from approximately 1850 through the 1960s. See Shalaby, N., Abu El-Azm, H., Damarany, A., Kaiser, J., Abdallah, H. S., Abu El-Yazid, M., Abd El-Raziq, Y., Baker, F., Hashesh, Z., Ibrahim, W., Minor, E., Regelein, R. and Tarek, A. 2018. The lost papers: rewriting the narrative of early Egyptology with the Abydos Temple Paper Archive. *ARCE Bulletin Online*. Available at: https://www.arce.org/abydos-paper-archive [accessed 17 June 2018].

Appendix A:
Legislation relating to the excavation and export of Egyptian antiquities

Year	Law	Summary
1835	Antiquities Ordinance High Order of Muhammed Ali	• Envisaged a museum in Cairo to house finds • Established an Egyptian Antiquities Service • Prohibited export of antiquities from Egypt without a permit
1869	High Order of Ismail Pasha	• Regulated excavations
1874	By-law	• All antiquities yet to be discovered (unearthed) belong to the government
1880	Decree of Muhammed Tawfik on the Prohibition of the Export of Antiquities	• Enacted a national ownership statute making all monuments and objects of antiquity property of the state
1884	Ottoman Antiquities Law	• Established national ownership of all artefacts in the Ottoman Empire
1897	Law No. 12	• Included punishments for people excavating without a permit • Looted artefacts must be returned to the government
1912	Law of Antiquities No. 14	• Clarified and unified previous laws regarding excavation, ownership, and sale of antiquities • Stated that Egyptian antiquities were the property of the state and could only leave Egypt with proper permits issued by the government • Finds to be divided equally into two shares: one for the state and one for the excavator • Division to be made by the Antiquities Service

Year	Law	Summary
1951	Law 215 Protection of Antiquities	• Stated that no antiquity could leave Egypt unless Egypt owned one or more objects similar to that being exported
1973	Egypt signs UNESCO Convention on the Means of Prohibiting and Preventing the Illicit Import, Export and Transfer of Ownership of Cultural Property 1970	• Introduced need for appropriate certificates in which an exporting State would specify that the export of the cultural property in question is authorized
1983	Law of Antiquities No. 117	• Abolished all antiquity exports from Egypt • All antiquities discovered by foreign archaeological excavation missions were state owned • The Egyptian Antiquities Authority could allow outstanding foreign missions to donate some of the movable antiquities which they have uncovered to museums (up to 10 per cent of all finds) • Outlawed trade in antiquities in Egypt
2010	Law 3 Promulgating the Antiquities' Protection Law	• Cancelled the 10 per cent of ownership granted to foreign excavation missions that discovered them

The above is a summary of the parts of legislation most relevant to the excavation and distribution of finds.[1]

Appendix B:
Ancient Egyptian chronology

Date	Period	Subdivisions
400,000–8000 BC	Palaeolithic	Lower/Middle/Upper
8000–4000 BC	Neolithic	
4500–3800 BC	Badarian	
3800–3100 BC	Predynastic	Naqada I–III
3100–2686 BC	Early Dynastic	Dynasties 1–3
2686–2181 BC	Old Kingdom	Dynasties 4–6
2181–2025 BC	First Intermediate Period	Dynasties 7–10
2025–1700 BC	Middle Kingdom	Dynasties 11–12
1700–1550 BC	Second Intermediate Period	Dynasties 13–17
1550–1069 BC	New Kingdom	Dynasties 18–20
1069–664 BC	Third Intermediate Period	Dynasties 21–25
664–525 BC	Late Period	Dynasty 26
525–404 BC	First Persian Period	Dynasty 27
404–343 BC	Late Dynastic Period	Dynasties 28–30
343–332 BC	Second Persian Period	
332–305 BC	Macedonian Period	
323–30 BC	Ptolemaic Period	
30 BC–395 AD	Roman Period	
395–641	Byzantine Period	
641–1517	Islamic Period	
1517–1805	Ottoman Period	
1805–1919	Khedival Period	
1919–1953	Monarchy	
1953–today	Republic	

Notes

1 For further information see: Ikram, S. 2011. Collecting and repatriating Egypt's past: toward a new nationalism. In H. Silverman (ed.), *Contested Cultural Heritage. Religion, Nationalism, Erasure, and Exclusion in a Global World*. New York: Springer, 141–54; Khater, A. 1960. *Le regime juridique des fouilles et des antiquités en Égypt*. Cairo: Institut Français d'Archéologie Orientale.

Bibliography

Abbreviations

BAA	British Academy Archives
BSAE	British School of Archaeology in Egypt
EEF	Egypt Exploration Fund
EES	Egypt Exploration Society
EES.COR	Egypt Exploration Society Archives, correspondence files
EES.DIST	Egypt Exploration Society Archives, distribution files
ERA	Egyptian Research Account
PMA	Petrie Museum Archives
TNA	The National Archives, UK

Abt, J. 2012. *American Egyptologist: The Life of James Henry Breasted and the Creation of the Oriental Institute*. Chicago: University of Chicago Press.

Abungu, G. 2004. The declaration: a contested issue. *ICOM News* 1: 5.

Adam, T. 2016. *Transnational Philanthropy: The Mond Family's Support for Public Institutions in Western Europe from 1890 to 1938*. Arlington: Palgrave Macmillan.

Adams, B. 1993. Potmark forgery: a serekh of Semerkhet from Abydos. *Discussions in Egyptology* 25: 1–12.

Adams, W. Y. 1997. Anthropology and Egyptology: divorce and remarriage? In Lustig, J. (ed.) *Anthropology and Egyptology: A Developing Dialogue*. Sheffield: Sheffield Academic Press, pp. 25–32.

Aitken, E. D. 1948. Egyptian antiquities at Huguenot University College. *Die Hugenoot,* 1948: 26.

Alberti, S. J. M. M. 2012. *Nature and Culture: Objects, Disciplines and the Manchester Museum*. Manchester: Manchester University Press.

Aldred, C. 1979. *Scenes from Ancient Egypt in the Royal Scottish Museum Edinburgh*. Edinburgh: Royal Scottish Museum.

Allan, D. A. 1960. The museum and its functions. In UNESCO (ed.) *The Organization of Museums*. Paris: United Nations, pp. 13–26.

Allan, D. A. 1949. Museums and education. *Journal of the Royal Society of Arts* 97: 86–106.

Allen, L. A. 2001. *A Bluestocking in Charleston: The Life and Career of Laura Bragg*. Colombia: University of South Carolina Press.

Allen, T. G. 1923. *A Handbook of the Egyptian Collection*. Chicago: University of Chicago Press.

Allison-Bunnell, S. W. 1998. Making nature 'real' again: natural history exhibits and public rhetorics of science at the Smithsonian Institution in the early 1960s. In MacDonald, S. (ed.) *The Politics of Display: Museums, Science, Culture*. London and New York: Routledge, pp. 77–83.

Anderson, M. and Reeves, A. 1994. Contested identities: museums and the nation in Australia. In F. E. S. (ed.) *Museums and the Making of Ourselves: The Role of Objects in National Identity*. London and New York: Leicester University Press, pp. 79–124.

Anthony, S. 2016. Ambition and anxiety: the Science Museum 1950–1983. In Morris, P. J. T. (ed.) *Science for the Nation: Perspectives on the History of the Science Museum*. London: Palgrave Macmillan, pp. 90–110.

Appadurai, A. 1986. Introduction: commodities and the politics of value. In Appadurai, A (ed.) *The Social Life of Things: Commodities in Cultural Perspective*. Cambridge: Cambridge University Press, pp. 3–63.

Arrowsmith, R. R. 2011. *Modernism and the Museum: Asian, African, and Pacific Art and the London Avant-Garde*. Oxford: Oxford University Press.

Ashmawi, A. 2012. *Legal Thefts: Stories of Thefts of Egyptian Antiquities, Their Smuggling and Attempts to Recover Them*. Cairo: Egyptian Lebanese Publishing House [in Arabic].

Ashton, S. A. 2013. *Origins of the Afro Comb: 6,000 Years of Culture, Politics and Identity*. Cambridge: Fitzwilliam Museum.

Attfield, J. 1999. Bringing modernity home: open plan in the British domestic interior. In Ciearaad, I. (ed.) *At Home: An Anthropology of Domestic Space*. New York: Syracuse University Press, pp. 73–82.

Bagh, T. 2011. *Finds from W.M.F. Petrie's Excavations in Egypt in the Ny Carlsberg Glyptotek*. Copenhagen: Ny Carlsberg Glyptotek.

Baird, J. and McFadyen, L. 2014. Towards an archaeology of archaeological archives. *Archaeological Review from Cambridge* 29(2): 14–32.

Barker, E. 1999. Exhibiting the canon: the blockbuster show. In Barker, E. (ed.) *Contemporary Cultures of Display*. New Haven and London: Yale University Press, pp. 127–46.

Basu, P. 2012. A museum for Sierra Leone? Amateur enthusiasms and colonial museum policy in British West Africa. In Longair, S. and McAleer, J. (eds.) *Curating Empire: Museums and the British Imperial Experience*. Manchester: Manchester University Press, pp. 145–67.

Bayly, C. A., Beckert, S., Connelly, M., Hofmeyr, I., Kozol, W. and Seed, P. 2006. AHR Conversation: on transnational history. *The American Historical Review* 111(5): 1441–64.

Bell, L. 2009. Engaging the public in public policy. *Museum and Social Issues. A Journal of Reflective Discourse* 4(1): 21–36.

Benjamin, W. 1985 [1928]. Manorially furnished ten-room apartment. In Benjamin, W. *One Way Street and Other Writings*, translated by Jephcott, E. and Shorter, K. London: Verso, pp. 48–9.

Bennett, T. 2014. Liberal government and the practical history of anthropology. *History and Anthropology* 25 (2): 150–70.

Bennett, T. 2004. *Pasts Beyond Memory: Evolution, Museums, Colonialism*. London and New York: Routledge.

Bennett, T. 1995. *The Birth of the Museum: History, Theory, Politics*. London and New York: Routledge.

Bennett, T., Cameron, F., Dias, N., Dibley, B, Harrison, R., Jacknis, I. and McCarthy, C. 2017. *Collecting, Ordering, Governing: Anthropology, Museums, and Liberal Government*. Durham, NC: Duke University Press.

Benson, J. 1994. *The Rise of Consumer Society in Britain, 1880–1980*. London: Longman.

Berger, C. 1983. *Science, God, and Nature in Victorian Canada*. Toronto: University of Toronto Press.

Berman, L. M. 2002. The prehistory of the Egyptian Department of the Museum of Fine Arts, Boston. In Eldamaty, M. and Trad, M. (eds.) *Egyptian Museum Collections Around the World. Volume Two*. Cairo: American University in Cairo Press, pp. 119–32.

Betrò, M. 2004. History of the collections. In Bresciani, E. and Betrò, M. (eds.) *Egypt in India. Egyptian Antiquities in Indian Museums*. Pisa: Pisa University Press, pp. 63–71.

Bhatti, S. 2007. *Translating Museums: A Counterhistory of South Asian Museology*. Walnut Creek: Left Coast Press.

Bierbrier, M. 2012. *Who Was Who in Egyptology*. Fourth Revised Edition. London: Egypt Exploration Society.

Bilbey, D. and Trusted, M. 2010. 'The question of casts': collecting and later reassessment of the cast collections at South Kensington. In Frederiksen, R. and Marchand, E. (eds.) *Plaster Casts: Making, Collecting and Display from Classical Antiquity to the Present*. Berlin and New York: De Gruyter, pp. 465–84.

Black, J. B. 2000. *On Exhibit: The Victorians and Their Museums*. Charlottesville and London: University Press of Virginia.

Blunck, L., Savoy, B. and Shalem, A. (eds.) *The Museum is Open: Towards a Transnational History of Museums 1750–1940*. Berlin and Boston: De Gruyter.

Boas, F. 1907. Some principles of museum administration. *Science* n.s. 25(650): 921–33.

Born, P. 2002. The canon is cast: plaster casts in American museum and university collections. *Art Documentation: Journal of the Art Libraries Society of North America* 21(2): 8–13.

Bowman, B. 2008. Transnational crimes against culture: looting at archaeological sites and the 'grey' market in antiquities. *Journal of Contemporary Criminal Justice* 24(3): 225–42.

Bragg, L. 1922. Exhibit and lecture notes. *Bulletin of the Charleston Museum* 17(3): 22.

Breasted, J. H. and Petrie, W. M. F. 1897. Professor Petrie's 'Egyptian Research Account'. *The Biblical World* 9(2): 138–42.

Brodie, N. 2015. The internet market in antiquities. In Desmarais, F. (ed.) *Countering Illicit Traffic in Cultural Goods: The Global Challenge of Protecting the World's Heritage*. Paris: ICOM, pp. 11–20.

Brodie, N. 2014. Auction houses and the antiquities trade. In Choulia-Kapeloni, S. (ed.) *Third International Conference of Experts on the Return of Cultural Property*. Athens: Archaeological Receipts Fund, pp. 71–82.

Brodie, N. 2012. Uncovering the antiquities market. In Skeates, R., McDavid, C. and Carman, J. (eds.) *The Oxford Handbook of Public Archaeology*. Oxford: Oxford University Press, pp. 230–52.

Bronk Ramsey, C., Dee, M. W., Rowland, J. M., Higham, T. F. G., Harris, S. A., Brock, F., Quiles, A., Wild, E. M., Marcus, E. S. and Shortland, A. J. 2010. Radiocarbon-based chronology for dynastic Egypt. *Science* 328 (5985): 1554–59.

Bronk Ramsey, C., Higham, T., Brock, F., Baker, D., Ditchfield, P. and Staff, R. 2015. Radiocarbon dates from the Oxford AMS system: Archaeometry datelist 35. *Archaeometry*, 57(1): 177–216.

Brunton, G. 1937. *Mostagedda and the Tasian Culture*. London: British School of Archaeology in Egypt.

Brunton, G. and Caton-Thompson, G. 1928. *The Badarian Civilisation*. London: British School of Archaeology in Egypt.

Brusius, M. 2012. Misfit objects: Layard's excavations in ancient Mesopotamia and the biblical imagination in mid-nineteenth century Britain. *Journal of Literature and Science* 5: 45–6.

Bryant, M. and Eaverly, M. A. 2007. Egypto-Modernism: James Henry Breasted, H.D., and the New Past. *Modernism/Modernity* 14(3): 434–53.
Bud, R. 2016. Infected by the bacillus of science. In Morris, P. J. T. (ed.) *Science for the Nation. Perspectives on the History of the Science Museum.* London: Palgrave Macmillan, pp. 250–72.
Bull, L. 1933. Two groups of prehistoric Egyptian objects. *The Metropolitan Museum of Art Bulletin* 28(7): 119–20.
Burton, R. 1879. Stones and bones from Egypt and Midian. *The Journal of the Anthropological Institute of Great Britain and Ireland* 8: 290–319.
Caddie, A. J. 1910. The board of education and provincial museums. *Museums Journal* 10(11): pp. 128–9.
Cameron, F. R. 2014. From 'dead things' to immutable, combinable mobiles: H.D. Skinner, the Otago Museum and University and the Governance of Māori populations. *History and Anthropology* 25(2): 208–26.
Candea, M. 2013. The fieldsite as device. *Journal of Cultural Economy* 6(3): 241–58.
Candlin, F. 2016. *Micromuseuology: An Analysis of Small Independent Museums.* London: Bloomsbury.
Carruthers, W. 2016. Multilateral possibilities: decolonization, preservation, and the case of Egypt. *Future Anterior: Journal of Historic Preservation, History, Theory, and Criticism* 13(1): 37–48.
Carruthers, W. 2015. Introduction: thinking about histories of Egyptology. In Carruthers, W. (ed.) *Histories of Egyptology. Interdisciplinary Measures.* London and New York: Routledge, pp. 1–18.
Carter, H. 1976. *Wonderful Things: The Discovery of Tutankhamun's Tomb.* Metropolitan Museum of Art: New York.
Caton-Thompson, G. and Gardiner, E. 1934. *The Desert Fayum.* London: Royal Anthropological Institute of Great Britain and Ireland.
Çelik, Z. 2016. *About Antiquities: Politics of Archaeology in the Ottoman Empire.* Austin: University of Texas Press.
Challis, D. 2015. What's in a face? Mummy portrait panels. In Carruthers, W. (ed.) *Histories of Egyptology: Disciplinary Measures.* London and New York: Routledge, pp. 227–41.
Challis, D. 2013. *The Archaeology of Race: The Eugenic Ideas of Francis Galton and Flinders Petrie.* London: Bloomsbury.
Challis, D. 2008. *From the Harpy Tomb to the Wonders of Ephesus: British Archaeologists in the Ottoman Empire 1840–1880.* London: Duckworth.

Childe, G. V. 1929. *The Most Ancient East: The Oriental Prelude to European Prehistory*. New York: Alfred A. Knopf.

Chubb, M. 1998. *Nefertiti Lived Here*. London: Libri Publications.

Cohen, D. 2006. *Household Gods: The British and their Possessions*. New Haven: Yale University Press.

Coleman, L. V. 1939. *The Museum in America: A Critical Study*. Three Volumes. Washington DC: The American Association of Museums.

Colla, E. 2007. *Conflicted Antiquities: Egyptology, Egyptomania, Egyptian Modernity*. Durham: Duke University Press.

Conforti, M. 1997. Deaccessioning in American Museums: II – some thoughts for England. In Weil, S. E. (ed.) *A Deaccession Reader*. Washington: American Association of Museums, pp. 73–85.

Conn, S. 2010. *Do Museums Still Need Objects?* Philadelphia: University of Pennsylvania Press.

Conn, S. 1998. *Museums and Intellectual Life, 1876–1926*. Chicago and London: The University of Chicago Press.

Crawford, O. G. S. 1927. Editorial notes. *Antiquity* 1(1): 1–4.

Crawford, O. G. S. 1929. Editorial notes. *Antiquity* 3(12): 385–8.

Crinson, M. 2001. Nation-building, collecting and display: the National Museum, Ghana. *Journal of the History of Collections* 13(2): 231–50.

Croly, J. C. 1886. *Sorosis. Its Origin and History*. New York: Press of J. J. Little and Co.

Cuno, J. 2008. *Who Owns Antiquity? Museums and the Battle Over Our Ancient Heritage*. Princeton: Princeton University Press.

Curran, B. A. 2007. *The Egyptian Renaissance: The Afterlife of Ancient Egypt in Early Modern Italy*. Chicago: The University of Chicago Press.

Curran, K. 2016. *The Invention of the American Art Museum: From Craft to Kulturgeschichte. 1870–1930*. Los Angeles: Getty Research Institute.

Curtis, N. 2006. Universal museums, museum objects and repatriation: the tangled stories of things. *Museum Management and Curatorship* 21(2): 117–27.

Daly, N. 1994. The obscure object of desire: Victorian commodity culture and fictions of the mummy. *NOVEL: A Forum on Fiction* 28(1): 24–51.

Daly, M. W. 1998. The British occupation, 1882–1922. In Daly, M. W. (ed.) *The Cambridge History of Egypt, Volume Two: Modern Egypt from 1517 to the End of the Twentieth Century*. Cambridge: Cambridge University Press, pp. 239–51.

Daston, L. 2004. Introduction: speechless. In Daston, L. (ed.) *Things That Talk: Object Lessons from Art and Science*. London and Cambridge: The MIT Press, pp. 9–24.

Daston, L. 1999. Introduction: the coming into being of scientific objects. In Daston, L. (ed.) *Biographies of Scientific Objects*. Chicago: The University of Chicago Press, pp. 1–14.

D'Auria, S. 2007. The American branch of the Egypt Exploration Fund. In Hawass, Z. A. and Richards, J. (eds.) *The Archaeology and Art of Ancient Egypt: Essays In Honor of David B. O'Connor*. Cairo: American Research Center in Egypt, pp. 185–98.

Davies, T. W. 2003. Levantine Archaeology. In Richard, S. (ed.) *Near Eastern Archaeology Reader*. Winona Lake: Eisenbraun, pp. 54–9.

Dawson, J. W. 1893. Notes on useful and ornamental stones of ancient Egypt. *Journal of the Transactions of the Victoria Institute* 26: 265–82.

Delamaire, M-S. 2003. Searching for Egypt: Egypt in 19th Century American World Exhibitions. In Humbert, J-M. and Price, C. (eds.) *Imhotep Today: Egyptianizing Architecture*. London: UCL Press, pp. 123–34.

Deetz, J. 1977. *In Small Things Forgotten: The Archaeology of Early American Life*. New York: Anchor Books.

Derrida, J. 1995. *Archive Fever: A Freudian Impression*. Translated Eric Prenowitz. Chicago and London: University of Chicago Press.

Diaz-Andreu, M. 2012. *Archaeological Encounters: Building Networks of Spanish and British Archaeologists in the 20th Century*. Newcastle upon Tyne: Cambridge Scholars Publishing.

Diaz-Andreu, M. 2007. *A World History of Nineteenth-century Archaeology: Nationalism, Colonialism and the Past*. Oxford: Oxford University Press.

Diaz-Andreu, M. and Champion, T. (eds.) 1996. *Nationalism and Archaeology in Europe*. Boulder and San Francisco: Westview Press.

Dibley, B. 1997. Telling times: narrating the nation at the New Zealand International Exhibition 1906–07. *Sites* 34 (Autumn 1997): 1–17.

Dietzler, J. 2013. On 'organized crime' in the illicit antiquities trade: moving beyond the definitional debate. *Trends in Organized Crime* 16(3): 329–42.

Diop, C. A. 1974. *The African Origin of Civilization: Myth or Reality*. New York: Lawrence Hill and Company.

Dirks, N. 2015. *Autobiography of an Archive: A Scholar's Passage to India*. New York: Columbia University Press.

Dixon, D. M. 2003. Some Egyptological sidelines on the Egyptian War of 1882. In Jeffreys, D. (ed.) *Views of Ancient Egypt Since Napoleon Bonaparte: Imperialism, Colonialism and Modern Appropriations*. London: UCL Press, pp. 87–94.

Doyon, W. 2018. The history of archaeology through the eyes of Egyptians. In Effros, B. and Lai, G. (eds.) *Unmasking Ideology in Imperial and Colonial Archaeology*. Los Angeles: Cotsen Institute of Archaeology Press, pp. 173–200.

Doyon, W. 2013/2014. Egyptology in the shadow of class. *Egyptological Documents, Archives and Libraries* 4: 261–72.

Droop, J. P. 1915. *Archaeological Excavation*. Cambridge: Cambridge University Press.

Drower, M. 1985. *Flinders Petrie: A Life in Archaeology*. London: Victor Gollancz.

Drower, M. 1982. Gaston Maspero and the birth of the Egypt Exploration Fund (1881–3). *Journal of Egyptian Archaeology* 68: 299–317.

Dudley, S. (ed.) 2010. *Museum Materialities: Objects, Engagements, Interpretations*. London and New York: Routledge.

Duffy, K. 2017. The dead curator: education and the rise of bureaucratic authority in natural history museums, 1870–1915. *Museum History Journal* 10(1): 29–49.

Dunne, J., Evershed, R. P., Salque, M., Cramp, L, Bruni, S., Ryan, K., Biagetti, S. and di Lernia, S. 2012. First dairying in green Saharan Africa in the fifth millennium BC. *Nature* 485: 390–4.

Edwards, A. B. 1891a. My home life. *Arena Magazine* 4: 299–311.

Edwards, A. B. 1891b. *Pharaohs, Fellahs and Explorers*. New York: Harper and Brothers.

Edwards, C. 2005. *Turning Houses into Homes: A History of the Retailing and Consumption of Domestic Furnishings*. London: Ashgate.

Edwards, E. 2014. Photographic uncertainties: between evidence and reassurance. *History and Anthropology* 25(2): 171–88.

Edwards, E. 2009. Photography and the material performance of the past. *History and Theory* 48(4): 130–50.

Edwards, E. and Morton, C. 2015. Between art and information: towards a collecting history of photographs. In Edwards, E. and Morton, C. (eds.) *Photographs, Museums Collections: Between Art and Information*. London: Bloomsbury Publishing, pp. 8–10.

Efrat, A. 2016. Thieves: art law, war and policy. In Charney, N. (ed.) *Art Crime: Terrorists, Tomb Raiders, Forgers and Thieves*. New York: Palgrave Macmillan, pp. 337–58.

Elias, C. 2012. Discovering Egypt: Egyptian antiquities at the University of Melbourne. *University of Melbourne Collections* 10: 9–14.

Ellis, H. 2017. Collaboration and knowledge exchange between scholars in Britain and the Empire, 1830–1914. In Jöns, H., Meusbruger, P. and Heffernan, M. (eds.) *Mobilities of Knowledge*. Dordrecht: Springer, pp. 141–55.

Ellsworth, W. W. 1891. Spoiling the Egyptians. *Century Magazine* 41: 152–3.

Ellwood, R. S. 1973. *Religious and Spiritual Groups in Modern America*. Englewood Cliffs: Prentice-Hall.

Emmitt, J. and Hellum, J. 2015. A Predynastic vessel with a potmark in the Auckland War Memorial Museum. *Records of the Auckland Museum* 50: 33–7.

Engelbach, R. and Gunn, B. 1923. *Harageh*. London: British School of Archaeology in Egypt.

Erman, A. 1929. *Mein Werden und mein Wirken: Erinnerungen eines alten Berliner Gelehrten*. Leipzig: Quelle and Meyer.

Eskildsen, K. R. 2012. The language of objects: Christian Jürgensen Thomsen's Science of the past. *Isis* 103(1): 24–53.

Evans, C. 2007. Delineating objects: nineteenth-century antiquarian culture and the project of archaeology. In Pearce, S. (ed.) *Visions of Antiquity: The Society of Antiquaries of London 1707–2007*. London: Society of Antiquaries of London, pp. 267–305.

Evans, C. 1989. Digging with the pen: novel archaeologies and literary traditions. *Archaeological Review from Cambridge* 8(20): 186–211.

Exell, K. 2015. Innovation and reaction: a discussion of the proposed re-display of the Egyptian galleries at the Manchester Museum. In Kousoulis, P. and Lazaridis, N. (eds.) *Proceedings of the Tenth International Congress of Egyptologists*. Leuven: Peeters Publishers, pp. 2187–97.

Fiskesjo, M. 2010. Commentary: the global repatriation debate and the new 'universal museums'. In Lydon, J. and Rizvi, U. Z. (eds.) *Handbook of Postcolonial Archaeology*. London and New York: Routledge, pp. 303–10.

Fletcher, W. M. R. 1892. *Egyptian Sketches*. Adelaide: E. A. Petherick and Co.

Fluck, C. 2014. Findspot known: treasures from excavation sites in Egypt in the Museum für Byzantinische Kunst, Berlin. *British Museum Studies in Ancient Egypt and Sudan* 21: 1–30.

Fogelman, A. 2008. Colonial legacy in African museology: the case of the Ghana National Museum. *Museum Anthropology* 31(1): 19–27.

Fonck, L. 1908. Review of Nach Petra und zum Sinai. Zwei Reiseberichte nebst Beiträgen zur biblischen Geographie und Geschichte by Ladislaus Szczepański. *Zeitschrift für katholische Theologie* 32(4): 727–9.

Forest, R. W. 1929. How museums can most wisely dispose of surplus material. *The Metropolitan Museum of Art Bulletin* 24(6): 158–60.

Fox, C. 1959. The gallery shop. *The Brooklyn Museum Bulletin. Annual Report 1957–58*: 27–8.

Foucault, M. 1989 [1966]. *The Order of Things*. English reprint. London and New York: Routledge.

Francis, D. 2015. 'An arena where meaning and identity are debated and contested on a global scale': narrative discourses in British Museum exhibitions, 1972–2013. *Curator: The Museum Journal* 58(1):41–58.

Frankfort, H. and Pendlebury, J. 1933. *The City of Akhenaten II: The North Suburb and the Desert Altars*. London: Egypt Exploration Society.

Fuller, H. 2015. Father of the nation: Ghanaian nationalism, internationalism and the political iconography of Kwame Nkrumah, 1957–2010. *African Studies Quarterly* 16(1): 39–75.

Fuller, H. 2014. *Building the Ghanaian Nation-State: Kwame Nkrumah's Symbolic Nationalism*. New York: Palgrave Macmillan.

Gange, D. 2013. *Dialogues with the Dead: Egyptology in British Culture and Religion 1822–1922*. Oxford: Oxford University Press.

Gange, D. 2006. Religion and science in late nineteenth-century Egyptology. *The Historical Journal* 49(4): 1083–103.

Geismar, H. 2015. The art of anthropology: questioning contemporary art in ethnographic display. In Message, K. and Witcomb, A. (eds.) *The International Handbook of Museum Studies: Museum Theory*. Malden: Blackwell Publishing, pp. 183–210.

Gero, J. 1985. Socio-politics and the woman-at-home ideology. *American Antiquity* 50(2): 342–50.

Gerstenblith, P. 2017. Implementation of the 1970 UNESCO Convention by the United States and other market nations. In Anderson, J. and Geismar, H. (eds.) *The Routledge Companion to Cultural Property*. London and New York: Routledge Press, pp. 70–88.

Gertzen, T. 2017. *Einführung in die Wissenschaftsgeschichte der Ägyptologie*. Münster: LIT Verlag.

Gertzen, T. 2015. The Anglo-Saxon branch of the Berlin School. In Carruthers, W. (ed.) *Histories of Egyptology*. London and New York: Routledge, pp. 34–49.

Gertzen, T. L. 2009. Ägyptologie zwischen Archäeologie und Sprachwissenschaft: die Korrespondenz zwischen A. Erman und W.M. Flinders Petrie. *Zeitschrift fur Ägyptische Sprache und Altertumskunde* 136: 114–69.

Gidiri, A. 1974. Imperialism and archaeology. *Race* 15(4): 431–59.

Giguere, J. 2014. *Characteristically American: Memorial Architecture, National Identity, and the Egyptian Revival.* Knoxville: University of Tennessee Press.

Gill, D. W. J. 2015. Egyptian antiquities on the market. In Hassan, F. A., Tassie, G., Owens, L. S., de Trafford, A., van Wetering, J. and el Daly, O. (eds.) *The Management of Egypt's Cultural Heritage, Volume 2.* London: ECHO and Golden House Publications, pp. 67–77.

Glanville, S. R. K. 1947. *The Growth and Nature of Egyptology. An Inaugural Lecture.* Cambridge: Cambridge University Press.

Goldhill, S. 2014. *The Buried Life of Things.* Cambridge: Cambridge University Press.

Gooch, J. 2013. *The Boer War: Direction, Experience and Image.* London and New York: Routledge.

Goode, G. B. 1895. *The Principles of Museum Administration.* York: Coultas and Volans.

Goode, J. F. 2007. *Negotiating for the Past: Archaeology, Nationalism, and Diplomacy in the Middle East, 1919–1941.* Austin: University of Texas Press.

Goodnow, K., Lothman, J. and Bredekamp, J. 2006. *Challenge and Transformation: Museums in Cape Town and Sydney.* New York and Oxford: Berghahn Books.

Gore, J. M. 2004. A lack of nation? The evolution of history in South African Museums, c.1825–1945. *South African Historical Journal* 51(1): 24–46.

Gorman, J. M. 2011. Universalism and the new museology: impacts on the ethics of authority and ownership. *Museum Management and Curatorship* 26(2): 149–62.

Gosden, C. and Larson, F. 2007. *Knowing Things: Exploring the Collections at the Pitt Rivers Museum 1884–1945.* Oxford: Oxford University Press.

Gosden, C. and Marshall, Y. 1999. The cultural biography of objects. *World Archaeology* 31(2): 169–78.

Grundon, I. 2007. *The Rash Adventurer: A Life of John Pendlebury.* London: Libri Publications Limited.

Guha, S. 2015. *Artefacts of History: Archaeology, Historiography and Indian Pasts.* New Dehli: Sage.

Guidotti, M. C. (ed.) 2006. *Materiale predinastico del Museo Egizio di Firenze*. Maat. Materiali del Museo Egizio di Firenze 4. Firenze: Giunt.

Hagen, F. and Ryholt, K. 2016. *The Antiquities Trade in Egypt 1880–1930. The H.O. Lange Papers*. Copenhagen: The Royal Danish Academy of Science and Letters.

Hall, K. M. 1901. The smallest museum. *Museums Journal* 1(1): 38–40.

Hamada, K. 1923a. Egyptian archaeological objects that has recently arrived at the Kyoto Imperial University. *Shirin* 8(1): 122–31 [in Japanese].

Hamada, K. 1923b. Excavations in Egypt and their archaeological results. *Taiyo* 29(5): xx–yy [in Japanese].

Hamada, K. and Chiba, T. 1914. The late Professor Tsuboi and Egyptology in Japan. *Ancient Egypt* 1914: 59–60.

Hamilakis, Y. 2016. From ethics to politics. In Hamilakis, Y. and Duke, P. (eds.) *Archaeology and Capitalism: From Ethics to Politics*. London and New York: Routledge, pp. 15–40.

Hamilton, S. 2007. Women in practice: women in British contract field archaeology. In Hamilton, S., Whitehouse, R. and Wright, K. I. (eds.) *Archaeology and Women: Ancient and Modern Issues*. Walnut Creek: Left Coast Press, pp. 121–46.

Hanna, M. 2013. Looting heritage: losing identity. *Al Rawi* 5: 22–5.

Hanna, M. 2016. Documenting looting activities in Post-2011 Egypt. In Desmarais, F. (ed.) *Countering Illicit Traffic in Cultural Goods: The Global Challenge of Protecting the World's Heritage*. Paris: International Council of Museums, pp. 47–64.

Harden, D. B. 1955. The cult of the known. *Museums Journal* 55(6): 152–4.

Hardwick, T. 2011. Five months before Tut: purchasers and prices at the MacGregor sale, 1922. *Journal of the History of Collections* 32(1): 179–92.

Harer, W. B. 2008. The Drexel collection: from Egypt to the diaspora. In D'Auria, S. (ed.) *Servant of Mut: Studies in Honor of Richard A. Fazzini*. Leiden and Boston: Brill, pp. 111–19.

Harris, V. and Goto, K. (eds.). 2003. *William Gowland: The Father of Japanese Archaeology*. Tokyo: Asahi Shinbunsha and London: British Museum Press.

Harrison, R. 2013. Reassembling ethnographic museum collections. In Harrison, R., Byrne, S. and Clarke, A. (eds.) *Reassembling the Collection: Ethnographic Museums and Indigenous Agency*. Santa Fe: SAR Press, pp. 3–36.

Hasinoff, E. 2011. *Faith in Objects: American Missionary Expositions in the Early Twentieth Century*. New York: Palgrave Macmillan.

Hassett, B., Birch, S. P., Herridge V. and Wragg Sykes, R. 2018. TrowelBlazers: accidentally crowdsourcing an archive of women in archaeology. In Apaydin, V. (ed.) *Shared Knowledge, Shared Power*. New York: Springer, pp. 129–142.

Hayes, W. 1990. *The Scepter of Egypt: A Background for the Study of the Egyptian Antiquities of the Metropolitan Museum of Art From the Earliest Times to the End of the Middle Kingdom*. New York: Metropolitan Museum of Art.

Henare, A. 2005. *Museums, Anthropology and Imperial Exchange*. Cambridge: Cambridge University Press, pp. 121–46.

Hennessy, P. 2006. *Having It So Good: Britain in the Fifties*. London: Allen Lane.

Henning, M. 2006. *Museums, Media and Cultural Theory*. Maidenhead: Open University Press.

Hickey, T. M. and Kennan, J. G. 2016. At the creation: seven letters from Grenfell, 1897. *Analecta Papyrologica* 28: 352–82.

Hicks, D. 2016. Pitt Rivers AD2065: the future of museums, past and present. *Museum iD* 19: 31–7.

Hinsley, C. M. and Wilcox, D. R. (eds.) 2016. *Coming of Age in Chicago: The 1893 World's Fair and the Coalescence of American Anthropology*. Lincoln and London: University of Nebraska Press.

Hill, K. 2016. *Women and Museums 1850–1914: Modernity and the Gendering of Knowledge*. Manchester: Manchester University Press.

Hill, K. 2005. *Cultural and Class in English Public Museums, 1850–1914*. London: Ashgate.

HMI 1899. *Revised Instructions Issued to Her Majesty's Inspectors, and Applicable to the Code of 1899*. London: Eyre & Spottiswoode.

Hoberman, R. 2003. In quest of a museal aura: turn of the century narratives about museum-displayed objects. *Victorian Literature and Culture* 31(2): 467–82.

Hodder, I. 1986. *Reading the Past*. Cambridge: Cambridge University Press.

Holger K. 2011. Tarifi Zor Bay Whittemore: Erken Dönem, 1871–1916. The elusive Mr. Whittemore: The early years 1871–1916. In Holger, K., Ousterhout, R. and Pitarakis, B. (ed.) *The Kariye Camii Reconsidered*. Istanbul: İstanbul Araştırmaları Enstitüsü, pp. 478–9.

Hooper-Greenhill, E. 1992. *Museums and the Shaping of Knowledge*. London and New York: Routledge.

Hoving, T. 1993. *Making the Mummies Dance: Inside the Metropolitan Museum of Art*. New York: Simon and Schuster.

Hoyle, W. E. 1908. The arrangement of an Egyptological collection. *The Museums Journal* 8(11): 152–62.

Huang, P. 2016. Early museological development within the Japanese Empire. *Journal of the History of Collections* 28(1): 125–35.

Hubert, J. 1989. A proper place for the dead: a critical review of the 'reburial' issue. In Layton, R. (ed.) *Conflict in the Archaeology of Living Traditions*. London and New York: Routledge, pp. 131–66.

Husband, T. 2013. *Creating the Cloisters*. New York: Metropolitan Museum of Art.

Hutchison, S. and Brown, R. (eds.) 2015. *Monsters and Monstrosity from the Fin de Siècle to the Millennium: New Essays*. Jefferson: McFarland.

Il Pai, H. 2010. Resurrecting the ruins of Japan's mythical homelands: colonial archaeological surveys in the Korean Peninsula and heritage tourism. In Lydon, J. and Rizvi, U. Z. (eds.) *Handbook of Postcolonial Archaeology*. London and New York: Routledge, pp. 93–112.

Ikram, S. 2010. Collecting and repatriating Egypt's past: toward a new nationalism. In Silverman, H. (ed.) *Contested Cultural Heritage: Religion, Nationalism, Erasure and Exclusion*. New York: Springer, pp. 141–54.

Ingold, T. 2000. Ancestry, generation, substance, memory, land. In Ingold, T. (ed.) *The Perception of the Environment: Essays in Livelihood, Dwelling and Skill.* London and New York: Routledge, pp. 132–51.

Iriye, A. and Saunier, P-Y. (eds.) 2009. *The Palgrave Dictionary of Transnational History: From the Mid-19th Century to the Present Day*. Basingstoke: Palgrave.

Irwin, J. T. 1980. *American Hieroglyphics: The Symbol of the Egyptian Hieroglyphs in the American Renaissance*. New Haven: Yale University Press.

Jacknis, I. 2006. A new thing? The NMAI in historical and institutional perspective. *American Indian Quarterly* 30(3/4): 511–42.

James, T. G. H. (ed.) 1982. *Excavating in Egypt: The Egypt Exploration Society*. London: Egypt Exploration Society.

Janssen, R. 1992. *The First Hundred Years: Egyptology at University College London 1892–1992*. London: UCL Press, pp. 98–102.

Jasanoff, M. 2006. *Edge of Empire: Conquest and Collecting in the East 1750– 1850*. London: Harper Perennial.

Johnson, W. A. 2012. The Oxyrhynchus distributions in America: papyri and ethics. *The Bulletin of the American Society of Papyrologists*. 49: 209–22.

Jørgensen, M. 2015. *How it All Began: The Story of Carl Jacobsen's Egyptian Collection, 1884–1925*. Copenhagen: Ny Carlsberg Glyptotek.

Joy, J. 2009. Reinvigorating object biography: reproducing the drama of object lives. *World Archaeology* 41(4): 540–6.

Jukes Brown, A. J. 1878. On some flint implements from Egypt. *The Journal of the Anthropological Institute of Great Britain and Ireland* 7: 396–412.

Kamerling, B. 1992. How Ellen Scripps brought ancient Egypt to San Diego. *The Journal of San Diego History* 38(2): 73–91.

Kaplan, F. E. S. (ed.) 1994. Introduction. In Kaplan, F. E. S. (ed.) *Museums and the Making of Ourselves: The Role of Objects in National Identity*. London and New York: Leicester University Press, pp. 1–15.

Karp, I. 1991. Other cultures in museum perspective. In Karp, I. and Lavine, S. D. (eds.) *Exhibiting Cultures: The Poetics and Politics of Museum Display*. Washington: Smithsonian Institution Press, pp. 373–85.

Kavanagh, G. 2000 *Dream Spaces: Memory and the Museum*. London: Leicester University Press.

Kavanagh, G. 1990. *History Curatorship*. Leicester and London: Leicester University Press.

Kawai, N. 2017. Egyptological landscape in Japan: past, present, and future. *CiPEG Journal* 1: 51–9.

Kersel, M. M. 2015. Storage wars: solving the archaeological curation crisis? *Journal of Eastern Mediterranean Archaeology and Heritage Studies* 3(1): 42–54.

Khater, A. 1960. *Le regime juridique des fouilles et des antiquités en Égypt*. Cairo: Institut Français d'Archéologie Orientale.

Kitchin, J. G. 1893. *The Bible Student in the British Museum*. London: Cassell and Company.

Kitchin, J. G. 1891. *Scripture Teaching, Illustrated by models and objects*. London: Church of England Sunday School Institute.

Knowles, C. 2014. Negative space: tracing absent images in the National Museums Scotland's collections. In Edwards, E. and Lien, S. (eds.) *Uncertain Images: Museums and the Work of Photographs*. Farnham; Ashgate, pp. 73–91.

Kohl, P. L. and Fawcett, C. 1996. *Nationalism, Politics and the Practice of Archaeology*. Cambridge: Cambridge University Press.

Kopytoff, I. 1986. The cultural biography of things: commoditization as process. In Appadurai, A. (ed.) *The Social Life of Things: Commodities in Cultural Perspective*. Cambridge: Cambridge University Press, pp. 64–91.

Kriegel, L. 2008. *Grand Designs: Labour, Empire, and the Museum in Victorian Culture*. Durham and London: Duke University Press.

Kristiansen, K. 2014. Toward a new paradigm? The third science revolution and its possible consequences in archaeology. *Current Swedish Archaeology* 22: 11–34.

Kroenke, K. R. 2010. *The Provincial Cemeteries of Naga-ed-Deir: A Comprehensive Study of Tomb Models Dating from the Late Old Kingdom to the Late Middle Kingdom*. Berkeley: UC Berkeley Electronic Theses and Dissertations.

Kröger, M. 1991. *Le bâton égyptien – Der ägyptische Knüppel: Die Rolle der ägyptischen Frage in der deutschen Außenpolitik von 1875/76 bis zur 'Entente Cordiale'*. Frankfurt am Main: Peter Lang.

Kuklick, B. 1996. *Puritans in Babylon: The Ancient Near East and American Intellectual Life, 1880–1930*. Princeton: Princeton University Press.

Kume, K. 2009. *Japan Rising: The Iwakura Embassy to the USA and Europe*. Edited by Tsuzuki, C. and Young, R. J. Cambridge: Cambridge University Press.

Kyoto University 2016. *Proceedings of the International Symposium on From Petrie to Hamada*. University of Kyoto: Kyoto.

Lane Fox [Pitt-Rivers], A. H. 1875a. On the principles of classification adopted in the arrangement of his anthropological collection, now exhibited in the Bethnal Green Museum. *Journal of Anthropological Institute* 4: 293–308.

Lane Fox [Pitt-Rivers], A. H. 1875b. On early modes of navigation. *The Journal of the Anthropological Institute of Great Britain and Ireland* 14: 399–437.

Lange, J. 1892. *Billedkunstens Fremstilling af Menneskeskikkelsen i dens ældste Periode*. Copenhagen: Bianco Lunos Kgl. Hof-Bogtrykkeri (F. Dreyer).

Larsen, H. 1961. Finds from Badarian and Tasian Civilizations. *Medelhavsmuseet Bulletin* 1: 9–19.

Larson, F. 2009. *An Infinity of Things. How Sir Henry Wellcome Collected the World*. Oxford: Oxford University Press.

Larson, F., Petch, A. and Zeitlyn, D. 2007. Social networks and the creation of the Pitt Rivers Museum. *Journal of Material Culture* 12(3): 211–39.

Larson, J. A. 2010. *Letters from James Henry Breasted to His Family. August 1919–July 1920*. Chicago: The Oriental Institute of the University of Chicago.

Latour, B. 2005. *Reassembling the Social: An Introduction to Actor-Network-Theory*. Oxford: Oxford University Press.

Latour, B. 1987. *Science in Action: How to Follow Scientists and Engineers Through Society.* Cambridge: Harvard University Press.

Latour, B. 1986. Visualization and cognition: drawing things together. *Knowledge and Society Studies in the Sociology of Culture Past and Present* 6(1): 1–40.

Latour, B. and Love, A. 2010. The migration of the aura or how to explore the original through its facsimiles. In Bartscherer, T. (ed.) *Switching Codes: Thinking Through Digital Technology in the Humanities and the Arts.* Chicago: University of Chicago Press, pp. 275–97.

Lawn, M. 2013. A pedagogy for the public: the place of objects, observation, mechanical production and cupboards. *Revista Linhas* 14(26): 244–64.

Lawn, M. 2005. A pedagogy for the public: the place of objects, observation, mechanical production and cupboards. In Lawn, M. and Grosvenor, I. (eds.) *Materialities of Schooling: Design, Technology, Objects, Routines.* Didcot: Symposium Books, pp. 145–62.

Lawrence, A. W. and Merrifield, R. 1957. The National Museum of Ghana. *Museums Journal* 57(7): 88–96.

Lewis, H. S. 1929. *Rosicrucian Questions and Answers.* San Jose: Rosicrucian Press.

Lawson, B. 1999. Exhibiting agendas: anthropology at the Redpath Museum (1882–1899). *Anthropologica* 41: 53–65.

Leahy, T. 2014. Kushites at Abydos: the royal family and beyond. In Pischikova, E., Budka, J. and Griffin, K. (eds.) *Thebes in the First Millennium BC.* Cambridge: Cambridge Scholars Publishing, pp. 62–70.

Lepsius, R. 1870. Ueber die Annahme eines sogenannten prähistorischen Steinalters in Aegypten. *Zeitschrift für Ägyptische Sprache und Altertumskunde* 8: 89–107.

Lesko, B. S. 2004a. Caroline Louise Ransom Williams, 1872–1952. In *Breaking Ground: Women in Old World Archaeology.* Web resource available at: https://www.brown.edu/Research/Breaking_Ground/bios/Ransom%20Williams_Caroline%20Louise.pdf [accessed 24 September 2017].

Lesko, B. S. 2004b. Sara Yorke Stevenson. In *Breaking Ground: Women in Old World Archaeology.* Web resource available at: https://www.brown.edu/Research/Breaking_Ground/bios/Stevenson_Sara%20Yorke.pdf [accessed 24 September 2017].

Lester, H. A. 1912. *Sunday School Teaching: Its Aims and its Methods.* London: Longmans, Green and Co.

Lewis, G. 1992. Museums in Britain: a historical survey. In Thompson, J. M. A. (ed.) *Manual of Curatorship: A Guide to Museum Practice.* Oxford and Boston: Butterworth-Heinemann, pp. 22–46.

Libby, W. F. 1954. Chicago radiocarbon dates, IV. *Science* 119: 135–40.

Licence, T. 2015. *What the Victorians Threw Away.* Oxford: Oxbow Books.

Livingstone, D. 2014. *Dealing with Darwin: Place, Politics, and Rhetoric in Religious Engagements with Evolution.* Baltimore: Johns Hopkins University Press.

Livingstone, D. N. 2003. *Putting Science in its Place: Geographies of Scientific Knowledge.* Chicago and London: University of Chicago Press.

Lockyer, A. 2008 National Museums and other cultures in modern Japan. In Sherman, D. J. (ed.) *Museums and Difference.* Bloomington: Indiana University Press, pp. 97–132.

Longair, S. and McAleer, J. (eds.) 2016. *Curating Empire: Museums and the British Imperial Experience.* Manchester: Manchester University Press.

Lubar, S., Rieppel, L., Daly, A. and Duffy, K. 2017. Lost museums. *Museum History Journal* 10(1): 1–14.

Lubbock, J. 1875. Notes on the discovery of stone implements in Egypt. *The Journal of the Anthropological Institute of Great Britain and Ireland* 4: 215–22.

Lucas, A. 1924. *Antiquities: Their Restoration and Preservations.* London: Arnold & Co.

Lucas, G. 2001. *Critical Approaches to Fieldwork: Contemporary and Historical Archaeological Practice.* London and New York: Routledge.

Luckhurst, R. 2012. Counter-narrative in the Egyptian rooms of the British Museum. *History and Anthropology* 23(2): 257–69.

Lutz, D. 2015. *Relics of Death in Victorian Literature and Culture.* Cambridge: Cambridge University Press.

McAlister, M. 1996. 'The common heritage of mankind': race, nation, and masculinity in the King Tut exhibit. *Representations* 54: 80–103.

McCarthy, C. 2009. 'Our works of ancient times': history, colonisation and agency at the 1906–07 New Zealand International Exhibition. *Museum History Journal* 2(2): 119–42.

McCarthy, K. 1991. *Women's Culture: American Philanthropy and Art, 1830–1930.* Chicago: University of Chicago Press.

MacDonald, S. 2003. Lost in time and space: ancient Egypt in museums. In MacDonald, S. and Rice, M. (eds.) *Consuming Ancient Egypt.* London: UCL Press, pp. 87–99.

Macdonald, S. 1998. Exhibitions of power and powers of exhibition. In MacDonald, S. (ed.) *The Politics of Display: Museums, Science, Culture*. New York: Routledge, pp. 9–15.

MacKenzie, J. M. 2009. *Museums and Empire: Natural History, Human Cultures and Colonial Identities*. Manchester: Manchester University Press.

Mackenzie, S. and Yates, D. 2016. What is grey about the 'grey market' in antiquities. In Beckert, J. and Dewey, M. (eds.) *The Architecture of Illegal Markets: Towards an Economic Sociology of Illegality in the Economy*. Oxford: Oxford University Press, pp. 70–86.

MacLauchlan, J. 1903. Technical museums. *Museums Journal* 2(12): 163–74.

McLeod, M. 2004. Museums without collections: museum philosophy in West Africa. In Knell, S. (ed.) *Museums and the Future of Collecting*. Ashgate: Farnham, pp. 52–61.

MacLeod, S., Hanks, L. H. and Hale, J. (eds.) 2012. *Museum Making: Narratives, Architectures, Exhibitions*. London and New York: Routledge.

MacMullen, R. 1982. The epigraphic habit in the Roman Empire. *The American Journal of Philology* 103(3): 233–46.

Malley, S. 2012. *From Archaeology to Spectacle in Victorian England: The Case of Assyria, 1845–1854*. Farnham: Ashgate.

Mandela, N. 1994. *Long Walk to Freedom*. New York: Back Bay Books.

Marchand, S. 2003. *Down from Olympus: Archaeology and Philhellenism in Germany, 1750–1970*. Princeton: Princeton University Press.

Marchand, S. 2000. The end of Egyptomania: German scholarship and the banalization of Egypt, 1830–1914. In Seipel, W. (ed.) *Ägyptomanie Europäische Ägyptenimagination von der Antike bis heute*. Wien: Kunsthistorisches Museum, pp. 125–33.

Marchand, S. 1998. Orientalism as Kulturpolitik. German archaeology and cultural imperialism in Asia Minor. In Stocking, G. W. (ed.) *Volksgeist as Method and Ethic*. Madison: University of Wisconsin Press, pp. 298–336.

Marcus, G. E. 1995. Ethnography in/of the world system: the emergence of multi-sited ethnography. *Annual Review of Anthropology* 24: 95–117.

Mariette, A. 1876. *Notice des principaux monuments exposés dans les galeries provisoires de S. A. le Khédive a Boulaq*. Sixth Edition. Le Caire: A. Mourès.

Markham, S. F. 1938. *A Report on the Museums and Art Galleries of the British Isles (other than National Museums)*. Edinburgh: Constable.

Markham, S. F. and Hargreaves, H. 1936. *The Museums of India*. London: The Museums Association.

Marstine, J. 2011. The contingent nature of the new museum ethics. In Marstine, J. (ed.) *The Routledge Companion To Museum Ethics. Redefining Ethics Of The Twenty-First Century Museum*. London and New York: Routledge, pp. 3–25.

Masters, S. 2017. Museum space and displacement: collecting classical antiquities in South Africa. In Parker, G. (ed.) *South Africa, Greece and Rome: Classical Confrontations*. Cambridge: Cambridge University Press, pp. 293–94.

Melman, B. 1992. *Women's Orients: English Women and the Middle East, 1718–1918, Sexuality, Religion and Work*. Ann Arbour: University of Michigan Press.

Merrillees, R. S. 1990. *Living with Egypt's Past in Australia*. Victoria: Museum of Victoria.

Merrington, P. 2017. The 'Mediterranean' Cape: reconstructing an ethos. In Parker, G. (ed.) *South Africa, Greece and Rome: Classical Confrontations*. Cambridge: Cambridge University Press, 114–37.

Meskell, L. 2005. Pharaonic legacies: postcolonialism, heritage and hyperreality. In Kane, S. (ed.) *The Politics of Archaeology and Identity in a Global Context*. Los Angeles: AIA Monographs/Cotsen Institute, pp. 149–71.

Meskell, L. 1998. *Archaeology Under Fire: Nationalism, Politics and Heritage in the Eastern Mediterranean and Middle East*. London and New York: Routledge.

Meskell, L. 1999. *Archaeologies of Social Life*. Oxford: Blackwell.

Mew, S. 2016. Managing the cultural past in the newly independent state of Mali and Ghana. In Craggs, R. and Wintle, C. (eds.) *Cultures of Decolonisation: Transnational Productions and Practices, 1945–70*. Manchester: Manchester University Press.

Mew, S. 2012. *Rethinking Heritage and Display in National Museums in Ghana and Mali*. PhD thesis. SOAS, University of London.

Meyerowitz, A. 1960. *The Divine Kingship in Ghana and Ancient Egypt*. London: Faber and Faber.

Miers, H. A. 1928. *A Report on the Public Museums of the British Isles (Other Than the National Museums)*. Dunfermline: Carnegie United Kingdom Trust.

Miers, H. A. and Markham, S. F. 1932. *A Report on the Museums and Art Galleries of British Africa*. The Museums Association Survey of Empire Museums. Edinburgh: T. and A. Constable.

Miskell, L. 2016. *Meeting Places: Scientific Congresses and Urban Identity in Victorian Britain*. London and New York: Routledge.

Mizoguchi, K. 2004. Identity, modernity, and archaeology: the case of Japan. In Meskell, L. and Preucel, R. W. (eds.) *A Companion to Social Archaeology*. Oxford: Blackwell Publishing, pp. 396–414.

Mitchell, S. 2004. *Frances Power Cobbe: Victorian Feminist, Journalist, Reformer*. Charlottesville and London: University of Virginia Press.

Mitchell, T. 2004. Orientalism and the exhibitionary order. In Preziosi, D. and Farago, C. J. (eds.) *Grasping the World: The Idea of the Museum*. Aldershot: Ashgate Publishing, pp. 442–61.

Mond, R. 1937. *Cemeteries of Armant*. London: Egypt Exploration Society.

Montebello, P. 2009. And what do you propose should be done with those objects? In Cuno, J. (ed.) *Whose Culture? The Promise of Museums and the Debate Over Antiquities*. Princeton: Princeton University Press, pp. 55–77.

Montserrat, D. 2000. *Akhenaten: History, Fantasy and Ancient Egypt*. London and New York: Routledge.

Moon, B. 2006. *More Usefully Employed: Amelia B. Edwards, Writer, Traveller and Campaigner for Ancient Egypt*. London: Egypt Exploration Society.

Moore, H. 1982. *Henry Moore at the British Museum*. London: H. N. Abrams.

Moore, M. 1924. *Observations*. New York: Dial Press.

Morfini, I. 2016. An Egyptian collection held in the National Museum in Accra. *Göttinger Miszellen* 249: 125–9.

Moser, S. 2016. Archaeology and ancient Egypt. In Prettejohn, E. and Trippi, P. (eds.) *Lawrence Alma-Tadema: At Home in Antiquity*. Munich: London and New York: Prestel, pp. 52–3.

Moser, S. 2015. Reconstructing ancient worlds: reception studies, archaeological representation and the interpretation of ancient Egypt. *Journal of Archaeological Method and Theory* 22(4): 1263–308.

Moser, S. 2006. *Wondrous Curiosities: Ancient Egypt at the British Museum*. London and Chicago: University of Chicago Press.

Moser, S. 1996. Science, stratigraphy and the deep sequence: excavation vs regional survey and the question of gendered practice in archaeology. *Antiquity,* 70(270): 813–23.

Mullins, P. R. 2002. Racializing the parlor: race and Victorian bric-a-brac consumption. In Orser, C. E. (ed.) *Race and the Archaeology of Identity*. Salt Lake City: University of Utah Press, pp. 158–76.

Muñoz, R. 2017. Amelia Edwards in America: a quiet revolution in archaeological science. *Bulletin of the History of Archaeology* 27(1): 1–10.

Murray, M. 1912. *Guide for 'Egyptian Research Students' Association' and a Catalogue of Loan Collection of Egyptian Antiquities Held in Kelvingrove Museum*. Glasgow: Glasgow Museums.

Murray, T. 1993. Archaeology and the threat of the past: Sir Henry Rider Haggard and the acquisition of time. *World Archaeology* 25(2): 175–86.

Murray, T. and Spriggs, M. 2017. The historiography of archaeology: exploring theory, contingency and rationality. *World Archaeology* 49(2): 151–7.

Nahum, A. 2010. Exhibiting Science: changing conceptions of Science Museum display. In Morris, P. J. T. (ed.) *Science for the Nation: Perspectives on the History of the Science Museum*. London: Palgrave Macmillan, pp. 178–86.

Nakano, T. 2016. Small pieces can tell: the richness and diversity of the Kyoto university museum's Egyptian collection. *Proceedings of the International Symposium on From Petrie to Hamada. Egyptian Antiquities of Kyoto University*. Kyoto: Kyoto University, pp. 28–31.

National Museum of Ghana 1970. *National Museum of Ghana Handbook: Ethnographical, Historical and Art Collections*. Accra: Ghana Publishing Corporation.

Naville, E. 1885. *The Store-City of Pithom and the Route of the Exodus*. London: Egypt Exploration Fund.

Newsom, J. 1948. *The Education of Girls*. London: Faber.

Nicholas, G. and Hollowell, J. 2007. Ethical challenges to a postcolonial archaeology: the legacy of scientific colonialism. In Hamilakis, Y. and Duke, P. (eds.) *Archaeology and Capitalism: From Ethics to Politics*. Walnut Creek: Left Coast Press, pp. 59–82.

Nichols, C. A. 2016. Exchanging anthropological duplicates at the Smithsonian Institute. *Museum Anthropology* 39(2): 130–46.

Nishimura, Y. and Miyagawa, N. 2017. An early history of Egyptology in Japan with a focus on philological studies. In Langer, C. (ed.) *Global Egyptology: Negotiations in the Production of Knowledges on Ancient Egypt in Global Context*. London: Golden House Publications, pp. 147–60.

Nora, P. 2001. *Rethinking France: Les Lieux de memoire*, Vol. 1. *The State*. Translated by Jordan, D. P. Chicago: University of Chicago Press.

Norman, M. 2001. 'It is surprising that things can be preserved as well as they are'. In Oddy, A. and Smith, S. (eds.) *Past Practice–Future Prospects*. London: British Museum, pp. 159–66.

Nunoo, R. 1965. The National Museum of Ghana, Accra. *Museum. Quarterly Review Published by UNESCO*, 18(3): 155–9.

O'Connor, D. 1987. The earliest pharaohs and the University Museum. *Expedition* 29(1): 27–39.

Odegaard, N. and O'Grady, C. R. 2016. The conservation practices for archaeological ceramics of Sir Flinders Petrie and others between 1880–1930. In Roemich, H. and Fair, L. (eds.) *Recent Advances in Glass and Ceramics Conservation 2016*. Paris: International Council of Museums – Committee for Conservation, pp. 85–95.

Okajima, S. 1940. *A History of Egypt*. Tokyo: Heibonsya [in Japanese].

Oldfield, S. 2004. Eckenstein, Lina Dorina Johanna (1857–1931). In *Oxford Dictionary of National Biography (Online ed.)* Oxford: Oxford University Press. DOI: http://dx.doi.org/10.1093/ref:odnb/59940 [accessed 12 May 2016].

Orbell, M. 1998. Maori writing about the exhibition. In Thomson, J. M. (ed.) *Farewell Colonialism: The New Zealand International Exhibition*. Palmerston North: Dunmore Press, pp. 141–63.

Owen, D. 1952. The changing outlook. *Museums Journal* 52(5): 51–3.

Parcak, S., Gathings, D., Childs, C., Mumford, G. and Cline, E. 2016. Satellite evidence of archaeological site looting in Egypt: 2002–2013. *Antiquity* 90: 188–205.

Pearce, S. 1995. *On Collecting: An Investigation into Collecting in the European Tradition*. London and New York: Routledge.

Peet, E. T. 1934. *The Present Position of Egyptological Studies: An Inaugural Lecture Delivered Before the University of Oxford on 17 January 1934*. Oxford: Clarendon Press.

Peet, T. E. and Newberry, P. 1932. *Handbook and Guide to the Egyptian Collection on Exhibition in The Public Museums Liverpool*. Liverpool: Public Museums Liverpool.

Pelc, M. 2014. *Maria Stona und ihr Salon in Strzebowitz. Kultur am Rande der Monarchie, der Republik und des Kanons*. Opava: Schleisische Universität.

Penny, G. 2002. *Objects of Culture: Ethnology and Ethnographic Museums in Imperial Germany*. Chapel Hill: University of North Carolina Press.

Petrie, W. M. F. 1931. *Seventy Years in Archaeology*. London: Sampson, Low and Marston.

Petrie, W. M. F. 1922. *Tombs of the Courtiers*. London: British School of Archaeology in Egypt.

Petrie, W. M. F. 1909. *Memphis I*. London: British School of Archaeology in Egypt.
Petrie, W. M. F. 1907. *Gizeh and Rifeh*. London: British School of Archaeology in Egypt.
Petrie, W. M. F. 1907. *Janus in Modern Life*. London: G.P. Putnam.
Petrie, W. M. F. 1906. *Migrations: The Huxley Lecture of 1906*. London: Anthropological Institute of Great Britain.
Petrie, W. M. F. 1904. *Methods and Aims in Archaeology*. London: Macmillan and Co.
Petrie, W. M. F. 1901a. *Diospolis Parva*. London: Egypt Exploration Fund.
Petrie, W. M. F. 1901b. *The Royal Tombs of the Earliest Dynasties*. London: Egypt Exploration Fund.
Petrie, W. M. F. 1888a. *Tanis II*. London: Egypt Exploration Fund.
Petrie, W. M. F. 1888b. The treatment of small antiquities. *The Archaeological Journal* 45: 85–9.
Petrie, W. M. F. 1885. *Tanis. Part 1, 1883-84*. London: Egypt Exploration Fund.
Petrie, W. M. F. and Duncan, G. 1906. *Hyksos and Israelite Cities*. London: British School of Archaeology in Egypt.
Petrie, W. M. F. and Quibell, J. 1896. *Naqada and Ballas*. London: Bernard Quaritch.
Pezzati, A. 2015. Gold medals and grand prizes. *Expedition Magazine* 57(1): 19–21.
Piacentini, P. 2011. The dawn of museums and photography in Egypt. In Piacentini, P. (ed.) *Egypt and the Pharaohs: From Conservation to Enjoyment*. Milan: Skira, pp. 5–43.
Piquette, K. E. 2016. Documenting Early Egyptian imagery: analyzing past technologies and materialities with the aid of Reflectance Transformation Imaging. In Graff, G. and Serrano, A. J. (eds.) *Prehistories of Writing: Iconography, Graphic Practices and Emergence of Writing in Predynastic Egypt*. Marseille: Presses Universitaires de Provence, pp. 87–112.
Pitt-Rivers, A. H. L. F. 1890. *King John's House, Tollard Royal, Wilts*. Printed privately.
Pitt-Rivers, A. H. L. F. 1888. Presidential address British Association for the Advancement of Science, Section H, Anthropology, 1888. *Report of the British Association for the Advancement of Science*, pp. 825–8.
Pope, R. 2011. Processual archaeology and gender politics: the loss of innocence. *Archaeological Dialogues* 18(1): 59–86.

Pratt, M. 2009. *Imperial Egypt: Travel Writing and Transculturation*. London and New York: Routledge.
Preziosi, D. 2003. *Brain of the Earth's Body: Art, Museums, and the Phantasms of Modernity*. Minneapolis: University of Minnesota Press.
Quirke, S. 2010. *Hidden Hands: Egyptian Workforces in Petrie Excavation Archives, 1880–1924*. London: Duckworth.
Quirke, S. and Stevenson, A. 2015. The Sekhemka sale and other threats to antiquities. *British Archaeology* 145: 30–4.
Rader, K. A. and Cain, V. E. 2014. *Life on Display: Revolutionizing U.S. Museums of Science and Natural History in the Twentieth Century*. Chicago: Chicago University Press.
Ransom, C. L. 1912. The value of photographs and transparencies as adjuncts to museum exhibits. *The Metropolitan Museum of Art Bulletin* 7(7): 132–4.
Ransom, C. L. 1911 *Handbook to the Egyptian Rooms*. New York: Metropolitan Museum of Art.
Read, H. 1934. *Art and Industry*. London: Faber and Faber.
Redman, S. J. 2015. Museum tours and the origins of museums studies: Edward W. Gifford, William R. Bascom, and the remaking of an anthropology museum. *Museum Management and Curatorship* 30(5): 444–61.
Reid, D. 2015. *Contesting Antiquity in Egypt: Archaeologies, Museums and the Struggle for Identities from World War I to Nasser*. Cairo: The American University in Cairo Press.
Reid, D. 2002. *Whose Pharaohs? Archaeology, Museums and Egyptian National Identity from Napoleon to World War I*. Berkeley and Los Angeles: University of California Press.
Reisner, G. 1908. *The Early Dynastic Cemeteries of Naga-ed-Der Part I*. Leipzig: J. C. Hinrichs.
Renfrew, C. 2006. Museum acquisitions: responsibilities for the illicit traffic in antiquities. In Brodie, N., Kersel, M. M., Luke, C. and Tubb, K. W. (eds.) *Archaeology, Cultural Heritage and the Antiquities Trade*. Gainesville: University Press of Florida, pp. 245–57.
Renfrew, C. 2000. *Loot, Legitimacy and Ownership*. London: Duckworth.
Rieser, A. C. 2003. *The Chautauqua Moment: Protestants, Progressives and the Culture of Modern Liberalism*. New York: Columbia University Press.
Riggs, C. 2017a. Shouldering the past: photography, archaeology and collective effort at the tomb of Tutankhamun. *History of Science* 55(3): 336–63.

Riggs, C. 2017b. *Egypt. Lost Civilizations*. London: Reaktion Books.

Riggs, C. 2017c. The body in the box: archiving the Egyptian mummy. *Archival Science* 17(2): 125–50.

Riggs, C. 2013. Colonial visions: Egyptian antiquities and contested histories in the Cairo Museum. *Museum Worlds: Advances in Research* 1: 65–84.

Riggs, C. 2014. *Unwrapping Ancient Egypt*. London: Bloomsbury

Riggs, C. 2010. Ancient Egypt in the museum: concepts and constructions. In Lloyd, A. (ed.) *A Companion to Ancient Egypt*. Chichester: Blackwell, pp. 1129–53.

Rivers, W. H. R. 1917. The government of subject peoples. In Seward, A. C. (ed.) *Science and the Nation: Essays by Cambridge Graduates*. Cambridge: Cambridge University Press, pp. 306–7.

Robertson, I. 1995. Infamous deaccessions. In Fahy, A. (ed.) *Collections Management*. London and New York: Routledge, pp. 168–71.

Robson, E. 2017. Old habits die hard: writing the excavation and dispersal history of Nimrud. *Museum History Journal* 10(2): 217–32.

Rozeik, C. 2012. 'A maddening temptation': The Ricketts and Shannon collection of Greek and Roman antiquities. *Journal of the History of Collections* 24(3): 369–78.

Ruffle, J. and Moignard, E. 1972. *City of Akhenaten: Object Index*. Birmingham: City Museum and Art Gallery.

el Saddik, W. 2017. *Protecting Pharaoh's Treasures: My Life in Egyptology*. Cairo: The American University Press in Cairo.

Said, E. 1978. *Orientalism*. New York: Pantheon Books.

Sayce, A. 1923. *Reminiscences*. London: Macmillan.

Scheinfeldt, T. 2016. The first years: the Science Museum at war and peace. Morris, P. J. T. (ed.) *Science for the Nation. Perspectives on the History of the Science Museum*. London: Palgrave Macmillan, pp. 41–60.

Schork, R. J. 2008. The singular circumstance of an errant papyrus. *Arion* 16: 25–47.

S.E. 1938. Hamada Kosaku (1881–1938) *Harvard Journal of Asiatic Studies* 3(3/4): 407–29.

Seligman, C. G. 1930. *Races of Africa*. Oxford: Clarendon Press.

Serpico, M. 2013/2014. Re-excavating Egypt: unlocking the potential in ancient Egyptian collections in the UK. *Egyptian and Egyptological Documents Archives Libraries* 4: 131–42.

Serpico, M. 2006. *Past, Present and Future: An Overview of Ancient Egyptian and Sudanese Collections in the UK*. London: Museums, Libraries and Archives Council.

Serpico, M. and El Gawad, H. 2016. *Beyond Beauty. Transforming the Body in Ancient Egypt*. London: Two Temple Place.

Shalaby, N., Abu El-Azm, H., Damarany, A., Kaiser, J., Abdallah, H. S., Abu El-Yazid, M., Abd El-Raziq, Y., Baker, F., Hashesh, Z., Ibrahim, W., Minor, E., Regelein, R. and Tarek, A. 2018. The lost papers: rewriting the narrative of early Egyptology with the Abydos Temple Paper Archive. *ARCE Bulletin Online*. Available at: https://www.arce.org/abydos-paper-archive [accessed 17 June 2018].

Shapin, S. 1989. The invisible technician. *American Scientist* 77(6): 554–63.

Shaw, T. 1990. A personal memoir. In Robertshaw, P. (ed.) *A History of African Archaeology*. London: James Currey Ltd, pp. 205–20.

Shaw, W. 2003. *Possessors and Possessed: Museums, Archaeology and the Visualization of History in the Late Ottoman Empire*. Berkeley: University of California Press

Shears, J. and Harrison, J. (eds.) 2013. *Literary Bric-à-Brac and the Victorians: From Commodities to Oddities*. London and New York: Routledge.

Sheets-Pyenson, S. 1987. Cathedrals of science: the development of colonial natural history museums during the late nineteenth century. *History of Science* 25(3): 279–300.

Shelton, A. 2000. Museum ethnography: an imperial science. In Hallam, E. and Street, B. (eds.) *Cultural Encounters: Encountering Otherness*. London and New York: Routledge, pp. 181–93.

Sheppard, K. L. (ed.) 2018. *My Dear Miss Ransom: Letters between Caroline Ransom Williams and James Henry Breasted, 1898–1935*. Oxford: Archaeopress.

Sheppard, K. L. 2013. *The Life of Margaret Alice Murray: A Woman's Work in Archaeology*. Lanham: Lexington Books.

Shinnie, P. L. 1990. A personal memoir. In Robertshaw, P. (ed.) *A History of African Archaeology*. London: James Currey Ltd, pp. 221–35.

Siapkas, J. and Sjogren, L. 2014. *Displaying the Ideals of Antiquity: The Petrified Gaze*. London and New York: Routledge, p. 101–11.

Snape, R. 2010. Objects of utility: cultural responses to industrial collections in municipal museums 1845–1914. *Museum and Society* 8(1): 18–36.

Sparks, R. 2013. Flinders Petrie through word and deed: re-evaluating Petrie's field techniques and their impact on object recovery in British Mandate Palestine. *Palestine Exploration Quarterly* 145(2): 143–59.

Spencer, N. 2007. Naville at Bubastis and other sites. In Spencer, P. (ed.) *The Egypt Exploration Society: The Early Years*. London: Egypt Exploration Society, pp. 1–30.

Staley, D. J. 2010. *History and Future: Using Historical Thinking to Imagine the Future*. Lanham: Lexington Books.

Star, S. L. and Griesemer, J. R. 1989. Institutional ecology, 'translations', and boundary objects: amateurs and professionals in Berkeley's Museum of Vertebrate Zoology, 1908–39. *Social Studies of Science* 19: 387–420.

Stevenson, A. 2015. Connecting across the centuries: fragments from Abydos. In Stevenson, A. (ed.) *The Petrie Museum of Egyptian Archaeology: Characters and Collections*. London: UCL Press, p. 64.

Stevenson, A. 2015. Egyptian archaeology and the museum. In *The Oxford Handbook of Archaeology Online*. Oxford and New York: Oxford University Press. Available at: DOI: 10.1093/oxfordhb/9780199935413.013.25 [accessed 21 June 2017].

Stevenson, A. 2014. The object of study: Egyptology, anthropology and archaeology at the University of Oxford, 1860–1960. In Carruthers, W. (ed.) *Histories of Egyptology: Interdisciplinary Measures*. London and New York: Routledge, pp. 19–33.

Stevenson, A. 2012. 'We seem to be working in the same line': A.H.L.F Pitt-Rivers and W.M. Flinders Petrie. *Bulletin of the History of Archaeology* 22(1): 4–13.

Stevenson, A., Libonati, E. and Baines, J. 2017. Object habits: legacies of fieldwork and the museum. *Museum History Journal* 10(2): 113–26.

Stevenson, A., Libonati, E. and Williams, A. 2016. 'A selection of minor antiquities': a multi-sited view on collections from excavations in Egypt. *World Archaeology* 48(2): 282–95.

Stevenson, A. and Dee, M. 2016. Confirmation of the world's oldest woven garment: the Tarkhan dress. *Antiquity* 90, Project gallery. Available at: http://antiquity.ac.uk/projgall/stevenson349 [accessed 22 July 2017].

Stocking, G. 1996. *After Tylor: British Social Anthropology, 1888–1951*. Madison: University of Wisconsin Press.

Stocking, G. W. 1985. *Objects and Others: Essays on Museums and Material Culture*. Madison: University of Wisconsin Press.

Stoler, A. L. 2010. *Along the Archival Grain: Epistemic Anxieties and Colonial Common Sense*. Princeton: Princeton University Press.

Sutherland, C. H. 1936. A late Roman coin-hoard from Kiddington, Oxon. *Oxoiensia* I: 70–80.

Svedberg, E. 1949. Museum display. *Journal of the Royal Society of Arts* 97: 850–65.
Swain, H. 2007. *An Introduction to Museum Archaeology*. Cambridge: Cambridge University Press.
Swanton, E. W. 1947. *A Country Museum: The Rise and Progress of Sir Jonathan Hutchinson's Educational Museum* at Haslemere. Haslemere: Educational Museum.
Swenson, A. and Mandler, P. 2013. *Britain and the Heritage of Empire, c.1800–1940*. Oxford: Oxford University Press.
Swigg, R. 2012. *Quick, Said the Bird: Williams, Eliot, Moore, and the Spoken Word*. Iowa City: University of Iowa Press.
Teeter, E. 2010. Egypt in Chicago: A story of three collections. In Hawass, Z. and Wegner, J. (eds.) *Millions of Jubilees: Studies in Honor of David P. Silverman*. Cairo: Conseil Suprême des Antiquitiés de l'Egypt, 303–14.
Thomas, D. W. 2004. *Cultivating Victorians: Liberal Culture and the Aesthetic*. Philadelphia: University of Pennsylvania Press.
Thomas, N. 1991. *Entangled Objects: Exchange, Material Culture, and Colonialism in the Pacific*. Cambridge, MA: Harvard University Press.
Thomas, N., Scott, G. D. and Trigger, B. (eds.) 1996. *The American Discovery of Ancient Egypt*. Los Angeles: Los Angeles County Museum.
Thomas, R. 1990. *The Commodity Culture of Victorian England: Advertising and Spectacle 1851–1914*. Stanford: Stanford University Press.
Thompson, J. 2016. *Wonderful Things: A History of Egyptology 2. The Golden Age 1881–1914*. Cairo: American University Press.
Thompson, J. 2015. *Wonderful Things: A History of Egyptology 1: From Antiquity to 1881*. Cairo: American University Press in Cairo.
Thomson, J. M. (ed.) *Farewell Colonialism: The New Zealand International Exhibition*. Palmerston North: Dunmore Press.
Thornton, A. 2015. Exhibition season: annual archaeological exhibitions in London, 1880s–1930s. *Bulletin of the History of Archaeology* 25(2): 1–18.
Thornton, A. 2013. '…a certain faculty for extricating cash': collective sponsorship in late 19th and early 20th century British archaeology. *Present Pasts* 5(1): 1–12.
Tlili, A. 2016. Encountering the creative museum: museographic creativeness and the bricolage of time materials. *Educational Philosophy and Theory* 48 (5): 443–58.
Tomkins, C. 1970. *Merchants and Masterpieces: The Story of the Metropolitan Museum of Art*. New York: E. P. Dutton.

Trask, J. 2012. *Things American: Art Museums and Civic Culture in the Progressive Era*. Philadelphia: University of Pennsylvania Press.

Trigger, B. G. 2006. *A History of Archaeological Thought*. Second Edition. Cambridge: Cambridge University Press.

Trumpour, M. and Schultz, T. 2008. The 'Father of Egyptology' in Canada. *Journal of the American Research Center in Egypt* 44: 159–67.

Tseng, A. 2008. *The Imperial Museums of Meiji: Architecture and Art of the Nation*. University of Washington Press: Washington.

Tsirogiannis, C. 2015. 'Due diligence'? Christies' antiquities auction, London, October 2015. *Journal of Art Crime* Fall: 27–37.

Tsirogiannis, C. 2016a. Mapping the supply: usual suspects and identified antiquities in 'reputable' auction houses in 2013. *Cuadernos de Prehistoria y Arqueología* 25: 107–44.

Tsirogiannis, C. 2016b. Reasons to doubt: misleading assertions in the London antiquities market. *Journal of Art Crime* Spring: 67–72.

Tufnell, O. 1982. Reminiscences of a 'Petrie Pup'. *Palestine Exploration Quarterly* 114(2): 81–6.

Tully, C. J. 2010. Walk like an Egyptian: Egypt as authority in Aleister Crowley's reception of the book of law. *The Pomegranate: International Journal of Pagan Studies* 12(1): 20–47.

Tully, G. 2011. Re-presenting ancient Egypt: re-engaging communities through collaborative archaeological methodologies for museum displays. *Archaeological Review from Cambridge* 26(2): 137–52.

Twain, M. and Warner, C. D. 1873. *The Gilded Age: A Tale of Today*. Chicago: American Pub. Co., F. G. Gilman.

Tylor, E. B. 1885. Presidential address to the Anthropology Section. *Report of the Fifty-Fourth Meeting of the British Association for the Advancement of Science held at Montreal in August and September 1884*. London: John Murray, pp. 899–910.

Ucko, P. 2003. (ed.) *Encounters with Ancient Egypt*. London: UCL Press.

Urry, J. 1990. *The Tourist Gaze*. London: Sage Publications.

van Rheeden, H. 2001. The rise and fall of the plaster-cast collection at the Hague Academy of Fine Arts (1920–1960): a personal enterprise of the Dutch dilettante and classicist, Constant Lunsingh Scheurleer (1881–1941). *Journal of the History of Collections* 13(2): 215–29.

Varutti, M. 2018. 'Authentic reproductions': museum collection practices as authentication. *Museum Management and Curatorship* 33(1): 42–56.

Veronika, D. 2015. The lost and forgotten Opava collection of Egyptian finds: the story of objects from digging conducted by famed Flinders

Petrie. In Lazar, I. (ed.) *Egypt and Austria VIII: Meeting point Egypt*. Koper: Univerza na Primorskem, pp. 17–31.

Villing, A. n.d. Reconstructing a 19th-century excavation: problems and perspectives. http://www.britishmuseum.org/research/online_research_catalogues/ng/naukratis_greeks_in_egypt/introduction/reconstructing_an_excavation.aspx [accessed 28 Jan 2015].

Vinson, S. and Gunn, J. 2015. Studies in esoteric syntax: the enigmatic friendship of Aleister Crowley and Battiscombe Gunn. In Carruthers, W. (ed.) *Histories of Egyptology: Interdisciplinary Measures*. London: Routledge, pp. 96–112.

Virenque, H. 2015. Edouard Naville (1844–1926) in the Delta. In Cooke, N. and Daubney, V. (eds.) *Every Traveller Needs a Compass: Travel and Collecting in Egypt and the Near East*. Oxford: Oxbow Books, pp. 190–5.

Voss, B. 2012. Curation as research: a case study in orphaned and underreported archaeological collections. *Archaeological Dialogues* 19(2): 145–69.

Voss, S. 2017. *Die Geschichte der Abteilung Kairo des DAI im Spannungsfeld deutscher politischer Interessen. Band 2, 1929 bis 1966*. Rahden/Westf: VML, Verlag Marie Leidorf.

Voss, S. 2016. Wissenshintergründe ... – Die Ägyptologie als ‚völkische' Wissenschaft entlang des Nachlasses Georg Steindorffs von der Weimarer Republik über die NS- bis zur Nachkriegszeit. In Voss, S. and Raue, D. (eds.) *Georg Steindorff und die deutsche Ägyptologie im 20. Jahrundert Wissenshintergründe und Forschungstransfers*. Berlin: De Gruyter, pp. 105–332.

Wainwright, G. A. 1920. *Balabish*. London: Egypt Exploration Society.

Wakefield, H. and White. G. 1959. *Handbook for Museum Curators. Part F Section I: Circulating Exhibitions*. London: Museums Association.

Wallach, A. 1998. *Exhibiting Contradiction: Essays on the Art Museum in the United States*. Amherst: University of Massachusetts Press.

Waller, L. 2016. Curating actor-network theory testing object-oriented sociology in the Science Museum. *Museum and Society* 14(1): 193–206.

Warner, N. 2016. *Collecting for Eternity: R. G. Gayer-Anderson and the Egyptian Museum in Stockholm*. Stockholm: National Museum of World Culture.

Watrall, E. 2018. Public heritage at scale: building tools for authoring mobile digital heritage and archaeology experience. *Journal of Community Archaeology and Heritage* 5(2): 114–27.

Wegner, J. and Wegner, J. H. 2015. *The Sphinx That Travelled to Philadelphia: The Story on the Colossal Sphinx in the Penn Museum*. Philadelphia: University of Pennsylvania Press.

Weil, S. E. (ed.) 1997. *A Deaccession Reader*. American Association of Museums: Washington.

Weightman, B. and Wilson, M. 2016. Janet May Buchanan. Scotland's forgotten heroine of Egyptology. Available at: http://egyptartefacts.griffith.ox.ac.uk/?q=resources/janet-may-buchanan-scotlands-forgotten-heroine-egyptology [accessed 9 August 2016].

Wengrow, D. 2003. Landscapes of knowledge, idioms of power: the African foundations of ancient Egyptian civilization reconsidered. In O'Connor, D. and Reid, A. (eds.) *Ancient Egypt in Africa*. London: UCL Press, pp. 121–36.

Wheeler, M. R. E. 1954. *Archaeology from the Earth*. Oxford: Oxford University Press.

Whitehead, C. 2009. *Museums and the Construction of Disciplines: Art and Archaeology in Nineteenth-Century Britain*. London: Duckworth.

Whitelaw, A. 2013. Women, museums and the problems of biography. In Hill, K. (ed.) *Museums and Biographies: Stories, Objects, Identities*. Woodridge: Brewer and Brewer, pp. 75–86.

Wilkinson, J. G. 1857. *The Egyptians in the Time of the Pharaohs: Being a Companion to the Crystal Palace Egyptian Collections*. London: Bradbury and Evans.

Willard, F. E. 1897. *Occupations for Women: A Book of Practical Suggestions for the Material Advancement, The Mental And Physical Development, and the Moral and Spiritual Uplift Of Women*. New York: The Success Company.

Willis, M. 2011. *Vision, Science and Literature, 1870–1920*. London: Pickering and Chatto.

Wilson, D. M. 2002. *The British Museum: A History*. London: British Museum Press.

Wimmer, A. and Schiller, N. G. 2002. Methodological nationalism and beyond: nation-state building, migration and the social sciences. *Global Networks* 2(4): 301–34.

Wingfield, C. 2018. Collection as (Re)assemblage: refreshing museum archaeology. *World Archaeology*. 49(5): 594–607.

Wingfield, C. 2011. From Greater Britain to Little England: the Pitt Rivers Museum, the Museum of English Life, and their six degrees of separation. *Museum History Journal* 4(2): 245–66.

Winlock, H. E. 1939. New galleries of Egyptian art. *The Metropolitan Museum of Art Bulletin* 34(5): 118–22.

Winslow, W. C. 1903. *The Truth About the Egypt Exploration Society. The Singular Reorganization of the American Branch*. Boston: Self published.

Wintle, C. 2017. De-colonising UK world art institutions, 1945–80. *On Curating* 35. Available at: http://www.on-curating.org/issue-35-reader/decolonising-uk-world-art-institutions-1945-1980-371.html#.Wm2i6pOFhPM [accessed 28 January 2018].

Witcomb, A. 2003. *Re-Imagining the Museum: Beyond The Mausoleum*. London and New York: Routledge.

Wolfe, S. J. 2016. Bringing Egypt to America: George Gliddon and the 'Panorama of the Nile'. *Journal of Ancient Egyptian Interconnections* 8: 1–20.

Worringer, W. 1928. *Egyptian Art*. London: Putnam.

Yamashita, S. 2006. Reshaping anthropology: a view from Japan. In Ribeiro, G. L. and Escobar, A. (eds.) *World Anthropologies: Disciplinary Transformations within Systems of Power*. London: Bloomsbury, pp. 29–48.

Yatabe, R. 1879. *Omori Kaikyo Kobutsu Hen*. Tokyo: University of Tokyo [in Japanese].

Yates, D. 2016. The global traffic in looted cultural objects. In Rafter, N. and Carribine, E. (eds.) *The Oxford Encyclopedia of Crime, Media, and Popular Culture*. Oxford: Oxford University Press. Available at: DOI: 10.1093/acrefore/9780190264079.013.124 [accessed 19 January 2018].

Young, J. 2007. Cultures and cultural property. *Journal of Applied Philosophy* 24(2): 111–24.

Ytterberg, N. 2016. Analysing museum collections in Scandinavia. *Museum Worlds* 4(1): 126–37.

Zimmerman, L. J. 2002. A decade after the Vermillion Accord: what has changed and what has not. In Fford, C., Hubert, J. and Turnbull, P. (eds.) *The Dead and Their Possessions: Repatriation in Principle, Policy and Practice*. London and New York: Routledge, pp. 91–8.

Ziter, E. 2003. *The Orient on the Victorian Stage*. Cambridge: Cambridge University Press.

Zytaruk, M. 2017. American's first circulating museum: the object collection of the library company of Philadelphia. *Museums History Journal* 10(1): 68–82.

Index

Abbott, Henry 72
Aboriginal material culture 124
abstract art 196
Abu Dhabi 253–4
Abu Simbel 200
Abydos 8, 11–14, 19–20, 47–8, 52, 58–61, 84, 92–6, 123, 135–6, 153, 173, 184, 186, 191, 224, 239–43, 255
accelerator mass spectrometry (AMS) 240–1
Actor-Network-Theory (ANT) 3
Adams, Barbara 20
Adams, W.Y. 201
aesthetics 171
Akhenaten 148–9, 153, 169–70
Alberti, Sam 56
Aldred, Cyril 196
Alexandria Graeco-Roman Museum 107
Ali, Muhammed, Khedive of Egypt 219
Allan, Douglas A. 185–6
Alma-Tadema, Lawrence 49
Amarna 146–9, 154–66, 170, 186, 190, 192, 194, 198, 204, 227
America and Britain, circulation of finds between 14, 93, 254
American influence on Egyptian archaeology 91
American museums 69–100, 172, 188–91, 196
ancient texts 11, 32, 108–11
Anglo-American relations 79
Anquandah, James 210
Anthropological Institute of Great Britain and Ireland 42
anthropology 41, 86, 95, 109, 122–3, 200–1
antiquities: assemblages broken up 13–14; legal accountability for 16; *major* and *minor* 36, 38–9, 88, 120, 229, 254; restrictions on export from Egypt of 11, 18, 33–4, 145–6, 151, 171, 175, 221–3; undocumented 226
Antiquity (journal) 173–4
Antiquus Mysticus Ordo Rosae Crucis (AMORC) 169–70
Appadurai, Arjun 3
Appiah, Kwame 231
archaeological practices 200, 232
archaeological principles 254
archaeological profession 147, 247
archaeological societies 8
archaeology: as a discipline 32, 37, 137, 199; public reception of 173; status in Britain and in France 29

archival research 14–16, 238–9
Armistead, Emily 119
art market 154, 223–8, 243, 255
artefacts, archaeological: allure of 210; attitudes to 183; central to one's view of the past 111; driving enterprise 7; exclusive focus on 109, 219; research based on 44; shaping of attitudes to 106; status of 201–2, 217; used in education 53; *see also* antiquities
'arts and crafts' movement 40, 49
Ashmolean Museum 48, 159, 169, 197
Astor, John Jacob 157
Aswan Dam 199, 209
auction houses 226–7
audience research by museums 242
Australia 124–5, 138, 150–4
Ayrton, Edward 91

baksheesh 19
Baltimore 93
Bankfield Museum 43, 186
Baring, Sir Evelyn 35, 124, 129
Barlow, Annie 57
Bayesian statistics 240
Bell, Larry 198
Belzoni, Giovanni 30
Benjamin, Walter 168, 202
Bennett, Tony 39, 49
the Bible, authority and truth of 52
biblical remains 78
Bicknell, Clarence 112
Bildt, Harald 175
Birch, Samuel 33
Birmingham 40, 183, 186
Bismarck, Otto von 108
black market in artefacts 226
Blackden, Marcus W. 52
Bloomsbury district 202
Boas, Franz 200–1
Bolton 40, 168
Bolton, Herbert 150
bomb damage 181–3
Bombay 130
Borchardt, Ludwig 107
Bordighera 112–13
Boston Museum of Fine Arts (MFA) 20, 36, 70–2, 75–8, 87, 90, 93–4, 166, 187, 222, 231
Botti, Giuseppe 107
'boundary objects' 106

Bradbury, Kate 82
Bragg, Laura (and 'Bragg boxes') 87–8
Braun, Edmund Wilhelm 116
Breasted, James Henry 83–5, 89, 91, 99, 110
Breccia, Evaristo 107
Brexit 254
'bricolage' 218, 243
Bristol 38, 181, 186
British Academy 199
British Association for the Advancement of Science (BAAS) 120–2
British influence in Egypt 6–7, 29, 128–9, 137, 147, 198
British Museum 28–38, 44–5, 48, 52, 57, 72, 99, 132, 154–5, 158–9, 166–9, 174, 220, 222, 231–5; Department of Egypt and Sudan 234; Naukratis project 237–8
British School of Archaeology in Egypt (BSAE) 11, 45–6, 57, 78, 87, 92–3, 112–14, 118, 123, 131, 135, 161, 173–5, 184, 193, 195, 223–4, 228, 232, 246
Brocklehurst, Marianne 41, 57
Brodie, Neil 116
Brooklyn Museum 17–18, 89–90, 187–91
Broome, Myrtle 169
Broughton Beck School 54
Brown, Percy 130
Brown University 191
Browning, Robert 10
Brugsch, Heinrich 73, 107
Brunton, Guy and Winifred 118, 173–4
Bubastis 26, 108, 218
Buchanan, May 61–2, 185
Buckinghamshire Museum 61, 223
Buckman, Marie 83, 93, 96–7, 150, 163, 165, 169, 173
Bulaq Museum 33–4
Burkitt, Miles 173

Cairo Declaration on the Protection of Cultural Property (2004) 222
Cairo Museum 227
Canada 119–24
Carnarvon, Lord 10, 90, 145–6, 152
Carruthers, William 198–9
Cartailhac, Emile 105
Carter, Howard 130, 145
casts, use of 166–71
Caton-Thompson, Gertrude 173–4
Cedar Rapids Masonic Lodge 93–4
Centre d'Étude et de Documentation sur l'Ancienne Égypte (CEDAE) 199
Cesnola, Luigi 77
Challis, Debbie 54
Charleston Museum 87–8
Charterhouse School 224, 229

Chautauqua Assembly 75, 190–1, 224
Chhatrapatī Shivaji Mahārāj Vastu Saṅrahālay (CSMVS) 130–1, 246
Chicago 77, 83–4, 89, 91, 169; Columbian Exposition (1893) 73–4
Childe, Gordon 173–4
China 253–4
Christianity 52–3
Chubb, Mary 165–6, 169–70
circulation of antiquities 14, 93, 254
Cleopatra's Needle, New York 74, 78, 94
Cleveland Museum of Art 171
Cobbe, Frances Power 58
codes of ethics 225–8
Colla, Elliot 5, 82, 230
Colombian National Museum, Bogota 18
colonialism 82, 107, 175, 245
Colorado College 191
commercial sales of artefacts 223–5, 229
Compton, Winifred 245
Conn, Stephen 76, 86–9, 196
conservation 158
contemporary art 234–6
contexere 61
context and contextualization 226, 254
Conze, Alexander 111
Cook, Clarence 49
Cook, Thomas (company) 6–7, 42, 223
Cooke, Ashley 183
Copenhagen 114
Coxe, Eckley B. Jr. 87, 91
Croly, Jane Cunningham 82
Crompton, Winifred 56, 162, 170
Crowley, Aleister 52
cultural shifts 201–2
Cuno, James 230–1
'curation crisis' 239
Currelly, Charles Trick 123–4

Dall, Caroline Healey 81
Danquah, Joseph B. 207
Darwin, Charles (and Darwinism) 120–3
Davidian people 128
Davies, Norman de Garis 124–5, 208
Davis, Theodore 90–1
Dawson, John William 120–3
'deaccessioning' 188
'decluttering' museums and homes 202
De Forest, Robert W. 172, 188
Deir el-Bahri 54, 108, 123, 130, 133, 155, 157, 239
Dennis, James Tackle 93
department stores 49, 172, 202
Derrida, Jacques 14–16
destructive sampling 239
Detroit 77
Dickens, Charles 82

digs, organisation of 17, 97
Diop, Cheikh Anta 208
dioramas 196–7, 205
dispersal of artefacts from Egypt 7–20, 27, 35, 38, 47–8, 55, 82, 105–8, 150, 183, 217–19, 223–4, 229
disposal of artefacts by museums 183–9
division parties 13
documentation in museums 195
Dominion Museum, Wellington 127
Donati, Vitaliano 107
Doyle, Arthur Conan 50
Doyon, Wendy 97
Droop, John 219
Drovetti, Bernardino 107
Drower, Margaret 223
Duncan, Garrow 17, 53, 223
Dunham, Dows 187
'duplicate' artefacts from digs 33–4, 48, 185, 187, 223

eBay 224–5
Eckenstein, Lina 52, 58
Eckenstein, Oskar 52
Edinburgh 185, 196, 231
Edwards, Amelia 10, 25, 29, 36–8, 50–3, 57–8, 70–1, 238; lectures in America 79–82, 89; opinion of modern-day Egyptians 82–3
Edwards, Elizabeth 97
Edwards, I.E.S. 187, 198
Effland, Andreas 241
Egypt: image of 52; interest in 41–5; infrastructure 6
Egypt Exploration Fund (EEF) 1, 8–11, 14, 19, 27–31, 35–42, 45, 48, 52–8, 69–84, 89–99, 108, 110, 118–21, 125–7, 130, 133–4, 148, 155, 183, 195, 218, 223, 237; American branch of 76, 83, 90, 96–7; local honorary secretaries 105
Egypt Exploration Society (EES) 10, 16, 38, 119, 123–4, 146–75, 186, 198–200, 205, 222, 224; American branch of 190; Graeco-Roman branch of 191
Egypt Research Account (ERA) 11, 57, 83–4
Egyptian Antiquities Service 29, 107, 166, 175, 219
Egyptians: collaborating in generation of new knowledge 241–2; foremen 97; workmen 18–20, 112, 146–7
Egyptology 6, 32, 41, 58, 62, 108–12, 135, 137, 201, 254; local societies for 203; public interest in 184–5
El Gawad, Heba Abd 18
Ellsworth, W.W. 217–19

Elshahed, Mohamed 234
Emery, Walter B. 200
Epstein, Jacob 154–5
Erman, Adolf 84, 105, 109–10
ethics see codes of ethics
eugenics 54
Evans, Sir Arthur 159
Evans, Christopher 55
Evans, Sir John 32, 100, 224
exhibition design 243–5
experimental archaeology 232

Faenza Museo Internazionale delle Ceramiche 112, 183
Fairman, H.W. 166, 194
Falmouth Museum 192, 232
Fannin, Kate 117
feminism 4, 86–7
field logging methods 92
field notes 18, 163, 200
fieldwork practices 33, 35, 200–1
First World War 94, 98–100
Firth, Cecil 146
Fitzwilliam Museum 243–4
Fletcher, William Roby 124
Fonck, Leopold 112
Foucault, Michel 39, 56
France 107–8
freemasonry 93–4
futurism 203

Galton, Francis 54
Gange, David 6, 52
Ganguli, Babu Ganga Dhar 130
Gardiner, Alan 110, 145–6, 237
Garrod, Dorothy 173
Garstang, John 11–13, 54, 91, 117–18, 130, 194–5, 223
Garstang Museum 16, 194
Geismar, Haidy 236
Geldart, Alice 185
Germany 107–11, 138
Gertzen, Thomas 110
Ghana 207–10, 246
Glanville, Stephen 219
Glasgow 61–2, 181
Gliddon, George 72, 219
global financial crisis 227–8
globalization 138
'golden age' of archaeology 174–5
Goode, G.B. 230
Gorringe, Henry H. 94
Gowland, William 133
Grace, William Russell 74
Great Exhibition (1851) 39
Green, Frederick 91
Grenfell, Bernard P. 10–11, 17

INDEX 299

Grenfell, Francis 99, 119, 124
'grey trade' in artefacts 226–7
Gunn, Battiscombe 52
Gustaf VI Adolf, King of Sweden 175

Hafez, Khaled 234
Haffenreffer Museum 191
Haggard, H. Rider 14–15, 50, 55
hakubutsukan 132
Hall, Henry 136, 191–2
Hall, Kate Marion 191
Hamada, Kōsaku 133–7
Hamilakis, Yannis 228
Hamilton, Augustus 127
Hamitic hypothesis 208
Hancock Museum, Newcastle 168
Hansard, Freda 58, 61
Harden, Donald H. 187
Harlem Renaissance 155
Harris, Neil 172
Hawass, Zahi 222, 229
Haweis, Mary 49
Haworth, Jesse 11, 56
Hay, Robert 72
Heal's department store 202
Hearst, Phoebe 83, 90–2
Henare, Amiria 44
Henning, Michelle 5
Higgins Museum, Bedford 192
Hill, Kate 37, 57
Hogarth, David 237
Holman, William A. 151
Hope, Charles 57
Horniman Museum 192
Hoving, Thomas 188, 221
Howe, Julia Ward 81
Hoyle, William E. 46
Hull Museum 181
Hunt, Arthur 10–11
Hutchinson, Sir Jonathan 54
Huxley, Thomas 10
hyperreality in museum displays 242

Ideal Home magazine 202
Illustrated London News 153–4
imperialism 132, 136
India 246
India Museum 128–9
'industrial art' 40, 202
'initial art' 114
Institut Français d'Archaéologie Orientale (IFAO) 107
International Museums Office 167
internet market in artefacts 224–5
interpretation of finds 164, 186, 232
Ipswich Museum 195
Italy 107, 111–12

Iziko Museums 246
Iziko Slave Lodge 117–18

Jacobsen, Carl 113–14
Japan 107, 131–8; 'Japanese Exhibition' (London, 1910) 134
Jermyn Street Museum 46
jewellery 98–9
Johnson, Diane 232
Jonas, Mary 153, 162–71
Jones, Sir William 128
Journal of Egyptian Archaeology 97–8, 173

Katsumi, Kuroita 136
Kelvingrove Museum, Glasgow 181
Kemp, Barry 194
Kennard, Henry Martyn 11, 56, 105
Kenyon, Frederic 100
Kintore, Earl of 125
Kipling, John Lockwood 130
Kipling, Rudyard 75–6, 130
Kircher, Athanasius 111
Kitchin, J.G. 53
Kohere, Reweti 126
Kopytoff, Igor 3
Korea 136
Kulturgeschicte model 46, 78, 200
Kyoto University 131–7

Lacau, Pierre 145–6
Lahore Museum 130
Lambert, George 127
Lange, Julius 114
Lanzone, Rodolfo Vittorio 112
Larson, Frances 194
Latour, Bruno 3, 169
Lawes, Henrietta 58, 61
Lawrence, Arnold W. 207–8
Lawrence, T.E. 17
Layard, Sir Austen Henry 10, 29
Leahy, Tony 239
Le Corbusier 202
Leeds Museum 181
legacy collections 237–9
Leicester 228
Lepsius, Richard 107
Lévi-Strauss, Claude 243
Levy, Joseph M. 155
Lewis, Spencer 169–70
Lieblein, Jens Daniel Carolus 113
Livermore, Mary A. 81
Liverpool Museum 14–15, 38–9, 61, 168–9, 181–6, 194, 253
Livingstone, David 44, 122
local institutions 55; *see also* museums, local and regional
Lockyer, Angus 135

'London Season', the 35
looting 227–8
the Louvre, Abu Dhabi 253
the Louvre, Paris 108
Love, A. 169
Lucas, Alfred 158
Lucknow Museum 130
Lutfi, Huda 234
Luxor 28
Lyons, Henry 168, 204–5
Lythgoe, Albert 90, 99

McAlister, Melani 221
McCarthy, Kathleen 88
Macclesfield 41, 57
Mace, Arthur 91
McGill University, Montreal 119–23
McIntosh, Hugh 150–3
MacKenzie, John 5, 129
McLean Museum and Art Gallery, Greenock 56, 186
McLeod, Malcolm 210
McManus Museum and Art Gallery, Dundee 17, 41
Macmillan, Harold 202
Malinowski, Bronislaw 200
Manchester 41, 56, 162, 169, 186, 231
Mandela, Nelson 246
Māori culture 126–7, 138
Mareotis (steamship) 25
Mariette, Auguste 6, 42
Markham Report (1938) 172, 174, 186, 195
marking of artefacts 60
Maspero, Gaston 10, 29–35
material culture 50, 124, 127, 255
mementos acquired by participants in digs 16
metal detecting 220
Metropolitan Museum of Art, New York 76–8, 83–7, 90, 92, 98–9, 167, 171–4, 188–9, 224, 231
Meyerowitz, Eva 207
Midgely, Thomas 169
Miers Report (1928) 172, 174, 186, 195
military operations 25, 30, 198
Minneapolis Institute of Fine Arts 196–8
Mitchell-Furness coterie 85
modern art 196–8
modernism 154–5, 175, 202–3
Mond, Robert 124
Montserrat, Dominic 55, 153, 244–5
Moody, Ronald 155
Moore, Henry 154–5
Moore, Marianne 154
Morgan, Henri de 90
Morris, William 40
Morse, Edward 133
Mortimer, Dunstan 196

Moser, Stephanie 5–6, 28, 147
Mukherjee, Sabyasachi 246
Mullens, Josiah 125
multi-sited projects 2
mummies 11, 16, 34, 42, 72, 89, 114–18, 246
mummy portraits 44, 54, 115
municipal museums 37–40, 43
Murray, Margaret 52, 58, 61–2, 245
Murray, Tim 55, 254
'museum effect' 170
Museum of Modern Art (MoMA), New York 196
museum practices 184, 186, 195–8, 206
museum profession 195
'museum taphonomy' 190
museums: absence of modern Egypt from 233–4; Asian 129–32; colonial 107, 116–17, 120, 138; control of 28, 116, 129; of fine art 70, 168, 254; intellectual prestige of 172–3; local and regional 37–9, 42, 56–7, 126, 138; loss of 190–4; measuring the worth of 236; modernization of 186; professionalism in 28; public enthusiasm for visits to 54, 220; public image of 172; public trust in 227; role of 5, 235–7, 242, 256
Museums Association 202, 227

Naguib, Amgad 234
al-Nahhas, Mostafa 199
Naqada 105, 110, 113
Nasser, Gamal Abdel 209
National Gallery, London 64
nationalism: American 85; Egyptian 9, 145, 171; Japanese 132–6; methodological 106
Natural History Museum 16
Naville, Édouard 30–5, 39, 52–3, 108, 123, 157, 191
Nefertiti 148–9, 153, 155, 229
New Walk Museum, Leicester 228
New Zealand 125–8, 138
Newberry, Percy 91, 205
Newton, Charles 35
Newton, Francis G. 150
Nichols, Catherine 48
Nicholson, Sir Charles 125
Nicholson Museum, Sydney 125
Nile steamers 6
Nkrumah, Kwame 207–9
Nora, Pierre 204
Northampton Borough Council 254–5
Northbrook, Lord 129
Norwich Castle Museum 156, 186
Nunoo, Richard 207

'object biographies' concept 242–3
'object habits' 2–5, 9, 28, 49, 55, 74, 106, 108, 114, 120, 168, 218, 236, 253–4

object-led knowledge 92
object lessons 53–4
Offord, J. 36
Okajima, Seitaro 137
Opava Museum 116
Orientalism 230
Orme, Beatrice 58, 60
'orphaned' collections 183–4, 194–5
Osman, Aly 96–7
Otago Museum 128

Packard, Alpheus Spring Jr. 191
Paisley Museum 156
'partage' arrangements 7–9, 14, 16, 18, 27, 77, 88, 107, 112, 145, 147, 175, 199, 217–23, 229, 231, 242; returning to 230–2, 236
Pasadena 190, 198
Paterson, Emily 50, 134, 162–3, 188
Peabody Essex Museum, Salem 72
Peet, Eric 201
Peet, Thomas E. 173
Pendlebury, John 165
Pennsylvania 77–8, 85, 90–1
Pepper, William 85–6
Pestalozzi, J.H. 53–4
Petrie, Flinders 1–2, 11, 17–20, 27–8, 31–40, 44–6, 49, 52–60, 73–4, 78–9, 83–91, 98–9, 105, 109–18, 122–3, 128–9, 133–7, 146, 157, 159, 174, 183–4, 187, 190–3, 200–5, 223, 245–6, 254
Petrie, Hilda 11–12, 17, 52, 58–62, 116, 184, 223
Petrie Museum 16, 58, 169, 194, 202, 231–2, 240–1
Philadelphia 86–9; Centennial Exhibition (1876) 73
Philips, Ellen 57
philology 108–11
photographs, use of 163
Picasso, Pablo 154
Pitt-Rivers, A.H. Lane Fox 32, 41–2, 158
Pitt Rivers Museum, Oxford 3, 46, 48, 122, 203–4, 245
Poole, Reginald Stuart 10, 34
Pope, Rachel 203
popularization 147
postage stamps 209
Poynter, Edward 49
preservation of delicate and fragmentary objects 158
Price, Campbell 239
Price, Hugh 17
Prichard, Matthew 96, 166–7
Princess Henry of Battenberg 14
pro rata dispersal system 16
Protestantism 53
provenance 187, 226

psychometry 51–2
public schools 54

Quibell, James and Kate 17, 91
Quirke, Stephen 13
Qurna burial group 45

radiocarbon dating 239–41
Ramesses II 70–1
Ransom, Caroline 83–5, 90, 92, 110, 225
Rawnsley, Hardwicke 52
Read, Herbert 202
Reading 61, 186–7
Ready, Augustus P. 158
Ready, William Talbot 158
Redpath Museum 119–23, 138
reflectance transformation imaging 239
Reid, Donald 18
Reisner, George 90–2, 99, 110
'relational museum' model 3
relic culture 51, 55
repatriation claims 229
replica objects 166
reproductions 165–71
restoration 157–62; styles of 160
Rhode Island School of Design 93
Rhodes, Cecil 117
Riggs, Christina 18
Riley, N.T. 32
Roberts, David 30
Robinson, Edward 167
Robson, Eleanor 154
Rochdale 57
Rochester Theological Seminary 75
Rockefeller, John D. 91
Roosevelt, Theodore 69
Rorimer, James 188
Rosetta Stone 229
Roussel, Raphael 196
Rowe, Louis Earle 93
Royal Anthropological Society 174
Royal Archaeological Institute 32, 35
Royal Asiatic Society 130
Royal College of Surgeons 181
Royal Commission on National Museums and Galleries (1928) 167
Royal Ontario Museum (ROM) 123
Rudolf, Cyprian 118
Ruskin, John 40

Saffron Walden Museum 234
St Louis Museum 229
'saloon' style displays 196
San Diego Museum 156
San el-Hagar *see* Tanis
Saqqara 198
Sayaji Rao III 129

Sayce, Archibald 134–6
Scandinavia 113, 175
Scheurleer, C.W. Lunsingh 193
Schiaparelli, Ernesto 107
Schliemann, Heinrich 10, 29
Schmidt, Valdemar 114
Schmitz, Jon 190–1
Science Museum, London 168, 204–5
'scientific colonialism' 241
'scientific racism' 208
Scott, John 56
Scripps, Ellen Browning 156
Seddon, Richard 126
seizing of finds 150
Senenmut 239
Service des Antiquités de l'Égypte *see* Egyptian Antiquities Service
Sethe, Kurt 109–10
Seymour, Beauchamp 29
shabtis 14–15, 54, 83, 184, 223
Shapin, Steven 146–7, 157
Shaw, Charles Thursten 207
Shelton, Anthony 5
Sheppard, Kate 61
Sheppard, Kathleen 85
Sheppard, Thomas 181
sherds of pottery 240–1
Shinnie, Peter 209
Shropshire Museum 186
Simon, Norton 198
Sinker, Caroline 87
Sithathoryunet, Princess 98
Skinner, H.D. 128
Smith, Cecil 46
Somerville College, Oxford 81
Sorosis Club 82
South Africa 117–19, 138
South Kensington Museum 41, 45–6, 78, 89, 99, 132, 166
Spiegelberg, Wilhelm 110
Spriggs, M. 254
Spurrell, Flaxman 113
Staley, David 203
Stead, William T. 52
Steindorff, Georg 110
Stepney Borough Council 192–3
Stevenson, Sara Yorke 83–6
Stockholm 175
Stoker, Bram 50
Stona, Maria 116
Suefi, Ali 18
Suez Canal 6, 198–9
suffrage movement 57–62, 81–2
Sunday School movement 53
Sunday School Teachers' Institute 192–3
Swain, H. 3
Swenson, Astrid 136
Sydney 125

Taj-Eddin, Zahed 235
Tale of Sinuhe 231
Tanis 31, 36, 38, 40, 125, 181
technological developments affecting museums 239–40
Tell el-Amarna *see* Amarna
Tell el-Maskhuta 30, 53
temporary exhibitions 35–6, 114, 200
Tewfik, Muhammed 30
theosophy 52
Thompson, Jason 6
Thomsen, Christian Jürgensen 113
Tlili, Anwar 243
Toledo Museum of Art 225, 243
'tomb cards' 92–3
tools, discovery of 42
Toronto 123–4
trafficking in antiquities 228
transnational analyses 106
Tsuboi, Shōgorō 133
Tufnell, Olga 11
Tully, Gemma 234
Turin Egyptian Museum 107
Tutankhamun, tomb of 9, 145–53, 158, 175, 220–1
Tuthmose III 169
'Tutmania' 175
Twain, Mark 69
Tylor, Edward 44, 120

United Nations Educational, Scientific and Cultural Organization (UNESCO) 195, 199–200, 209; 1970 Declaration on Cultural Property 220, 225, 228
'Universal Museum' declaration (2002) 217–18, 222, 226
universities, role of 172
University College London (UCL) 11, 13–14, 54, 58, 61, 99, 134, 183–4, 202
'Urabi, Ahmad 6
Urlin, Amy 59–62
ushabtis see shabtis

Valley of the Kings 145, 148, 151
Vermillion Accord on Human Remains (1989) 230–1
Verne, Jules 203
Victorian culture and the Victorian era 7–8, 40, 48–50, 55, 62, 202, 245
Villing, Alexandra 238

Wainwright, Gerald A. 94–7
Waite, Fred 128
Wallis, Henry 49
Ward, John 224

Ward, Joseph 126
Warhol, Andy 198
Warner, Charles Dudley 69, 77
Warrington Museum 39
Washington Monument 72–3
Wellcome, Sir Henry 193–4
Wellesley College 190
Wellington (New Zealand) 127
Wells, H.G. 203
West Park Museum, Macclesfield 57
Wheeler, Mortimer 173, 201
White, Henry 79
Whitechapel Museum 191
Whitehead, Christopher 44
Whitman, Walt 72
Whittemore, Thomas 94–6, 225
Wiedemann, Alfred 110
Wilkinson, Gardner 41
Willet, Henry 40–1
Willis, Martin 55
Wilmarth, Mary 84
Wilson, Sir Erasmus 10, 31
Wingfield, Chris 3, 201
Winlock, Herbert 171, 174
Winslow, William Copley 70–1, 74–7, 90
Wintle, Clare 206
Witcomb, Andrea 5
women in the home 203
women's contribution to archaeology and museum practice 3–4, 28, 57–61, 83, 88, 109, 203
women's movements 69–70
women's rights 57, 81; *see also* suffrage movement
women's status and role 58, 62
World Archaeological Congress 230–1
world culture, collections of 245
world fairs 39
Worringer, Wilhelm 78
Worsaae, Jens 42, 113
Wright, G.E. 175

Yates, Donna 228
Young, William H. 159–62, 169
'Young Turks' 173

Zaghoul, Saad 145
Zionism 75

www.ingramcontent.com/pod-product-compliance
Lightning Source LLC
Jackson TN
JSHW081257100426
100637JS00007B/43